Physics of Digital Photography

IOP Series: Emerging Technologies in Optics and Photonics

Series Editor

R Barry Johnson a Senior Research Professor at Alabama A&M University, has been involved for over 40 years in lens design, optical systems design, electro-optical systems engineering, and photonics. He has been a faculty member at three academic institutions engaged in optics education and research, employed by a number of companies, and provided consulting services.

Dr Johnson is an SPIE Fellow and Life Member, OSA Fellow, and was the 1987 President of SPIE. He serves on the editorial board of Infrared Physics & Technology and Advances in Optical Technologies. Dr Johnson has been awarded many patents, has published numerous papers and several books and book chapters, and was awarded the 2012 OSA/SPIE Joseph W Goodman Book Writing Award for Lens Design Fundamentals, Second Edition. He is a perennial co-chair of the annual SPIE Current Developments in Lens Design and Optical Engineering Conference.

Foreword

Until the 1960s, the field of optics was primarily concentrated in the classical areas of photography, cameras, binoculars, telescopes, spectrometers, colorimeters, radiometers, etc. In the late 1960s, optics began to blossom with the advent of new types of infrared detectors, liquid crystal displays (LCD), light emitting diodes (LED), charge coupled devices (CCD), lasers, holography, fiber optics, new optical materials, advances in optical and mechanical fabrication, new optical design programs, and many more technologies. With the development of the LED, LCD, CCD and other electo-optical devices, the term 'photonics' came into vogue in the 1980s to describe the science of using light in development of new technologies and the performance of a myriad of applications. Today, optics and photonics are truly pervasive throughout society and new technologies are continuing to emerge. The objective of this series is to provide students, researchers, and those who enjoy self-teaching with a wide-ranging collection of books that each focus on a relevant topic in technologies and application of optics and photonics. These books will provide knowledge to prepare the reader to be better able to participate in these exciting areas now and in the future. The title of this series is Emerging Technologies in Optics and Photonics where 'emerging' is taken to mean 'coming into existence,' 'coming into maturity,' and 'coming into prominence.' IOP Publishing and I hope that you find this Series of significant value to you and your career.

Physics of Digital Photography

Andy Rowlands

IOP Publishing, Bristol, UK

ISBN   978-0-7503-1242-4 (ebook)
ISBN   978-0-7503-1243-1 (print)
ISBN   978-0-7503-1244-8 (mobi)

DOI   10.1088/978-0-7503-1242-4

Version: 20170401

IOP Expanding Physics
ISSN 2053-2563 (online)
ISSN 2054-7315 (print)

British Library Cataloguing-in-Publication Data: A catalogue record for this book is available from the British Library.

Published by IOP Publishing, wholly owned by The Institute of Physics, London

IOP Publishing, Temple Circus, Temple Way, Bristol, BS1 6HG, UK

US Office: IOP Publishing, Inc., 190 North Independence Mall West, Suite 601, Philadelphia, PA 19106, USA

For my parents, Ann and Gareth.

Contents

Preface

My aim in writing this book is to provide a theoretical overview of the photographic imaging chain. The book is intended for use by graduate students and researchers entering imaging science, and for photographers with a graduate level technical background. For existing researchers, it should serve as a link between imaging science and photographic practice.

Chapter 1 works through the photographic formulae used to describe concepts such as image formation, field of view, and depth of field. This leads to the definition of the photometric exposure distribution formed at the camera sensor plane. Chapter 2 continues the imaging chain by providing an introduction to digital output, before going on to discuss exposure strategy in digital photography. The aim is to produce a digital output image file with specified characteristics such as a standard brightness.

Chapter 3 gives insight into the physical phenomena which affect the nature of the raw data produced by the camera. Such phenomena include diffraction, sensor resolution and aliasing, noise, and analog-to-digital conversion. Linear systems theory is used as the mathematical framework, and this provides a formal description of the point spread and optical transfer functions needed for the discussion of image quality in chapter 5.

Chapter 4 describes the physical principles behind some of the main steps involved in converting the raw data into a viewable output image. A large part of the chapter is devoted to colour theory and the implementation of white balance in digital cameras.

Chapter 5 explains the theory required for interpreting image quality metrics used by reviewers of digital cameras and lenses. Theory for cross-format comparisons is described in detail. Practical strategies for maximising the full image quality potential of a camera system are also discussed.

Data obtained from the Olympus® E-M1 camera has been used to illustrate various examples in this book.

Certain topics have been omitted which I believe are already well-covered elsewhere. In particular, I have chosen to concentrate on the physics of digital photography itself rather than the underlying camera technology. The book *Camera Technology: the Dark Side of the Lens* by N Goldberg is an excellent resource on this topic. Although it is written about film cameras, many of the concepts carry over to digital cameras. Furthermore, many excellent books have been written about sensor technology and signal processing, and I highly recommend *Image Sensors and Signal Processing for Digital Still Cameras* edited by J Nakamura.

I would like to thank Professor R Barry Johnson and Dr Rafal Mantiuk for helpful discussions and suggestions. Dave Coffin provided some useful information about his *dcraw* raw converter, and the late Dr Hubert Nasse kindly gave permission to reproduce several figures from his articles. Finally, I would like to thank the production staff at IOP Publishing, and in particular Dr John Navas, for overseeing the commissioning and publication of this book.

Andy Rowlands, January 2017

About the author

Derwyn Andrew Rowlands

Andy Rowlands gained a first class joint honours degree in Mathematics and Physics in 2000, and received his PhD in Physics in 2004 from the University of Warwick, UK. For his PhD he developed a method for treating short-range order in the first-principles quantum description of substitutionally disordered metallic systems.

He was subsequently awarded a Fellowship in Theoretical Physics from the Engineering and Physical Sciences Research Council (EPSRC) which he held at the University of Bristol, UK, from 2004 to 2007. This was followed by a further postdoctoral position at Lawrence Livermore National Laboratory (LLNL) in California, USA, in 2008.

In 2009, Andy moved to China to pursue his interest in travel photography. During this time he studied Mandarin Chinese at Shanghai Jiao Tong University, and between 2012 and 2014 continued his physics research at Tongji University, Shanghai. His combined interests in physics and photography inspired the writing of this book.

www.andyrowlands.com

Acronyms

1D	one dimension/one-dimensional
2D	two dimensions/two-dimensional
ADC	analog-to-digital converter
ADU	analog-to-digital units
AFoV	angular field of view
AHD	adaptive homogeneity-directed
AS	aperture stop
AV	aperture value
AW	adopted white
BV	brightness value
CAT	chromatic adaptation transform
CCD	charge-coupled device
CCE	charge collection efficiency
CCT	correlated colour temperature
CFA	colour filter array
CIE	Commission Internationale de l'Eclairage
CIPA	Camera and Imaging Products Association
CMOS	complimentary metal-oxide semiconductor
CoC	circle of confusion
CRT	cathode ray tube
DCNU	dark current non-uniformity
DN	digital number
DNG	Digital Negative
DoF	depth of field
DOL	digital output level
dpi	dots per inch
DR	dynamic range
DSC/SMI	digital still camera/sensitivity metamerism index
DSNU	dark signal non-uniformity
EC	exposure compensation
EP	entrance pupil
ETTR	expose to the right
EV	exposure value
EW	entrance window
EXIF	Exchangeable Image File
FF	fill factor
FoV	field of view
FPN	fixed pattern noise
FS	field stop
FT	Fourier transform
FWC	full-well capacity
HVS	human visual system
ICC	International Color Consortium
IP	image plane
IQ	image quality
ISO	International Standards Organisation
LCD	liquid crystal diode

LENR	long-exposure noise reduction
LRS	least resolvable separation
LSI	linear shift-invariant
LUT	look-up table
MOS	metal-oxide semiconductor
MTF	modulation transfer function
OECF	opto-electronic conversion function
OLPF	optical low-pass filter
OP	object plane
OPD	optical path difference
OTF	optical transfer function
PCS	Profile Connection Space
PDR	photographic dynamic range
PGA	programmable gain amplifier
PPG	patterned pixel grouping
ppi	pixels per inch
PRNU	pixel response non-uniformity
PSF	point-spread function
PTF	phase transfer function
rms	root mean square
QE	quantum efficiency
RA	relative aperture
REI	recommended exposure index
RI	relative illumination
RP	resolving power
SQF	subjective quality factor
SNR	signal-to-noise ratio
SOS	standard output sensitivity
SP	sensor plane
SPD	spectral power distribution
SV	speed value
TR	tonal range
TV	time value
UCS	uniform chromaticity scale
VNG	variable number of gradients
WB	white balance
XP	exit pupil
XW	exit window

IOP Publishing

Physics of Digital Photography

Andy Rowlands

Chapter 1

Fundamental optical formulae

A digital camera provides control over the light from the photographic scene as it flows through the lens to the sensor plane where an optical image is formed. The nature of the optical image along with the choice of shutter duration determines the exposure distribution. The exposure distribution stimulates a response from the imaging sensor, and it is the magnitude of this response along with subsequent signal processing which ultimately defines the appearance of the output digital image.

A photographer must balance a variety of technical and aesthetic factors when controlling the nature of the optical image formed at the sensor plane. For example, the field of view (FoV) of a camera and lens combination is an important geometrical factor which influences photographic composition. For a given sensor format, this is primarily controlled by the choice of lens focal length. Another fundamental aesthetic aspect of a photograph is the choice of focus point and the depth of field (DoF), which is the depth of the photographic scene which appears to be in focus. DoF is primarily controlled by the object distance along with the lens aperture diameter which restricts the size of the light bundle passing through the lens. Another aspect is subject motion. This can appear frozen or blurred depending on the choice of shutter duration.

This chapter begins with the basics of image formation and works through the optical principles which determine the fundamental nature of the optical image and subsequent exposure distribution formed at the sensor plane. Many of these principles can be described using simple photographic formulae. Photographic formulae use photometry to quantify light, and Gaussian optics to describe light propagation in terms of rays. Gaussian optics is a branch of geometrical optics which assumes ideal imaging by neglecting lens aberrations and their associated image defects. Although aberrations are an inherent property of spherical surfaces, modern photographic lenses are generally well-corrected for residual aberrations through skilful lens design, particularly at small lens aperture diameters. Formulae based on Gaussian optics predict the position and size of the image representative of a well-corrected photographic lens.

In practice, an exposure distribution is required which stimulates a useful response from the imaging sensor. This is one of the fundamental aims of a photographic exposure strategy which forms the subject of chapter 2. One of the key quantities involved is the lens f-number. Although photography is usually carried out in air, the derivation of the f-number presented in this chapter does not make any assumption about the nature of the refractive media surrounding the lens. The aim is to help provide deeper insight into its physical significance.

A variety of physical phenomena such as diffraction are beyond the scope of geometrical optics and are instead introduced in chapter 3. Such phenomena profoundly affect image quality (IQ), which is the subject of chapter 5.

1.1 Image formation

1.1.1 Refraction

Geometrical optics uses rays to represent the propagation of light as it traces paths through the optical system. The ability of a lens to bend rays is explained by Fermat's principle which infers that light rays will choose a path between any two points which is stationary with respect to variations in the path length [1]. Usually, the path is a time minimum. If a light ray travels more slowly in one medium compared to another, the quickest path may result in a change of direction at the interface between the media. This is known as *refraction*. It follows that the shape and material of a refractive medium such as a lens can be used to control the direction of light rays. The equation of central importance is Snell's law of refraction,

$$n' \sin I' = n \sin I.$$

Here the first medium is described by its *refractive index n*,

$$n = \frac{c_0}{c},$$

where c_0 is the speed of light in a vacuum, and c is the speed of light in the medium. The second medium is similarly described by its refractive index n', and a refracting surface separates the media. The angles I and I' are the angles of incidence and refraction, respectively. These angles are measured from the *normal to the refracting surface* at the point of ray intersection, as shown in figure 1.1 for a single spherical surface. Only rotationally symmetric systems will be considered in this chapter. The axis of symmetry is known as the *optical axis* and is conventionally taken along the z direction. The refracting surface is defined by its radius of curvature R centred at position C on the optical axis. Other angles of fundamental importance are U and U' which are measured relative to the optical axis.

The tracing of real rays through the surfaces of an optical system to determine the precise location and nature of the image is a complex computational task undertaken by lens designers [2]. Unfortunately, spherical surfaces inherently cause

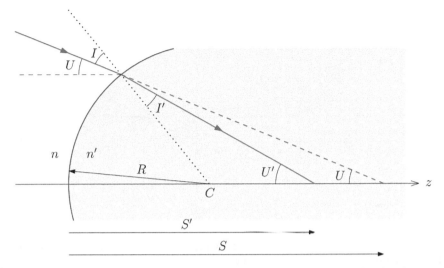

Figure 1.1. Snell's law of refraction. The incident ray (blue) is refracted at the spherical surface (magenta). The dotted line is the surface normal.

aberrations or image defects. The simplest example conceptually is that of spherical aberration which is illustrated in figure 1.2. Rays entering the lens parallel to the optical axis will generally not meet at a unique point on the optical axis after refraction. Aberrations degrade IQ but their effects can be balanced and therefore reduced through skilful lens design.

1.1.2 Gaussian optics

Photographic formulae are based upon *Gaussian optics* which describes image formation in the absence of aberrations. The physical significance of Gaussian optics is described in this section by considering a single refracting surface separating two refractive media. Lenses will subsequently be treated in section 1.1.3.

Object and image planes
Lens aberrations arise from the higher order terms in the expansion of the sine function,

$$\sin \theta = \theta - \frac{\theta^3}{3!} + \frac{\theta^5}{5!} - \frac{\theta^7}{7!} + \cdots. \tag{1.1}$$

Gaussian optics is based upon the fact that a great deal of useful information such as the position of the ideal image relative to the object can be obtained by considering the so-called *paraxial* region. This is an infinitesimal region of the lens around the optical axis where all angles are infinitesimally small. In particular the following relation holds,

$$\sin \theta = \theta. \tag{1.2}$$

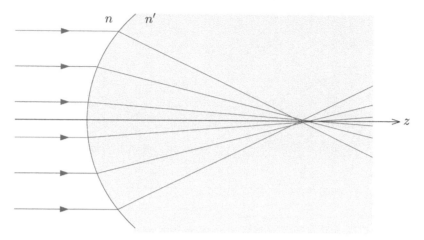

Figure 1.2. Spherical aberration for a single spherical surface. Rays entering parallel to the optical axis do not cross the optical axis at exactly the same point after refraction.

The effects of aberrations are similarly infinitesimal in this region and so the image-forming properties are ideal. Paraxial distances and angles are conventionally denoted using lower-case symbols,

$$S \to s$$
$$S' \to s'$$
$$I \to i$$
$$I' \to i'$$
$$U \to u$$
$$U' \to u'.$$

From equation (1.2) it follows that Snell's law reduces to

$$\boxed{n'\, i' = n\, i}. \tag{1.3}$$

Figure 1.3 shows a point object p positioned at the optical axis at a distance s from a single spherical surface separating two refractive media. The plane perpendicular to the optical axis at p is defined as the *object plane*. Consider a paraxial ray making an infinitesimal angle u with the optical axis. After refraction, this ray will intersect the optical axis again at point p' a distance s' from the surface. The point p' is defined as the image of p. The plane perpendicular to the optical axis at p' is defined as the *image plane*. Later in this section, lenses comprised of many spherical surfaces will be considered; in that case the image plane will be located after the final surface.

Graphical consideration of figure 1.3 together with equation (1.3) can be used to derive the following relationship [1],

$$\boxed{\frac{n}{s} + \frac{n'}{s'} = \Phi}. \tag{1.4}$$

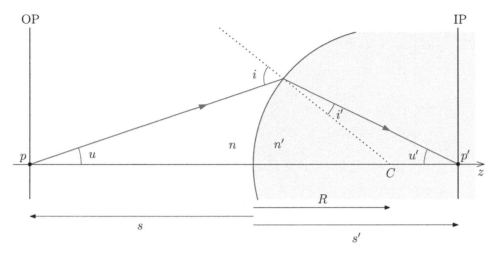

Figure 1.3. Snell's law in the paraxial region where all angles $i, i', u, u' \to 0$ and all rays become infinitesimally close to the optical axis. The dotted line is the surface normal. Here the object is positioned at the optical axis; u is positive, u' is negative, s and s' are both positive. The object plane and image plane have been denoted by OP and IP.

Here Φ is the *surface power*, which is the optical or refractive power of the surface measured in diopters (inverse metres),

$$\Phi = \frac{n' - n}{R}.$$

A surface with a positive power (a converging surface) can bend a ray travelling parallel to the optical axis so that it intersects with the optical axis. On the other hand, a surface with negative power (a diverging surface) will bend such a ray away from the optical axis. Alternatively if $R \to \infty$ then the spherical surface takes the form of a plane surface positioned perpendicular to the optical axis. In this case the surface has zero refractive power. A ray travelling parallel to the optical axis cannot be bent by such a plane surface irrespective of the value of n'.

Given a single spherical surface and the object-plane distance s, the significance of equation (1.4) is that only knowledge of the surface power is needed to locate the corresponding image plane.

Extension of the paraxial region

For a given object plane and spherical surface, equation (1.4) can be used to locate the position of the corresponding image plane. However, the rays involved are paraxial and so strictly speaking the object and image can only be points on or infinitesimally close to the optical axis. In practice the relation $\sin \theta = \theta$ is satisfied reasonably well for angles of incidence and refraction up to about $\pi/9$ radians (20°) as shown in figure 1.4. However, this is not generally sufficient for imaging real objects.

A way forward is suggested by the following relation which is also valid in the paraxial region,

$$\tan \theta = \theta.$$

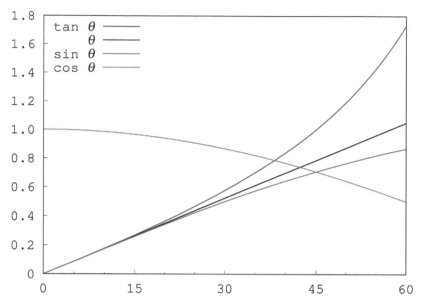

Figure 1.4. Trigonometrical functions of angle θ (degrees).

This means that the paraxial angles measured relative to the optical axis satisfy

$$u = \tan u$$
$$u' = \tan u'.$$

When considering arbitrary *non-paraxial* heights above the optical axis, Gaussian optics maintains this relationship by performing a fictitious extension of the paraxial region [3]. The extension proceeds by projecting a given spherical surface onto a tangent plane at the optical axis in order to leave the effects of aberrations out of consideration. The new geometry is illustrated in figure 1.5 for a single surface. The angles u and u' measured relative to the optical axis become

$$u = \tan^{-1}\left(\frac{y}{s}\right) = \frac{y}{s} \tag{1.5a}$$

$$u' = \tan^{-1}\left(\frac{-y}{s'}\right) = \frac{-y}{s'}. \tag{1.5b}$$

This means that outside the paraxial region, the ray angles u and u' *must be interpreted as ray tangent slopes rather than angles* [2, 3].

Since the normal to the tangent plane is parallel to the optical axis, the ray tangent slopes u and u' are equivalent to the angles of incidence and refraction i and i'. However, it was noted earlier that a plane surface itself has no refractive power. Therefore, the refractive power of the original spherical surface is retained when

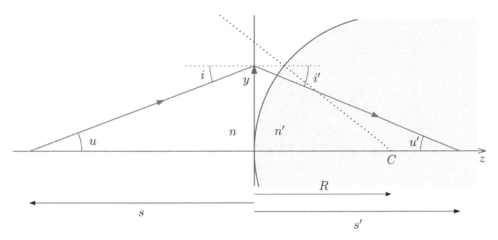

Figure 1.5. The point of ray intersection with the spherical surface (magenta curve) at height y is projected onto a tangent plane (red line) at the same height y. Here the ray slope u is positive and u' is negative.

performing the above projection. Substituting equation (1.5) into equation (1.4) yields

$$\boxed{n'u' = nu - y\Phi}. \tag{1.6}$$

This is the form of Snell's law obtained by extending the paraxial region. The significance of this equation is the *linear* relationship between the ray slopes and heights; all ray slopes and heights can be scaled without affecting the positions of the object and image planes. In other words, Fermat's principle must be violated in order to leave aberrations out of consideration.

Equation (1.4) is now formally valid for imaging of points positioned at arbitrary height above the optical axis and therefore real objects of finite size. Figure 1.6 shows the object and image planes defined by the axial (on-axis) paraxial rays of figure 1.5. These planes have been labeled OP and IP. Now rays from a point at the top of the object of height h at OP will meet at a unique point on IP. Therefore IP defines the plane where the image of OP can be said to be in *sharp focus*.

Equation (1.6) can be used as a basis for tracing paraxial rays through a general compound lens which may consist of a large number of surfaces of various curvatures and spacings. This is known as a *ynu raytrace* [2, 3]. Only angles measured relative to the optical axis are needed together with the points of ray intersection with each tangent plane.

Interpretation of Gaussian optics
Gaussian optics is often viewed as an approximation and phrases such as 'paraxial approximation' are frequently used. However this is not really the case; equation (1.6) is exact for the paraxial region close to the optical axis [3]. The idea of Gaussian optics is to represent the imaging properties of the lens at larger radial distances outwards from the optical axis by the ideal imaging properties of the paraxial region.

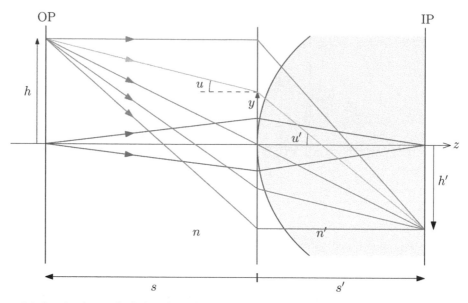

Figure 1.6. Imaging by a spherical surface after extending the paraxial region. Example rays for an object point on the optical axis and at the top of the object of height h are shown. The ray slopes and intersection height have been indicated for the grey ray. In this case both u and u' are negative. The object plane and image plane have been denoted by OP and IP.

In fact, a paraxial ynu raytrace is typically performed as a first step in lens design [2, 3]. Properties such as the Gaussian image location are used as ideal reference coordinates when controlling residual aberrations which affect the nature and quality of the real image. Aberrations arise from the higher order terms in the expansion of $\sin\theta$ given by equation (1.1) that are absent in the paraxial region,

$$\sin\theta = \theta - \frac{\theta^3}{3!} + \frac{\theta^5}{5!} - \frac{\theta^7}{7!} + \cdots.$$

For this reason, Gaussian optics is also referred to as first-order optics. Depending on the final aberration content of the lens design, the optimized image location may not be identical to the Gaussian location. Nevertheless, modern photographic lenses are very well-corrected for aberrations and so the optimized image location will be almost identical to that predicted by photographic formulae based on Gaussian optics.

1.1.3 Lens refractive power

A simple lens or element can be defined as a transparent medium with refractive index n_{lens} bounded by two refracting surfaces. A compound lens comprises an assembly of such simple lenses or elements. Photographic formulae are concerned only with the overall properties of the compound lens in projecting the image onto the imaging sensor.

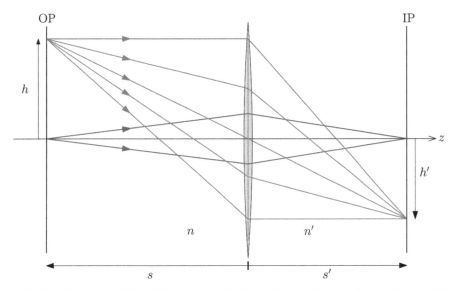

Figure 1.7. The object plane (OP) and image plane (IP) for a thin lens. Here s and s' are both positive, h is positive and h' is negative.

It is useful to consider quantities in the *object space* of the compound lens before the rays undergo refraction, and in the *image space* of the compound lens after all refraction has taken place. It is customary to indicate image-space quantities with an added prime symbol, for example n' represents the image-space refractive index. Various sign conventions are in use. In this book the sign convention illustrated in figure 1.7 will be adopted:

- *Image-space distances are positive when measured from left to right.*
- *Object-space distances are positive when measured from right to left.*
- *All heights are positive when measured upwards from the optical axis and negative below.*

Equation (1.4) for refraction at a surface can be generalised to the case of a compound lens,

$$\frac{n}{s} + \frac{n'}{s'} = \Phi. \tag{1.7}$$

Here n and n' are the object-space and image-space refractive indices, and Φ is the *total* refractive power. This depends upon the nature of the component lenses, their spacings and all refractive media. The value of Φ can be obtained by performing a ynu raytrace through all surfaces.

In the case of refraction at a single surface described in section 1.1.2, the surface power Φ was projected onto a tangent plane which defined the point from which the object and image distances s and s' were measured. In the case of a compound lens, it is not obvious from where s and s' should be measured. This issue will be addressed below starting with the simple case of a thin lens before moving on to thick and compound lenses.

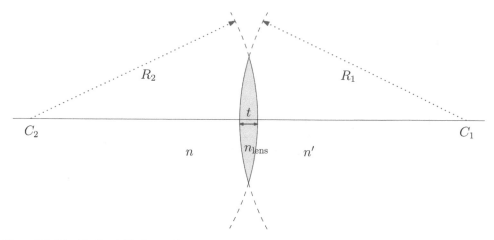

Figure 1.8. The idealised thin lens with $t \to 0$. R_1 and R_2 are the radii of curvature of the first and second refracting surfaces, respectively. The corresponding centres of curvature are labelled C_1 and C_2. Here R_2 is negative because C_2 lies to the left of the second surface.

Thin lens imaging

As a first step, it is useful to introduce the so-called *thin lens* illustrated in figure 1.8 which has negligible thickness compared to its diameter. The shapes of the two spherical surfaces are described by their radii of curvature R_1 and R_2. The refractive index of the lens medium is denoted by n_{lens}.

For a thin lens the total refractive power Φ is simply the sum of the individual surface powers [1],

$$\Phi = \Phi_1 + \Phi_2 \tag{1.8a}$$

$$\Phi_1 = \frac{n_{\text{lens}} - n}{R_1} \tag{1.8b}$$

$$\Phi_2 = \frac{n' - n_{\text{lens}}}{R_2}. \tag{1.8c}$$

Equation (1.7) with Φ defined by equation (1.8) is known as *Descartes' thin lens formula*. The terms Φ_1 and Φ_2 are the refractive powers of the first and second surfaces of the lens. The tangent planes of the two spherical surfaces shown in figure 1.8 are coincident 'at the lens' since $t \to 0$. Therefore the distance s can only be measured 'from the lens' to the object plane, and the distance s' can only be measured from the lens to the corresponding image plane. This is illustrated in figure 1.7. Given s, the distance s' can be found by solving equations (1.7) and (1.8).

Air has a refractive index equal to 1.000 277 at standard temperature and pressure (0 °C and 1 atm). In comparison, water has a refractive index equal to 1.3330 at standard temperature (20 °C). A value of 1 for the refractive index of air is often assumed to simplify photographic formulae. For precise calculations, refractive indices may be defined relative to air rather than to a vacuum. In either case, if the lens is surrounded by air then equations (1.7) and (1.8) simplify to

$$\frac{1}{s} + \frac{1}{s'} = (n_{\text{lens}} - 1)\left(\frac{1}{R_1} - \frac{1}{R_2}\right).$$

This is known as the *lensmakers' formula*. In analogy with refraction at a single surface, the significance of the lensmakers' and Descartes' formulae is that, for a given object plane, *only the total refractive power is required to locate the image plane.*

It should also be mentioned that objects in the scene lying in front of or behind the chosen object plane have their own corresponding object plane and image plane. For example, consider the planes labeled OP and IP in figure 1.7. Objects lying in front of or behind OP will not be in sharp focus at IP. Nevertheless, such objects can still appear to be acceptably sharp at IP provided the object-plane separation falls within the DoF of the imaging system. This will be discussed in section 1.3 later.

Thick lens imaging
In practice, a lens is only treated mathematically as a thin lens for preliminary calculations or if neglecting its thickness does not affect the accuracy of the calculation [3]. For a *thick lens* a third term Φ_{12} must be included to obtain the total refractive power,

$$\Phi = \Phi_1 + \Phi_2 - \Phi_{12} \tag{1.9a}$$

$$\Phi_{12} = \frac{t}{n_{\text{lens}}}\Phi_1\Phi_2. \tag{1.9b}$$

Here t is the lens thickness at the optical axis as illustrated in figure 1.9. Equation (1.7) with Φ defined by equation (1.9) is known as *Gullstrand's equation*. Significantly, Φ is no longer simply the sum of the surface powers because it also depends on the lens thickness t. Unlike the thin lens treatment, Φ can no longer be associated with the tangent planes to the refracting surfaces. Two new planes need to be defined; the first and second *principal planes* H and H'. These are planes from where the overall refractive power of the lens can be imagined to originate.

The locations of H and H' for an example thick lens are shown in figure 1.9. The position of H' can be found by considering a ray entering the lens at a height y_1 parallel with the optical axis travelling from left to right ($u_1 = 0$). The ray has a slope u_2 after the final refraction; H' is located by extending this ray backwards to height y_1. The location of H can similarly be determined by considering a ray entering the lens parallel with the optical axis from right to left.

The principal planes serve as equivalent refracting surfaces representing the lens; replacing the lens with H and H' together with the object-space and image-space refractive media will result in the same overall refractive properties. Depending on the radii of curvature of the surfaces, H and H' are not necessarily located inside the lens. The second principal plane is often located to the left of the first principal plane, and so the terms 'front' and 'rear' are not used to avoid confusion. An important

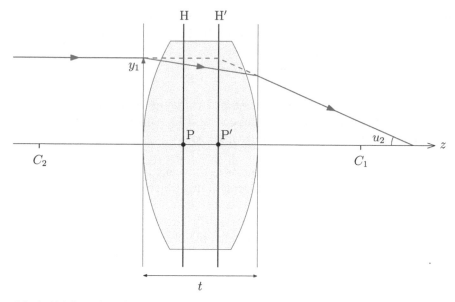

Figure 1.9. A thick lens with thickness t. The dashed line represents the imaginary path that would be taken if the lens were to be replaced by the hypothetical principle planes H and H'. The principal points P and P' are shown. The red lines are the tangent planes.

property of H and H' is that they are planes of unit magnification since rays travel parallel between them in this equivalent refracting scenario. It must be emphasised that the rays do not necessarily follow the path indicated by the dashed lines in figure 1.9 and that this equivalent refracting scenario must be treated as hypothetical.

The first and second *principal points* P and P' are positioned where H and H' intersect the optical axis. Significantly, the relationship between the positions of the object plane and image plane for a thick lens are determined by equations (1.7) and (1.9) provided that the object and image distances s and s' are measured from P and P', respectively.

Compound lens imaging

A *compound lens* such as a photographic lens is comprised of an assembly of component lenses or elements. References [4, 5, 6] provide details of standard layouts for various types of photographic lenses.

A compound lens can be treated analogously to a thick lens by *defining a pair of principal planes for the compound lens*. The compound lens principal planes and points can be located by performing a ynu raytrace through all surfaces. The slope u_k used to locate H' will be the value after refraction by the final surface as illustrated in figure 1.10. The total refractive power Φ depends upon the nature of the component lenses, their spacings and all refractive media. Its value can be obtained from the raytrace data. Note that Gullstrand's equation would result from a raytrace performed for a single thick lens. Similarly, Descartes' formula would result from a raytrace performed for a single thin lens, in which case the principal planes would be coincident with the tangent planes 'at the lens'.

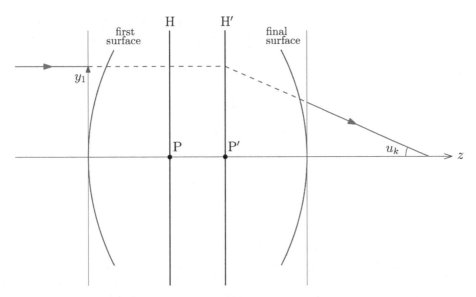

Figure 1.10. Principal planes and principal points for a compound lens.

After the principal planes and points have been located, equation (1.7) again determines the relationship between the positions of the object plane and image plane provided that the object and image distances s and s' are measured from P and P', respectively.

1.1.4 Magnification

Lateral or *transverse magnification* m is defined as the ratio of the image height to the object height,

$$m = \frac{h'}{h}. \tag{1.10}$$

The image plane projected onto the imaging sensor by a photographic lens is real and inverted. Accordingly in optics, the object height h and image height h' measured from the optical axis are typically defined to be positive and negative, respectively. Therefore m will be negative.

Within Gaussian optics the transverse magnification can also be calculated from the object and image distances s and s',

$$m = -\left(\frac{n}{n'}\right)\frac{s'}{s}. \tag{1.11}$$

Again since the sign convention here is that the object distance s and image distance s' are both positive, m is negative for a photographic lens.

In contrast, photographic formulae conventionally take m to be a positive value even though the image is inverted. This means that '$-m$' in optical formulae appears as '$+m$' in some photographic formulae. To avoid confusion, this book defines magnification according to the optics convention but uses its absolute value when possible. Therefore '$-m$' is presented in the form '$+|m|$'. This approach should yield formulae which are recognisable within both optics and photography. Equation (1.11) will therefore be presented in the form

$$\boxed{|m| = \left(\frac{n}{n'}\right)\frac{s'}{s}}.$$ (1.12)

1.1.5 Focal length

A physically more useful way of representing the ability of a lens to bend light rays is in terms of *focal length* rather than refractive power.

Front and rear effective focal lengths
Lens refractive power was determined in section 1.1.3 by considering rays entering the lens parallel to the optical axis. Rays which are parallel to each other are said to be *collimated*. In practice, rays entering the lens will be collimated when arriving from an object positioned at an infinite distance in front of the lens. Furthermore, the rays will be collimated with respect to the optical axis provided the object at infinity is positioned on the optical axis itself. To see this, consider the rays leaving the axial (on-axis) point on the object plane in figure 1.12 and observe the effect on the rays entering the lens when $s \to \infty$.

The above situation is shown in the upper diagram of figure 1.11. Within Gaussian optics, these rays will converge to a single point known as the *rear focal point*, F'. The plane perpendicular to the optical axis at F' is known as the *rear focal plane*. With $s \to \infty$, the physical distance s' from the second principal point (P') to F' is defined as the second effective focal length [3], posterior focal length [2], or *rear effective focal length* [7] denoted by f_R'. This is the minimum possible distance over which the lens can bring rays to a focus. From equation (1.7) it follows that

$$\frac{n'}{f_R'} = \Phi.$$ (1.13)

In this situation the image plane will coincide with the rear focal plane. This important concept is known as *infinity focus* or *focus at infinity*.

Now consider the lower diagram of figure 1.11 which shows a point in front of the lens referred to as the first or *front focal point* (F) from which all rays passing through the lens emerge collimated. In this situation $s' \to \infty$ and so the image plane is situated at an infinite distance behind the lens. The plane perpendicular to the optical axis at F is known as the *front focal plane*. The physical distance from the first principal point (P) to F is defined as the first effective focal length [3], anterior focal length [2], or *front effective focal length* [7] denoted by f_F. A lens is unable to focus on an object placed at F or closer. From equation (1.7) it follows that

$$\frac{n}{f_F} = \Phi.$$ (1.14)

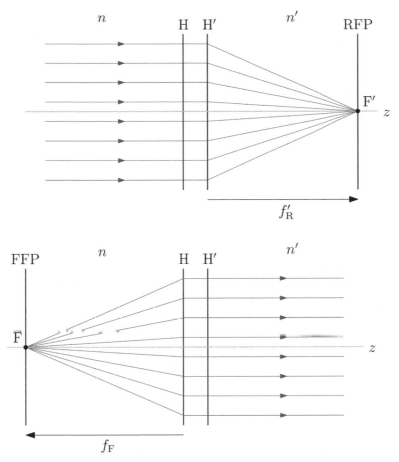

Figure 1.11. Top: Rear effective focal length f'_R and rear focal point F' for a compound lens. The rear focal plane has been denoted by RFP. Bottom: Front effective focal length f_F and front focal point F. The front focal plane has been denoted by FFP.

The front and rear effective focal lengths are equal only if $n = n'$. The term 'effective' is used because f_F and f'_R are the physical distances from the principal points to the respective focal points, the principal point locations being determined from imaginary or hypothetical equivalent refracting planes.

Combining equations (1.7), (1.13), and (1.14) yields the *Gaussian conjugate equation* for the object and image distances expressed in terms of the front and rear effective focal lengths instead of Φ,

$$\boxed{\frac{n}{f_F} = \frac{n}{s} + \frac{n'}{s'} = \frac{n'}{f'_R}} \, .$$

The Gaussian conjugate equation describes the behaviour illustrated in figure 1.12. If the object plane at s is brought forward from infinity, the distance s' increases and so the image plane moves further away from the rear focal plane.

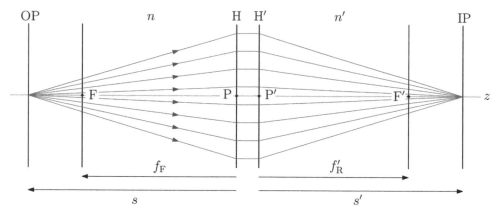

Figure 1.12. Imaging according to the Gaussian conjugate equation.

Effective focal length

The effective focal length f_E is defined as the reciprocal of the total refractive power [7],

$$f_E = \frac{1}{\Phi}. \tag{1.15}$$

Combining equations (1.13), (1.14), and (1.15) yields the relation

$$\boxed{\frac{n}{f_F} = \frac{n'}{f_R'} = \frac{1}{f_E}}. \tag{1.16}$$

Unlike f_F and f_R', the effective focal length f_E is not a physically representable length in general. However in photography the usual case is that the object-space and image-space refractive media are both air. Then $f_E = f_R' = f_F$ and these terms are used interchangeably. If no distinction is made, the term 'focal length' usually refers to the rear effective focal length in air.

In order to illustrate the relationship between the focal lengths, Descartes' formula has been used to calculate the example data given in table 1.1 for a thin lens. In particular, it can be seen that if either of n or n' are changed then the total refractive power Φ will change and *this affects the values of both f_F and f_R'.*

Front and back focal distances

The *front focal distance* is measured from the point where the first surface of the lens intersects the optical axis to the axial position on the object plane. The rear or *back focal distance* is measured from the point where the final surface of the lens intersects the optical axis to the axial position on the image plane [7].

These distances are sometimes referred to as the front and back focal lengths and so care should be taken not to confuse them with f_F and f_R' which are 'effective' quantities measured from hypothetical refracting surfaces.

Table 1.1. Focal lengths and surface powers for a thin lens calculated using equation (1.8) assuming $R_1 = 0.1$ m, $R_2 = -0.1$ m, and $n_{lens} = 1.5$. All powers and focal lengths are measured in diopters and metres, respectively.

	air–lens–air	water–lens–water	water–lens–air	air–lens–oil
n	1	1.33	1.33	1
n'	1	1.33	1	1.5
Φ_1	5	1.7	1.7	5
Φ_2	5	1.7	5	0
Φ	10	3.4	6.7	5
f_E	0.1	0.294	0.149	0.2
f_F	0.1	0.391	0.199	0.2
f'_R	0.1	0.391	0.149	0.3

Nodal points

Photographers often refer to the nodal points of a lens rather than the principal points. The nodal points can be visualised intuitively; a ray aimed at the first nodal point in object space will emerge from the second nodal point in image space with the same slope. The nodal points are therefore points of unit angular magnification. The front nodal point is often assumed to be the no-parallax point in panoramic photography; in fact the no-parallax point is the lens entrance pupil [8].

The front and rear effective focal lengths are always defined from the principal points [1,7]. Nevertheless, they can be measured from the nodal points provided the definition is reversed [4]; the distance from the first nodal point to the front focal point is equal to the magnitude of the *rear* effective focal length f'_R, and the the distance from the second nodal point to the rear focal point is equal to the magnitude of the *front* effective focal length f_F. This is illustrated in figure 1.13.

If the object-space and image-space refractive indices n and n' are equal, then the first nodal and first principal points coincide, the second nodal and second principal points coincide, and $f_F = f'_R$. This is naturally the case in air and the *nodal slide* is a method for experimental determination of effective focal lengths [1].

1.1.6 Lens focusing movement

The imaging sensor is fixed in position at the *sensor plane*. This term will be used instead of 'film plane', traditionally used for film cameras. *The sensor plane is positioned to coincide with the rear focal plane when focus is set at infinity.*

From the preceding discussion of image formation and in particular the Gaussian conjugate equation, it is clear that when the object plane is brought forward from infinity, the image plane will no longer coincide with the rear focal plane and sensor plane but will naturally be positioned behind them. In order to

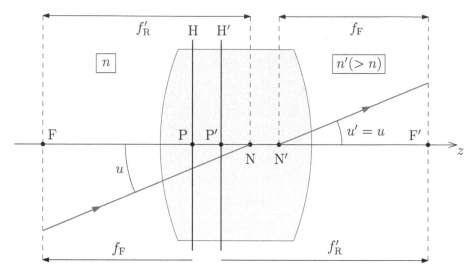

Figure 1.13. Lens nodal points; a ray aimed at the first nodal point N emerges from the second nodal point N′ at the same angle u. In this example, image space has a higher refractive index than object space.

record an image in sharp focus, the image plane must be brought forward to coincide with the sensor plane. This is achieved by moving the optical elements of the lens in order to bring the rear focal plane forward until the image plane and sensor plane coincide. The optical elements can be moved either manually by adjusting the lens barrel, or via an autofocus motor linked to the autofocus system. Traditionally the whole lens barrel is moved, however many modern lenses use front-cell focusing or are internally focusing [5]. These types of lenses have groups of floating optical elements which move relative to each other so that the front of the lens does not extend.

It should now be clear that the sensor plane and image plane coincide after achieving sharp focus, but only coincide with the rear focal plane when focus is set at infinity. Accordingly, these terms should not be used interchangeably.

Provided the distances s and s' are measured from the respective principal points, the Gaussian conjugate equation can be used to calculate the required focusing movement for a traditional photographic lens in which the whole lens barrel moves upon focusing. For simplicity, it will be assumed that the lens is surrounded by air so that $n = n' = 1$ and therefore $f_F = f'_R = f_E$. For clarity, the symbol f will be used to represent effective focal length. The following formulae derived within Gaussian optics are almost exact for a photographic lens that has been well-corrected for aberrations.

Object distance measured from first principal point
First assume that focus is set at infinity so that the rear focal plane, sensor plane, and image plane all coincide. This is illustrated in figure 1.14(a). If the object plane is then brought forward, the image plane will move behind the sensor plane a distance denoted here by e. This is illustrated in figure 1.14(b). The aim is to eliminate e by

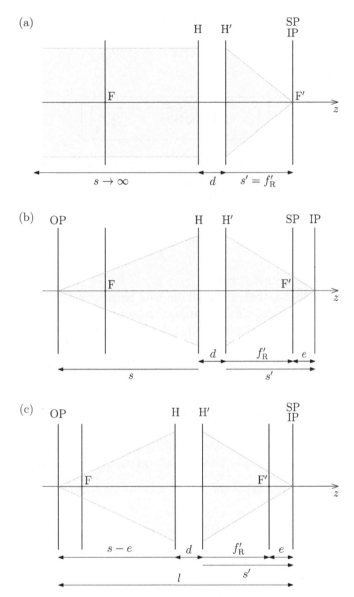

Figure 1.14. Geometry for lens focusing movement. The sensor plane has been denoted by SP.

moving the lens barrel forward, however the value of e itself will be affected as the distance s between the first principal point and object plane is reduced. Denoting the required movement by e, the final geometry is illustrated in figure 1.14(c). It can be seen that e satisfies

$$\frac{1}{s-e} + \frac{1}{f+e} = \frac{1}{f}. \qquad (1.17)$$

This can be rearranged in the quadratic form

$$e^2 - (s - f)e + f^2 = 0.$$

The required solution is

$$e = \frac{1}{2}\left[(s - f) - \sqrt{(s - f)^2 - 4f^2}\right]. \tag{1.18}$$

Here s is the original object distance before the focusing movement. Note that e here is defined relative to the infinity focus position so that $e \to 0$ when $s \to \infty$.

The magnification can be found by substituting equation (1.12) into the Gaussian conjugate equation with $s' = f + e$,

$$|m| = \frac{e}{f}.$$

Therefore $|m| \to 0$ at infinity focus.

Equation (1.18) shows that if the whole lens barrel moves forwards, the lens is unable to focus on an object plane positioned closer than an original object distance $s = 3f$ from the first principal point. At this minimum focus distance, $e = f$, and so the minimum possible object-to-image distance is $4f + d$ after the focusing movement. For an ideal thin lens, $d \to 0$ and the minimum possible object-to-image distance is $4f$.

In the case of an internal focus design, the movement of floating elements can cause the focal length to change upon focusing. Even though the front element does not move, the relative and absolute positions of both the first and second principal points may change and so the required focusing movement depends on the details of the lens design. References [6, 9] provide information about focusing movement in these types of lenses.

Object distance measured from sensor plane
Manual focusing scales on lenses are calibrated using the distance from the sensor plane to the object plane. The location of the sensor/film plane is commonly indicated with a -⊖- symbol on the camera body.

Again consider the situation where focus is set at infinity so that the rear focal plane, sensor plane, and image plane all coincide. If the object plane is then brought towards the lens, the discussion leading up to equation (1.17) again applies if the whole lens barrel moves forward upon focusing. Using the new distance measures, equation (1.17) is replaced by

$$\frac{1}{l - (d + f + e)} + \frac{1}{f + e} = \frac{1}{f}.$$

Here l is the final distance between the sensor plane and object plane. The distance d is the measured length between the first and second principal points of the compound lens and may be positive or negative depending on their order. The value of d can be obtained from the lens design data. The above equation can be rearranged in the quadratic form

$$e^2 - (l - 2f - d)e + f^2 = 0.$$

The required solution is

$$e = \frac{1}{2}\left[(l - 2f - d) - \sqrt{(l - 2f - d)^2 - 4f^2}\right].$$

Again e is defined relative to the infinity focus position. It can be seen that the solution for e when the object distance is measured from the sensor plane rather than the first principal point is obtained by making the substitution $s - f = l - 2f - d$.

1.2 Field of view

The field of view (FoV) is the extent of the object plane that can be imaged by the lens. It is formed by a specific light cone subtended by the object plane with its apex situated at the lens *entrance pupil*. In photography a more useful way to express the FoV is via the angle of the FoV or *angular FoV* (AFoV) [3]. The AFoV describes the angular extent of the light cone and can be measured along the horizontal, vertical, and diagonal directions.

Equation (1.15) defined the effective focal length f_E as the reciprocal of the total refractive power. The shorter the effective focal length of a lens, the more strongly it is able to bend the incoming light rays and hence the wider the AFoV. Conversely, the longer the effective focal length, the narrower the AFoV.

A number of important concepts will be introduced through the derivation of the FoV formulae. These include stops, chief and marginal rays, entrance and exit pupils, pupil magnification, bellows factor, and focus breathing.

Figure 1.15. Adjustable iris diaphragm which acts as an aperture stop.

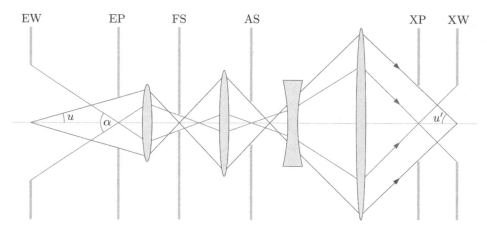

Figure 1.16. The chief ray (green) defines the AFoV (α). The marginal ray (blue) defines the maximum acceptance angles u and u' for a given object plane. Shown are the entrance window (EW), entrance pupil (EP), field stop (FS), aperture stop (AS), exit pupil (XP), and exit window (XW).

1.2.1 Entrance and exit pupils

Modern lenses typically include an iris diaphragm which acts as an adjustable *aperture stop* in the lens. An example is illustrated in figure 1.15. Adjusting the aperture stop alters the amount of light passing through the lens but does not affect the AFoV. This is because the AFoV is determined by a type of ray which passes through the centre of the aperture stop, as discussed below.

A compound lens may have optical elements situated in front of and behind the physical aperture stop. The image of the physical aperture stop seen through the front of the lens due to any optical elements in front of the physical aperture stop is known as the *entrance pupil*. The image of the physical aperture stop seen through the back of the lens formed by any optical elements behind the physical aperture stop is known as the *exit pupil*. Within Gaussian optics, the entrance and exit pupils are ideal images. An example is shown in figure 1.16. The pupils may be located in any order and may not necessarily be inside the lens. In photographic lenses the pupils are typically virtual as opposed to real images. Figure 1.17 shows a lens design with pupils that are reversed and virtual.

The following quantity m_p known as the pupil factor or *pupil magnification* is used in photographic formulae [4, 5, 6],

$$m_p = \frac{\text{diameter of the exit pupil}}{\text{diameter of the entrance pupil}}.$$

If $m_p = 1$, the centres of the entrance and exit pupils are coincident with the first and second principal points. In real photographic lenses this is rarely the case; generally $m_p \neq 1$ and the pupils will be displaced from the principal planes. For example, $m_p < 1$ in telephoto lenses.

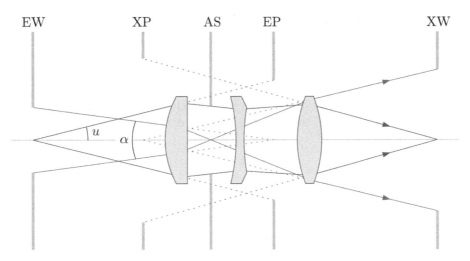

Figure 1.17. Virtual exit pupil and entrance pupil for an example photographic lens design.

1.2.2 Chief and marginal rays

One or more *field* stops may be present in the lens which block the passage of rays. One of these field stops will be the limiting field stop. The Gaussian images of the limiting field stop seen through the front and back of the lens are referred to as the *entrance window* and *exit window*, respectively. In photography, these typically coincide with the object plane and sensor plane.

The *meridional plane* contains the optical axis. The *chief ray* is the incoming meridional ray from the scene which passes by the edge of the limiting field stop, as illustrated in figure 1.16. The chief ray passes through the *centre* of the aperture stop. Consequently, the chief ray also passes through the centre of the entrance and exit pupils. The entrance pupil is situated in front of the first lens surface in figure 1.16, however in photographic lenses the entrance pupil is usually virtual as in figure 1.17. In this case the virtual extension of the entering chief ray will pass through the centre of the entrance pupil. Similarly if the exit pupil is virtual, the virtual extension of the exiting chief ray will pass through the centre of the exit pupil.

The *marginal ray* is the meridional ray from the axial position on the object plane which passes through the entrance window and the *edge* of the aperture stop. Consequently, the marginal ray also passes by the edges of the entrance and exit pupils. In other words, the base of the entrance pupil defines the maximum cone of light accepted by the system, and the base of the exit pupil defines the maximum cone of light which exits the system. This is important for determining exposure which will be quantified in section 1.4.

The chief ray defines the AFoV of the lens as the angle α subtended by the edges of the entrance window from the centre of the entrance pupil. In other words, the apex of the light cone forming the AFoV is located at the entrance pupil. If a lens designer moves the position of the aperture stop, the pupil positions and pupil magnification will change. This will alter the AFoV, but the FoV defined by the entrance window will remain unchanged.

Adjusting the diameter of the aperture stop restricts the size of the ray bundle formed by the marginal rays. This will affect the amount of light reaching the sensor plane but will not affect the AFoV.

In Gaussian optics, all rays including the chief and marginal rays are treated mathematically as paraxial ray tangent slopes by extending the paraxial region.

1.2.3 Angular field of view

The AFoV has been defined in the previous section as the angle subtended by the edges of the entrance window from the centre of the entrance pupil. Consider a photographic lens with an image circle designed for a given sensor format with the corresponding exit window coincident with the imaging sensor. The geometry is shown in figure 1.18. The dimension of the imaging sensor in the vertical direction is $d = 2h'$. When focused at the object plane, the corresponding AFoV in the vertical direction has been denoted by α. An expression for α can be obtained in terms of the object-space quantities h, s and s_{ep},

$$\tan\frac{\alpha}{2} = \frac{h}{s - s_{ep}}. \tag{1.19}$$

Here s is the distance from the first principal plane to the object plane, and s_{ep} is the distance from the first principal plane to the entrance pupil. Since $d = 2h'$, the magnification expressed in the form of equation (1.10) can be used to obtain h,

$$h = \frac{d}{2|m|}.$$

Substituting into equation (1.19) and re-arranging yields

$$\alpha = 2\tan^{-1}\frac{d}{2|m|(s - s_{ep})}. \tag{1.20}$$

The remaining piece of information to be determined is the distance $s - s_{ep}$.

The first step is to substitute the Gaussian magnification expressed in the form of equation (1.12) into the Gaussian conjugate equation. This yields the following expressions for the object and image distances measured from the principal planes,

$$s = \left\{1 + \frac{1}{|m|}\right\}f_F \tag{1.21a}$$

$$s' = (1 + |m|)f_R'. \tag{1.21b}$$

Let the distance from the second principal plane to the exit pupil be s_{xp}'. The distances s_{ep} and s_{xp}' can be obtained in terms of the pupil magnification m_p by considering focus set at infinity, thus eliminating the magnification variable [10]. In

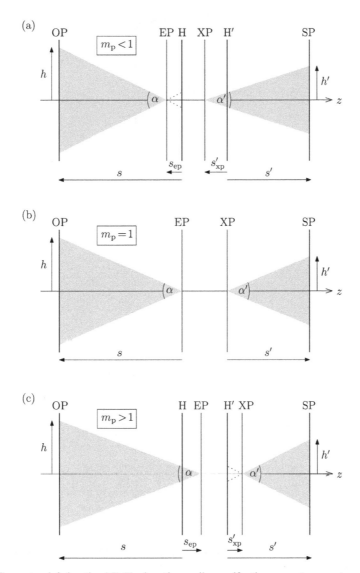

Figure 1.18. Geometry defining the AFoV when the pupil magnification $m_p < 1$, $m_p = 1$, and $m_p > 1$. The pupils and principal planes are not required to be in the order shown.

this case, rays leave the exit pupil which has diameter $m_p D$ and converge at the rear focal point, thus forming a cone as illustrated in figure 1.19. Since the principal planes are planes of unit magnification, the cone has diameter D at the intersection with the second principal plane, where D is the diameter of the entrance pupil. Since the second principal point lies a distance f'_R from the rear focal point, the exit pupil will be positioned a distance $m_p f'_R$ from the sensor plane. Therefore

$$s'_{xp} = (1 - m_p)f'_R. \tag{1.22}$$

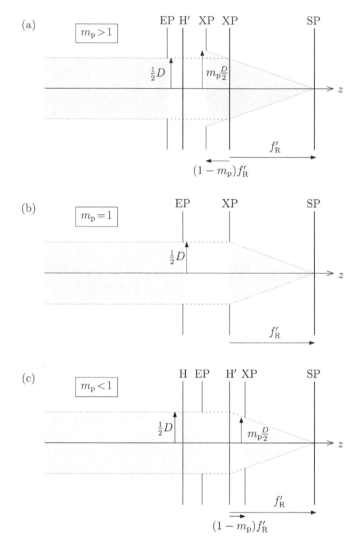

Figure 1.19. Gaussian pupil and focal plane distances at infinity focus. The pupils and principal planes are not required to be in the order shown.

Now by solving the Gaussian conjugate equation

$$\frac{n}{s_{ep}} + \frac{n'}{s'_{xp}} = \frac{1}{f_E}$$

and using the relationship between the focal lengths defined by equation (1.16), the following expression for s_{ep} is obtained,

$$s_{ep} = \left(1 - \frac{1}{m_p}\right) f_F. \tag{1.23}$$

Therefore the distance from the entrance pupil to the object plane is

$$s - s_{ep} = \left\{ \frac{1}{|m|} + \frac{1}{m_p} \right\} f_F.$$

(1.24)

Now substituting equation (1.24) into equation (1.20) yields [11]

$$\boxed{\alpha = 2 \tan^{-1} \left(\frac{d}{2 b f_F} \right)}.$$

(1.25)

Here b is the *bellows factor*,

$$\boxed{b = 1 + \frac{|m|}{m_p}}.$$

(1.26)

More generally, the AFoV can be defined in the horizontal, vertical, and diagonal directions. Equation (1.25) is equally valid for any of these directions simply by replacing the height h and sensor size d with h_k and d_k, where k represents the horizontal (x), vertical (y), or diagonal direction.

Bellows factor

The AFoV according to equation (1.25) depends upon a combination of the front effective focal length of the lens, the dimensions of the imaging sensor, the magnification, and the pupil magnification. The magnification and pupil magnification are contained within the bellows factor b. The fact that the magnification affects the AFoV may be surprising. For a fixed framing, the AFoV actually becomes smaller when focusing on an object positioned closer to the lens than infinity. Consequently, the object appears to be *larger* than expected.

The contribution from the bellows factor can be considerable at close focusing distances. For example, $|m| = 1$ is referred to as 1:1 magnification. In this case $b = 2$ assuming $m_p = 1$. For the 35 mm full-frame format, the diagonal AFoV for a 50 mm macro lens at 1:1 magnification is seen to decrease from 46.8° to 24.4°.

The AFoV is maximised at infinity focus where $|m| = 0$ and the AFoV formula reduces to

$$\alpha = 2 \tan^{-1} \left(\frac{d}{2 f_F} \right).$$

(1.27)

Focus breathing

An effect which opposes the bellows factor is characteristic of some lens designs, for example lenses which focus internally so that the front element does not move. In this case the focal length of the lens is reduced as the object plane moves closer to the lens, and so α *increases* for a fixed framing. This can partially compensate for the reduction in α due to the bellows factor. In the case that the bellows factor is over-compensated for, there will be an overall increase in α and objects appear to shrink. This is known as *focus breathing*.

1.2.4 Field of view area

Although the FoV is defined at the object plane, the FoV area can in principle be measured at any plane positioned at an arbitrary distance l from the first principal plane. Referring to such a plane as an FoV plane, the area of the FoV plane is a function of both l *and* the position of the object plane on which the lens is focused,

$$\text{FoV} = 4(l - s_{\text{ep}})^2 \tan\left(\frac{\alpha_x}{2}\right) \tan\left(\frac{\alpha_y}{2}\right).$$

Here α_x and α_y are the AFoVs calculated in the horizontal and vertical directions using equation (1.25) for a lens focused at a specific object plane which specifies the bellows factor b. The distance s_{ep} is defined by equation (1.23),

$$s_{\text{ep}} = \left(1 - \frac{1}{m_{\text{p}}}\right) f_{\text{F}}.$$

If the lens is focused at infinity, $b = 1$ for any focal length, in which case there is a simple relationship between focal length and FoV. For example, if the focal length f_{F} is doubled, the FoV area measured at finite l is reduced by a factor of 4. Figure 1.20 illustrates the relative difference in FoV at a selection of focal lengths when the lens is focused at infinity.

Figure 1.20. Relative difference in FoV for a selection of focal lengths (mm) corresponding to a 35 mm full-frame system. Focus is set at infinity in all cases.

The relationship between focal length and FoV is not as simple when the lens is focused on a closer object plane because the bellows factor b will become a function of magnification and focal length. This can be seen from the following formula obtained by combining the Gaussian conjugate and magnification equations,

$$|m| = \frac{f_F}{s - f_F}.$$ (1.28)

1.2.5 Focal-length multiplier

Given the lens effective focal length f_E and camera system sensor format, equation (1.25) can be used to determine the AFoV. In order to obtain the same AFoV using a camera system with a different sensor format, a different effective focal length would be required. This is referred to as the *equivalent* focal length required on the other system.

In order to aid comparison between different camera systems, the equivalent focal length required on a 35 mm full-frame sensor is commonly referred to. A full-frame sensor has the same dimensions as 35 mm full-frame film. The relationship is defined as

$$\boxed{f_{E,35} = m_f f_E}.$$ (1.29)

Here f_E is the effective focal length on the given system, $f_{E,35}$ is the effective focal length on a 35 mm full-frame system that would yield the same AFoV, and m_f is the *focal-length multiplier*. The quantity $f_{E,35}$ is referred to as the 35 mm equivalent or *full-frame equivalent* focal length. It has been assumed that the camera is being used in air so that $f_F = f_E$.

By definition, $m_f = 1$ for a 35 mm full-frame sensor. Approximate values for other sensor formats are given in figure 1.21. These all assume that the focus is set at

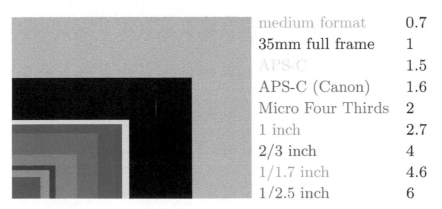

medium format	0.7
35mm full frame	1
APS-C	1.5
APS-C (Canon)	1.6
Micro Four Thirds	2
1 inch	2.7
2/3 inch	4
1/1.7 inch	4.6
1/2.5 inch	6

Figure 1.21. Common sensor formats scaled larger than actual size for clarity. The corresponding approximate value of the infinity-focus focal-length multiplier m_f is indicated.

infinity when comparing the AFoV. At closer focus distances, equation (1.29) is no longer exact. According to equation (1.28), the magnification of the two systems will not be identical when focus is set on the same object plane. The generalised formula is

$$f_{E,35} = \frac{m_f f_E}{1 + \beta}.$$

The correction β is defined by

$$\beta = \frac{(m_f - 1)(f_E/s)}{m_p - (m_p - 1)(f_E/s)}.$$

This corrects for the magnification difference so that α is the same for both systems. The distance s is defined from the first principal plane of the smaller format to the object plane. This equation will be derived in chapter 5 where cross-format comparisons are discussed in detail.

The term *crop factor* can be used in place of focal-length multiplier when a lens is used which has a wider imaging circle than the sensor format on which it is mounted. For example 35 mm full-frame lenses can be used on APS-C cameras. Strictly speaking, the term should not be used for sensor formats where the lens image circle is optimised for the sensor format and is not being cropped, an example being the Micro Four Thirds^{TM} format.

1.3 Depth of field

In section 1.1.3 it was mentioned that for a given object plane and corresponding image plane, an object lying in front or behind that object plane can still appear acceptably sharp at the image plane. The requirement is that the object must lie within a distance from the object plane known as the *depth of field* (DoF). More precisely, an object behind the object plane must lie within the far DoF, and an object in front of the object plane must lie within the near DoF. It is possible to derive simple equations for the DoF within Gaussian optics. However, geometrical optics does not take into account the wave phenomenon of diffraction and so these equations will only yield approximate results in practice.

1.3.1 Circle of confusion

Consider the geometry illustrated in figure 1.22. A lens with pupil magnification m_p will be considered for generality [10]. The object plane is positioned at a distance s from the first principal point P. The corresponding image plane coincides with the sensor plane at a distance s' from the second principal point P'.

Now consider the upper diagram where a point object is placed at the optical axis *in front* of the object plane at a distance s_n from P. The rays from this point will converge *behind* the sensor plane at a distance s_n' from P'. At the sensor plane the image of the point will be a *blur spot* with diameter c.

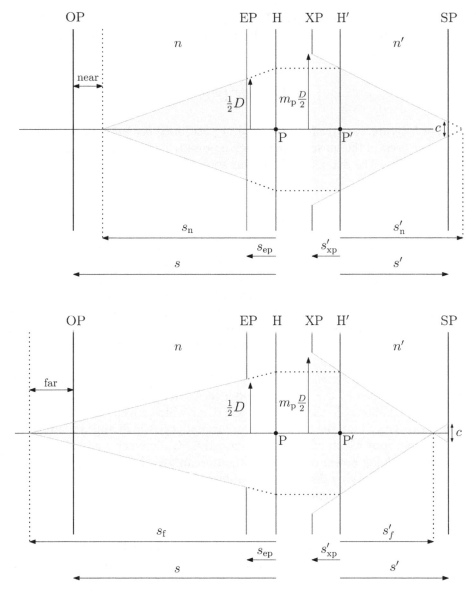

Figure 1.22. Geometry for the DoF equations. The pupil magnification $m_p > 1$ in this example. The near DoF and far DoF boundaries are defined by the distances where the blur spot diameter is equal to the acceptable CoC diameter c.

In order to derive an expression for c, recall from section 1.2.3 that the exit pupil has diameter $m_p D$ and lies a distance from P′ defined by equation (1.22),

$$s'_{xp} = (1 - m_p)f'_R.$$

The exit pupil therefore lies a distance $s'_n - s'_{xp}$ from the point of sharp focus. From the upper diagram it can be seen that the exit pupil forms the base of a triangle with the point of sharp focus at its apex. The blur spot forms the base of a scaled triangle with the same apex, but situated at a distance $s'_n - s'$ from the point of sharp focus. Therefore c is given by

$$c = \left(\frac{s'_n - s'}{s'_n - s'_{xp}}\right) m_p D. \tag{1.30}$$

In the lower figure, rays from a point object positioned *behind* the object plane will converge *in front* of the sensor plane. Such a point will also appear as a blur spot at the sensor plane. The diameter of the blur spot will be

$$c = \left(\frac{s' - s'_f}{s'_f - s'_{xp}}\right) m_p D. \tag{1.31}$$

Provided the diameter c does not exceed a prescribed value, objects situated between s_n and s_f will remain acceptably sharp or in-focus at the sensor plane. The blur spot with this prescribed diameter c is known as the acceptable *circle of confusion* (CoC).

The criterion for defining the CoC size is based upon the assumption that detail smaller than the CoC will be undetectable to a human *observer of the output image* from the camera under standard viewing conditions. The output image may be on a display or print, and the viewing conditions include a standard viewing distance and enlargement. Points positioned in the photographic scene which appear on the sensor plane as blur spots *smaller* than the CoC will not affect the appearance of the output image as seen by the observer under these viewing conditions. On the other hand, points positioned in the photographic scene which appear on the sensor plane as blur spots *larger* than the CoC will produce imagery which appears out of focus. Viewing conditions which affect the prescribed CoC diameter c include:

- The resolving power or acuity of the human visual system (HVS).
- The image viewing distance and ambient conditions.
- The enlargement factor from the sensor dimensions to the viewed output image dimensions.

Smaller sensors require a smaller CoC because the enlargement factor will be greater. A common value chosen by camera manufacturers based upon an assumed set of viewing conditions is $d/1500$, where d is the size of the sensor diagonal. Table 1.2 lists example CoC diameters for various sensor formats. Chapter 5 will discuss the concept of the CoC in greater detail.

1.3.2 Depth of field equations

A straightforward way to derive the DoF equations is to first project the CoC onto the *object* plane according to the magnification between the object and image planes [5]. The geometry shown in the upper diagram of figure 1.22 reveals that

$$\frac{c}{|m|} = \left(\frac{s - s_n}{s_n - s_{ep}}\right) D. \tag{1.32}$$

Table 1.2. Example CoC diameters for various sensor formats.

Sensor format	Sensor dimensions (mm)	CoC (mm)
35 mm full frame	36 × 24	0.030
APS-C	23.6 × 15.7	0.020
APS-C (Canon®)	22.2 × 14.8	0.019
Micro Four Thirds™	17.3 × 13	0.015
1 inch	13.2 × 8.8	0.011
2/3 inch	8.6 × 6.6	0.008
1/1.7 inch	7.6 × 5.7	0.006
1/2.5 inch	5.76 × 4.29	0.005

Similarly from the lower diagram of figure 1.22,

$$\frac{c}{|m|} = \left(\frac{s_f - s}{s_f - s_{ep}} \right) D. \tag{1.33}$$

The distance s_{ep} has been defined by equation (1.23),

$$\boxed{s_{ep} = \left(\frac{m_p - 1}{m_p} \right) f_F}.$$

Near depth of field
The distance s_n can be found by rearranging equation (1.32),

$$s_n = \frac{|m|Ds + cs_{ep}}{|m|D + c}.$$

Any object positioned closer than the distance s_n from the first principal plane is considered to be out of focus.

The *near DoF* is the distance $s - s_n$. This is given by

$$\boxed{\text{near DoF} = \frac{c(s - s_{ep})}{|m|D + c}}. \tag{1.34}$$

Any object positioned closer than the object plane with a separation distance greater than $s - s_n$ from the object plane is considered to be out of focus.

Far depth of field
The distance s_f can be found by rearranging equation (1.33),

$$s_f = \frac{|m|Ds - cs_{ep}}{|m|D - c}$$

Any object positioned further than the distance s_f from the first principal plane is considered to be out of focus.

The *far DoF* is the distance $s_f - s$. This is given by

$$\text{far DoF} = \left| \frac{c(s - s_{ep})}{|m|D - c} \right|. \tag{1.35}$$

Any object positioned beyond the object plane with a separation distance greater than $s_f - s$ from the object plane is considered to be out of focus.

Total depth of field
The *total DoF* is the distance between the near and far boundaries, $s_f - s_n$, and can be obtained by adding together the near and far DoF equations,

$$\text{total DoF} = \left| \frac{2|m|Dc(s - s_{ep})}{m^2 D^2 - c^2} \right|. \tag{1.36}$$

DoF depends upon the following:

- Object distance s. Reducing s by moving closer to the object plane reduces the DoF. The location of the first principal plane from which the object distance is measured can be found from the lens design data, however its precise location is unimportant beyond macro to portrait object distances.
- Entrance pupil diameter D. This can be written

$$D = \frac{f_F}{N},$$

where N is the lens *f-number*. Section 1.4 covers exposure and will discuss the f-number in detail. Reducing N for a fixed focal length increases D and so the DoF is reduced according to equations (1.34) and (1.35). Similarly, increasing the focal length for a fixed f-number increases D and reduces DoF.

- Magnification m. This can be calculated using the formula

$$|m| = \frac{f_F}{s - f_F}.$$

The front effective focal length f_F determines the minimum possible object distance s. In air, $f_F = f_E$. According to equations (1.34) and (1.35), mD influences the distribution of the near and far DoF. This is discussed below in the section on hyperfocal distance.

- Acceptable CoC diameter c. This depends upon the sensor format. Standard values assumed by the camera or lens manufacturer are listed in table 1.2. In chapter 5, the equation will be given for calculating a more appropriate value for c if the intended print enlargement and viewing distance are known. Chapter 5 also discusses cross-format comparisons including how DoF relates to sensor format.

- Pupil magnification m_p. The distance s_{ep} depends upon m_p and can be calculated using equation (1.23),

$$s_{ep} = \left(\frac{m_p - 1}{m_p} \right) f_F.$$

The pupil magnification is important when using a dedicated macro or portrait lens and its value can be found from the lens design data. Beyond these working distances, s_{ep} can be neglected.

Alternative expressions

Various alternative forms of the DoF equations can be found [5, 10]. One example arises from defining the following quantity,

$$h = \frac{f_F^2}{cN}. \tag{1.37}$$

This is an approximation of the *hyperfocal distance H* to be discussed in the section below. In terms of h, the DoF equations can be written

$$\boxed{\begin{aligned}
\text{near DoF} &= \frac{(s - f_F)(s - s_{ep})}{h + (s - f_F)} \\[2mm]
\text{far DoF} &= \frac{(s - f_F)(s - s_{ep})}{h - (s - f_F)} \\[2mm]
\text{total DoF} &= \frac{2h(s - f_F)(s - s_{ep})}{h^2 - (s - f_F)^2}
\end{aligned}}$$

Unity pupil magnification

If $m_p = 1$ then the pupils coincide with the principal planes and $s_{ep} = 0$. However, the pupil magnification in real photographic lenses is rarely unity. Nevertheless, the pupil magnification has negligible effect on the DoF formulae when the object plane is positioned sufficiently far from the lens, typically beyond macro to portrait distances as mentioned above. In this case the s_{ep} term can be dropped. For example, the above form of the DoF equations reduces to

$$\boxed{\begin{aligned}
\text{near DoF} &= \frac{(s - f_F)s}{h + (s - f_F)} \\[2mm]
\text{far DoF} &= \frac{(s - f_F)s}{h - (s - f_F)} \\[2mm]
\text{total DoF} &= \frac{2h(s - f_F)s}{h^2 - (s - f_F)^2}
\end{aligned}}$$

An illustration of these equations for the 35 mm full-frame format with CoC diameter $c = 0.030$ mm and example s, f_F, and N values is given in figure 1.23. The green horizontal dashed line indicates the CoC, and the intersection of the graph with this line marks the boundaries of the DoF.

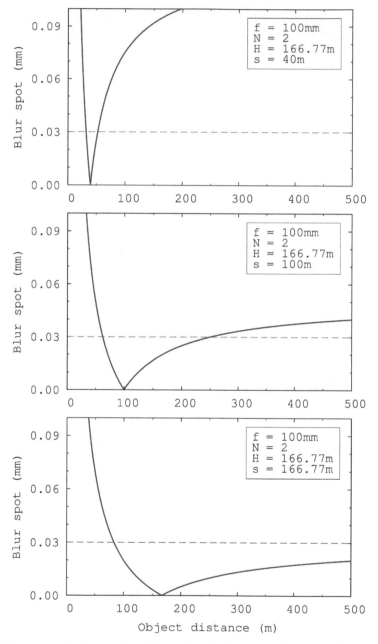

Figure 1.23. Blur spot as a function of object distance from the first principal point after focusing on the object plane positioned at distance s. The horizontal dashed line indicates an acceptable CoC with diameter $c = 0.030$ mm.

1-36

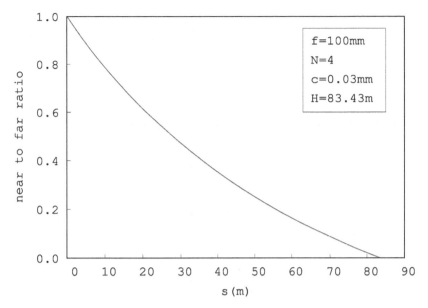

Figure 1.24. Near DoF divided by the far DoF as a function of distance s from the first principal plane for example f_F, N, and c values. At the minimum focus distance past $s = f_F$, the near and far DoF are almost equal and so the ratio is 1:1. At the hyperfocal distance H, the ratio is 1: ∞ and so the fraction is zero.

1.3.3 Hyperfocal distance

Figure 1.24 shows the ratio of the near DoF to the far DoF as a function of object-plane distance s for example f_F, N and c values. The pupil magnification has been set to unity. It can be seen that the near DoF and far DoF are equal only when $s = f_F$ which is 100 mm in this example. In fact the magnification is infinite at this object distance and the lens is unable to achieve focus. As the object plane moves further away from the lens, focus can in principle be achieved and the ratio of the near to far DoF is seen to decrease from unity. For example, $|m| = 1$ when $s = 2f_F$, and the near to far DoF ratio is $(D - c)/(D + c)$ or equivalently $(h - f_F)/(h + f_F)$.

As the object-plane distance increases further, a distance $s = H$ is eventually reached where the near to far DoF ratio reduces to zero because the far DoF extends to infinity. This value $s = H$ is known as the *hyperfocal distance* [5]. From equation (1.35), the far DoF extends to infinity when

$$|m| = \frac{c}{D}. \tag{1.40}$$

Substituting equation (1.28) for $|m|$ with s equal to H yields

$$\frac{f_F}{H - f_F} = \frac{c}{D} = \frac{cN}{f_F}.$$

This can be re-arranged to give

$$\boxed{H = h + f_F}. \tag{1.41}$$

Note that the hyperfocal distance H is independent of the pupil magnification m_p. The quantity h is an approximation to H defined by equation (1.37) earlier,

$$h = \frac{f_F^2}{cN}.$$

When s is equal to H, the corresponding near DoF is given by $H - s_n$. Substituting the above expression for H into the near DoF equation and working through the algebra yields

$$H - s_n = \frac{H - s_{ep}}{2}.$$

Since the distance between the entrance pupil and first principal plane is negligible compared to the hyperfocal distance, the s_{ep} term can be neglected. This leads to the following result,

$$\boxed{H - s_n = \frac{H}{2}}.$$

Therefore when the object plane is positioned at the hyperfocal distance $s = H$, the far DoF extends to infinity and the near DoF extends to half the hyperfocal distance. According to Gaussian optics, focusing at the hyperfocal distance yields the maximum available DoF for a given combination of camera settings. This is useful for landscape photography. This is also the focus setting for fixed-focus cameras which rely on maximising the DoF to produce in-focus images.

Figure 1.23 illustrates the hyperfocal distance for the 35 mm full-frame format with CoC diameter $c = 0.030$ mm and example s, f_F, and N values. When $s = H$, the blur spot never reaches the value 0.030 mm behind s, but it reaches 0.030 mm at a distance $H/2$ in front of s. In reality, the blur spot will never vanish due to the effects of diffraction. Diffraction will be discussed in chapters 3 and 5.

1.3.4 Focus and recompose limits

A widely used technique for setting the focus on *static* subjects is the *focus and recompose* method. Typically the centre autofocus point in the viewfinder is used to focus on the subject, the focus is locked by pressing the shutter, and then the camera is pivoted to recompose the scene before the shutter is released. While this method is adequate for landscape photography, it can lead to error in close-up photography. In particular, the object will become out of focus if it pivots outside the near DoF after recomposing. This can be particularly problematic in portrait photography which typically requires precise focus on the eye nearest to the camera. An example is shown in figure 1.25.

Consider the geometry illustrated in figure 1.26. First the focus is set on the object at point p using the centre autofocus point. This defines the object plane and the near DoF. Assuming the camera is pivoted about the lens entrance pupil when

Figure 1.25. Accurate focus is critical when the DoF is narrow.

recomposing, the maximum pivot angle φ allowed before p falls outside the near DoF limit is given by

$$\varphi = \cos^{-1}\left[\frac{s_n - s_{ep}}{s - s_{ep}}\right].$$

This angle is valid in any pivot direction. The distance $s_n - s_{ep}$ can be found by re-arranging the near DoF equation (1.34),

$$s_n - s_{ep} = \frac{|m|D(s - s_{ep})}{|m|D + c}.$$

Therefore

$$\varphi = \cos^{-1}\left[\frac{D}{D + (c/|m|)}\right].$$

This can be manipulated into the alternative form

$$\boxed{\varphi = \cos^{-1}\left[\frac{h}{h + s - f_F}\right].}$$

The pivot angle is seen to be independent of the pupil magnification.

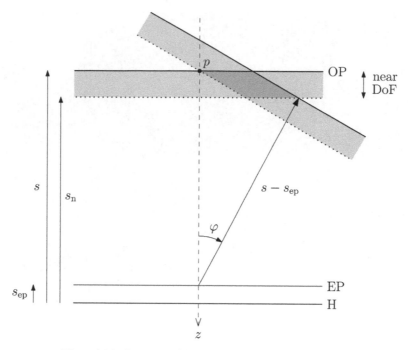

Figure 1.26. Geometry of the focus and recompose technique.

For the special case that the lens is focused at the hyperfocal distance H, equation (1.40) reveals that $c/|m| = D$, and equation (1.41) reveals that $s - f_F = h$, and so the maximum allowed pivot angle is

$$\varphi = \cos^{-1}(0.5) = 60°.$$

Generally, if the calculated φ is too small for the required recomposition, it is advisable to first compose the scene and then set focus by using an alternative viewfinder autofocus point that lies as close as possible to the location of the subject. This can be achieved more easily using a camera which allows quick repositioning of the focus point. An advantage of digital cameras which use contrast-detect autofocus is that the available focus points cover the entire viewfinder area. Some of these cameras have facial recognition algorithms which allow automatic detection of, and focusing on, the eye nearest to the camera.

1.3.5 Keystone distortion

The object plane has remained perpendicular to the optical axis throughout the theory discussed so far. Figure 1.27 shows a situation where the intended object plane has been tilted by an angle θ. The new object plane visible within the AFoV is shown by the thick black line in object space. The corresponding image plane shown by the thick black line in image space is tilted relative to the sensor plane. Significantly, the ratio s'/s changes with height from the optical axis so that the

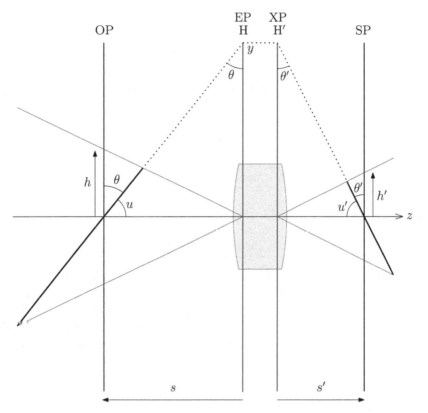

Figure 1.27. Keystone distortion is caused by the magnification varying across the image plane. Here the pupil magnification is unity for simplicity.

magnification varies across the image plane. This leads to *keystone distortion* when the image is projected onto the sensor plane [2, 3].

The relationship between θ and θ' is known as the *Scheimpflug condition*. An expression can straightforwardly be found within Gaussian optics [2, 3]. One argument proceeds by using the linearity of the paraxial region to perform a hypothetical extension of the principal planes as shown in figure 1.27. A paraxial ray leaving the optical axis with tangent slope u will intersect the first principal plane at height y, and therefore

$$u = \frac{y}{s}.$$

Since the principal planes are planes of unit magnification, the ray must emerge from the second principal plane at the same height y. The ray will intersect the optical axis at a distance s' from the second principal plane, and so the paraxial tangent slope u' is given by

$$u' = \frac{y}{s'}.$$

Therefore

$$u = \left(\frac{s'}{s}\right) u' = mu',$$

where m is the Gaussian magnification at the optical axis. From the geometry it can be seen that

$$\tan \theta = \frac{s}{y} = \frac{1}{u}$$

$$\tan \theta' = \frac{s'}{y} = \frac{1}{u'}.$$

Combining these equations yields the Scheimpflug condition,

$$\boxed{\tan \theta' = m \tan \theta}.$$

If the object plane is tilted relative to the camera, a large tilt angle may cause the object plane to extend beyond the DoF. On the other hand, the Scheimpflug principle can be utilised by special purpose lenses. For example, tilt-shift lenses can be used to control the orientation of the object plane relative to the image plane. In particular, the object plane can be set parallel to the ground while avoiding keystone distortion. This is useful for extending apparent DoF in architectural or landscape photography [5].

1.4 Exposure

Exposure is a measure of the amount of light per unit area which reaches the sensor plane while the camera shutter is open. In particular, *photometric exposure* includes a weighting which takes into account the spectral sensitivity of the HVS. Photometric exposure depends upon a number of factors:

- A measure of the light from the photographic scene which passes through the lens to the sensor plane in terms of the rate of energy flow. This can be quantified using *photometry*.
- The ability of the lens to bend light rays. This depends upon the total refractive power of the lens which can be described in terms of the effective focal length f_E introduced in section 1.1.5.
- The lens aperture stop opening which restricts the size of the ray bundle entering and exiting the lens. From a given object position, this ray bundle is formed between the chief and marginal rays defined in section 1.2.
- The transmissive properties of the lens.
- The nature of the object-space and image-space refractive media n and n'.
- The time duration the imaging sensor is exposed to the light which emerges from the lens.

Based on the above considerations, a formal expression for the photometric exposure at the sensor plane will be derived in this section. This will be used as a basis for developing a photographic exposure strategy in chapter 2. The familiar f-number will emerge as one of the fundamental quantities.

1.4.1 Photometry

The 'amount' of light from the photographic scene which passes through the lens to the sensor plane can be quantified in terms of power or flux. Photometric or *luminous flux* Φ_v is the rate of flow of electromagnetic energy emitted from or received by a specified surface area, appropriately weighted to take into account the spectral sensitivity of the HVS. The unit of measurement is the lumen (lm). Table 1.3 lists various other photometric quantities which are useful for describing the flow of flux from the photographic scene to the sensor plane.

The luminous flux *per unit area* received by a specified surface is known as *illuminance* E_v. The unit of measurement is the lux (lx), which is equivalent to lm m^{-2}. Integrating illuminance over a surface area yields the total flux for that area. In photography, the illuminance at the sensor plane is of primary interest.

Now consider the flux emerging from the scene being photographed. When flux is *emitted* from an area, the quantity analogous to illuminance is *luminous exitance* M_v. However, luminous exitance does not depend on direction and so it is not a convenient quantity for measuring the light emitted from the scene in the direction of the lens entrance pupil. A more useful quantity is *luminous intensity* I_v, which is the flux emitted from a *point* source into a *cone*. Luminous intensity takes into account the direction of propagation. The cone is defined per unit solid angle measured in steradians (sr) as illustrated in figure 1.28. The unit of measurement of luminous intensity is the candela (cd), equivalent to lm/sr.

When the source is extended, luminous intensity can be spread out over an infinitesimal area. This defines *luminance* L_v as the luminous flux per unit solid angle per unit projected area. Appropriately integrating luminance over source area and solid angle yields the flux received by the observer. Importantly, the *scene luminance distribution* can now be defined as an array of infinitesimal luminance patches representing the photographic scene, and each scene position subtends a solid angle with the lens entrance pupil. The lens transforms the flux defined by the scene

Table 1.3. Common photometric quantities with their symbols and SI units.

Photometry		
Quantity	Symbol	Unit
Luminous flux	Φ_v	lm
Illuminance	E_v	lx $\equiv$ lm m^{-2}
Luminous exitance	M_v	lx $\equiv$ lm m^{-2}
Luminous intensity	I_v	cd $\equiv$ lm sr^{-1}
Luminance	L_v	cd m^{-2}

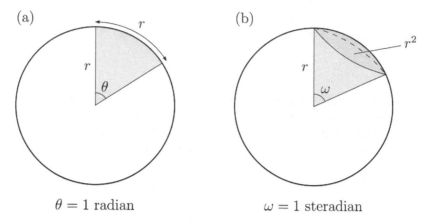

$\theta = 1$ radian $\qquad\qquad \omega = 1$ steradian

Figure 1.28. (a) An angle of 1 radian (rad) is defined by an arc length r of a circle with radius r. Since the radius of a circle is $2\pi r$, the angle corresponding to a whole circle is 2π radians. (b) A solid angle ω projects a point source onto the surface of a sphere, thus defining a cone. For a cone of radius r, a surface area of r^2 defines a solid angle of 1 steradian (sr). Since the surface area of a whole sphere is $4\pi r^2$, the solid angle corresponding to a whole sphere is 4π steradians.

luminance distribution into an array of infinitesimal illuminance patches on the sensor plane referred to as the *sensor-plane illuminance distribution*.

1.4.2 Flux emitted into a cone

The expression for the flux emitted from a small plane source into a cone is an important optical result needed for deriving various quantities related to exposure such as f-number. In this section, the derivation is performed using *real* angles [4, 12]. Subsequently, an expression will be obtained which is valid within Gaussian optics.

First recall from the previous section that the flux emitted into a cone from a *point source* is defined by

$$\Phi = I\omega. \tag{1.42}$$

Here I is the luminous intensity and ω is the solid angle defining the cone. An isolated point source of flux would have the same luminous intensity when viewed from any angle.

In contrast, consider a typical photographic scene where a source of flux such as the Sun is illuminating a *plane surface*. An ideal diffuse or *Lambertian* surface will scatter the flux into many different directions. For a point on such a surface, *Lambert's cosine law of intensity* states that the luminous intensity will fall off as the cosine of the angle θ between the scattered direction and the surface normal. Mathematically, this means that *the luminous intensity is dependent on θ*,

$$I(\theta) = I \cos \theta. \tag{1.43}$$

In figure 1.29, the plane surface is represented by the object plane. Consider a point on the object plane situated at the optical axis. The *luminance* at the optical axis can

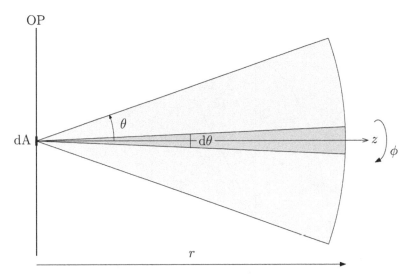

Figure 1.29. The angle element $d\theta$ is integrated from 0 to θ. The angle ϕ revolves around the optical axis z.

be associated with an infinitesimal area element dA. Note that the projected surface area seen by an observer at an angle θ from the surface normal is also reduced by the cosine of the angle θ,

$$dA(\theta) = dA \cos \theta.$$

It follows that the *luminance* of a Lambertian surface is independent of θ and hence the same when viewed from any direction,

$$L = \frac{I(\theta)}{dA(\theta)} = \frac{I}{dA}.$$

However, since the luminous *intensity* is dependent on θ according to equation (1.43), *angular integration is required in order to determine the flux emitted into a cone from the surface area element* dA. Equation (1.42) must be modified to

$$\Phi = \int_{\theta=0}^{\theta} \int_{\phi=0}^{2\pi} I_v(\theta_1) \, d\omega(\theta_1, \phi) \, d\theta_1 \, d\phi. \tag{1.44}$$

Here θ is the vertical angle of the cone from the optical axis, θ_1 is a dummy variable, and ϕ is the horizontal angle which revolves around the optical axis.

To determine the expression for an infinitesimal change in solid angle $d\omega$, consider the geometry illustrated in figure 1.30. The spherical surface area element dS for an infinitesimal (differential) change in vertical angle θ and infinitesimal change in horizontal angle ϕ is

$$dS = r \, d\theta_1 \times r \sin \theta_1 \, d\phi.$$

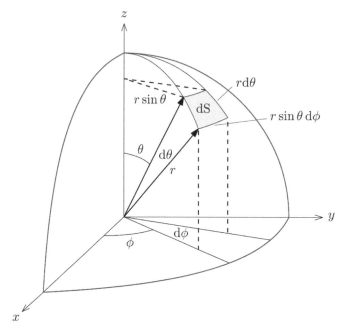

Figure 1.30. Surface area element dS of a cone of flux. Here the z-axis representing the optical axis is in the vertical direction.

Therefore

$$d\omega = \frac{r\,d\theta_1 \times r \sin \theta_1\,d\phi}{r^2} = \sin \theta_1\,d\theta_1\,d\phi. \tag{1.45}$$

Substituting equations (1.43) and (1.45) into equation (1.44) and performing the integration over ϕ yields

$$\Phi_v = 2\pi \int_0^\theta I \cos \theta_1 \sin \theta_1\,d\theta_1 = \pi L\,dA \int_0^\theta (2 \sin \theta_1 \cos \theta_1)d\theta_1. \tag{1.46}$$

Here θ_1 is the dummy variable. Performing this integration yields the following result,

$$\boxed{\Phi = \pi L \sin^2 \theta\,dA}. \tag{1.47}$$

Recall that dA is the infinitesimal area associated with a plane source at the optical axis, L is the luminance associated with dA, and θ is the *real* vertical angle subtended by the cone with the optical axis.

In the paraxial region, the dummy variables appearing in equation (1.46) become $\cos \theta_1 = 1$ and $\sin \theta_1 = u_1$, where u_1 is a paraxial ray tangent slope. Consequently, the expression for the flux emitted into a cone from a small plane surface valid within Gaussian optics is given by

$$\boxed{\Phi = \pi L \, u^2 \, \mathrm{d}A}.$$ (1.48)

This means that the base of the cone illustrated in figure 1.29 becomes flat within Gaussian optics.

1.4.3 Relative aperture

Figure 1.31 shows a ray bundle entering and exiting a lens from the *axial* position on the object plane. The ray tangent slopes u and u' correspond to the marginal ray in object space and image space, respectively. Recall that the paraxial marginal ray just makes it past the edge of the Gaussian entrance and exit pupils. In figure 1.31, the marginal ray is brought to a focus at the corresponding axial position on the Gaussian image plane. After lens focusing movement, the Gaussian image plane will coincide with the sensor plane. The infinitesimal areas $\mathrm{d}A$ and $\mathrm{d}A'$ associated with the axial positions just mentioned are shown in the figure.

The flux entering the lens from the axial position on the object plane is defined by equation (1.48) derived in the previous section,

$$\Phi = \pi L \, u^2 \, \mathrm{d}A.$$

Since the flux arriving at the sensor plane is the central quantity of interest, a relationship needs to be found between $\mathrm{d}A$ and $\mathrm{d}A'$.

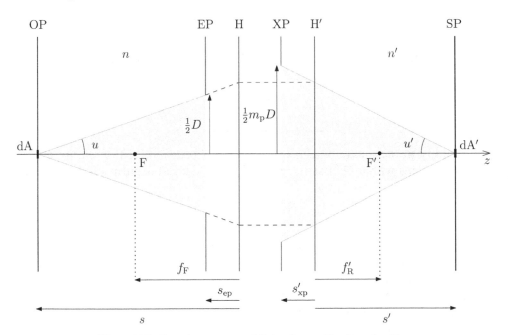

Figure 1.31. Gaussian geometry defining the working f-number N_w.

First note that dA and dA' may be expressed as the product of infinitesimal heights in the x and y directions,

$$dA = dh_x\, dh_y$$
$$dA' = dh'_x\, dh'_y.$$

The ratio of dA' to dA can therefore be expressed in terms of the Gaussian magnification,

$$\frac{dA'}{dA} = \frac{dh'_x}{dh_x}\frac{dh'_y}{dh_y} = m^2.$$

Substituting for dA in equation (1.48) now yields

$$\Phi = \pi L\, \frac{dA'}{m^2}\, u^2.$$

Further progress can be made by utilising the *Lagrange theorem* [1, 2] which defines an optical invariant valid within Gaussian optics. Application of the invariant provides a relationship between the magnification and the tangent slopes u and u',

$$m = \frac{nu}{n'u'}. \tag{1.49}$$

It follows that the flux at the axial area element on the sensor plane is given by

$$\Phi = \pi L\, dA'\left[\left(\frac{n'}{n}\right)u'\right]^2.$$

The corresponding *illuminance* at this axial position is $E = \Phi/dA'$ or

$$\boxed{E = \frac{\pi}{4}L\left[\left(\frac{n'}{n}\right)2u'\right]^2} . \tag{1.50}$$

The quantity in the square brackets is a general expression for the *relative aperture* (RA) of the lens within Gaussian optics which is valid at arbitrary focus distance,

$$\mathrm{RA} = \left(\frac{n'}{n}\right)2u'.$$

In order to arrive at a more convenient expression for the illuminance which is useful in practice, the tangent slope u' needs to be expressed in terms of axial distances. In photography it is useful to consider two cases:

1. Focus set at infinity. In this case E can be expressed in terms of the *f-number*.
2. Focus set closer than infinity. In this case E can be expressed in terms of the *working f-number*.

1.4.4 f-number

When focus is set at infinity, the object distance $s \to \infty$ and the image distance $s' \to f_R'$, where f_R' is the rear effective focal length. The corresponding geometry is illustrated in figure 1.32. The tangent slope u' is seen to be

$$u' = \frac{D}{2f_R'}.$$

Here D is the diameter of the *entrance* pupil. Substituting into equation (1.50) yields the following expression for the illuminance at dA',

$$E = \frac{\pi}{4} L \left[\left(\frac{n'}{n} \right) \frac{D}{f_R'} \right]^2 .$$

The refractive indices can be removed by utilising the relationship between the front and rear effective focal lengths defined by equation (1.16),

$$\frac{f_R'}{f_F} = \frac{n'}{n}.$$

Therefore

$$E = \frac{\pi}{4} L \left(\frac{D}{f_F} \right)^2 .$$

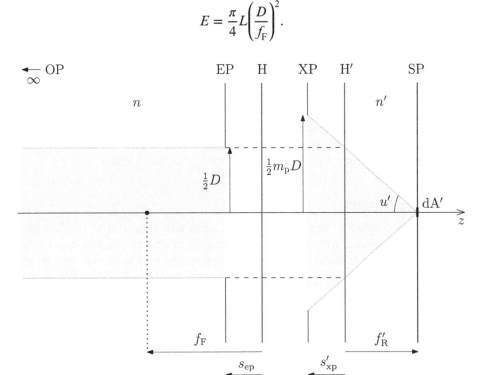

Figure 1.32. Gaussian geometry defining the f-number N for a lens focused at infinity. In this illustration the pupil magnification $m_p > 1$.

In the nineteenth century, the quantity D/f_{F} was defined as the *apertal ratio* [13], however this term has not come into widespread use. The apertal ratio is the specific case of the RA when the lens is focused at infinity. In photography it is numerically more convenient to consider the reciprocal of the apertal ratio instead which is defined as the *f-number N*,

$$N = \frac{f_{\mathrm{F}}}{D} \qquad (1.51)$$

RA and f-number therefore have a reciprocal relationship [14]. The f-number is usually marked on lens barrels using the symbols *f/N* or 1:*N*, where *N* is the f-number. (In order to avoid confusion with the focal length, the symbol *N* will be used for f-number in this book.) The expression for the illuminance at the *axial* area element on the sensor plane when focus is set at infinity becomes

$$E = \frac{\pi}{4} L \frac{1}{N^2}. \qquad (1.52)$$

Equation (1.51) shows that the f-number is defined as the *front* effective focal length divided by the diameter of the entrance pupil [2, 15]. The f-number is commonly but incorrectly defined as the effective focal length f_{E} or rear effective focal length f'_{R} divided by the diameter of the entrance pupil. In the former case, the correct numerical value for *N* would be obtained only if the object-space medium is air. In the latter case, the correct numerical value for *N* would be obtained only if the object-space and image-space media both have the same refractive index.

It is often assumed that the Gaussian expression for the f-number is an approximation. It will be shown in section 1.4.10 that the Gaussian expression is exact for a lens that is free of spherical aberration and coma. It will also be shown that the minimum value of the f-number in such a lens is limited to $N = 0.5$ in air.

1.4.5 Working f-number

At closer focus distances, lens focusing movement will ensure that the flux emitted from the object plane will be brought to a sharp focus at the sensor plane. Consequently, the rear focal point will no longer lie on the sensor plane and so $s' \neq f'_{\mathrm{R}}$. The relevant geometry is shown in figure 1.31. Simple trigonometry reveals that

$$u' = \frac{m_{\mathrm{p}}D/2}{\left(s' - s'_{\mathrm{xp}}\right)}.$$

Here *D* is the diameter of the entrance pupil, m_{p} is the pupil magnification, s' is the image distance measured from the second principal plane, and s'_{xp} is the distance from the second principal plane to the exit pupil. Expressions for s' and s'_{xp} were found earlier when deriving the FoV equations in section 1.2.3,

$$s' = (1 + |m|)f'_R$$
$$s'_{xp} = (1 - m_p)f'_R.$$

Here $|m|$ is the absolute value of the Gaussian magnification and f'_R is the rear effective focal length. Therefore

$$s' - s'_{xp} = (m_p + |m|)f'_R$$

and so

$$u' = \frac{m_p D}{2(m_p + |m|)f'_R}.$$

Substituting this equation into equation (1.50) and again utilising the relationship between the front and rear effective focal lengths defined by equation (1.16) leads to the following expression for the illuminance at the axial area element on the sensor plane,

$$E = \frac{\pi}{4}L\left(\frac{D}{bf_1}\right)^2. \tag{1.53}$$

The *bellows factor* b has previously been defined by equation (1.26),

$$\boxed{b = 1 + \frac{|m|}{m_p}}.$$

It is convenient to rewrite equation (1.53) in the form

$$\boxed{E = \frac{\pi}{4}L\frac{1}{N_w^2}}. \tag{1.54}$$

The *working f-number* N_w is defined by

$$\boxed{N_w = bN}. \tag{1.55}$$

At infinity focus, $|m| = 0$ and the bellows factor $b = 1$. The working f-number then reduces to the f-number N.

As the object plane is brought closer towards the lens, $|m|$ increases and so N_w also increases. This means that the illuminance *decreases* at closer focus distances. The contribution from the bellows factor can become significant at very close focus distances in the same way that it affects the AFoV. For example, macro photography involves reproduction ratios of 1:1 or larger so that $|m| \geqslant 1$. If $m_p = 1$ and $|m| = 1$ the bellows factor becomes $b = 2$ and equation (1.54) reveals that the flux arriving at the axial area element on the sensor plane is reduced to one quarter of the amount expected according to the value of the f-number N. In macro photography the pupil magnification m_p can also have a significant effect.

Photographic exposure strategy will be discussed in chapter 2. The traditional strategy is based upon the exposure value (EV), and this uses N rather than N_w. In other words, traditional exposure calculations assume that the object plane is located at infinity, and so only N is marked on lens barrels. Knowledge of $|m|$ and m_p for a given lens and working object distance will enable a photographer to compensate for any illuminance decrease at closer focus distances by using N_w in place of N in exposure calculations. This is useful when using a hand-held exposure meter. In the case of through-the-lens (TTL) metering systems, the illuminance decrease will be automatically taken into account [5].

1.4.6 f-stop

It has been shown that when the object plane is positioned at infinity, the illuminance at the *axial* area element dA' on the sensor plane is defined by

$$E = \frac{\pi}{4} L \frac{1}{N^2}.$$

Here L is the scene luminance at the axial area element on the object plane and N is the f-number,

$$N = \frac{f_F}{D}.$$

The flux collected at dA' is given by

$$\Phi = E \, dA'.$$

Provided the combination of front effective focal length f_F and entrance pupil diameter D is such that N is kept constant and the scene luminance L is time-independent, the flux or luminous power Φ incident at dA' will also remain constant.

Now consider adjusting the f-number N. Since E is inversely proportional to the square of N, the f-number must decrease by a factor $\sqrt{2}$ in order to double the flux Φ. Similarly, the f-number must increase by a factor $\sqrt{2}$ in order to halve Φ. Adjustable iris diaphragms are constructed so that successive increments will double or halve the flux Φ. This leads to the following series of possible f-numbers when the surrounding medium is air:

N:	0.5	0.7	1	1.4	2	2.8	4	5.6	8	11	16	22	32	etc

Changing the f-number by a single increment in this series is referred to as an increase or decrease by one *f-stop*. Modern iris diaphragms also allow fractional f-stops.

1.4.7 Natural vignetting

The f-number, working f-number, and f-stop have been derived based upon the flux emitted from the *axial* position on the object plane. Equations (1.52) and

(1.54) therefore give the illuminance only at the axial area element on the sensor plane.

For an arbitrary off-axis source position on the object plane, geometrical considerations dictate that the cone of flux subtended with the lens entrance pupil will be distorted. Even if the object plane is a Lambertian surface with a *uniform* scene luminance distribution, the illuminance at the corresponding off-axis area element on the sensor plane will be *reduced* compared to the axial value.

In order to obtain an expression for the illuminance valid at an arbitrary position on the sensor plane, equations (1.52) and (1.54) need to be modified to describe the cone of flux emitted from an arbitrary off-axis source position. This can be achieved through a straightforward modification of the derivation for the flux emitted into a cone given in section 1.4.2. Referring to the geometry of figure 1.33, the following modifications are required:

- The object plane area element normal to the centre of the entrance pupil is reduced by a factor $\cos\varphi$ so that $dA(\varphi) = dA\cos\varphi$.
- The radial distance r is extended by a factor $\cos\varphi$. This increases the projected differential solid angle element by a factor $\cos^2\varphi$.
- The differential area element on the surface of the cone at the entrance pupil is *approximately* reduced by a factor $\cos\varphi$. This approximation is valid provided the source point is far from the entrance pupil; the precise relation is given in [16].

Performing these modifications to the derivation given in section 1.2 leads to the following Gaussian formula,

$$\Phi(\varphi) = \pi L \, dA \, u^2 \cos^4\varphi. \tag{1.56}$$

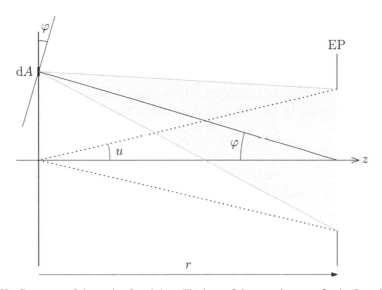

Figure 1.33. Geometry of the cosine fourth law. The base of the cone becomes flat in Gaussian optics.

This is the generalised expression for the flux entering the lens from an arbitrary source position on the object plane. Equation (1.54) now becomes

$$E = \frac{\pi}{4} L \frac{1}{N_w^2} \cos^4 \varphi \ .$$

If focus is set at infinity, N_w can be replaced by N. In this equation it is implicit that L and E are both functions of position, the system is rotationally symmetric, and the value of φ depends on the position of the area element under consideration on the object plane. Although the result is approximate, it is known as the *cosine fourth law*. The $\cos^4 \varphi$ factor takes into account the reduction in flux at the lens entrance pupil as the source position on the object plane moves away from the optical axis. This leads to natural darkening with radial distance from the centre of the resulting image, and is referred to as *fall-off*, *roll-off*, or *natural vignetting*. Examples are illustrated in figure 1.34.

The angle φ is an object-space angle [17, 18], however the cosine fourth law is often quoted with φ replaced by the image-space angle φ' subtended from the exit pupil by the corresponding off-axis position on the image plane. In fact, $\varphi = \varphi'$ only under the conditions that the pupil magnification $m_p = 1$ and the refractive indices of the object-space and image-space media are equal, $n = n'$. Since φ and φ' define the chief rays in object space and image space, the relationship between these angles can be found by applying the Lagrange invariant,

$$\varphi = \frac{n'}{n} m_p \, \varphi'.$$

1.4.8 Photometric exposure

Photometric exposure H_v at the sensor plane is defined as the time integral of the sensor-plane illuminance E over the exposure duration t,

$$H = \int_0^t E(t') \mathrm{d}t'.$$

Again the 'v' subscript has been dropped. If the illuminance does not change during the exposure duration, the time-integral can be replaced by the product,

$$\boxed{H = E \, t} \ . \tag{1.57}$$

Substituting equation (1.54) into equation (1.57) yields the following expression for H,

$$\boxed{H = \frac{\pi}{4} L \, T_{\text{lens}} \frac{t}{N_w^2} \cos^4 \varphi} \ . \tag{1.58}$$

A lens transmission factor $T_{\text{lens}} \leqslant 1$ has been included which takes into account light loss through the lens. This factor can also be included in the illuminance formulae. As described in the previous section, the angle φ is the object-space angle subtended

Figure 1.34. Natural cosine-fourth falloff for a rectilinear lens focused at infinity in air. The upper and lower diagrams show effective focal lengths of 24 mm and 50 mm, respectively, on a camera with a 35 mm full-frame sensor.

from the optical axis by the scene area element under consideration on the object plane.

Since illuminance E is the power or flux received per unit area weighted by the spectral response of the HVS, photometric exposure is the electromagnetic energy received per unit area weighted by the same response. It is implicit in equation (1.58) that L is a function of position on the object plane. Even if the scene luminance distribution is uniform, the illuminance E and hence exposure H will vary across the sensor plane for a given exposure duration t. Therefore photometric exposure H is also a function of position, and each position is associated with an infinitesimal area element dA' on the sensor plane. This dependence is not typically indicated in photographic formulae.

For a given scene luminance distribution L, the magnitude of the photometric exposure distribution at the sensor plane depends upon the exposure strategy of the photographer. A photographic exposure strategy includes both artistic and technical considerations and relies on the imaging sensor providing the required response. The user-controlled camera settings t and N, together with the ISO setting S to be defined later, are together known as the *camera exposure*.

A photometric measure of exposure is adequate for developing a photographic exposure strategy because camera metering is based upon photometry, and the sensitivity of the camera output to electromagnetic radiation (light) is similarly based upon photometry. A more complete description of camera output will be described in chapter 3 based upon a radiometric measure of exposure.

1.4.9 Exposure value

Traditional exposure calculations assume that the lens is focused at infinity so that the working f-number appearing in equation (1.58) is replaced by the f-number. The fraction t/N^2 can be related to a quantity known as the exposure value or EV. This is a convenient way of labelling the camera exposure and is defined by

$$\frac{t}{N^2} = \frac{1}{2^{\text{EV}}}. \tag{1.59}$$

This can be rearranged in a more useful form,

$$\boxed{\text{EV} = \text{AV} + \text{TV}}. \tag{1.60}$$

The *aperture value* (AV) and *time value* (TV) are defined by

$$\boxed{\begin{aligned} \text{AV} &= \log_2 N^2 \\ \text{TV} &= -\log_2 t \end{aligned}}.$$

The following table lists example values of f-number N and corresponding AV,

N:	0.5	0.7	1	1.4	2	2.8	4	5.6	etc
AV:	−2	−1	0	1	2	3	4	5	

It can be seen that a 1 AV change describes a 1 f-stop change in the axial flux. However it should be remembered that AVs are specific numbers to be associated with specific values of N.

The following table lists example values of t and corresponding TV,

t:	8	4	2	1	1/2	1/4	1/8	etc
TV:	−3	−2	−1	0	1	2	3	

It can be seen that a 1 TV increase corresponds to a halving of the exposure duration. TVs are specific numbers to be associated with specific values of t. When the exposure duration $t = 1$ s, the illuminance is numerically equal to the photometric exposure according to equation (1.57) and so EV = AV in this case.

From equation (1.60) it is evident that many combinations of t and N exist which have the same EV and therefore the same camera exposure. Modern digital cameras allow fractional EVs such as 1/3 and 1/2 EV. An increase or decrease by 1 EV corresponds to a doubling or halving, respectively, of the axial exposure. Nevertheless it should be remembered that each EV describes a set of possible N and t combinations. A *change* in EV can be quantified in terms of the *photographic stop* such that a difference of 1 EV defines 1 stop. The f-stop described previously in section 1.4.6 is the specific case of a photographic stop where the AV is adjusted.

1.4.10 f-number for aplanatic lenses

Further insight into the physical significance of the f-number requires going beyond Gaussian optics by considering a real ray bundle entering and exiting the lens. Figure 1.35 shows such a ray bundle leaving the axial position on the object plane. The ray angles U and U' are *real* angles which correspond to the real marginal ray in object space and image space, respectively. Real angles are defined by real rays which are traced through the optical system using exact trigonometrical relations [2, 3].

An *aplanatic* lens is defined as a lens that is free of spherical aberration and coma. Expressions for the RA and f-number are derived below that are valid for aplanatic lenses. In particular, it will be shown that the Gaussian expression is exact for an aplanatic lens.

In section 1.4.3, the Lagrange theorem was utilised in order to obtain a relationship between the Gaussian magnification and the paraxial ray tangent slopes u and u' defined by equation (1.49),

$$m = \frac{nu}{n'u'}.$$

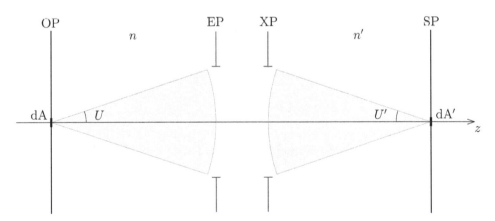

Figure 1.35. The object-space and image-space numerical apertures are defined in terms of the half-cone angles U and U' formed by the real marginal ray which makes it past the edge of the lens aperture. In this diagram the acceptance angles of the cones have been extended up to the entrance and exit pupils.

This equation, valid within Gaussian optics, was used to obtain an expression for the RA. By replacing u and u' with the sines of the real ray angles U and U', the Lagrange theorem can be extended to the *sine theorem* which is valid for real rays [1, 2]. This leads to the following expression for the magnification M defined by the *real* marginal ray,

$$M = \frac{n \sin U}{n' \sin U'} = \frac{\text{NA}}{\text{NA}'}. \tag{1.62}$$

The quantity NA is the *object-space numerical aperture*, and NA' is the *image-space numerical aperture*.

In an aplanatic lens, $M = m$. In other words, the real marginal magnification is equal to the Gaussian magnification and so the position of the image plane defined by the real marginal ray will be identical with the Gaussian image plane position. In this case the sine theorem takes the form

$$\boxed{\frac{\sin U'}{u'} = \frac{\sin U}{u}}. \tag{1.63}$$

This is *Abbe's sine condition* [1, 2, 12] for a lens to be free of spherical aberration and coma.

Now consider the flux entering an aplanatic lens from the axial position on the object plane. This is given by the expression for the flux emitted into a cone derived in section 1.4.2 and defined by equation (1.47) with $\theta = U$,

$$\Phi = \pi L \sin^2 U \, dA.$$

Substituting the Gaussian magnification $m^2 = dA'/dA$ yields

$$\Phi = \pi L \frac{dA'}{m^2} \sin^2 U.$$

Now substituting for m using Abbe's sine condition [12] yields the following expression for the flux collected at the axial area element dA',

$$\Phi = \frac{\pi}{4} L \left[\left(\frac{n'}{n} \right) 2 \sin U' \right]^2 dA'.$$

The illuminance at dA' is $E = \Phi/dA'$ or

$$E = \frac{\pi}{4} L \left[\left(\frac{n'}{n} \right) 2 \sin U' \right]^2. \tag{1.64}$$

This may be written more compactly in the form

$$\boxed{E = \frac{\pi}{4} L \left[\frac{2 \, \text{NA}'}{n} \right]^2}. \tag{1.65}$$

This equation, derived using real rays, has similarities to the Gaussian expression defined by equation (1.50) which was derived using paraxial ray tangent slopes. The bracketed quantity here is a generalisation of the RA valid for real rays,

$$ \mathrm{RA} = \frac{2n' \sin U'}{n} = \frac{2\,\mathrm{NA}'}{n}. $$

This equation is valid for arbitrary object-plane distance. The angle U' is maximised at infinity focus. When the object plane is brought forward from infinity, the object-space angle U and object-space numerical aperture NA both become larger and the magnification increases according to equation (1.62). On the other hand, the image-space angle U' and image-space numerical aperture NA' both become smaller which reduces the illuminance at the axial area element on the sensor plane. The maximum achievable magnification will in theory be higher if the object-space medium has a higher refractive index than the image-space medium. This principle is utilised in microscopes by immersing the objective in immersion oil, typically with a refractive index $n \approx 1.5$. Conversely for a given scene luminance, the maximum achievable illuminance at the axial area element on the sensor plane could in principle be increased by using an image-space medium with a higher refractive index than the object-space medium.

The f-number is defined as the reciprocal of the RA when the lens is focused at infinity [14]. In the case of an aplanatic lens, this may be written

$$ N = \frac{n}{2\,\mathrm{NA}'_\infty}. $$

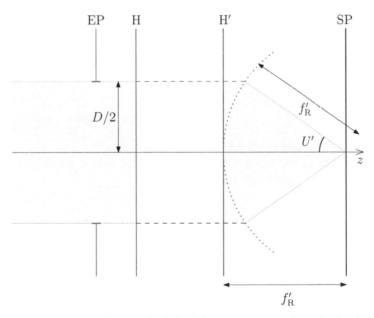

Figure 1.36. In a real aplanatic lens the second principal plane becomes part of a perfect hemisphere centred at the rear focal point (dashed blue curve) when the lens is focused at infinity. The entrance pupil diameter is D; the exit pupil is not involved.

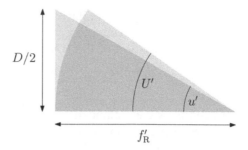

Figure 1.37. Remembering that u' must be interpreted as a tangent when the paraxial region is extended, the sine of the real angle U' must equal u' when an aplanatic lens is focused at infinity.

In order to show that this is equivalent to the Gaussian expression $N = f_F/D$, the first step is to consider Abbe's sine condition defined by equation (1.63) when the object plane approaches infinity. The object-space angles $\sin U$ and u will approach zero, however the ratio $\sin U/u$ approaches unity and Abbe's sine condition reduces to an interesting form [19],

$$\frac{\sin U'}{u'} = 1 \quad \text{when} \quad s \to \infty.$$

Since the image plane is positioned a distance f'_R from the second principal point and u' is a *tangent* slope, the real image-space ray bundle must be associated with an equivalent refracting surface that takes the form of a *hemisphere* centred at the rear focal point in order for this equation to hold. The geometry is shown in figure 1.36. In other words, the second principal plane defined in Gaussian optics is in reality a surface that is part of a perfect sphere. Since this principal surface has *radius* f'_R and is centred at the rear focal point when focus is set at infinity, the following relation holds exactly [1, 2, 5, 9],

$$\sin U' = \frac{D}{2f'_R} \quad \text{when} \quad s \to \infty. \tag{1.66}$$

The relationship between U' and u' is illustrated in figure 1.37.

The illuminance at the axial area element on the sensor plane can be found by substituting equation (1.66) into equation (1.64),

$$E = \frac{\pi}{4}L\left[\left(\frac{n'}{n}\right)\frac{D}{f'_R}\right]^2 \quad \text{when} \quad s \to \infty.$$

The refractive indices can be accounted for by utilising the relationship between the front and rear effective focal lengths defined by equation (1.16). This yields

$$E = \frac{\pi}{4}L\left(\frac{D}{f_F}\right)^2 \equiv \frac{\pi}{4}L\frac{1}{N^2} \quad \text{when} \quad s \to \infty.$$

This means that the Gaussian expression for the f-number is seen to hold exactly for a lens that is free of spherical aberration and coma,

$$N = \frac{n}{2\,NA'_\infty} = \frac{f_F}{D}.$$

Writing $N = f_F/D$ can lead to the incorrect assumption that the f-number can be made arbitrarily small. However, the equivalent expression $N = n/(2\,NA'_\infty)$ reveals that the lowest possible f-number for a well-corrected lens is $N = 0.5$ in air. This limit can be lowered by using an image-space medium with a higher refractive index than object space, $n' > n$. This will increase the value of the infinity-focus image-space numerical aperture NA'_∞ relative to the value of the object-space refractive index n. For example, if an image-space medium is used with a refractive index $n' = 1.5$ and the object-space medium is air, the lowest possible f-number would be $N = 0.33$ [2].

Bibliography

[1] Jenkins F A and White H E 1976 *Fundamentals of Optics* 4th edn (New York: McGraw-Hill)
[2] Kingslake R and Johnson R B 2010 *Lens Design Fundamentals* 2nd edn (New York: Academic)
[3] Smith W J 2007 *Modern Optical Engineering* 4th edn (New York: McGraw-Hill)
[4] Kingslake R 1983 *Optical System Design* 1st edn (New York: Academic)
[5] Kingslake R 1992 *Optics in Photography* (Bellingham, WA: SPIE) (*SPIE Press Monograph* vol PM06)
[6] Ray S F 2002 *Applied Photographic Optics: Lenses and Optical Systems for Photography, Film, Video, Electronic and Digital Imaging* 3rd edn (London: Focal)
[7] Greivenkamp J E 2004 *Field Guide to Geometrical Optics* (Bellingham, WA: SPIE) (*SPIE Field Guides* vol FG01)
[8] Johnson R B 2008 Correctly making panoramic imagery and the meaning of optical center *Proc. SPIE* **7060** 70600F
[9] Blahnik V 2014 *About the Irradiance and Apertures of Camera Lenses* Carl Zeiss Camera Lens Division http://lenspire.zeiss.com/en/overview-technical-articles
[10] van Walree P Derivation of the depth of field equations http://toothwalker.org/optics/dofderivation.html Retrieved 31.01.2017
[11] van Walree P Center of perspective http://toothwalker.org/optics/cop.html#fov Retrieved 31.01.2017
[12] Born M and Wolf E 1999 *Principles of Optics: Electromagnetic Theory of Propagation Interference and Diffraction of Light* 7th edn (Cambridge: Cambridge University Press)
[13] Sutton T and Dawson G (ed) 1867 *A Dictionary of Photography* (London: Sampson Low, Son, & Marston)
[14] Hecht E 2003 *Optics* (Pearson)
[15] Hatch M R and Stoltzmann D E The f-stops here *Opt. Spectra* **June 1980** 88–91
[16] Foote P 1915 *Bull. Bur. Stand.* **12** 583

[17] Koyama T 2006 *Image Sensors and Signal Processing for Digital Still Cameras* ed J Nakamura (Boca Raton, FL/London: CRC Press/Taylor and Francis)

[18] Kerr D 2007 Derivation of the "Cosine Fourth" law for falloff of illuminance across a camera image http://dougkerr.net/

[19] Sasian J 2012 *Introduction to Aberrations in Optical Imaging Systems* (Cambridge: Cambridge University Press)

Chapter 2

Exposure strategy

Chapter 1 introduced the optical formulae required to define the illuminance distribution formed by an optical image at the sensor plane. Subsequently, the photometric exposure distribution was defined as the illuminance distribution multiplied by the exposure time or duration t.

For any given scene, there is no universal definition for what constitutes a correct photometric exposure distribution. This very much depends upon the aesthetic and technical requirements of the individual photographer. Nevertheless, the exposure distribution must at least generate a useful response from the imaging sensor so that a satisfactory digital output image can be obtained.

Modern exposure strategy as defined by the International Standards Organisation (ISO) 12232 photographic standard [1] is based on the digital output image produced by the camera (typically JPEG) and not the raw data. Based on analysis of the scene luminance distribution and knowledge of the sensitivity of the digital output to photometric exposure, standard exposure strategy aims to provide the photographer with an output image with specified characteristics such as a standard brightness. This can be used as a starting point for further adjustments to compensate for non-typical scenes, or for further adjustments based on other technical requirements or aesthetic considerations.

In order to understand the development of modern exposure strategy in digital photography, this chapter begins with an introduction to digital output. Simplified descriptions of the concepts are given where possible, and many of these concepts will be expanded upon in later chapters. Average photometry and exposure indices are then discussed in detail, and the final section describes use of the exposure modes found on modern digital cameras.

Finally, it should be mentioned that the exposure strategy developed in this chapter is based on the output from the in-camera image-processing engine, and it is not a strategy that aims to produce the highest image quality (IQ) that the camera is capable of delivering. Technical IQ can be maximised by following an exposure strategy based on the expose-to-the-right (ETTR) technique used in conjunction with raw output, along with subsequent processing of the raw file. IQ in relation to photographic practice will be discussed in chapter 5.

2.1 Digital output

2.1.1 Sensor response

The photometric exposure distribution H at the sensor plane generates photo-electrons at the photosensitive area of the photosites or sensor pixels. The total number of photoelectrons or charge signal $n_{e,j}$ generated at a given photosite j during a camera exposure is proportional to the average photometric exposure per photosite H_j,

$$n_{e,j} \propto H_j.$$

This relation is valid only for exposure levels which produce a useful response from the sensor. Furthermore, this relation assumes that the camera is fitted with ideal infra-red cut-off and ultraviolet filters to block light wavelengths outside of the visible spectrum. (A more complete equation will be derived later using radiometry in chapter 3.) The photoelectrons generate a voltage signal proportional to $n_{e,j}$,

$$V_j \propto n_{e_j}.$$

This voltage is converted into a digital number (DN) by an analog-to-digital converter (ADC). Each DN represents a raw level, and the DNs associated with all photosites comprise the raw data which can be processed into an output image file for viewing. The raw data together with camera metadata can be stored in a raw file.

Each DN is specified by a string of binary digits or *bits*, each of which can be either 0 or 1. The length of the string is known as the *bit depth*. For a bit depth equal to M, the number of possible DNs that can be represented is 2^M. A raw file with a bit depth equal to M is referred to as an M-bit raw file. An M-bit raw file therefore provides 2^M possible raw levels per photosite. Typically $M = 10$, 12, or 14 in consumer cameras.

Figure 2.1 shows an idealised sensor response curve. The linear relation between scene luminance and signal is evident, and this is an important requirement for

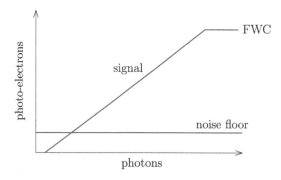

Figure 2.1. Model sensor response curve.

faithful reproduction of scene luminance. Most modern sensors are linear to a high precision until near the top of the sensor response curve. However, a useful response to photometric exposure is obtained only between charge signal values $n_{e,j}$ referred to as the *noise floor* and *full-well capacity* (FWC). The noise floor is defined as the signal noise due to the electronic readout circuitry, and such noise will be present every time charge readout occurs even in the absence of photometric exposure. It therefore defines the minimum usable output signal from an engineering perspective. FWC is the maximum number of photoelectrons which can be stored at a photosite during a camera exposure. When FWC is reached, the sensor is said to be saturated.

2.1.2 Colour

A colour can be specified by its luminance and *chromaticity*. Luminance only defines the achromatic or greyscale component of a colour, and so full colour reproduction requires a strategy for detecting chromaticity.

The most common practical approach is similar to that used by the human visual system (HVS). One of three different types of colour filter are placed above each photosite on the sensor. The pattern of colour filters forms a *colour filter array* (CFA). For example, figure 2.2 illustrates a Bayer CFA which uses a pattern of red, green, and blue filters [2]. When the signal produced by each photosite is quantised by the ADC, a raw value or DN *associated with each type of filter* will be recorded. These values will be denoted here by $\mathcal{R}$, $\mathcal{G}$, and $\mathcal{B}$. Since only one type of filter can be placed over each photosite, full $\mathcal{RGB}$ information will not be recorded at each photosite location. This missing information can be obtained through interpolation by carrying out a computational process known as *colour demosaicing*.

After the colour demosaic has been performed, there will be 2^M levels for each $\mathcal{RGB}$ colour component per photosite. As well as contributing to the total luminance, each colour component also contributes *chromaticity information* at each photosite because the $\mathcal{RGB}$ components specify a colour in the *camera raw space*, which in principle defines the internal *colour space* of the camera. Colour spaces are similar to mathematical vector spaces.

Unfortunately, the camera raw space is not a suitable colour space for viewing images. However, the camera raw space can be transformed into a standard *output-referred colour space* designed for viewing images on a standard display/monitor. Familiar examples include sRGB [3] and Adobe® RGB.

Figure 2.2. Bayer CFA showing the red, green, and blue mosaics.

The linear RGB components of the output colour space denoted by R_L, G_L, and B_L, can be referred to as *relative tristimulus values*. The raw $\mathcal{RGB}$ components at a given photosite can be transformed into relative tristimulus values by applying the following linear matrix transformation,

$$\begin{bmatrix} R_L \\ G_L \\ B_L \end{bmatrix} = \underline{M}_R \underline{D} \begin{bmatrix} \mathcal{R} \\ \mathcal{G} \\ \mathcal{B} \end{bmatrix}.$$

Here $\underline{M}_R$ is a *colour rotation matrix*,

$$\underline{M}_R = \begin{bmatrix} M_{11} & M_{12} & M_{13} \\ M_{21} & M_{22} & M_{23} \\ M_{31} & M_{32} & M_{33} \end{bmatrix}.$$

The matrix entries are colour-space and camera-dependent, however each row will always sum to unity. The diagonal matrix $\underline{D}$ takes care of *white balance* (WB) which will be discussed in chapter 4.

The total luminance Y per photosite is given as a weighted sum of the relative tristimulus values. In the case of the sRGB colour space, the weighting is defined as

$$Y = 0.2126\, R_L + 0.7152\, G_L + 0.0722\, B_L.$$

This is a normalised measure of luminance referred to as *relative luminance*.

2.1.3 Digital output levels

Ultimately most output images will be viewed on 8-bit per-channel displays which can show a total of $(2^8)^3 = 16\,777\,216$ possible colours, and so in-camera image-processing engines usually produce 8-bit per-channel output image files, typically JPEG. In this case, the colour of an image pixel corresponding to a given photosite is specified by three colour components in the output-referred colour space, each taking one of 256 possible values ranging from 0 to 255.

It may appear that a significant amount of data would be lost when reducing bit depth from $M = 10$, 12, or 14 down to 8. Indeed, performing the reduction in a linear manner would drastically lower the IQ. Luminance information and dynamic range (DR) would potentially be lost, and more importantly, unwanted banding or *posterisation* effects would appear because the tonal transitions would no longer appear smooth.

Instead, the bit-depth reduction is performed in a *nonlinear* manner in conjunction with a process known as gamma compression or *gamma encoding* [4, 5]. A type of nonlinear tone curve known as a *gamma curve* is applied to the relative tristimulus values. The nonlinearity takes the form of a power law,

$$R' \propto (R_L)^\gamma$$
$$G' \propto (G_L)^\gamma$$
$$B' \propto (B_L)^\gamma.$$

The bit depth of the gamma-encoded values R', G', and B' is subsequently reduced to 8 by quantising to the range [0,255]. These 8-bit values are *nonlinearly* related to the raw data and are referred to as *digital output levels* (DOLs). In fact, *a gamma curve is incorporated into the definition of standard output-referred colour spaces* such as sRGB [3] and Adobe® RGB. The gamma curve must be applied *after* the linear transformation from the camera raw space to the relative tristimulus values of the output-referred colour space.

The nonlinear representation by DOLs can prevent unwanted posterisation artefacts from appearing, and moreover can preserve image attributes such as DR. However, the nonlinearity introduced will ultimately need to be compensated for by the display device. This is known as gamma expansion or *gamma decoding*.

Dynamic range, tonal range, gamma curves, and tone curves are discussed in the remainder of this section.

2.1.4 Dynamic range

Dynamic range (DR) is an important concept fundamental to the development of a photographic exposure strategy. This section gives a brief description of DR in terms of its transfer through several important stages in the photographic imaging chain.

Scene dynamic range

Scene luminance ratio or *scene DR* is specified as the ratio between the highest and lowest non-clipped scene luminance values. For example, a typical daylight scene may have a DR of 128:1. Since this is a luminance ratio, scene DR can also be specified in terms of the photographic stop defined previously in section 1.4.9 of chapter 1. Since each stop corresponds to a doubling or halving of luminance, the daylight scene here has a DR of $\log_2 128 = 7$ stops. In other words, the lowest luminance value needs to be doubled seven times in order to equal the highest luminance value in this example.

The aim of a photographic exposure strategy is to appropriately position the scene DR on the sensor response curve.

ADC dynamic range

The ADC quantises the analog voltage into a DN which represents a raw level. A linear ADC uses DNs that are linearly related to the voltage and therefore linearly related to scene luminance up to the quantisation step.

An M-bit linear ADC provides 2^M DNs and can therefore quantise $\log_2 2^M = M$ stops of DR in principle, assuming that the sensor itself provides a perfectly linear voltage response. In this case, the DR provided by a linear ADC is directly given by its bit depth. For example, DN = 4096 represents a scene luminance level 4096 times greater than DN = 1. In this case DN = 1 needs to be doubled 12 times in order to equal DN = 4096, and so the raw levels from DN = 1 to DN = 4096 represent 12 stops of DR.

ADC saturation occurs when the input voltage is quantised to the highest available DN.

Raw dynamic range

Raw DR is the maximum DR that can be represented by the raw data. If the sensor response and ADC are both perfectly linear, the raw DR cannot be greater than the ADC DR. Raw DR is limited by the noise floor from below, and by FWC or ADC saturation from above. Ideally the scene DR will be less than the raw DR, otherwise scene information will be clipped irrespective of the photographic exposure strategy.

In this chapter it is more straightforward to think in terms of DNs rather than photoelectrons. In this case, raw DR per photosite can be defined as

$$
\begin{aligned}
\text{raw DR (ratio)} &= \frac{n_{\text{DN, clip}}}{\sigma_{\text{DN, read}}} : 1 \\
\text{raw DR (stops)} &= \log_2\!\left(\frac{n_{\text{DN, clip}}}{\sigma_{\text{DN, read}}}\right)
\end{aligned}.
$$

Here $n_{\text{DN, clip}}$ is the *raw clipping point* expressed in DN, which is the maximum usable raw level in the raw data. The noise floor (or read noise) in DN has been denoted by $\sigma_{\text{DN, read}}$.

Image dynamic range

The *image DR* is the maximum DR that can be represented by the DOLs of the output image file such as JPEG or TIFF.

Image DR depends upon the available raw DR along with the nature of the tone curve used to encode the data. If a *nonlinear* tone curve (such as a gamma curve) is used so that the DOLs have a nonlinear relationship with luminance, the represented DR is no longer restricted by the bit depth of the image file. For example, an 8-bit image file can encode *any* amount of DR if the appropriate nonlinear tone curve is used, even though only 256 DOLs are available per colour component. Image DR for an 8-bit image file can be defined in the following way:

$$
\begin{aligned}
\text{image DR (ratio)} &= \frac{L(\text{DOL} = 255)}{L(\text{DOL} = 1)} : 1 \\
\text{image DR (stops)} &= \log_2\!\left(\frac{L(\text{DOL} = 255)}{L(\text{DOL} = 1)}\right)
\end{aligned}.
$$

Here $L(\text{DOL} = 1)$ is the luminance represented by DOL = 1, and $L(\text{DOL} = 255)$ is the luminance represented by DOL = 255.

Since the raw DR defines the maximum possible DR *available* for producing an output image, the image DR cannot be greater than the raw DR in practice.

Display dynamic range

The *display DR* is the maximum DR that can be represented by the luminance output from the display. A high image DR may need to be compressed into the display DR. This is discussed further in section 2.1.7.

Figure 2.3. The upper diagram shows a wide DR but narrow TR. The lower diagram shows a narrow DR but wide TR.

2.1.5 Tonal range

Tonal range (TR) is defined as the number of tonal levels which divide up the DR. This relationship is illustrated in figure 2.3. During the process of raw data capture, DR is necessarily dependent on TR. For an M-bit ADC, the upper limit for the *raw TR* will be 2^M where typically $M = 10$, 12, or 14, and so the upper limit for the raw DR will be M stops if the ADC and sensor response are both perfectly linear.

After the process of raw data capture has been completed, the raw data will be converted into the DOLs of the output image. Unlike the relationship between DR and TR during raw data capture, the image DR is *independent* of the *image TR*. If the image file is encoded using a nonlinear tone curve, the DOLs are tonal levels which have a nonlinear relationship with the raw data and therefore a nonlinear relationship with scene luminance. For example, *all* of the raw DR can be transferred to an 8-bit image file provided an appropriate nonlinear tone curve is used, even though an 8-bit file only has a TR of 256. Similarly, photographers who use raw conversion or post-processing software may prefer to use 16-bit image files. Again the DR of the image cannot be greater than the raw DR, however a 16-bit image file has many more tonal levels available which can improve the appearance of fine tonal transitions and prevent posterisation when manipulating the data.

2.1.6 Tone reproduction

Tone reproduction describes how tones in the scene are reproduced in the output image. Ideally the image presented to the viewer will appear to be an identical reproduction of the scene. For many reasons, this is not possible in conventional photography. For example, DR limitations imposed by the camera and display medium will inhibit *objective* tone reproduction. Furthermore, the range of viewing conditions encountered will often differ from those at the photographic scene and will inhibit *subjective* tone reproduction. For simplicity, viewing conditions will be ignored in this section and tone reproduction will be categorised either as being *accurate* or as *preferred*.

In nature, the scene luminance distribution is presented linearly, or in other words it appears with a linear gamma. Accurate tone reproduction similarly aims for a linear reproduction of scene luminance. This means that the overall input–output luminance relationship must be *linear* over the luminance range which can be reproduced by the display medium. On the other hand, preferred tone reproduction simply aims to present the viewer with a pleasing image. Often this reproduction will be designed to address DR limitations, or extreme tonal adjustments may be made for creative effect.

The following section on gamma discusses accurate tone reproduction, and the subsequent section on tone curves discusses preferred tone reproduction.

Recall that raw levels expressed as DNs can take integer values in the range [0, RCP] where RCP $\leqslant 2^M - 1$ is the raw clipping point and M is the bit depth of the ADC, and 8-bit DOLs can take integer values in the range [0,255]. It is often convenient to normalise these values to the range [0,1] when applying gamma curves, and so the following notation will be adopted:

R_L, G_L, B_L	Relative tristimulus values (linear)
R', G', B'	DOLs (gamma encoded)
V	$R_L, G_L,$ or B_L normalised to the range [0,1]
V'	$R', G',$ or B' normalised to the range [0,1]
γ_E	Encoding gamma
γ_D	Decoding or display gamma (typically $\gamma_D \approx 1/\gamma_E$).

2.1.7 Gamma

A *gamma curve* is a type of nonlinear tone curve which is generally defined by a power law with exponent denoted by γ,

$$V' = V^\gamma.$$

Here V is the linear input function and V' is the nonlinear output function, both normalised to the range [0,1]. In the present context, $V = R_L, G_L,$ or B_L and $V' = R'$, G', or B', similarly normalised to the range [0,1]. The exponent γ is the *encoding gamma* γ_E incorporated into the definition of the standard output-referred colour space. For example, figure 2.4 shows a curve defined by an encoding gamma $\gamma_E = 1/2.2$. This is similar to the gamma curve used by the sRGB colour space discussed in chapter 4.

It has already been mentioned that the effect of gamma encoding on luminance reproduction must be cancelled through gamma expansion or *gamma decoding* by the display device so that the overall input–output luminance relationship will be linear. The compensating gamma curve γ_D applied by the display device is known as the *display gamma*. For example, a display gamma defined by a curve with $\gamma_D = 2.2$ will compensate for an encoding gamma $\gamma_E = 1/2.2$. This is shown

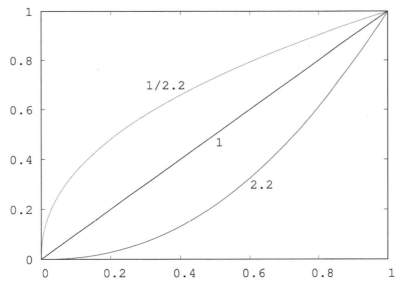

Figure 2.4. Gamma curves: $\gamma_E = 1/2.2$ (green), $\gamma = 1$ (black), and $\gamma_D = 2.2$ (magenta).

graphically in figure 2.4. Mathematically, the relationship can be modelled in the following way,

$$L_n = C\{V'\}^{\gamma_D} + B. \tag{2.1}$$

Here L_n represents the normalised luminance output from the display, C is a gain, and B is a black-level offset. The later section on display gamma will discuss this equation in further detail. The important result is that if the display gamma γ_D is the reciprocal of the encoding gamma γ_E, the overall gamma will be unity and L_n will be linearly related to V. In order to compensate for environmental viewing factors such as flare, an overall gamma slightly higher than unity will normally be used in practice [4].

When digital photography first evolved, images were commonly displayed on cathode-ray tube (CRT) monitors. The output luminance from CRT monitors has a *nonlinear* relationship with input electron-gun voltage, typically obeying a gamma law with a γ value in the range 2.35 to 2.55 [4]. This meant that gamma encoding was naturally required to compensate for the nonlinearity. However, the nonlinearity turned out to be highly fortuitous because it has since been recognised that the process of gamma encoding and decoding has advantages which relate to IQ.

In fact, the output luminance relationship with the input signal does not naturally follow a CRT-type power law in modern displays, however a power law relationship represented by a display gamma γ_D is maintained through calibration so that the process of gamma encoding and decoding can be performed. The IQ benefit arises from the fact that gamma encoding and decoding makes efficient use of the limited TR provided by an 8-bit image file [4]. In particular, visible banding or posterisation artefacts can be avoided. Posterisation occurs when an insufficient number of tonal levels are used to represent relative luminance ranges which the HVS is most sensitive to, as discussed in further detail below. An added benefit is that a nonlinearly-encoded 8-bit image file can represent more of the raw DR than possible with a linear encoding, as previously mentioned when discussing the relationship between DR and TR.

In conclusion, the process of gamma encoding and decoding (or gamma compression and expansion) is not actually required for accurate tone reproduction on modern displays. Its purpose relates to IQ, in particular:

(i) Bit depth can be reduced while minimising destructive effects such as posterisation. This is the primary reason for using gamma.

(ii) Gamma-encoded images can represent more DR for a given bit depth than linearly encoded images.

Gamma and posterisation

When the ADC quantises the voltage signal, quantisation error is introduced [4]. The quantisation error arises from the fact that a range of analog voltages will be mapped or quantised to the same raw level. The quantisation step is smaller for higher bit depths. If the quantisation step is too large, tonal transitions may not be sufficiently smooth and visible banding or posterisation can occur. Raw data is never posterised because the bit depth of the ADC is sufficient for signal noise to exceed the quantisation step and smooth the tonal transitions. This is known as *dithering* [6]. However, posterisation can occur when the raw data is converted into an image file with a lower bit depth. Posterisation is illustrated in the middle and lower diagrams of figure 2.5.

The HVS does not perceive luminance linearly in terms of its physiological brightness response. According to the *Weber–Fechner law*, the relationship is approximately logarithmic and is generally represented as a power law with $\gamma \approx 1/3$ to $1/2.2$. Physically this means that *darker levels will appear lighter than their luminance values would suggest*, as shown by the linear luminance gradient in the upper diagram of figure 2.5. For example, 18% relative luminance lies mid-way on a lightness (relative brightness) scale and is commonly referred to as *middle grey*.

In order to minimise posterisation when converting to an image file with a lower bit depth, it makes sense to allocate more DOLs to luminance levels which the HVS is most sensitive to, and allocate fewer DOLs to luminance levels which the HVS cannot easily discern from neighbouring ones. Figure 2.6 shows a gamma curve defined by $\gamma_E = 1/2.2$ applied to linear raw data normalised to the range [0,1] and subsequently quantised to 8-bit output. Two example regions are shown. The first region with normalised raw level between 0.0 and 0.1 has been allocated 90 DOLs on account of the relatively high sensitivity of the HVS to this luminance range. On the other hand, the second region between 0.9 and 1.0 has only been allocated 12 levels on account of the lower sensitivity of the HVS to this luminance range.

The linear luminance gradient shown in the upper diagram of figure 2.5 has been constructed using gamma-encoded DOLs. It will therefore appear correctly as a linear luminance gradient when viewed on a display with a compensating nonlinear

Figure 2.5. The upper diagram shows a linear gradient of 8-bit gamma-encoded DOLs; this appears correctly as a linear luminance gradient on a display with a compensating nonlinear display gamma. The middle and lower diagrams show posterisation when the data are truncated to 6 bits or 64 tonal levels, and 5 bits or 32 tonal levels, respectively.

display gamma. In particular, tonal transitions will appear to be smooth. However, an 8-bit gamma-encoded image can become posterised through image processing. For example, the middle diagram of figure 2.5 shows the gradient processed by reducing the TR to 64. This is equivalent to re-quantising the data to 6 bits, and posterisation becomes apparent. Posterisation is even more apparent in the lower diagram which has a TR of 32.

Gamma and dynamic range
Compared to a linear encoding, gamma encoding can compress more DR into a representation by DOLs of a given bit depth. This means that more of the available raw DR can be transferred to an 8-bit JPEG output image file than the maximum eight stops that can ordinarily be accommodated by a linear encoding. Since the gamma decoding by the display device occurs *after* quantisation, this DR can in principle be preserved when the image is displayed.

The actual amount of DR represented by a gamma curve can be calculated by taking the ratio of the highest represented luminance to the lowest represented non-clipped luminance. For 8-bit per-channel output, these are represented by DOL = 255 and 1, where DOL = R', G', or B'. Given gamma-encoded data normalised to

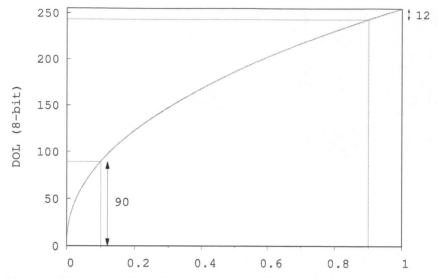

Figure 2.6. A $\gamma_E = 1/2.2$ curve applied to linear raw data normalised to the range [0,1] subsequently quantised to 8-bit output.

the range [0,1], these DOLs can be obtained by multiplying by 255 and taking the integer part. The represented normalised luminances are

$$\left(\frac{1}{255}\right)^{1/\gamma_E} \to \text{DOL} = 1$$

$$1 \to \text{DOL} = 255.$$

In other words, a normalised luminance $(1/255)^{1/\gamma_E}$ is quantised to DOL = 1, and a normalised luminance of 1 is quantised to DOL = 255. For $\gamma_E = 1/2.2$, the represented DR is therefore $\log_2(255^{2.2}) \approx 17.6$ stops. In practice, this may differ depending on the rounding strategy used.

Although the above calculation gives an upper limit for the DR which can be represented by an encoding gamma $\gamma_E = 1/2.2$, the actual amount represented in practice cannot be greater than the raw DR. This is because the available levels in the raw file have discrete spacing on a normalised luminance axis. For 14-bit and 12-bit linear raw files, the raw DR that can be transferred to the image file is naturally limited to 14 and 12 stops, respectively.

Display gamma
The luminance output from a conventional CRT display or liquid crystal display (LCD) can be expressed in the following way [7]

$$L = (L_{peak} - L_{black})\{V'\}^{\gamma_D} + L_{black} + L_{refl}. \tag{2.2}$$

Here L is the absolute luminance output as a function of V' measured in cd m^{-2}, L_{peak} is the peak luminance output in a completely dark room (around 500 cd m^{-2} for LCD displays), and L_{refl} is the luminance due to ambient light reflected from the surface of the display. The luminance emitted by an LCD for a black pixel L_{black}

cannot be reduced to zero and is typically in the range 0.1 to 1 cd m^{-2}. The display gamma γ_{D} is not necessarily the same as the inherent display nonlinearity, γ. The required nonlinearity $\{V'\}^{\gamma_{\mathrm{D}}}$ can be accommodated through use of a look-up table (LUT) determined by experimental measurement.

Dividing equation (2.2) throughout by L_{peak} defines the normalised luminance $L_{\mathrm{n}} = L/L_{\mathrm{peak}}$ which can be written in the form of equation (2.1),

$$L_{\mathrm{n}} = C\{V'\}^{\gamma_{\mathrm{D}}} + B.$$

The gain C and offset B are defined as

$$C = \frac{L_{\mathrm{peak}} - L_{\mathrm{black}}}{L_{\mathrm{peak}}}$$

$$B = \frac{L_{\mathrm{black}} + L_{\mathrm{refl}}}{L_{\mathrm{peak}}}.$$

The gain C is controlled by the 'contrast' setting on the display, and the offset B is controlled by the 'brightness' setting [4].

The *display DR* is the maximum DR that can be represented by the luminance output with $L_{\mathrm{refl}} = 0$. Since $V' = 1$ and $V' = 0$ correspond to the maximum and minimum output, the display DR expressed in terms of stops is given by

$$\boxed{\text{display DR (stops)} = \log_2\left(\frac{L_{\mathrm{peak}}}{L_{\mathrm{black}}}\right).}$$

The ratio $(L_{\mathrm{peak}}/L_{\mathrm{black}})$: 1 is referred to as the *contrast ratio*. If $L_{\mathrm{black}} = 0$ then the display DR is calculated using the first controllable level above zero instead [7].

In practice, the display DR is limited by the ambient light that is reflected from the surface of the display. This becomes apparent when the term L_{refl} is included in the expression for the display DR,

$$\text{display DR (stops)} = \log_2\left(\frac{L_{\mathrm{peak}} + L_{\mathrm{refl}}}{L_{\mathrm{black}} + L_{\mathrm{refl}}}\right).$$

For LCD displays, the display DR remains unchanged by adjusting the display gamma γ_{D} because the value $V' = 0$ ultimately corresponds with L_{black}. In this case the overall gamma can only redistribute the tonal levels within the output luminance range.

The display DR for conventional displays is often lower than the image DR. However, this does not imply that the image DR will necessarily be clipped. If the black-level offset in the above model is greater than zero, $L_{\mathrm{black}} > 0$, the gain will be less than unity, $g < 1$. The gain has been set to compensate for the black-level offset and ensure that $V' = 1$ is mapped to L_{peak}, as shown in figure 2.7. In other words, the image DR is compressed into the display DR through contrast reduction. This is a simple example of *global tone-mapping*.

An image with high DR can appear to lack contrast when viewed on a conventional low DR display [7]. This is one reason for applying additional tone curves beyond a gamma curve. Tone curves are discussed in the next section.

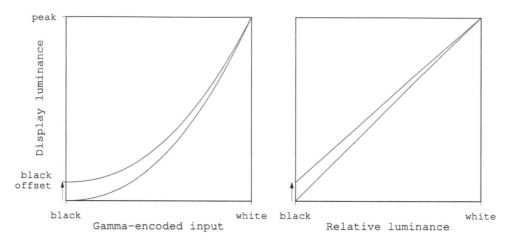

Figure 2.7. Overall system gamma $\gamma = 1$ for an LCD display shown in terms of gammaencoded DOLs V' (left) and normalised raw level V (right). The black-level offset B and gain C are related via $C + B = 1$ so that the image DR is compressed into the display DR. Here L_{refl} has been set to zero.

Summary
- If the image file has a lower bit depth than the raw file, gamma encoding and decoding (or gamma compression and expansion) is an efficient way to make use of the limited TR. In particular, IQ as perceived by the HVS can be optimised by minimising visible posterisation.
- Gamma-encoded DOLs can represent more DR than linearly encoded DOLs of the same bit depth.
- Gamma encoding must be appropriately compensated for by the display gamma in order to render linear output for viewing.

An added benefit to photographers is that gamma-encoded image data is easier to interpret and manipulate than linear data. This will be discussed in section 2.1.9.

2.1.8 Tone curves

A gamma curve can be considered to be a special type of tone curve. Images viewed on a display with the appropriate compensating display gamma will appear to be accurate or photometrically correct. When plotted on axes representing gamma-encoded values, a gamma curve appears as a diagonal straight line. This is illustrated for $\gamma_E = 1/2.2$ by the black curve in figure 2.8.

The application of any tone curve beyond a gamma curve will produce in an image that is no longer accurate or photometrically correct. This is known as preferred tone reproduction. In-camera image-processing engines are designed to render images considered to be more pleasing to the HVS than accurate images. A common type of applied curve known as an *s-curve* has an 's'-shape when plotted on axes representing gamma-encoded values. The blue curve in figure 2.8 is an example s-curve. The lower part of the s-curve is known as the toe, and the upper part as the knee or shoulder. An s-curve increases mid-tone contrast which gives the

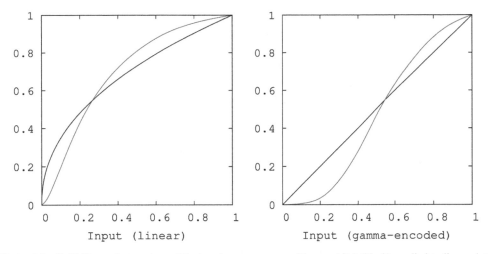

Figure 2.8. (Left) Example tone curve (blue) and gamma curve with $\gamma_E = 1/2.2$ (black) applied to linear data normalised to the range [0,1]. (Right) Corresponding curves plotted using gamma-encoded axis values with $\gamma_E = 1/2.2$.

image more 'punch' at the expense of contrast in the shadows and highlights which become compressed. On the other hand, an *inverted s-curve* increases the contrast in the shadows and highlights but the resulting image will have reduced mid-tone contrast and appear 'flat'.

Tone curves and dynamic range

The application of a tone curve can be used to control the amount of raw DR transferred to the output image file in place of that provided by the gamma curve of the chosen output-referred colour space. An s-curve generally raises the black clipping level, which is the luminance level at which the output clips to DOL = 0. This *lowers* the DR compared to that provided by the gamma curve. Conversely, an inverted s-curve generally lowers the black clipping level which in turn *increases* the DR compared to that provided by the gamma curve.

For several reasons, in-camera image-processing engines usually apply tone curves which do not make full use of the available raw DR. For example, the applied tone curve may be suited to represent the DR of typical scenes or the DR of a typical display. For such reasons, in-camera image-processing engines typically use s-curves which compress the shadows. For example, the s-curve shown in figure 2.8 has heavily compressed the shadows and raised the black clipping level, which in turn has lowered the represented DR compared to that of the gamma curve.

The procedure for calculating the DR represented by a gamma curve detailed previously in section 2.1.7 similarly applies to a general tone curve. The gradient near the black level effectively determines the DR. In the present example, the blue s-curve can accommodate approximately 7.7 stops of DR after quantising to 8-bit output compared to the 17.6 stops provided by the gamma curve with $\gamma_E = 1/2.2$. In this example, the value is slightly less than the eight stops provided by an 8-bit linear encoding. This is explained by the diagram on the left-hand side of figure 2.8 which shows that the gradient of the curve near the black level is slightly less than unity when plotted on linear axes.

It is impossible to know the DR represented by an 8-bit JPEG file which has already had an arbitrary tone curve applied unless the relationship between the raw levels (or more precisely the flux at the sensor plane) and the output image file DOLs is known. This relationship is described by the opto-electronic conversion function (OECF) which can be measured in practice by photographing a calibrated step wedge [8]. As discussed in section 2.3.4 later, the total DR provided by the tone curve can be split into *highlight DR* and *shadow DR* components which are, respectively, measured above and below middle grey. The raw DR minus the sum of the highlight and shadow DR gives an indication of the available *raw headroom*. For scenes with a higher DR than the amount which can be accommodated by the tone curve of the JPEG file produced by the camera, raw converters allow the photographer to apply a more suitable tone curve which can utilise any available raw headroom as required.

2.1.9 Histograms

Nature and the raw data are both linear ($\gamma_E = 1.0$). Some non-commercial raw converters such as *dcraw* can output linear demosaiced images[1]. Such images will appear correctly if viewed on a display with a linear display gamma ($\gamma_D = 1$), but will appear too dark if viewed on a typical display with $\gamma_D = 2.2$.

Even though linear output would appear correctly when shown on a linear gamma display, the image histogram itself would be difficult to interpret. Because a typical scene has an average luminance that is approximately 18% of the maximum, the histogram levels for a typical scene would be distributed heavily towards the left-hand side. The grey histogram shown in figure 2.9 corresponds to an example raw file that was converted to an 8-bit output image file encoded using a linear gamma.

On the other hand, standard DOLs are gamma-encoded according to the gamma curve of the selected standard output-referred colour space. The blue histogram shown in figure 2.9 corresponds to the same example raw file, but this time demosaiced and then converted to an 8-bit image file encoded using the sRGB colour space. The sRGB colour space uses a gamma encoding similar to a gamma curve defined by $\gamma_E = 1/2.2$. This time the image will appear too dark if viewed on a display with a linear display gamma, but will appear correctly if viewed on a display with $\gamma_D = 2.2$. However, the histogram will be gamma encoded and therefore much easier to interpret, the reason being that the levels will be distributed more in line with lightness (relative brightness) perception rather than luminance. In other words, the levels will typically be distributed around the centre of the histogram for a typical scene. This is illustrated by the blue histogram in figure 2.9.

Histograms provided by commercial raw converters will be gamma encoded even if a 'linear' tone curve is selected. This gamma may be that of the internal working

---

[1] The freeware raw converter *dcraw* by D Coffin is available at https://www.cybercom.net/~dcoffin/dcraw.

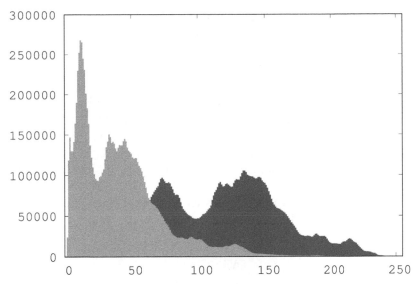

Figure 2.9. Luminance histogram corresponding to example 8-bit output with linear gamma (grey), and sRGB gamma-encoded histogram showing corresponding DOLs (dark blue). The vertical axis represents pixel count.

colour space used by the raw converter, or that of the selected standard output-referred colour space such as sRGB, Adobe® RGB, or ProPhoto RGB. Histograms of images already converted to a standard output-referred colour space will already be gamma-encoded according to the gamma curve used by that colour space.

2.2 Average photometry

The aim of a photographic exposure strategy is to appropriately place the scene DR on the sensor response curve. As discussed in the introduction to this chapter, an appropriate placement of the scene DR depends upon the strategy of the individual photographer. Nevertheless, the camera aims to provide the photographer with a starting point for further adjustments based on a digital output image with standardised characteristics. Two main factors contribute to the scene DR:

- The reflectance properties of the scene objects.
- Non-uniform scene illumination.

The reflectance of natural objects ranges between approximately 3% and 90%. Under uniform illumination and assuming the scene objects are Lambertian reflectors, scene luminance is proportional to reflectance and so the maximum DR can be $\log_2(90/3) \approx 4.9$ stops. Higher scene DR values occur when the scene illumination is non-uniform, for example when multiple light sources are present which illuminate different parts of the scene, and in particular when scene areas are shaded from a light source.

Recall from section 1.4 of chapter 1 that the photometric exposure distribution at the sensor plane is described by equation (1.58),

$$H = \frac{\pi}{4} L \, T_{\text{lens}} \frac{t}{N^2} \cos^4 \varphi.$$

Here H is a function of position on the sensor plane, and the object plane is assumed to be at infinity so that $N_{\text{w}} = N$. The variables which can be controlled by the photographer are the f-number N and the exposure duration (or 'shutter speed') t. For a given framing, luminance L can also be controlled to a certain extent by altering the scene illumination, for example through the addition of external lighting.

Combinations of N and t can be expressed as an exposure value (EV) defined by equation (1.59) of chapter 1,

$$\frac{t}{N^2} = \frac{1}{2^{\text{EV}}}.$$

A technique that can be used to quantify the scene luminance distribution is *reflected-light metering*. Along with knowledge of the sensitivity of the digital image output to photometric exposure, reflected-light metering provides information which can be used to determine an appropriate EV.

2.2.1 Reflected-light metering

One strategy that can be used to determine an appropriate EV is *reflected-light metering*. Traditional reflected-light metering is based upon *average photometry* which requires the use of a reflected-light meter to measure the *average* scene luminance $\langle L \rangle$. This is simply the arithmetic average of the scene luminance values detectable within the AFoV of the meter. Either a hand-held reflected-light meter or a simple in-camera metering mode can be used with average photometry. The meter will recommend suitable combinations of N and t which satisfy the reflected-light meter equation,

$$\boxed{\frac{t}{N^2} = \frac{K}{\langle L \rangle S_{\text{EI}}}} . \qquad (2.3)$$

The constant K is the *reflected-light meter calibration constant* for a hand-held reflected-light meter. In-camera reflected-light meters are calibrated according to the related *photographic constant P*. These constants will be discussed in the following section which covers meter calibration.

A form of *exposure index* S_{EI}, commonly referred to as the *ISO setting*, is designed to ensure that a specific digital output is obtained from the camera when the scene is metered using average photometry. In film photography, film speed is typically used as the exposure index, although film can be 'pushed' or 'pulled' by using an exposure index which differs from the ISO film speed rating.

Equation (2.3) can be recast in terms of EV. Substituting equation (1.59) of chapter 1 into equation (2.3) yields

$$EV = BV + SV. \tag{2.4}$$

The *brightness value* (BV) and *speed value* (SV) are defined by

$$BV = \log_2 \frac{3.125 \langle L \rangle}{K} \tag{2.5a}$$

$$SV = \log_2 \frac{S_{EI}}{3.125}. \tag{2.5b}$$

Since equation (2.4) and equation (1.60) of chapter 1 are equal, the reflected-light meter will recommend suitable combinations of N and t by solving

$$\boxed{EV = AV + TV = BV + SV}.$$

The photographer can select any combination of N and t which has the recommended EV. The particular combination selected may depend on factors such as a required shutter speed or DoF.

2.2.2 Meter calibration

Reflected-light meters need to be appropriately calibrated in order to recommend a suitable EV. For a given average luminance $\langle L \rangle$ and exposure index S_{EI}, hand-held reflected-light meters will recommend a suitable EV according to the value of the calibration constant K, and simple in-camera metering modes will recommend a suitable EV according to the value of the photographic constant P. These constants have been standardised based upon statistical analysis of typical scenes and user-preference for what is considered to be a well-exposed photograph.

In order to explain the origin and relationship between these constants, it is necessary to begin with a brief historical overview of several important definitions from film photography that were made before the emergence of digital photography.

Film speed

In film photography, the exposure index value is typically taken to be *film speed S* which is a sensitometric measure of a specified response to photometric exposure from photographic film. Around the time that the ANSI PH3.49-1971 photographic standard was issued in 1971 for calibration of hand-held exposure meters, film speed for colour-reversal (R) film was defined as

$$S = \frac{8}{H_R}. \tag{2.6}$$

Here H_R is the geometric average of the base 10 logarithm of the photometric exposure required to produce specific densities at two specific points on the film response curve.

In 1979 the ANSI PH2.21-1979 standard [9], now replaced by ISO 2240-2003 [10], changed the definition of film speed S for colour reversal film to

$$S = \frac{10}{H_R}.$$
(2.7)

This definition change is significant and will be discussed later.

Photographic constant
Equation (1.58) of chapter 1 is the defining equation for the photometric exposure distribution at the sensor plane. Replacing L by the metered arithmetic average luminance $\langle L \rangle$ yields

$$H = \frac{\pi}{4} \langle L \rangle\, T_{\text{lens}} \frac{t}{N_{\text{w}}^2} \cos^4 \varphi.$$
(2.8)

The problem with the use of this expression as part of an exposure strategy is that H varies over the sensor plane even though $\langle L \rangle$ is a constant. This is because of natural vignetting described by the $\cos^4 \varphi$ term. Ideally, a single value for an *arithmetic mean photometric exposure* $\langle H \rangle$ should be defined which corresponds with $\langle L \rangle$.

A way forward is to choose a fixed 'effective' value for $\cos^4 \varphi$ deemed most representative of the variation due to natural vignetting. The ANSI PH3.49-1971 standard [11], later replaced by ISO 2720 [12], selected a value $\cos^4 \varphi = 0.916$ with $\varphi = 12°$. Furthermore, various additional assumptions were made about light loss through a typical lens. Equation (2.8) could then be written in the form

$$\boxed{\langle H \rangle = q \langle L \rangle \frac{t}{N^2}}.$$
(2.9)

The parameter q groups together the various assumptions and is defined as

$$q = \frac{\pi}{4} \frac{F}{b^2}\, T_{\text{lens}} \cos^4(12°) = 0.65.$$

Here $F = 1.03$ is a lens flare correction factor, $T_{\text{lens}} = 0.9$ is a lens transmittance factor, and $b = 80/79$ is the bellows factor.

The most recent photographic standard on exposure, ISO 12232 [1], uses the same value for q but the assumptions made are slightly different,

$$q = \frac{\pi}{4} v\, T_{\text{lens}} \cos^4(10°) = 0.65.$$

Here $v = 0.98$ is a vignetting factor, $T_{\text{lens}} = 0.9$, the cosine fourth factor is $\cos^4 \varphi = 0.94$ with $\varphi = 10°$, and focus is set at infinity so that $b = 1$ and the working f-number reduces to the f-number. The significance of equation (2.9) is the *proportionality* between $\langle L \rangle$ and $\langle H \rangle$.

The product of the arithmetic mean photometric exposure $\langle H \rangle$ with the film speed S yields the *photographic constant* P,

$$\boxed{\langle H \rangle S = P = q \langle L \rangle \frac{t}{N^2} S}.$$
(2.10)

Through long-term statistical analysis of photographs of a large number of scenes, the most appropriate value for the photographic constant was settled upon [13]. It was found to be

$$P \approx 8. \tag{2.11}$$

In other words, exposure meters should be calibrated to aim for $P = 8$; this could be expected to yield the most suitable mean photometric exposure $\langle H \rangle$ for a typical scene. (Note that the equality between P and the constant appearing in equation (2.6) was coincidental.) The appropriate mean photometric exposure $\langle H \rangle$ can be referred to as the required *photographic exposure* [13].

The value chosen for P explains the so-called *sunny-16 rule* which states that a suitable exposure duration when a satisfactory photograph is taken with a camera set at $N = 16$ on a clear sunny day at a solar altitude of 40 degrees is approximately given by the reciprocal of the film speed [13]. In fact the sunny-16 rule corresponds with $P = 8.11$, the difference being negligible in practice.

Hand-held meter constant
The calibration constant K for *hand-held* reflected-light meters can be obtained by comparing equations (2.3) and (2.10). The value is found to be

$$K = \frac{P}{q} = 12.3.$$

This assumes $P = 8$ and $q = 0.65$ [13]. The sunny-16 rule corresponds with $K = 12.5$. The ANSI PH3.49-1971 photographic standard was replaced in 1974 by ISO 2720:1974 which included a tolerance on the allowed values of K from 10.6 to 13.4 [12].

In-camera metering systems
In 1982, the ISO 2721 standard was issued for calibration of simple *in-camera* metering systems [14]. The standard describes procedures for calibrating the arithmetic average photometric exposure $\langle H \rangle$ at the film plane consistent with average photometry.

Simple in-camera metering systems are calibrated in terms of the photographic constant P rather than the hand-held reflected-light metering constant K. The parameter q is not required because the actual arithmetic average photometric exposure at the film plane is being measured. According to equations (2.10) and (2.11), a calibration consistent with ISO 2720 should ensure that

$$\langle H \rangle S = P = 8.$$

However, the following definition was used by ISO 2721,

$$\boxed{\langle H \rangle S = 10}. \tag{2.12}$$

This 10/8 increase can be accounted for by the 1979 change in definition for colour reversal film speed from equation (2.6) to equation (2.7); an increase in the value of S by 10/8 accounts for the 10/8 increase in the value of P.

The change in definition for colour reversal film speed was made according to user preference because the general practice at the time was to average multiple hand-held meter EV readings according to the Zone System [15]. This effectively reduced the recommended $\langle H \rangle$ to a *geometric* average which is not consistent with the arithmetic average used in ISO 2720. In fact, a geometric average is approximately a factor 8/10 smaller for a typical scene than a true arithmetic average and so photographs generally appeared 1/3 of a photographic stop too bright [15]. The change in definition for colour reversal film speed therefore enabled practitioners of the Zone System to obtain correct exposure recommendations without the need for meter recalibration. On the other hand, in-camera metering systems perform an arithmetic average and must be consistent with the new film speed definition.

One consequence of the new film speed definition is that users of wide-angle reflected-light meters which perform an arithmetic average should increase the meter constants specified in ISO 2720 by a factor 10/8. For example $K = 12.5$ becomes

$$K = 15.4 \tag{2.13}$$

and the allowed tolerance now covers 13.25 to 16.75 [15].

For consistency between film and digital photography, the ISO 12232 [1] photographic standard on exposure adopted equation (2.12) for use in digital photography with exposure index replacing film speed,

$$\boxed{\langle H \rangle S_{\mathrm{EI}} = 10} \, . \tag{2.14}$$

2.2.3 Average scene luminance

It is often stated that reflected-light meters are calibrated to an 'average reflectance' expressed as a percentage, for example 18%. Average reflectance is meaningful when the scene illumination is *uniform*. Under uniform illumination, luminance is proportional to reflectance provided the scene objects within the FoV are perfect Lambertian reflectors. For non-Lambertian reflectors, luminance is proportional to *luminance factor*.

However, illumination in real scenes is generally *non-uniform*. Natural objects have a reflectance range between about 3% and 90%. Assuming the scene objects are perfect Lambertian reflectors, uniform illumination would result in a scene luminance ratio of 30:1 or scene DR of $\log_2(90/3) = 4.9$ stops, well below the 160:1 luminance ratio or 7.3 stops of DR often quoted for a typical scene. As mentioned in the introduction to this section, higher scene DR arises when multiple light sources are present which illuminate different parts of the scene, and in particular when scene areas are shaded from a light source.

Recall that reflected-light meters measure *average luminance* and are calibrated in terms of the metering constant K which was derived from the photographic constant P. These constants were determined through observer statistical analysis of photographs of *real scenes* and can therefore ultimately be associated with an *average luminance* rather than an average reflectance.

An estimate of this average luminance expressed as a percentage of the maximum scene luminance can be obtained by comparing the value of the hand-held reflected-light metering constant K with the value of the *incident*-light metering constant C recommended for calibration of hand-held incident-light meters [16],

$$\langle L \rangle \approx \pi \frac{K}{C}.$$

Using the value $C = 250$ common for flat receptors and within the range specified in ISO 2270 together with $K = 12.5$ yields an average scene luminance of approximately 16%. This is close to 18% which has special significance in relation to the HVS; 18% relative luminance corresponds to *middle grey* on a lightness scale according to the Weber–Fechner law discussed in section 2.1.7.

An interpretation of this result is that the scene luminance distribution for typical scenes approximately *averages to middle grey*, or an average luminance that is 18% of the maximum. Equivalently, the average scene luminance is always $\log_2(100/18) \approx 2.5$ stops below the maximum scene luminance, irrespective of the scene DR.

2.3 Exposure index

For a typical scene metered using average photometry, recall from section 2.2.2 that a well-exposed photographic film is considered to result from an exposure distribution which satisfies equation (2.12),

$$\langle H \rangle S = 10.$$

The ISO 12232 photographic standard [1] adopted the same equation for use in digital photography in the form of equation (2.14),

$$\boxed{\langle H \rangle S_{\mathrm{EI}} = 10}.$$

The exposure index S_{EI}, informally referred to as the ISO setting, replaces film speed S. The exposure index is evidently a numerical value which is inversely proportional to $\langle H \rangle$, the average photometric exposure provided to the imaging sensor [1].

However, the capability of digital cameras can vary widely, and so there are further considerations which must be taken into account when defining what can be considered a 'well-exposed' digital image, or more accurately a digital image that results from an 'appropriate' photometric exposure at the sensor plane. ISO speed, standard output sensitivity (SOS), and recommended exposure index (REI) are measured exposure index *values* which differ according to the nature of this objective. A specified digital output must be obtained from the camera, and the exposure indices define *how* this digital output is specified.

At a fundamental level, the sensitivity of the digital output to photometric exposure depends upon several factors which include the following:

- The rate at which the photosite electron wells fill with electrons in response to photometric exposure. This defines the sensitivity of the sensor itself and depends primarily upon its quantum efficiency (QE) and fill-factor (FF). These characteristics will be defined in chapter 3. The sensitivity of a given sensor is therefore fixed and cannot be adjusted.

- *Analog gain* applied to amplify the signal before it is quantised by the ADC. Doubling the gain enables the same digital image to be obtained from halving $\langle H \rangle$, and so the exposure index doubles according to equation (2.14).
- *Digital gain* which alters the DOLs such as gamma-curve and tone-curve processing.

For sensors which use the same technology and have equal QE and FF, the sensitivity is independent of photosite area or sensor pixel size. This is explained by figure 2.10.

Since 2004, Japanese camera manufacturers have been required to use either the SOS or REI methods first introduced by the Camera and Imaging Products Association of Japan (CIPA) [17]. The digital output is specified in terms of DOLs in the output image file, typically JPEG, and not in terms of raw levels.

2.3.1 ISO speed

Although no longer used by Japanese camera manufacturers, it is instructive to first describe *ISO speed* which remains part of the ISO 12232 standard [1].

ISO speed specifies an exposure index value designed to ensure a minimum IQ level. Two methods for determining ISO speed are available which relate to different aspects of IQ [18]. The noise-based method aims to ensure a minimum signal-to-noise ratio (SNR). However, this method cannot be used with lossy image formats such as JPEG and so this method will not be discussed here. The alternative is the *saturation-based* method which aims to avoid the clipping of highlights. Saturation-based ISO speed S_{sat} must be defined in accordance with equation (2.14),

$$S_{\text{sat}} = \frac{10}{\langle H \rangle}. \tag{2.15}$$

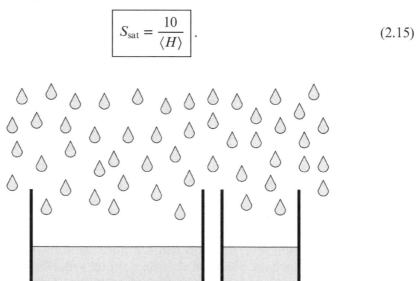

Figure 2.10. Sensor sensitivity is independent of photosite area for sensors that use the same technology with equal QE and FF. In this case the photosites will fill with electrons at the same rate. An analogy is commonly made to the fact that large and small buckets collect rainwater at the same rate.

Recall from section 2.2.3 that the photographic constant $P = 10$ contained in this equation indirectly implies an assumed 18% average luminance $\langle L \rangle / L_{\text{max}}$ for a typical scene, where $\langle L \rangle$ is the average scene luminance and L_{max} is the maximum scene luminance. Consistent with this assumption, the aim of saturation-based ISO speed is to ensure that the DR for a typical scene is placed on the sensor response curve such that the output image file will not contain clipped highlights. In this section it will be assumed that the output image file is an 8-bit JPEG file, however other file formats such as TIFF could be used in principle.

For a typical scene with 18% average luminance, a scene object with 100% relative luminance must be placed just below the JPEG clipping point in order to prevent highlights from clipping. In fact, the definition includes a safety factor so that a scene object with 100% relative luminance will be placed half a stop below the JPEG clipping point. In other words, the highlights will not actually clip until the average scene luminance drops to approximately 12.8% of the scene maximum.

ISO speed measurement
In order to measure S_{sat}, the internal analog gain must be fixed in a known setting. A uniform grey card of any reflectance must be *uniformly* illuminated. For a fixed combination of N and t, the maximum luminance L_{sat} which does not lead to JPEG saturation (highlight clipping) can then be measured.

The measurement should be carried out according to the procedures and ambient conditions detailed in the ISO 12232 standard [1]. In particular, the WB appropriate for the scene illumination should be used so that the DOLs for each RGB colour component will be equal. An 8-bit JPEG file clips when the DOL reaches 255. It is possible that the camera manufacturer could place the JPEG clipping point below the raw clipping point on the sensor response curve, and so this does not necessarily imply that FWC has been utilised.

Since the luminance is uniform, the photometric exposure H_{sat} corresponding to the measured L_{sat} can be calculated according to equation (2.9),

$$H_{\text{sat}} = q L_{\text{sat}} \frac{t}{N^2}.$$

In order to determine the value of the ISO speed, the 18% value for the average scene luminance is amended in the following way,

$$\frac{\langle L \rangle}{L_{\text{sat}}} = \frac{18}{100\sqrt{2}} \approx \frac{10}{78}.$$

The extra $\sqrt{2}$ factor has been inserted to provide $\log_2(\sqrt{2}) = 0.5$ stops of *exposure headroom* for use in situations where the actual average scene luminance falls below 18%. The JPEG output will not saturate until the average scene luminance drops to $10/78 \approx 12.8\%$, as mentioned above. Equivalently, $\langle L \rangle$ is assumed to always be $\log_2(78/10) \approx 3$ stops below the maximum scene luminance, irrespective of the scene DR. If the scene DR is larger than the DR which can be accommodated by the JPEG tone curve (the image DR), then the shadows will clip at the DOL corresponding to the base of the tone curve.

Since $\langle H \rangle$ is proportional to $\langle L \rangle$ according to equation (2.9), the relationship between $\langle H \rangle$ and H_{sat} is given by

$$\frac{\langle L \rangle}{L_{sat}} = \frac{\langle H \rangle}{H_{sat}} \approx \frac{10}{78}. \tag{2.16}$$

The ISO speed S_{sat} can now be determined from H_{sat} by substituting equation (2.16) into equation (2.15),

$$\boxed{S_{sat} = \frac{78}{H_{sat}}}. $$

This measured value should be rounded to the nearest standard value. The *base* ISO speed corresponds to the analog gain setting which allows full use of the sensor response curve.

ISO speed characteristics

There are several drawbacks associated with the use of saturation-based ISO speed as the exposure index:
- ISO speed is primarily affected by the position of the JPEG highlight clipping point on the sensor response curve.
- ISO speed is unaffected by tone-curve processing below the JPEG highlight clipping point.
- The half stop of exposure headroom is built into the measurement.

Figure 2.11 shows the 8-bit JPEG tone curves for two different camera models. Since both curves clip at exactly the same position, the measured ISO speed will be the

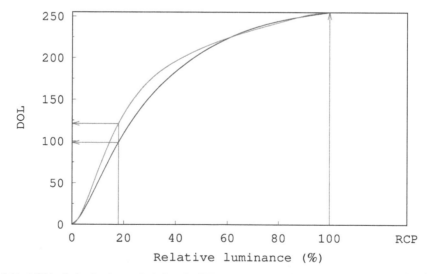

Figure 2.11. 100% relative luminance is tied to the JPEG highlight clipping point (DOL = 255 for 8-bit output) assuming an average scene luminance of 12.8%. The position of DOL = 255 determines the ISO speed. Both JPEG tone curves here define the same ISO speed but lead to different image brightness. It is possible that the JPEG clipping point could be placed below the raw clipping point (RCP).

same for both cameras [18]. However, each curve leads to a different image brightness because the DOL corresponding to 18% relative luminance is not the same. For photographers who primarily shoot JPEG, this is a disadvantage because an image obtained using the EV recommended by the meter may not produce an image with the expected brightness.

2.3.2 Standard output sensitivity

Standard output sensitivity (SOS) was introduced by CIPA in 2004. For consistency with film photography, this is again defined in accordance with equation (2.14),

$$S_{SOS} = \frac{10}{\langle H \rangle}.$$
(2.17)

The aim of SOS is to produce an image with a *standard brightness* rather than to ensure a minimum IQ level.

SOS relates the exposure index to a *mid-tone* DOL instead of the DOL at JPEG saturation used by saturation-based ISO speed. The particular mid-tone chosen is defined by DOL = 118, the reason being that this corresponds with middle grey (18% relative luminance) on the standard gamma curve of the sRGB colour space as shown in figure 2.12. In other words, if a typical scene with an *average* luminance of 18% is metered using average photometry, the output image will turn out to be photometrically correct.

The camera manufacturer is free to place middle grey at any desired position on the sensor response curve through use of both analog and digital gain, and the measured S_{SOS} value will adjust accordingly in order to ensure the standard image brightness. For example, the two JPEG tone curves shown in figure 2.11 would lead to different measured S_{SOS} values and hence a different recommended EV when metering the same scene. However, use of the recommended EV in both cases would lead to the same standard image brightness expected by the photographer. Furthermore, the shadow and highlight clipping points do not affect S_{SOS} and can be freely adjusted. This is discussed further in section 2.3.4 which discusses extended highlights.

Standard output sensitivity measurement
In order to calculate S_{SOS}, a uniform grey card of any reflectance must be *uniformly* illuminated according to the conditions specified by CIPA DC-004 or ISO 12232. The measured luminance is taken to represent the average scene luminance $\langle L \rangle$. For a fixed combination of N and t, the value $\langle L \rangle$ which produces DOL = 118 in the JPEG output should be obtained, again under the procedures specified by CIPA DC-004 or ISO 12232. In particular, the camera WB should be correctly set.

The corresponding average photometric exposure $\langle H \rangle$ must be consistent with equation (2.9),

$$\langle H \rangle = q \langle L \rangle \frac{t}{N^2}.$$

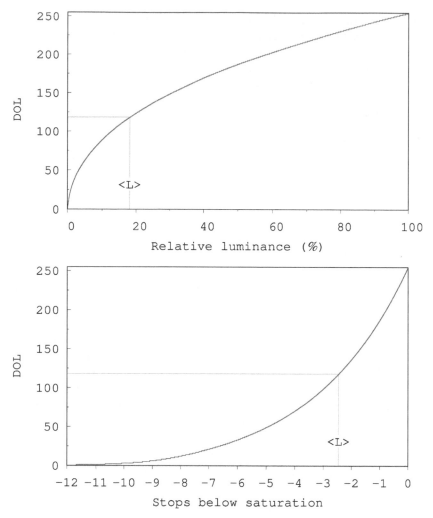

Figure 2.12. (Top) Standard sRGB gamma curve (magenta) with output quantised to 8 bits. Metered $\langle L \rangle$ corresponds to DOL = 118 assuming an 18% average scene luminance. (Bottom) Same curve plotted using base 2 logarithmic units on the horizontal axis; $\langle L \rangle$ lies approximately 2.5 stops below L_{sat} and the curve clips to black approximately 11.7 stops below L_{sat}.

Using $q = 0.65$ along with $K = 15.4$ as defined by equation (2.13) ensures that the photographic constant $P = 10$,

$$P = Kq = 15.4 \times 0.65 = 10.$$

Subsequently, SOS can be determined from equation (2.17). The calculated value should be rounded to the nearest standard value tabulated in CIPA DC-004 or ISO 12232. This means that the quoted S_{SOS} may differ from the calculated value to within a tolerance of ± 1/3 stop.

2.3.3 Recommended exposure index

Recommended exposure index (REI) allows camera manufacturers to use an arbitrary specification for the required digital output according to the manufacturer's own objective, for example a specification which the manufacturer considers produces the most pleasing image. Although digital gain and other image processing can be applied arbitrarily, the REI value must nevertheless be consistent with equation (2.14) which defines the average photometric exposure provided at the sensor plane,

$$\boxed{\langle H \rangle S_{\mathrm{REI}} = 10}.$$

Since REI must be defined using average photometry, its value can be determined experimentally [17]. A uniformly illuminated grey card can be photographed using a known AV and TV determined from the selected N and t, and the BV can be obtained by measuring the luminance using a hand-held reflected-light meter with known calibration constant K. The SV can then be determined by solving the EV equation,

$$SV = AV + TV - BV.$$

Subsequently, equation (2.5b) which defines SV can be rearranged to yield the REI,

$$S_{\mathrm{REI}} = 3.125 \times 2^{SV}.$$

The REI is provided by the camera manufacturer so that users of hand-held exposure meters and other accessories such as strobe lighting can correctly use the EV equation.

According to ISO 12232, if the camera does not provide a simple metering mode which functions using average photometry, then the REI value is not useful and should not be reported [1].

2.3.4 Extended highlights

The introduction of SOS has given camera manufacturers the freedom to use the sensor response curve in any desired fashion when rendering an output image provided the image turns out to have the standard brightness [19]. One consequence is that digital cameras now routinely appear with 'extended' low-ISO settings available below the base ISO setting. However, the JPEG output at the base ISO setting is found to have additional highlight headroom compared to the extended low-ISO output.

The diagram on the left-hand side of figure 2.13 was obtained by photographing a step wedge using the Olympus® E-620 [19]. The dark blue curve and the red curve are the JPEG tone curves at ISO 100 and ISO 200, respectively. The horizontal axis uses a base 2 logarithmic scale with respect to scene luminance and therefore represents stops. This representation is similar to the lower diagram of figure 2.12 except that the stop values have been normalised so that zero corresponds to middle grey, or DOL = 118. It can be seen that the highlights clip at approximately 2.5 stops above

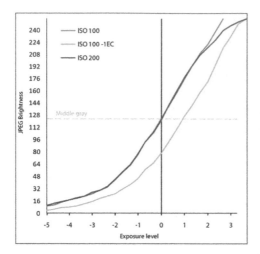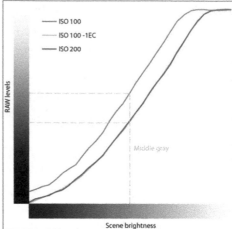

Figure 2.13. The diagram on the left shows DOL as a function of stops above and below middle grey (DOL = 118) for the Olympus® E-620. A JPEG image taken at ISO 200 has an extra stop of highlight headroom compared to an image taken at ISO 100. The diagram on the right shows the corresponding raw levels as a function of scene brightness. (Figure reproduced from [19] courtesy of www.dpreview.com)

middle grey on the ISO 100 curve. However, the highlights clip at approximately 3.5 stops above middle grey on the ISO 200 curve, and so an extra stop of highlight headroom is available before the JPEG output saturates.

Further information is provided by the light blue curve in the same diagram on the left-hand side. This is the JPEG tone curve obtained at ISO 100 when underexposing by one stop by using the shutter speed and f-number recommended by metering at ISO 200. Naturally the image is darker, but notably the highlights have the same clipping point as the ISO 200 curve.

The diagram on the right-hand side of figure 2.13 shows the corresponding raw levels. These curves are nonlinear only because the horizontal axis represents scene brightness rather than scene luminance. Surprisingly, it can be seen that ISO 100 and ISO 200 do not produce the same raw data. Furthermore, the ISO 100 curve underexposed by one stop coincides exactly with the ISO 200 curve.

The above investigation reveals that ISO 100 and ISO 200 are in fact using the same analog gain setting. The ISO 200 setting is defined by metering at ISO 100 and then reducing the metered EV by one stop. This effectively lowers the position of middle grey (18% relative luminance) on the sensor response curve by one stop. Digital gain is then utilised by applying a different tone curve to the 'underexposed' raw data. This tone curve renders JPEG output with the standard brightness by relating middle grey with DOL = 118, but with an additional stop of highlight headroom made accessible by the 'underexposing' of the scene luminance distribution.

For example, if the ISO 100 tone curve saturates at the same point as the standard sRGB curve, then the highlights at ISO 200 will clip at 200% relative luminance. Equivalently, the average scene luminance can drop to 9% before the highlights must clip. This additional stop of highlight headroom is lost if the ISO 100 'low-ISO' setting is selected. An equivalent viewpoint is that the ISO 100 setting is defined by 'overexposing' the raw data by one stop, which causes a loss of one stop of highlight headroom in the JPEG output at ISO 100 compared to ISO 200. In reality, neither viewpoint can be considered as underexposing or overexposing because SOS permits the application of both analog and digital gain [19].

When reviewing cameras, reviwers may investigate and report the nature of the JPEG tone curve. The number of stops provided by the tone curve above and below middle grey (DOL = 118) is referred to as the *highlight DR* and *shadow DR*, respectively [19]. This information is useful for photographers who rely on JPEG output. Since the application of digital gain adversely affects achievable SNR, camera manufacturers must balance various IQ trade-offs when designing an in-camera image-processing engine, and it is important to consider all aspects of the JPEG output when comparing cameras. Photographers who process the raw data themselves using raw-processing software are of course free to apply any desired tone curve to the raw data, and so information regarding aspects of the raw data such as raw DR will likely be of greater interest.

2.4 Exposure modes

Each of the several different camera exposure modes available on modern digital cameras can be useful depending on the type of photographic situation encountered. The descriptions given below are meaningful when the exposure is based upon the JPEG image produced by the camera. This does not necessarily provide the best IQ. As described in chapter 5, IQ can be optimised by using raw output in conjunction with the ETTR methodology and subsequent processing of the raw file.

2.4.1 Metering modes

There is no guarantee that any given photographic scene will match the characteristics of a typical scene defined to have an average luminance of 18% (middle grey). If the actual photographic scene luminance distribution does not average to middle grey, use of average photometry will lead to an image which appears lighter or darker than an image of standard brightness. In turn, this could lead to a loss of scene DR if the JPEG tone curve provides insufficient highlight or shadow DR.

Although traditional arithmetic average metering remains an option on some modern cameras such as Fuji® cameras, it has largely given way to more advanced forms of metering such as centre-weighted, spot, and matrix metering. Centre-weighted and spot metering can be classed as simple metering modes based on average photometry, however they aim to give more reliable results for scenes which are not typical. Centre-weighted metering applies a greater weighting to the centre of the scene when calculating the average luminance, and spot metering can be used to prioritise a particular subject in the scene.

On the other hand, a pattern or matrix metering mode will generally base its exposure recommendation on its own analysis of multiple parts of the scene. This analysis may include comparison with a database of known scene characteristics and the analysis will not in general be based upon an assumption that the luminance distribution averages to middle grey.

It should be remembered that exposure index or ISO settings such as SOS and REI are measured using average photometry when the programmable analog gain amplifier is fixed in a known state. In other words, the measured ISO setting corresponds with a particular analog gain. If a simple in-camera metering mode is used which functions using average photometry, the camera will recommend a suitable camera exposure by solving the EV equation,

$$EV = AV + TV = BV + SV.$$

Nevertheless, the camera can continue to function using the measured ISO settings when a matrix metering mode is selected. The matrix metering mode will determine appropriate combinations of exposure duration t and f-number N based on the analog gain setting corresponding to the selected ISO setting, the JPEG tone curve, and its own analysis of the scene luminance distribution. However, the suggested t and N combinations will not in general correspond with those calculated using the EV equation. As such, no correspondence can be expected with t and N values recommended by a simple in-camera metering mode or hand-held reflected-light meter.

2.4.2 Exposure compensation

Exposure compensation (EC) can be applied to adjust the camera exposure away from that recommended by the meter. This provides an additional means to deal with photographic scenes that are not typical. Because a lower EV corresponds to a greater average photometric exposure, positive EC will lower the metered EV, and negative EC will raise the metered EV. If a simple in-camera metering mode is selected or a hand-held reflected-light meter is used, the EC can be incorporated into the EV equation,

$$EV = AV + TV = SV + BV - EC.$$

However, it should be remembered that photographic scenes vary enormously in terms of content and DR, and there is no universal definition for what should be regarded as the most suitable exposure for an individual scene. Many photographers will use the camera exposure recommended by the meter simply as a starting point for further adjustments. In particular, the photographer may wish to darken or lighten the image according to artistic intent. Photographers aiming to optimise technical IQ may choose to follow the ETTR strategy used in conjunction with raw output which will be discussed in chapter 5.

2.4.3 Aperture priority (A or Av)

In aperture priority mode, the photographer controls the f-number N and ISO setting S_{EI}. The camera meter provides the exposure duration (or 'shutter speed') t. Aperture priority mode is designed to prioritise control over DoF.

The recommended t value can be adjusted by applying EC based on knowledge of the photographic scene and metering mode or by examining the image histogram. Once EC has been applied to obtain the desired image brightness, the exposure duration t provided by the camera may be too slow to prevent camera shake if the ambient lighting conditions are too dark and a tripod is not being used. For a photographer with steady hands, the usual rule of thumb is that camera shake can be prevented by using an exposure duration shorter than $t_{\max}$, where

$$t_{\max} = \frac{1}{m_f f_E}. \tag{2.18}$$

Here f_E is the effective focal length and m_f is the focal-length multiplier. This rule is referred to as the *reciprocal focal-length rule*. The value $t_{\max}$ can be lengthened if the camera or lens includes image stabilisation. In principle, M stops of image stabilisation allow $t_{\max}$ to be doubled M times. The reciprocal focal-length rule evolved before the advent of digital photography but remains useful. Nevertheless, if the sensor has a high pixel density then it is advisable to use a shorter exposure duration than $t_{\max}$ or ideally use a tripod in order to take advantage of the high resolving power on offer. Resolving power will be discussed in chapter 5.

The exposure duration can be shortened either by lowering the f-number or by raising the ISO setting. For IQ reasons it is advisable to lower the f-number if a lower value is available, however this will result in a shallower DoF which may not be suitable for certain photographic scenes such as landscapes. The photographer must judge the optimum balance between f-number and ISO setting. Some cameras feature an auto-ISO mode which will automatically raise the ISO setting once the metered t increases beyond a selected threshold value. When using a zoom lens, it is particularly useful if the threshold value can be tied to the lens focal length according to the reciprocal focal-length rule. The threshold maximum exposure duration is commonly referred to as the *minimum shutter speed*.

A maximum exposure duration or minimum shutter speed is similarly required when photographing moving subjects if the objective is to freeze the appearance of moving action in the image. Depending on the subject, a much shorter exposure duration may be required than $t_{\max}$. Shutter priority mode and manual mode can be more convenient than aperture priority mode when photographing moving subjects.

2.4.4 Shutter priority (S or Tv)

In time priority or shutter priority mode, the photographer controls the exposure duration (shutter speed) t and ISO setting S_{EI}. The camera meter provides the f-number N. Shutter priority mode is useful when the photographic conditions require a maximum exposure duration (minimum shutter speed) to be maintained, particularly when needing to freeze the appearance of moving action. However, there is less direct control over DoF.

An experienced photographer can judge the required exposure duration by considering factors such as the speed of the subject, the distance between the camera and the subject, and the lens focal length. Camera shake is not typically a major issue in shutter priority mode because the selected exposure duration will likely be much shorter than t_{max} defined by equation (2.18). However, camera shake can be an issue if a very long focal length is used. Image stabilisation can help prevent camera shake but will not help to freeze the moving action.

When a shorter exposure duration is selected or available light decreases, the camera will open up the aperture by lowering the f-number. If the f-number has been lowered to the minimum available value and the camera meter indicates that the target exposure cannot be achieved, the ISO setting will need to be raised accordingly. For IQ reasons with JPEG output, it makes sense to start by selecting the lowest ISO setting which allows the camera to obtain its target exposure for the selected t value.

Applying EC in shutter priority mode will adjust the target exposure and consequently change the f-number. If positive EC is applied when the camera has already selected the lowest available f-number, then the target exposure cannot be achieved. The camera meter will indicate this occurrence by a mark on the EV scale. In this case the ISO setting will need to be raised. If the camera has an auto-ISO mode, this will be performed automatically. The auto-ISO mode will prioritise lowering the f-number before raising the ISO setting.

2.4.5 Program mode (P)

The program exposure mode is a semi-automatic mode which will recommend a combination of N and t by metering the scene at the selected ISO setting S_{EI}. The particular combination presented will be based on analysis of the scene content. However, this combination can be overridden, and all combinations of N and t *with the same EV* can be cycled through and the desired combination selected.

If a simple metering mode is used based on average photometry, all available combinations of N and t will satisfy the EV equation,

$$EV = AV + TV = BV + SV - EC.$$

Note that in aperture priority mode the f-number will remain fixed when EC is applied, and in shutter priority mode the exposure duration t will remain fixed when EC is applied. If EC is applied in program mode, neither the f-number N nor shutter duration t will remain fixed and so all available combinations of N and t can be selected.

If auto-ISO is available in program mode, all available combinations of N and t at all available ISO settings can be cycled through, and the camera will automatically adjust the ISO setting according to the chosen combination.

2.4.6 Manual mode (M)

Manual mode provides complete control over the f-number N, shutter duration t, and ISO setting S_{EI}. The combination selected defines a *user* EV. By marking the EV scale, the camera meter will indicate the difference between the user EV and its own metered target exposure. This difference is the *user* EC.

If auto-ISO is available in manual mode, the camera will automatically adjust the ISO setting so that the user EV matches its own target exposure. In other words, auto-ISO in manual mode aims to eliminate the user EC. The camera will mark the EV scale to indicate when this cannot be achieved using the available ISO settings. Some cameras additionally allow *target* EC to be applied in order to adjust the target exposure away from the metered value.

Bibliography

[1] ISO 2006 Photography—Digital still cameras—Determination of exposure index, ISO speed ratings, standard output sensitivity, and recommended exposure index, ISO 12232:2006

[2] Bayer B E 1976 *Color imaging array US patent* **3971065**

[3] IEC 1999 Multimedia systems and equipment—Colour measurement and management—Part 2-1: Colour management—Default RGB colour space—sRGB, IEC 61966-2-1 1999

[4] Poynton C 2003 *Digital video and HDTV algorithms and interfaces* (San Francisco, CA: Morgan Kaufmann)

[5] Sato K 2006 *Image Sensors and Signal Processing for Digital Still Cameras* ed J Nakamura (Boca Raton, FL/London: CRC Press/Taylor and Francis)

[6] Martinec E 2008 Noise, dynamic range and bit depth in digital SLRs http://theory.uchicago.edu/~ejm/pix/20d/tests/noise/ and http://www.photonstophotos.net/emil%20martinec/noise.html

[7] Rafal K M, Mantiuk K and Sidel H-P 2015 *Wiley Encyclopedia of Electrical and Electronics Engineering* (New York: Wiley)

[8] ISO 2009 Photography—Electronic still-picture cameras—Methods for measuring opto-electronic conversion functions (OECFs), ISO 14524:2009

[9] ANSI 1979 Method for determining the speed of color reversal films for still photography, ANSI PH2.21-1979

[10] ISO 2003 Photography—Colour reversal camera films—Determination of ISO speed, ISO 2240:2003

[11] ANSI 1971 General-purpose photographic exposure meters (photoelectric type), ANSI PH3.49-1971

[12] ISO 1974 Photography—General purpose photographic exposure meters (photoelectric type)—Guide to product specification, ISO 2720:1974

[13] Connelly D 1968 Calibration levels of films and exposure devices *J. Photogr. Sci.* **16** 185

[14] ISO 1982 Photography—Cameras—Automatic controls of exposure, ISO 2721:1982

[15] Holm J 2016 private communication

[16] Stimson A 1962 An interpretation of current exposure meter technology *Photogr. Sci. Eng.* **6** 1

[17] CIPA 2004 Sensitivity of digital cameras, CIPA DC-004

[18] Yoshida H 2006 *Image Sensors and Signal Processing for Digital Still Cameras* ed J Nakamura (Boca Raton, FL/London: CRC Press/Taylor and Francis)

[19] Butler R 2011 Behind the scenes: extended highlights! http://www.dpreview.com/articles/2845734946

IOP Publishing

Physics of Digital Photography

Andy Rowlands

Chapter 3

Raw data model

Chapter 1 used photometry and Gaussian optics to describe the flow of light through the lens from the photographic scene to the sensor plane. This provided a framework enabling fundamental optical quantities to be defined which served as a basis for the photographic exposure strategy developed in chapter 2.

However, the above description does not provide any insight into the characteristics and quality of the digital raw data produced by the camera. This is affected by a variety of physical phenomena. One of the most important is diffraction. This is a wave phenomenon which causes light passing through the lens aperture to spread out. Diffraction imposes a fundamental limit on resolution because a point in the scene is prevented from being imaged as a point on the sensor plane. Diffraction requires a wave description of light which is beyond the scope of geometrical optics. Other physical phenomena which affect the raw data include those related to the imaging sensor itself. The sensor photosites are not point objects and must sample the optical image at a non-zero finite resolution. This leads to further blurring of scene detail because each photosite mixes together light collected from an area in the photographic scene. Furthermore, the sampling can lead to false detail appearing in the output image. This unwanted effect is known as aliasing and can be described using Fourier theory. One way to reduce aliasing to a minimal level is to pre-filter the light through an optical low-pass filter (OLPF) before it reaches the sensor plane. However, such filtering causes further blurring of scene detail.

Mathematically, the above phenomena can be modelled as a blurring and sampling of the ideal optical image formed at the sensor plane by using linear systems theory. Linear systems theory is widely used and has a variety of applications. In relation to photography, it can be applied as part of the design process when building an imaging system to a given specification. The central quantities of interest are the point-spread function (PSF) in the real domain, and the optical transfer function (OTF) in the Fourier domain. In the present chapter, a very simple camera model based on linear systems theory is described which includes basic PSFs for the optics, OLPF, and sensor components of a camera. Models for signal noise and the conversion of the analog signal into the digital raw data are also included.

The PSF and OTF are fundamental measures of image quality (IQ). In particular, the modulation transfer function (MTF) which can be obtained from the OTF is widely used in photography to interpret lens performance and to define camera system resolving power. The camera model derived in this chapter provides mathematical expressions which will be used to discuss IQ in chapter 5.

3.1 Linear systems theory

Linear systems theory is a mathematical framework which uses a linear operator to model a system [1], and is widely used in the simulation and design of optical and camera systems [2–7].

This section provides a brief introduction to linear systems theory beginning with a *radiometric* description of light. Recall that practical exposure strategy as described in chapter 2 is based on *photometry*. Photometric quantities include a spectral weighting according to the response of the human visual system (HVS). For example, luminance as measured by a reflected-light meter correlates logarithmically with the brightness response of the HVS. Sensitivity measures are defined according to the ISO 12232 standard in terms of the luminance required to obtain a specified digital output level (DOL) from the camera [8]. The measurement uses standard illumination (the D55 daylight illuminant or the studio tungsten illuminant) which have spectral characteristics assumed to be representative of typical photographic conditions.

Ideally the sensor will not respond to non-visible light. The response outside of the visible spectrum will be reduced by the infra-red cut-off filter fitted to the camera, along with an optional ultraviolet-blocking filter fitted to the lens. Nevertheless, the camera system and the HVS do not respond in the same way over the visible spectrum. Although satisfactory for defining an exposure strategy, inclusion of a spectral weighting in terms of the response of the HVS is unsuitable for modelling the precise nature of the camera raw data. This requires knowledge of the spectral composition of the illumination source which may differ from that assumed by the ISO standard, the spectral transmission of the lens and filters, and finally the spectral response of the imaging sensor itself. A suitable framework for quantifying light in this way is provided by *radiometry* which allows an arbitrary spectral weighting to be included [9].

This section begins by using radiometry to define an ideal reference image. This is the radiometric counterpart of the ideal optical image described using Gaussian optics and photometry in chapter 1. The difference between the ideal and real image can be described by the system PSF or OTF. After an introduction to the PSF and OTF, this section closes by introducing a simple model camera system. The system PSF consists of optics, OLPF, and sensor components which will be described in later sections of this chapter.

Table 3.1. Common radiometric and photometric quantities with their symbols and SI units.

Quantity	Symbol	Radiometry Unit
Spectral flux	$\Phi_{e,\lambda}$	$W\ nm^{-1}$
Spectral irradiance	$E_{e,\lambda}$	$W\ m^{-2}\ nm^{-1}$
Spectral exitance	$M_{e,\lambda}$	$W\ m^{-2}\ nm^{-1}$
Spectral intensity	$I_{e,\lambda}$	$W\ sr^{-1}\ nm^{-1}$
Spectral radiance	$L_{e,\lambda}$	$W\ sr^{-1}\ m^{-2}\ nm^{-1}$
Radiant flux	Φ_e	$W \equiv J\ s^{-1}$
Irradiance	E_e	$W\ m^{-2}$
Radiant exitance	M_e	$W\ m^{-2}$
Radiant intensity	I_e	$W\ sr^{-1}$
Radiance	L_e	$W\ sr^{-1}\ m^{-2}$

Photometry		
Quantity	Symbol	Unit
Luminous flux	Φ_v	lm
Illuminance	E_v	$lx \equiv lm\ m^{-2}$
Luminous exitance	M_v	$lx \equiv lm\ m^{-2}$
Luminous intensity	I_v	$cd \equiv lm\ sr^{-1}$
Luminance	L_v	$cd\ m^{-2}$

3.1.1 Radiometry

The energy flow of light can be rigorously described by electromagnetic optics using Maxwell's equations and the Poynting vector [10, 11]. Nevertheless, a satisfactory description in many circumstances is provided by radiometry [9]. All of the photometric quantities introduced in chapter 1 have radiometric counterparts as listed in table 3.1. The major difference is that radiometric quantities have not been spectrally weighted according to the spectral sensitivity of the HVS. Radiometric quantities are denoted with an 'e' subscript for 'energetic' to distinguish them from photometric quantities which are denoted with a 'v' subscript for 'visual'.

Traditional radiometry assumes that the light source is *incoherent*, a topic which will be discussed in section 3.2 later. Many light sources can be approximated as being incoherent, in particular extended sources such as the Sun. This enables radiometric quantities to be decomposed into their spectral representations as continuous functions of wavelength. Integrating over all wavelengths will restore the full radiometric quantity. For example, radiance L_e is obtained from spectral radiance $L_{e,\lambda}$ in the following manner,

$$L_e = \int L_{e,\lambda}\ d\lambda.$$

Here the wavelength dependence is denoted with a subscript because $L_{e,\lambda}$ is a derivative quantity. Non-spectral quantities which have a wavelength dependence written in the form $f(\lambda)$ are weighting factors rather than derivative quantities and should not be independently integrated over wavelength [9].

As mentioned in the introduction to this section, the spectral representation is required in this chapter so that the light reaching the sensor plane can be appropriately weighted according to the spectral response of the system components before the integration over wavelength is performed.

The spectral radiometric quantities of interest in this chapter are the *spectral radiant flux*, *spectral scene radiance*, and *spectral sensor-plane irradiance*. In the remainder of this chapter the 'e' subscript will be dropped for clarity.

From radiometry to photometry
It is useful to briefly show how the photometric quantities introduced in chapter 1 can be obtained from their corresponding radiometric counterparts.

The sensitivity of the HVS to electromagnetic radiation varies as a function of wavelength. In daylight, the relative sensitivity is described by the *standard luminosity function* for photopic vision $V(\lambda)$ shown in figure 3.1. The HVS cannot detect electromagnetic radiation outside the visible range which is from approximately $\lambda_1 \rightarrow \lambda_2$, where

$$\lambda_1 = 380 \text{ nm}$$
$$\lambda_2 = 780 \text{ nm}.$$

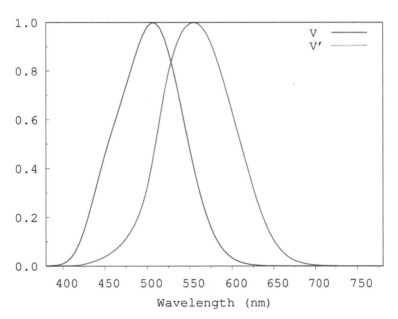

Figure 3.1. Standard 1924 CIE luminosity function for photopic vision $V(\lambda)$ (green curve). The curve is normalised to a peak value of unity at 555 nm. The 1951 CIE luminosity function for low-light or scotopic vision $V'(\lambda)$ is also shown (blue curve).

Photometric quantities by definition do not have a spectral representation but can be obtained from their spectral-radiometric counterparts by including the standard luminosity function as a weighting factor and then integrating over all wavelengths from $\lambda_1 \rightarrow \lambda_2$. For example, luminance can be obtained from spectral radiance $L_{e,\lambda}$ in the following manner,

$$L_v = K \int_{\lambda_1}^{\lambda_2} L_{e,\lambda} \, V(\lambda) \, d\lambda. \tag{3.1}$$

The luminous efficacy K is a normalisation constant,

$$K = 683 \text{ lm W}^{-1}.$$

A source of electromagnetic radiation with a high radiometric value will have zero photometric value if wavelengths in the visible spectrum are absent.

3.1.2 Ideal image

The coordinate representation must be introduced in order to express function values at precise locations in space. The following notation will be adopted in this chapter:

(x_{op}, y_{op}) Coordinates on the object plane

(x_{xp}, y_{xp}) Coordinates on the exit pupil plane

(x, y) Coordinates on the sensor plane.

The magnification m can be used to express the sensor-plane coordinates in terms of the object-plane coordinates,

$$(x_{op}, x_{op}) = \left(\frac{x}{m}, \frac{y}{m} \right).$$

The ideal geometrical spectral *irradiance* distribution at the sensor plane is the spectral radiometric counterpart of the illuminance formula derived previously using photometry in section 1.4 of chapter 1,

$$\boxed{E_{\lambda,\text{ideal}}(x, y) = \frac{\pi}{4} L_\lambda \left(\frac{x}{m}, \frac{y}{m} \right) \frac{1}{N_w} T_{\text{lens}} \cos^4 \varphi}. \tag{3.2}$$

Here N_w is the working f-number, m is the Gaussian magnification, and L_λ is the spectral scene radiance.

The cosine fourth term can be replaced with an image-space term $R(x, y, \lambda)$ referred to as the *relative illumination* (RI) factor which models the combined effects of the natural fall-off due to the cosine fourth law along with the vignetting arising from the specific real lens design [3]. The RI factor is normalised to unity at the optical axis. Vignetting arising from the lens design typically decreases as the f-number N increases, and so the RI factor is a function of N. Geometric *distortion* data for the specific lens design can also be incorporated into the definition of the ideal image [3].

3.1.3 Point-spread function

Unlike the ideal imaging scenario described above, a point on the object plane will not be imaged as a point on the sensor plane in reality. Light originating from a point on the object plane will always be distributed over an area surrounding the ideal image point. This leads to *blurring* of the ideal point image which can be described mathematically by a *point-spread function* (PSF) [1]. A variety of components in a camera system will contribute to this blurring effect. Each contribution can be modelled by its own PSF, and these can all be combined together to define an overall system PSF.

Figure 3.2 shows a selection of real lens PSFs obtained using a microscope [12]. The first six images represent moderate IQ and are typical point spreads for fast lenses used at maximum aperture or for wide-angle lenses at the edge of the frame, while image 7 shows a PSF representative of a lens with outstanding performance [12]. Image 8 includes the PSF contributed by an OLPF placed in front of the sensor plane along with the PSF of image 7. As described in section 3.4 later, OLPFs split the light into a number of spots in order to reduce an unwanted effect known as aliasing.

When light originating from the entire field of view is projected by the lens onto the sensor plane, every ideal point image will be blurred. In turn, the entire image will be blurred in comparison with the ideal optical image described by equation (3.2). It is useful to represent the ideal and real irradiance distributions at the sensor plane by the input and output functions $f(x, y)$ and $g(x, y)$,

$$f(x, y) = E_{\lambda,\text{ideal}}(x, y)$$
$$g(x, y) = E_{\lambda}(x, y).$$

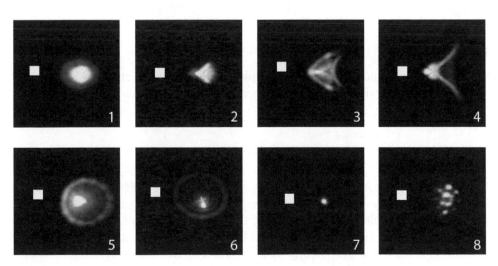

Figure 3.2. PSFs obtained using a microscope. The white square represents the size of a photosite with 8.5 μm pixel pitch. (Figure reproduced from reference [12] with kind permission.)

Since the PSFs associated with each position on the sensor plane will all overlap, evaluating the real blurred image $g(x, y)$ may seem an impossible task. However, it turns out that $g(x, y)$ can be straightforwardly determined provided two conditions are satisfied:

- The PSF denoted by $h(x, y)$ must not change functional form when it is shifted over the sensor plane. This condition is referred to as *shift invariance*.
- A *linear* mapping must exist between $f(x, y)$ and $g(x, y)$.

A system which is both linear and shift-invariant is referred to as *isoplanatic* or *linear shift-invariant* (LSI) [1, 2]. In practice, a camera system will only be approximately LSI. The first condition does not hold in the presence of residual lens aberrations, however this can be overcome in practice by treating the system as a group of subsystems which are LSI over specific regions of the sensor plane. The second condition holds in terms of irradiance provided the lighting is incoherent, which is a good approximation under normal photographic conditions.

When the camera system is treated as LSI, the output function $g(x, y)$ can be determined at an arbitrary position on the sensor plane via the following *convolution* integral,

$$g(x, y) = \int_{-\infty}^{\infty} \int_{-\infty}^{\infty} f(x', y')\, h(x - x')\, h(y - y')\, \mathrm{d}x'\, \mathrm{d}y'. \qquad (3.4)$$

This can be written more compactly by introducing the convolution operator $*$,

$$\boxed{g(x, y) = f(x, y) * h(x, y)}.$$

An informal derivation of the convolution integral is given below in one dimension (1D). Subsequently, the convolution operation will be illustrated with some simple examples.

3.1.4 Convolution

Mathematically, a point on the sensor plane can be represented by a Dirac delta function $\delta(x - x_0)$ which has the following properties,

$$\delta(x - x_0) = 0 \quad \text{when } x \neq x_0$$

$$\int_{-\infty}^{\infty} \delta(x - x_0)\, \mathrm{d}x = 1.$$

The first property states that $\delta(x - x_0)$ is zero everywhere except at the location x_0. The second property ensures that $\delta(x - x_0)$ defines an area of unity. This means that the height of the delta function approaches infinity as its width becomes infinitesimally small. Nevertheless, the important characteristic is the area, and so the delta function is represented graphically by an upward arrow with height equal to unity,

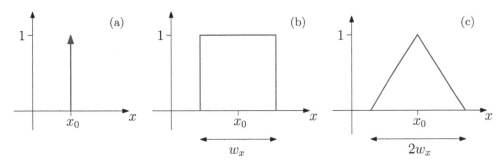

Figure 3.3. (a) Delta function of unit area positioned at x_0. (b) 1D rectangle function centred at x_0. (c) 1D triangle function centred at x_0.

as shown in figure 3.3(a). Weighting a function by $\delta(x - x_0)$ and integrating over all space yields the function *value* at x_0,

$$\int_{-\infty}^{\infty} f(x)\, \delta(x - x_0)\, \mathrm{d}x = \begin{cases} f(x_0), & x = x_0 \\ 0, & x \neq x_0. \end{cases} \tag{3.6}$$

For illustration purposes, first assume that the system is ideal apart from the existence of an *isolated* PSF centred at position x_0 on the sensor plane and denoted by $h(x - x_0)$. If the delta function at x_0 is replaced by the PSF, weighting $f(x)$ by $h(x - x_0)$ and integrating over all space will yield the *output* function value $g(x_0)$. However unlike the delta function, the PSF also has non-zero values at a range of positions $x = x_i$ surrounding x_0. Denoting the domain or kernel area of the PSF by A, it follows that

$$\int_{-\infty}^{\infty} f(x)\, h(x - x_0)\, \mathrm{d}x = \begin{cases} g(x_0), & x = x_0 \\ g(x_i), & x = x_i \in A \\ 0, & |x - x_0| \notin A. \end{cases}$$

Now consider a real system where blur exists at all positions on the sensor plane. In this case, all the PSFs associated with every point on the sensor plane will overlap. In order to determine the output function $g(x)$ at an arbitrary position x_0, all point spread *towards* position x_0 needs to be evaluated. In an LSI system, it turns out that this can be achieved simply by making the replacement $h(x - x_0) \rightarrow h(x_0 - x)$. This amounts to *flipping the PSF*,

$$\int_{-\infty}^{\infty} f(x)\, h(x_0 - x)\, \mathrm{d}x = g(x_0).$$

To see this graphically, consider the example PSF shown by the black curve in figure 3.4 centred at point x_0. This example PSF is symmetric for simplicity, but this need not be the case in general. Three example points x_1, x_2 and x_3 contained within the domain of the PSF are shown. The contribution to $g(x_0)$ from x_0 itself is the

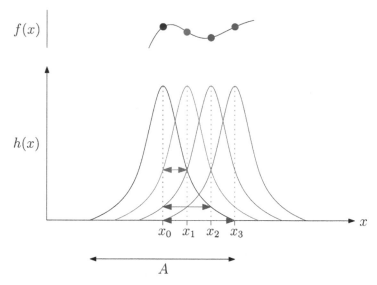

$$f(x)$$

$$h(x)$$

$$x_0 \quad x_1 \quad x_2 \quad x_3$$

$$x$$

$$A$$

Figure 3.4. Derivation of the convolution operation in 1D. The input function $f(x)$ is shown at positions $x_i = x_0, x_1, x_2,$ and x_3. The PSF denoted by $h(x)$ is assumed to be shift-invariant.

product $f(x_0)h(x_0 - x_0)$ or $f(x_0)h(0)$. The contribution from x_1 is seen to be the product $f(x_1)h(x_0 - x_1)$. Similarly, the contributions from x_2 and x_3 are seen to be $f(x_2)h(x_0 - x_2)$ and $f(x_3)h(x_0 - x_3)$, respectively. The PSF has insufficient width to contribute to $g(x_0)$ when centred at positions beyond x_3. In summary,

$$g(x_0) = f(x_0)h(x_0 - x_0) + f(x_1)h(x_0 - x_1)$$
$$+ f(x_2)h(x_0 - x_2) + f(x_3)h(x_0 - x_3).$$

Since x actually varies continuously between x_0 and x_3, there are many more contributions which must be accounted for,

$$g(x_0) = \int_{-x_3}^{x_3} f(x')h(x_0 - x')\, dx'.$$

The integration limits have been defined to take into account contributions from both the left-hand side and right-hand side of x_0. Moreover, the value x_3 must be replaced by infinity to take into account a PSF of infinite extent,

$$g(x_0) = \int_{-\infty}^{\infty} f(x')\, h(x_0 - x')\, dx'.$$

It has turned out that the output function $g(x_0)$ is given by the *product of the overlap of the input function $f(x)$ with the PSF centred at x_0*. In other words, the functional form of the spread around x_0 that contributes to the output at x_0 is defined by the PSF itself.

In an LSI system, the complete output function $g(x)$ can be obtained by performing the above calculation at every output position x,

$$g(x) = \int_{-\infty}^{\infty} f(x')\, h(x - x')\, dx'.$$

This result generalises to the two-dimensional (2D) expression given by equation (3.4).

Example 1 The ideal PSF is the delta function itself,

$$h(x - x') = \delta(x - x').$$

In this case, the PSF becomes infinitesimally narrow and its height extends to infinity in order to preserve an area of unity. Because there is no spread around x contributing to the output at x, the output function remains unchanged compared to the input function,

$$g(x) = \int_{-\infty}^{\infty} f(x')\, \delta(x - x')\, dx' = f(x).$$

The next simplest PSF is a scaled delta function where B is a constant,

$$h(x - x') = B\, \delta(x - x').$$

Again there is no spread around x contributing to the output at x and so the result is a simple multiplication,

$$g(x) = B \int_{-\infty}^{\infty} f(x')\, \delta(x - x')\, dx' = B\, f(x).$$

Example 2 When the PSF contributes point-spread, the convolution operation is no longer trivial. This is best illustrated by using a simple example. Consider the input function $f(x)$ defined by the rectangle function illustrated in figure 3.3(b),

$$f(x) = \text{rect}(x).$$

The rectangle function for general x_0 is defined by

$$\text{rect}\left(\frac{x - x_0}{w_x}\right) = \begin{cases} 1, & \left|\dfrac{x - x_0}{w_x}\right| < \dfrac{1}{2} \\[2mm] \dfrac{1}{2}, & \left|\dfrac{x - x_0}{w_x}\right| = \dfrac{1}{2} \\[2mm] 0, & \left|\dfrac{x - x_0}{w_x}\right| > \dfrac{1}{2}. \end{cases}$$

In the present example, the rectangle function is centred at $x_0 = 0$ and the width $w_x = 1$. Let the PSF similarly be a rectangle function centred at $x_0 = 0$,

$$h(x) = \text{rect}(x).$$

The output function is given by the following convolution integral,

$$g(x) = \int_{-\infty}^{\infty} \text{rect}(x')\text{rect}(x - x')\, dx'.$$

The solution can be determined graphically according to figure 3.5. Starting at $x = -\infty$, the function $f(x') = \text{rect}(x')$ along with the flipped PSF defined by $h(x - x') = \text{rect}(x - x')$ are plotted using x' as the dummy variable on the horizontal axis [1]. The output function $g(-\infty)$ is equal to the area of overlap of $\text{rect}(x')$ and $\text{rect}(x - x')$. A new value for x is chosen and the procedure is repeated. The flipped PSF shifts along the axis as x increases, and the overlap must be calculated at each value of x.

In the present example, the area of overlap is easily seen to be zero for $-\infty < x \leqslant -1$ and $1 \leqslant x < \infty$, but is positive for values of x between -1 and 1. For example, figure 3.5(a) shows the overlap area is 0 for $x = -1$, and figure 3.5(b) shows that the overlap area is 0.5 for $x = -0.5$. The overall result turns out to be the triangle function centred at $x_0 = 0$ shown in figure 3.5(c),

$$g(x) = \text{tri}(x).$$

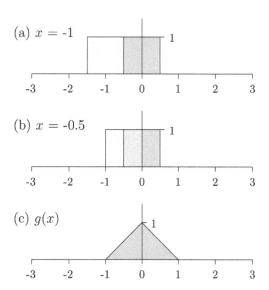

Figure 3.5. Graphical solution of the convolution integral of example 2. The input function $f(x')$ is shown by the blue rectangle function. The flipped PSF is shown in yellow. (a) For $x = -1$, the area of overlap is zero and so $g(-1) = 0$. (b) For $x = -0.5$, the area of overlap shown in grey is equal to 0.5 and so $g(-0.5) = 0.5$. (c) The complete output function $g(x)$ is a triangle function.

The triangle function for general x_0 is illustrated in figure 3.3(c) and is defined by

$$
\text{tri}\left(\frac{x - x_0}{w_x}\right) =
\begin{cases}
0, & \left|\dfrac{x - x_0}{w_x}\right| \geqslant 1 \\
1 - \left|\dfrac{x - x_0}{w_x}\right|, & \left|\dfrac{x - x_0}{w_x}\right| < 1.
\end{cases}
$$

3.1.5 Optical transfer function

PSFs give *qualitative* insight into IQ. Although some *quantitative* IQ measures are based on the PSF, the shape of a PSF can be very complicated and difficult to describe in simple numerical terms, as evident from figure 3.2. A much more useful quantitative description of IQ is provided by the *transfer function* which is the Fourier transform (FT) of the PSF. For an optical system such as a camera, a component transfer function is referred to as an *optical transfer function* (OTF) [10].

Consider a PSF denoted by $h(x, y)$ along with the ideal and real irradiance distributions at the sensor plane denoted by $f(x, y)$ and $g(x, y)$, respectively. The PSF and its corresponding OTF denoted by $H(\mu_x, \mu_y)$ are related by the following FT pair,

$$
h(x, y) = \int_{-\infty}^{\infty} \int_{-\infty}^{\infty} H(\mu_x, \mu_y)\, e^{i2\pi(\mu_x x + \mu_y y)} \mathrm{d}\mu_x\, \mathrm{d}\mu_y \tag{3.7a}
$$

$$
H(\mu_x, \mu_y) = \int_{-\infty}^{\infty} \int_{-\infty}^{\infty} h(x, y)\, e^{-i2\pi(\mu_x x + \mu_y y)} \mathrm{d}x\, \mathrm{d}y \tag{3.7b}
$$

Analogous expressions can be written for the FT pairs $f(x, y) \leftrightarrow F(\mu_x, \mu_y)$ and $g(x, y) \leftrightarrow G(\mu_x, \mu_y)$.

The FT gives the prescription for constructing an arbitrary function as a superposition of sinusoidal waveforms at various different *spatial frequencies* μ_x and μ_y, phases, and amplitudes. The spatial frequencies are expressed in units of cycles per unit distance, for example cycles/mm. These spatial frequencies, phases and amplitudes correspond to irradiance waveforms in a 2D plane but are ultimately characterised by the optical wave which travels from the object plane to the sensor plane.

A major advantage of the spatial frequency representation arises from the *convolution theorem* which infers that the convolution operation in the real domain is equivalent to a simple product in the Fourier domain. Equation (3.4) may therefore be written

$$
H(\mu_x, \mu_y) = \frac{G(\mu_x, \mu_y)}{F(\mu_x, \mu_y)}.
$$

Note that OTFs are always normalised to unity at (0,0). This corresponds with the total volume under the PSF normalised to unity [13],

$$\int\int h(x, y)\, dx\, dy = 1.$$

The OTF is seen to provide a simple relationship between the ideal input and real output irradiance distributions as a function of spatial frequency. Since the OTF is a complex quantity in general, more specific information can be extracted by expressing the OTF in terms of its modulus and phase,

$$H(\mu_x, \mu_y) = \left| H(\mu_x, \mu_y) \right| e^{i\phi(\mu_x, \mu_y)}.$$

The modulus $|H(\mu_x, \mu_y)|$ and phase $\phi(\mu_x, \mu_y)$ are defined as the *modulation transfer function* (MTF) and *phase transfer function* (PTF), respectively,

$$\boxed{\begin{aligned} \mathrm{MTF}(\mu_x, \mu_y) &= \left| H(\mu_x, \mu_y) \right| \\ \mathrm{PTF}(\mu_x, \mu_y) &= \phi(\mu_x, \mu_y) \end{aligned}}.$$

3.1.6 Modulation transfer function

The MTF has been defined above as the modulus of the OTF,

$$\mathrm{MTF}(\mu_x, \mu_y) = \left| H(\mu_x, \mu_y) \right| = \left| \frac{G(\mu_x, \mu_y)}{F(\mu_x, \mu_y)} \right|. \tag{3.9}$$

The MTF is commonly used as a performance metric in imaging. In order to gain physical insight into the significance of the MTF, consider imaging a sinusoidal target pattern at the object plane defined by a *single* spatial frequency. The ideal irradiance waveform $f(x, y)$ at the sensor plane is shown by the blue curve in figure 3.6. At the sensor plane, the spatial frequency of f is an *image-space* spatial frequency which depends upon the magnification. This spatial frequency has been denoted by μ_{x0}, μ_{y0}.

The *modulation depth* of f is defined as the ratio of the magnitude of the waveform (ac value) to the mean value (dc bias),

$$M_f = \frac{|f|}{\mathrm{dc}}.$$

Notice that the modulation depth is *independent* of the spatial frequency μ_{x0}, μ_{y0}. In an LSI system, convolving f with a PSF will yield a real output irradiance waveform $g(x, y)$ at the same spatial frequency μ_{x0}, μ_{y0} and with the same dc bias [1]. However, the magnitude and therefore the modulation depth will be attenuated according to equation (3.9),

$$M_g(\mu_{x0}, \mu_{y0}) = \frac{|g|}{\mathrm{dc}} = \frac{1}{\mathrm{dc}} \left| \frac{G(\mu_{x0}, \mu_{y0})}{F(\mu_{x0}, \mu_{y0})} f \right|.$$

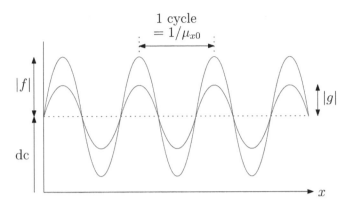

Figure 3.6. The blue curve shows an ideal input irradiance waveform $f(x, y)$ defined by a single spatial frequency μ_{x0}, μ_{y0} at the sensor plane. The magenta curve shows an example reduction in magnitude after convolving $f(x, y)$ with a PSF which partially fills in the troughs of the waveform. Phase differences have not been included.

In other words, the *modulation depth of the output waveform depends upon the spatial frequency μ_{x0}, μ_{y0}* [1, 14]. Combining the above equations yields

$$\left| H(\mu_{x0}, \mu_{y0}) \right| = \frac{M_g(\mu_{x0}, \mu_{y0})}{M_f}.$$

If the whole process is repeated but the spatial frequency of the sinusoidal target pattern is changed each time, the following general function of image-space spatial frequency will be obtained,

$$\boxed{\left| H(\mu_x, \mu_y) \right| = \frac{M_g(\mu_x, \mu_y)}{M_f}}.$$

This is precisely the MTF defined by equation (3.9).

Modulation depth can be interpreted by expressing the ac/dc ratio in the form of the Michelson equation [14],

$$M = \frac{E_{\max} - E_{\min}}{E_{\max} + E_{\min}}.$$

Here $E_{\min}$ and $E_{\max}$ are the minimum and maximum values of the irradiance waveform at a specified spatial frequency. Since neither $E_{\max}$ nor $E_{\min}$ can be negative, it must follow that $0 \leqslant M \leqslant 1$. This interpretation is synonymous with *contrast*, although the term contrast is applied to square waveforms rather than sinusoidal waveforms. If the camera component under consideration introduces point spread, then

$$0 \leqslant M_g(\mu_x, \mu_y) \leqslant M_f \leqslant 1$$

and

$$\boxed{0 \leqslant \text{MTF}(\mu_x, \mu_y) \leqslant 1}.$$

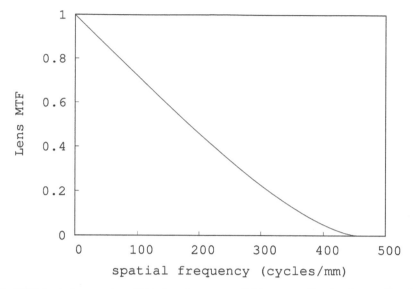

Figure 3.7. MTF due to lens aperture diffraction along one spatial frequency direction for a perfect aberration-free lens set at $N = 4$. The wavelength $\lambda = 550$ nm has been used for the lighting, and the cut-off frequency is defined by 455 cycles/mm.

Since most of the point spread is typically concentrated over a small blur spot surrounding the ideal image point, the MTF will only be reduced slightly from unity at low spatial frequencies. However, the MTF will drop significantly at higher spatial frequencies as the peak to peak separation approaches the size of the blur spot.

The spatial frequency at which the MTF drops to zero for the camera component under consideration is defined as its *cut-off frequency*. Image information cannot be transmitted above the cut-off frequency. This will be important for defining resolving power in chapter 5.

As an example, a perfect aberration-free lens has an associated PSF which arises due to lens aperture diffraction. For a circular lens aperture, the PSF is defined by the well-known Airy pattern illustrated in figure 3.14 of section 3.2.4. The corresponding MTF when the f-number is set at $N = 4$ is shown along one spatial frequency direction in figure 3.7. Section 3.2 will discuss lens aperture diffraction in detail.

3.1.7 Phase transfer function

As the modulus of the OTF, the MTF leaves phase information out of consideration. The PTF describes the change in the phase $\phi(\mu_x, \mu_y)$ of the output sinusoidal waveforms $G(\mu_x, \mu_y)$ relative to the input $F(\mu_x, \mu_y)$ as a function of spatial frequency. Since these waveforms combine to form the ideal and real irradiance distributions at the sensor plane, $f(x, y)$ and $g(x, y)$ respectively, any change in phase can have a significant effect on the nature of the output image.

The PTF takes values between $-\pi$ and $+\pi$. A PTF which is linear will shift the image [2]. For example, the sinusoidal waveforms shown in figure 3.6 have spatial frequency μ_{x0}, μ_{y0}. A linear PTF at μ_{x0}, μ_{y0} will shift the attenuated waveform shown in magenta relative to the input waveform shown in blue.

If the PSF is symmetric, the PTF will be either zero or $+\pi$. These values correspond to spatial frequency ranges where the OTF is positive or negative, respectively [14]. A phase reversal will reverse the contrast at the specified spatial frequency, meaning that peaks and troughs will switch places.

Certain residual lens aberrations such as coma are associated with real but *asymmetric* PSFs. In this case the PTF will be a nonlinear function. Nonlinearities cause phase distortions which can severely degrade the image.

Although not achievable in a camera system due to the presence of lens aperture diffraction, a perfect imaging system would in principle have $\mathrm{MTF}(\mu_x, \mu_y) = 1$ and $\mathrm{PTF}(\mu_x, \mu_y) = 0$ for all spatial frequencies.

3.1.8 Model camera system

It is instructive to introduce a model camera system consisting of lens, OLPF, and sensor components, each of which provide contributions to the system PSF. In linear systems theory, the system PSF is given simply as a convolution of each component PSF,

$$\boxed{h_{\mathrm{system}}(x, y) = h_{\mathrm{lens}}(x, y) * h_{\mathrm{OLPF}}(x, y) * h_{\mathrm{sensor}}(x, y)}.$$

Each of these component PSFs can be subdivided into further PSF contributions which are similarly convolved together. The model described in this chapter includes only the contribution to the lens PSF arising from lens aperture diffraction, and the contribution to the sensor PSF arising from the detector aperture at a photosite.

The aim is to determine the real irradiance distribution at the sensor plane. This is obtained by convolving the system PSF with the ideal irradiance distribution defined by equation (3.2),

$$E(x, y) = h_{\mathrm{system}}(x, y) * E_{\mathrm{ideal}}(x, y).$$

Physically it is useful to think of the system PSF as a *blur filter* similar to the blur filters available in image editing software. Defining the image in terms of the irradiance distribution, the convolution operation is analogous to sliding the blur filter over the ideal image to produce the real output image. The shape, diameter, and strength of the blur filter determines the level of blur present in the output. Most of the blur strength is concentrated in the region close to the ideal image point.

It will be shown in section 3.3 later that an additional process must be introduced in conjunction with the detector–aperture contribution to the sensor PSF, specifically a *sampling* of the real irradiance distribution. Ultimately this arises because the sensor photosites are not point objects and so the sensor signal is not a continuous function over the sensor plane. Mathematically, the sampling operation can be modelled as a multiplication with the so-called comb function. This is a 2D array of delta functions which restrict the output of the convolution operation to the appropriate grid of sampling positions defined by the photosite or sensor pixel spacings p_x and p_y,

$$\tilde{E}(x, y) = \left(h_{\text{system}}(x, y) * E_{\text{ideal}}(x, y)\right) \text{comb}\left[\frac{x}{p_x}, \frac{y}{p_y}\right].$$

The sampled real irradiance distribution $\tilde{E}(x, y)$ can then be used to model the sensor signal and subsequent raw data output.

It is often more convenient to perform calculations in the Fourier domain. Since the FT of each component PSF yields the component transfer function or OTF, the FT of the system PSF is the system transfer function or *system OTF*,

$$H_{\text{system}}(\mu_x, \mu_y) = \text{FT}\{h_{\text{system}}(x, y)\}.$$

From the convolution theorem introduced in section 3.1.5, the system OTF is given simply as a *multiplication* of the component OTFs,

$$H_{\text{system}}(\mu_x, \mu_y) = H_{\text{lens}}(\mu_x, \mu_y) H_{\text{OLPF}}(\mu_x, \mu_y) H_{\text{sensor}}(\mu_x, \mu_y).$$

The system PSF can then be straightforwardly calculated by taking the inverse FT. However, the system OTF provides additional information in the form of the MTF and PTF which can be used to assess IQ.

3.2 Optics

The *Airy pattern* is a famous pattern in optics which arises from the PSF due to diffraction at a lens aperture. Due to the importance of diffraction in relation to IQ in photography, this section traces the physical origins of the diffraction PSF starting from the wave equation. The mathematical expression for the diffraction PSF is arrived at in section 3.2.4.

This section also briefly shows how a description of lens aberrations can be included within the framework of linear systems theory by introducing the wavefront error, and closes by discussing the effects of polarising filters.

3.2.1 Wave optics

Electromagnetic waves are *transverse* waves with oscillating electric field **E** and magnetic field **H** components oriented perpendicular to each other and to the direction of wave propagation, as illustrated in figure 3.8. The fields themselves depend on position $\mathbf{r} = (x, y, z)$ and time t. Being vector fields, they have orthogonal components in the x, y, and z directions,

$$\mathbf{E}(\mathbf{r}, t) = \left(E_x(\mathbf{r}, t), E_y(\mathbf{r}, t), E_z(\mathbf{r}, t)\right)$$

$$\mathbf{H}(\mathbf{r}, t) = \left(H_x(\mathbf{r}, t), H_y(\mathbf{r}, t), H_z(\mathbf{r}, t)\right).$$

Electromagnetic waves are described by Maxwell's equations which form the basis of *electromagnetic optics*. However, the theory of electromagnetic optics greatly

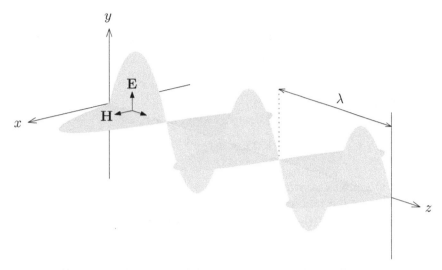

Figure 3.8. Electromagnetic wave at a given instant in time propagating in the z-direction. The electric and magnetic fields oscillate in phase and are perpendicular to each other and to the direction of propagation.

simplifies when the propagation medium satisfies four important properties. If the medium is linear, isotropic, uniform, and non-dispersive [10, 11] then Maxwell's equations reduce to the following two wave-type equations,

$$\nabla^2 \mathbf{E} - \frac{1}{c^2} \frac{\partial^2 \mathbf{E}}{\partial t^2} = 0$$

$$\nabla^2 \mathbf{H} - \frac{1}{c^2} \frac{\partial^2 \mathbf{H}}{\partial t^2} = 0.$$

Here c is the speed of light in the medium. Significantly, these equations are also satisfied by any of the individual vector-field components,

$$\boxed{\nabla^2 U(\mathbf{r}, t) - \frac{1}{c^2} \frac{\partial^2 U(\mathbf{r}, t)}{\partial t^2} = 0}. \tag{3.10}$$

Here $U(\mathbf{r}, t)$ can be any of E_x, E_y, E_z, H_x, H_y, or H_z. In other words, it is not necessary to solve for the full vector quantities when the medium satisfies the above properties, and instead only one scalar wave equation needs to be solved. This is the basis of the scalar theory of *wave optics* [10, 11].

At the interface between two dielectric media such as the lens aperture and the iris diaphragm, equation (3.10) no longer holds for the individual components. Nevertheless, the coupling at the interface can be neglected provided the aperture area is large compared to the wavelength [10, 11]. In this case wave optics remains a good approximation. On the other hand, the vector theory of electromagnetic optics based upon Maxwell's equations must be used when the medium does not satisfy one of the properties of linearity, isotropy, uniformity, or non-dispersiveness. For example, the vector theory is needed to describe polarisation.

Helmholtz equation

For *monochromatic* light, the complex solution of equation (3.10) can be written

$$U(\mathbf{r}, t) = U(\mathbf{r}) \, e^{i2\pi\nu t}.$$

Here:
- ν is the *optical frequency*.
- $U(\mathbf{r})$ is the complex field or *complex amplitude*,

$$U(\mathbf{r}) = A(\mathbf{r}) \, e^{i\phi(\mathbf{r})}.$$

- $A(\mathbf{r})$ is a complex constant.
- $|U(\mathbf{r})|$ defines the real amplitude.
- $\phi(\mathbf{r})$ is the phase which describes the position within an optical cycle or wavelength.

Figure 3.9 shows example *wavefronts* for a spherical wave. These are positions with the same phase. At a point on a wavefront, the vector normal to the wavefront at that point describes the direction of propagation. These vectors can be associated with the geometrical rays used in chapter 1.

Substituting $U(\mathbf{r}, t)$ into equation (3.10) reveals that the complex amplitude must satisfy the *Helmholtz equation*,

$$\boxed{(\nabla^2 + k^2)U(\mathbf{r}) = 0}.$$

The *wavenumber* k corresponding to λ is defined by

$$k = \frac{2\pi\nu}{c} = \frac{2\pi}{\lambda}.$$

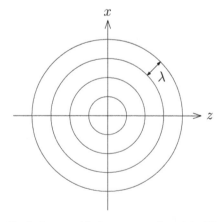

Figure 3.9. Cross section of a spherical wave with the source at the origin. The phase is $\phi = \arg(A) - kr$ and the wavefronts satisfy $kr = 2\pi n + \arg(A)$, where n is an integer. The spacing between consecutive wavefronts is given by $\lambda = 2\pi/k$.

An important characteristic of the Helmholtz equation is that it is *linear*. A linear combination of any two solutions of the Helmholtz equation is also a solution. This means that the principle of superposition applies and the sum of the individual complex amplitudes at any given position gives the total complex amplitude at that position [10, 11].

When imaging using *polychromatic* light, the range of wavelengths over which the camera system responds defines the *spectral passband*, $\lambda_1 \rightarrow \lambda_2$. In this case, the principle of superposition again applies to the complex amplitude provided the light is perfectly correlated or fully *coherent*. Coherent light can be produced by point sources such as lasers. On the other hand, extended sources such as the Sun give rise to random or *incoherent* light. In this case, the principle of superposition no longer applies to the complex amplitude [10, 11]. Instead, the system is linear in *irradiance*, which was defined in section 3.1.1 as the power per unit area received by a specified surface measured in $W\,m^{-2}$. For incoherent illumination, irradiance is simply the squared magnitude of the complex amplitude,

$$\boxed{E(\mathbf{r}) = |U(\mathbf{r})|^2}. \tag{3.11}$$

This relation is valid provided the irradiance is *stationary*, meaning that fluctuations will occur over very short time scales but the average value will be independent of time. In this case the time dependence of the wave solutions does not need to be considered.

In reality, light is generally *partially coherent* which requires a much more complicated analysis [11]. In this chapter, the light will be assumed to be polychromatic and fully incoherent, which is a reasonable approximation under typical photographic conditions. In this simplified approach, the light can be treated mathematically as monochromatic but incoherent, and the polychromatic effects can be taken into account simply by integrating over the spectral passband [2, 3].

In the theory of wave optics, power per unit area is commonly referred to as the *optical intensity* or simply the intensity. These terms will not be used in this book in order to avoid confusion with the radiant intensity which is a directional quantity involving solid angle [9].

3.2.2 Huygens–Fresnel principle

An important solution of the Helmholtz equation written in spherical coordinates is the *spherical wave* defined by

$$\boxed{U_{\text{sphere}}(\mathbf{r}) = \frac{A}{r}e^{-ikr}}.$$

Here A is a complex constant and r is the radial distance. As shown in figure 3.9, the wavefronts are spheres centred at the origin and so the wave propagates radially. The spherical wave is important because the Huygens–Fresnel principle states that all points on *any* wavefront actually spread out as spherical waves. In other words, the points on a wavefront are themselves sources of spherical waves, the super-position of which maintains the wavefront as it propagates.

The *Fresnel–Kirchhoff equation* is a mathematical expression of the Huygens–Fresnel principle within wave optics. Denoting the complex amplitude or field for a distribution of source points $\{x_1, y_1\}$ on a plane perpendicular to the optical axis by $U(x_1, y_1)$, the resulting field at points $\{x_2, y_2\}$ on a plane separated by a distance z from the source is given by

$$U(x_2, y_2) = \frac{1}{i\lambda} \int_{-\infty}^{\infty} \int_{-\infty}^{\infty} U(x_1, y_1) \frac{e^{ikR}}{|R|} \, dx_1 \, dy_1 \, .$$

Here R is the distance between (x_1, y_1) and (x_2, y_2),

$$|R| = \sqrt{(x_2 - x_1)^2 + (y_2 - y_1)^2 + z^2} \, .$$

Since R depends only on the distance perpendicular to the optical axis between the source points and the resulting field points rather than on their absolute positions in the plane, $R \equiv R(x_2 - x_1, y_2 - y_1)$, the Fresnel–Kirchhoff equation is seen to be a convolution of the source field with a spherical wave impulse response,

$$U(x_2, y_2) = U(x_1, y_1) * \left[\frac{1}{i\lambda} \frac{e^{ikR}}{|R|} \right] \, .$$

The impulse response is an example of a Green's function [10].

The Huygens–Fresnel principle can be observed when a wave passes through a narrow opening such as a lens aperture. Spherical waves are seen to propagate radially outwards, but the effects of superposition are restricted at points nearer to the edges of the aperture. Consequently the whole wavefront is distorted as shown in figure 3.10, leading to a visible *diffraction* pattern of constructive and destructive interference. The diffraction pattern leads to a blurring of the image at the sensor plane which can be modelled by a PSF.

3.2.3 Aperture diffraction PSF

Due to the importance of diffraction in relation to IQ in photography, a simplified derivation of the irradiance PSF due to aperture diffraction is given below in order to illustrate the basic underlying principles. Readers unfamiliar with wave optics may wish to omit this section and head straight to the result for a circular aperture defined by equation (3.20).

The following derivation proceeds by first determining the *amplitude* PSF due to diffraction which is valid for fully *coherent* illumination. This is achieved by considering a delta function source point at the axial position on the object plane, and treating the lens as a thin lens with the aperture stop at the lens. An expression is derived for the complex amplitude response at the sensor plane arising from the delta function input. The magnification is then used to project the input coordinates onto the sensor plane to form an LSI system valid for coherent illumination. For fully *incoherent* illumination, the *irradiance* PSF due to diffraction can then be straightforwardly obtained by taking the squared magnitude of the amplitude PSF, and normalising the volume under the PSF to unity.

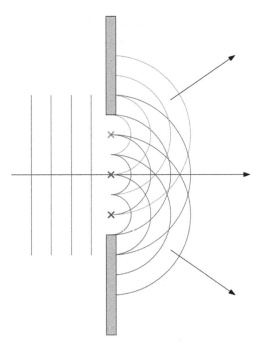

Figure 3.10. Diffraction of incoming plane waves at an aperture. Spherical waves propagating radially outward are shown from three example source points marked by crosses. Superposition of spherical waves is limited closer to the edges of the aperture leading to a spreading out of the waves and a visible diffraction pattern at the sensor plane.

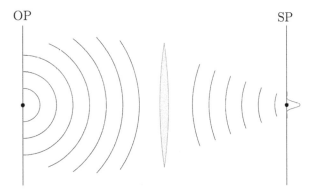

Figure 3.11. A spherical wave emerging from an axial source position is modified by the phase transmission function of the lens and converges towards the ideal image position at the sensor plane.

(1) Thin lens model

Figure 3.11 shows the wavefronts entering a lens from an object point positioned on the optical axis. The wavefronts are modified by the lens and converge towards the sensor plane. Because of diffraction at the lens aperture, the corresponding field at the sensor plane will be a distribution rather than a point.

Let the field $U(x_{op}, y_{op})$ at the object position (x_{op}, y_{op}) be described by a delta function. When the Fresnel–Kirchhoff equation is applied to this field, the integration vanishes and the field at the lens becomes

$$U(x_{ap}, y_{ap}) = \frac{1}{i\lambda} \frac{e^{ikR}}{|R|}.$$

Here R is the distance between the object position (x_{op}, y_{op}) and the position on the aperture plane (x_{ap}, y_{ap}),

$$R = \sqrt{(x_{ap} - x_{op})^2 + (y_{ap} - y_{op})^2 + s^2}.$$

The geometry is shown in figure 3.12. The lens modifies the spherical wavefront at the aperture plane in the following manner,

$$U'(x_{ap}, y_{ap}) = U(x_{ap}, y_{ap}) \, a(x_{ap}, y_{ap}) \, t_l(x_{ap}, y_{ap}).$$

Here t_l is the *phase transformation function* [10, 11] for a converging thin lens with focal length f,

$$t_l(x_{ap}, y_{ap}) = \exp\left(-i\frac{k}{2f}\left(x_{ap}^2 + y_{ap}^2\right)\right).$$

This form of t_l neglects aberrations and is strictly valid only in the paraxial region [10]. The *aperture function* $a(x_{ap}, y_{ap})$ restricts the size of the aperture by taking a value of unity where the aperture is clear, and zero where the aperture is blocked.

Now the Fresnel–Kirchhoff equation can be applied to the set of source points $\{(x_{ap}, y_{ap})\}$ lying in the aperture plane. The resulting field at the sensor plane is

$$U'(x, y) = \frac{1}{i\lambda} \int_{-\infty}^{\infty} \int_{-\infty}^{\infty} U'(x_{ap}, y_{ap}) \frac{e^{ikR'}}{|R'|} \, dx_{ap} \, dy_{ap}.$$

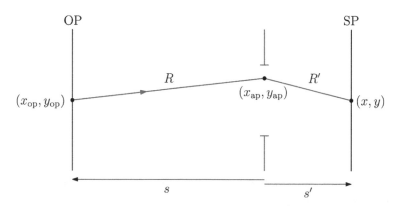

Figure 3.12. The set of coordinates $\{(x_{ap}, y_{ap})\}$ lie in the aperture plane for a thin lens with the aperture at the lens. The coordinates (x_{op}, y_{op}) and (x, y) denote the source and image positions, respectively. The distances R and R' are indicated for an example coordinate (x_{ap}, y_{ap}).

Here R' is the distance between (x_{ap}, y_{ap}) and (x, y),

$$R' = \sqrt{(x - x_{ap})^2 + (y - y_{ap})^2 + s'^2}.$$

The complex amplitude $U'(x, y)$ is the amplitude response due to the delta function input and can be denoted $h_{amp,diff}(x_{op}, y_{op}; x, y)$. This emphasises the dependence on the object-plane coordinates through R. Putting everything together leads to the following expression,

$$h_{amp,diff}(x_{op}, y_{op}; x, y) = \frac{1}{(i\lambda)^2} \int_{-\infty}^{\infty} \int_{-\infty}^{\infty} \frac{e^{ikR}}{|R|} t_l(x_{ap}, y_{ap})$$
$$\times a(x_{ap}, y_{ap}) \frac{e^{ikR'}}{|R'|} dx_{ap} dy_{ap}.$$

(3.12)

The response $h_{amp,diff}(x_{op}, y_{op}; x, y)$ is not a PSF because it is shift-variant, depending upon both the object-plane and sensor-plane coordinates. Before proceeding further, various simplifying approximations need to be made.

(2) Simplifying approximations

- Close to the object plane, the spherical wavefronts can be approximated as parabolic wavefronts. This is achieved by performing a Taylor expansion of R in the numerator of equation (3.12) and dropping higher order terms. At the lens, the parabolic phase term can be further expanded and terms dropped. This leads to a *plane wave* approximation,

$$\frac{e^{ikR}}{|R|} \approx \frac{e^{ikR_{plane}}}{s}$$

where

$$R_{plane} = s + \frac{x_{op}^2 + y_{op}^2}{2s} + \frac{x_{ap}^2 + y_{ap}^2}{2s} - \frac{x_{ap} x_{op} + y_{ap} y_{op}}{s}.$$

- After diffraction by the lens aperture, similar approximations can be made. The parabolic approximation in the so-called *near-field* region leads to a description of diffraction known as *Fresnel* diffraction. The plane-wave approximation in the *far-field* region where the sensor plane is located leads to a description known as *Fraunhofer* diffraction,

$$\frac{e^{ikR'}}{|R'|} \approx \frac{e^{ikR'_{plane}}}{s'}$$

where

$$R'_{plane} = s' + \frac{x^2 + y^2}{2s'} + \frac{x_{ap}^2 + y_{ap}^2}{2s'} - \frac{x_{ap} x + y_{ap} y}{s'}.$$

Substituting these expressions together with the phase transformation function t_l into equation (3.12) leads to an equation containing many terms,

$$h_{\text{amp,diff}}(x_{\text{op}}, y_{\text{op}}; x, y) \approx \frac{e^{ik(s+s')}}{(i\lambda)^2 ss'}$$

$$\times \int_{-\infty}^{\infty} \int_{-\infty}^{\infty} a(x_{\text{ap}}, y_{\text{ap}}) \exp\left\{\frac{ik}{2s'}(x^2 + y^2)\right\} \exp\left\{\frac{ik}{2s}(x_{\text{op}}^2 + y_{\text{op}}^2)\right\}$$

$$\times \exp\left\{\frac{k}{2}(x_{\text{ap}}^2 + y_{\text{ap}}^2)\left(\frac{1}{s} + \frac{1}{s'} - \frac{1}{f}\right)\right\}$$

$$\times \exp\left\{\frac{-ik}{s}(x_{\text{ap}}x_{\text{op}} + y_{\text{ap}}y_{\text{op}})\right\} \exp\left\{\frac{-ik}{s'}(x_{\text{ap}}x + y_{\text{ap}}y)\right\} dx_{\text{ap}} dy_{\text{ap}}.$$

Fortunately, this expression can be simplified. Arguments can be given for dropping the final exponential term on the second line [10]. Furthermore, the exponential term on the third line vanishes according to the Gaussian lens conjugate equation in air,

$$\frac{1}{s} + \frac{1}{s'} - \frac{1}{f} = 0.$$

The simplified expression becomes

$$h_{\text{amp,diff}}(x_{\text{op}}, y_{\text{op}}; x, y) \approx \frac{e^{ik(s+s')}}{(i\lambda)^2 ss'} \exp\left\{\frac{ik}{2s'}(x^2 + y^2)\right\} \int_{-\infty}^{\infty} \int_{-\infty}^{\infty} a(x_{\text{ap}}, y_{\text{ap}})$$

$$\times \exp\left\{\frac{-ik}{s}(x_{\text{ap}}x_{\text{op}} + y_{\text{ap}}y_{\text{op}})\right\} \exp\left\{\frac{-ik}{s'}(x_{\text{ap}}x + y_{\text{ap}}y)\right\} dx_{\text{ap}} dy_{\text{ap}}.$$

(3.13)

(3) Shift-invariance

The final line of equation (3.13) can be rewritten by substituting the magnification $m = -s'/s$ according to the optical rather than photographic sign convention,

$$h_{\text{amp,diff}}(x - mx_{\text{op}}, y - my_{\text{op}}) \approx \frac{e^{ik(s+s')}}{(i\lambda)^2 ss'} \exp\left\{\frac{ik}{2s'}(x^2 + y^2)\right\}$$

$$\times \int_{-\infty}^{\infty} \int_{-\infty}^{\infty} a(x_{\text{ap}}, y_{\text{ap}}) \exp\left\{\frac{-ik}{s'}(x - mx_{\text{op}})x_{\text{ap}}\right\} \exp\left\{\frac{-ik}{s'}(y - my_{\text{op}})y_{\text{ap}}\right\} dx_{\text{ap}} dy_{\text{ap}}.$$

The coordinates $(mx_{\mathrm{op}}, my_{\mathrm{op}})$ are image-space coordinates because the magnification projects the object-space coordinates onto the sensor plane, as described in section 3.1.2 earlier.

For fully *coherent* lighting, the system is now in a form that is LSI. In this case, the *amplitude* PSF due to diffraction is given by

$$
h_{\mathrm{amp,diff}}(x, y, \lambda) \approx \frac{e^{iik(s+s')}}{(i\lambda)^2 ss'} \exp\left\{\frac{ik}{2s'}(x^2 + y^2)\right\}
$$

$$
\times \int_{-\infty}^{\infty} \int_{-\infty}^{\infty} a(x_{\mathrm{ap}}, y_{\mathrm{ap}}) \exp\left\{-i2\pi\left(\frac{x}{\lambda s'}\right) x_{\mathrm{ap}}\right\} \exp\left\{-i2\pi\left(\frac{y}{\lambda s'}\right) y_{\mathrm{ap}}\right\} \mathrm{d}x_{\mathrm{ap}} \, \mathrm{d}y_{\mathrm{ap}}.
$$

(3.14)

In the second line, the wavenumber k has been replaced by making the substitution $k = 2\pi/\lambda$.

If the light is fully *incoherent*, the system is not linear in complex amplitude and so $h_{\mathrm{amp,diff}}(x, y, \lambda)$ does not define a PSF. Nevertheless, the irradiance PSF due to diffraction which is valid for incoherent lighting can be straightforwardly determined from $h_{\mathrm{amp,diff}}(x, y, \lambda)$, as shown in step (6) below.

(4) Fourier transformation

By comparing equation (3.14) with the FT defined by equation (3.7b), the second line should be recognisable as the *FT of the aperture function*,

$$
A(\mu_x, \mu_y) = \mathrm{FT}\{a(x, y)\}.
$$

This defines the *amplitude transfer function*. However, the spatial frequencies μ_x and μ_y are to be substituted by the following real-space quantities defined at the sensor plane,

$$
\mu_x = \frac{x}{\lambda s'}, \qquad \mu_y = \frac{y}{\lambda s'}.
$$

Now equation (3.14) may be written in the final form

$$
h_{\mathrm{amp,diff}}(x, y, \lambda) \approx \frac{e^{ik(s+s')}}{(i\lambda)^2 ss'} \exp\left\{\frac{ik}{2s'}(x^2 + y^2)\right\} A\left(\mu_x = \frac{x}{\lambda s'}, \mu_y = \frac{y}{\lambda s'}\right).
$$

When the illumination is *coherent*, this important result shows that *the real optical image at the sensor plane will be a convolution of the ideal image predicted by geometrical optics with a PSF that is the Fraunhofer diffraction pattern of the exit pupil* [10].

(5) Generalised model

For a general compound lens, the derivation for the thin lens model can be generalised to the case of a general compound lens by associating all diffraction effects with either the entrance pupil or the exit pupil [10].

Taking the viewpoint that all diffraction effects are associated with the exit pupil, the coordinates of the aperture function must now be considered on the exit pupil plane instead, and the aperture function must take a value of unity where the projected aperture is clear, and zero where the projected aperture is blocked. Therefore

$$
\boxed{
\begin{aligned}
h_{\text{amp,diff}}(x, y, \lambda) &\approx \frac{U_0\, e^{ikz'}}{i\lambda z'} \exp\left\{\frac{ik}{2z'}(x^2 + y^2)\right\} \\
&\times A\left(\mu_x = \frac{x}{\lambda z'}, \mu_y = \frac{y}{\lambda z'}\right)
\end{aligned}
}
\tag{3.15}
$$

Here U_0 is a complex constant, and $A(x/\lambda z', y/\lambda z')$ is the FT of the aperture function evaluated at the spatial frequencies $\mu_x = x/\lambda z'$ and $\mu_y = y/\lambda z'$.

The distance s' measured from the aperture plane to the sensor plane for the thin lens has been replaced by the distance z' measured from the exit pupil to the sensor plane. The Gaussian expression for z' is

$$
z' = s' - s'_{\text{xp}} = \frac{n'}{n} D_{\text{xp}} N_{\text{w}}.
\tag{3.16}
$$

Here s' and s'_{xp} are the distances from the second principal plane to the sensor plane and exit pupil respectively, D_{xp} is the diameter of the exit pupil, and N_{w} is the working f-number.

(6) Incoherent illumination

When the illumination is *incoherent*, the system is linear in irradiance rather than complex amplitude. An LSI system can be formed by introducing the *irradiance PSF due to diffraction*. According to equation (3.11), this is obtained simply by taking the squared magnitude of equation (3.15),

$$
\boxed{
h_{\text{diff}}(x, y, \lambda) = \frac{U_0^2}{(\lambda z')^2}\left| A\left(\mu_x = \frac{x}{\lambda z'}, \mu_y = \frac{y}{\lambda z'}\right)\right|^2.
}
\tag{3.17}
$$

The volume under the PSF can then be normalised to unity. This expression is valid for source points on or close to the optical axis.

This leads to the important result that for *incoherent* illumination, *the real optical image at the sensor plane will be a convolution of the ideal image predicted by geometrical optics with a PSF that is proportional to the squared magnitude of the Fraunhofer diffraction pattern of the exit pupil* [10].

3.2.4 Circular aperture: Airy disk

For a circular lens aperture, the aperture function describing the exit pupil plane can be modelled by a radially symmetric circle function of diameter $D_{\text{xp}} = m_{\text{p}}D$, where m_{p} is the pupil magnification and D is the diameter of the entrance pupil,

$$
a_{\text{circ}}(x_{\text{xp}}, y_{\text{xp}}) = \text{circ}\left[\frac{\sqrt{x_{\text{xp}}^2 + y_{\text{xp}}^2}}{D_{\text{xp}}}\right] = \text{circ}\left[\frac{r_{\text{xp}}}{D_{\text{xp}}}\right] = \begin{cases} 1, & r_{\text{xp}} < D_{\text{xp}}/2 \\ \frac{1}{2}, & r_{\text{xp}} = D_{\text{xp}}/2 \\ 0, & r_{\text{xp}} > D_{\text{xp}}/2. \end{cases}
$$

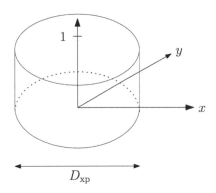

Figure 3.13. Circle function which models the aperture function.

The FT of an aperture function modelled by a circle function is the so-called jinc function,

$$A_{\mathrm{circ}}(\mu_x, \mu_y) = \mathrm{jinc}\left[D_{\mathrm{xp}}\sqrt{\mu_x^2 + \mu_y^2}\right] = \mathrm{jinc}\left[D_{\mathrm{xp}}\mu_r\right] = \frac{2J_1\left[\pi D_{\mathrm{xp}}\mu_r\right]}{\pi D_{\mathrm{xp}}\mu_r}. \qquad (3.18)$$

Here μ_r is the radial spatial frequency and J_1 is a Bessel function of the first kind.

For incoherent illumination, the diffraction PSF for a circular aperture is obtained by substituting equation (3.18) into equation (3.17),

$$h_{\mathrm{diff}}(x, y, \lambda) = \frac{U_0^2}{(\lambda z')^2} \left| \frac{\pi}{4} D_{\mathrm{xp}}^2 \, \mathrm{jinc}\left(D_{\mathrm{xp}}\sqrt{\left(\frac{x}{\lambda z'}\right)^2 + \left(\frac{y}{\lambda z'}\right)^2} \right) \right|^2. \qquad (3.19)$$

For the special case that focus is set at infinity, $z' \to m_{\mathrm{p}}f_{\mathrm{R}}' = D_{\mathrm{xp}} N$. Now substituting for z' yields

$$h_{\mathrm{diff}}(x, y, \lambda) = \left(\frac{U_0 \, \pi D_{\mathrm{xp}}}{4\lambda N}\right)^2 \left| \frac{2J_1[\alpha]}{\alpha} \right|^2. \qquad (3.20)$$

The quantity α is defined by

$$\alpha = \frac{\pi\sqrt{x^2 + y^2}}{\lambda N} = \frac{\pi \, r}{\lambda N}.$$

This PSF is illustrated in 1D in figure 3.14 and in 2D and 3D in figure 3.15. A sequence of diffraction rings where the PSF is zero are apparent. If the radial distance on the sensor plane r is measured in units of λN, these rings occur when $J_1[\pi r] = 0$. The first zero ring has solution

$$r = 1.22 \, \lambda N.$$

This defines the well-known *Airy disk*, and the diameter or *spot size* of the Airy disk is $2.44 \, \lambda N$.

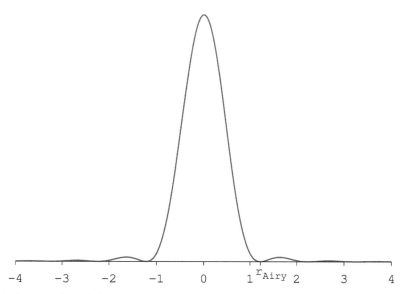

Figure 3.14. Cross-section of the irradiance PSF due to diffraction for a single wavelength with the lens focused at infinity. The lens aperture is unobstructed and circular, and the lighting is incoherent. The horizontal axis represents radial distance from the origin measured in units of λN. The first zero ring at a radial distance $r_{\text{Airy}} = 1.22\,\lambda N$ defines the Airy disk. The volume under the PSF can be normalised to unity.

The spot size contains the major contribution to the point spread associated with diffraction. Because the spot size becomes wider as N increases, increased blurring of the image occurs with increasing f-number. This is known as *diffraction softening*. Landscape photographers often need to maximise depth of field by using a small aperture while simultaneously avoiding noticeable diffraction softening. On a 35mm full-frame camera, around $N = 11$ is generally considered to achieve the optimum balance.

3.2.5 Aperture diffraction MTF

The diffraction OTF for incoherent illumination is obtained by taking the FT of the irradiance PSF due to diffraction defined by equation (3.17),

$$h_{\text{diff}}(x, y, \lambda) = \frac{U_0^2}{(\lambda z')^2}\left|A\left(\mu_x = \frac{x}{\lambda z'}, \mu_y = \frac{y}{\lambda z'}\right)\right|^2.$$

Recall that the square modulus of the FT of the aperture function, $|A(\mu_x, \mu_y)|^2$, is a real-space quantity because the spatial frequencies are substituted by real-space coordinates $x/(\lambda z')$, $y/(\lambda z')$. It follows that the FT of $|A(\mu_x, \mu_y)|^2$ will yield a function related to $a(x, y)$ which will be defined in the Fourier domain because the real-space

Figure 3.15. Irradiance PSF due to diffraction for a single wavelength λ with the lens focused at infinity. The lens aperture is unobstructed and circular, and the lighting is incoherent. No contrast adjustments have been made.

coordinates will be substituted by the spatial frequencies $(\lambda z'\mu_x, \lambda z'\mu_y)$. The following identity can be used to take the FT,

$$
\mathrm{FT}\left\{ \left| A\left(\frac{x}{\lambda z'}, \frac{y}{\lambda z'}\right) \right|^2 \right\} = \mathrm{FT}\left\{ A\left(\frac{x}{\lambda z'}, \frac{y}{\lambda z'}\right) A^*\left(\frac{x}{\lambda z'}, \frac{x}{\lambda z'}\right) \right\}
$$

$$
= (\lambda z')^2\, a(\lambda z'\mu_x, \lambda z'\mu_y)\ \otimes\ a^*(\lambda z'\mu_x, \lambda z'\mu_y).
$$

Here $*$ denotes the complex conjugate. The self cross-correlation or *auto-correlation* operation is denoted by the $\otimes$ symbol and is defined by

$$
g(x) = \int_{-\infty}^{\infty} f(x) h(x_0 - x)\, \mathrm{d}x_0.
$$

Compared to a convolution, the correlation operation does not flip the function h before the overlap is calculated.

Substituting the above identity into equation (3.17) yields the following expression for the incoherent diffraction OTF,

$$
\boxed{H_{\mathrm{diff}}(\mu_x, \mu_y, \lambda) = U_0^2\, a(\lambda z'\mu_x, \lambda z'\mu_y)\ \otimes\ a^*(\lambda z'\mu_x, \lambda z'\mu_y)}.
$$

After normalising to unity at (0,0), *the OTF is seen to be the normalised auto-correlation function of the amplitude transfer function* [10]. At the sensor plane, the Gaussian expression for z' was defined by equation (3.16),

$$
z' = s' - s'_{\mathrm{xp}} = \frac{n'}{n} D_{\mathrm{xp}} N_{\mathrm{w}}.
$$

For a circular lens aperture,

$$
a_{\mathrm{circ}}(\lambda z'\mu_x, \lambda z'\mu_y) = \mathrm{circ}\left[\frac{\lambda z'\sqrt{\mu_x^2 + \mu_y^2}}{D_{\mathrm{xp}}}\right] = \mathrm{circ}\left[\frac{\lambda z'\mu_r}{D_{\mathrm{xp}}}\right] = \mathrm{circ}\left[\frac{\mu_r}{\mu_c}\right].
$$

Here the radial spatial frequency μ_r and the quantity μ_c are defined by

$$\mu_r = \frac{\sqrt{x^2 + y^2}}{\lambda z'} = \frac{r}{\lambda z'}$$

$$\mu_c = \frac{D_{xp}}{\lambda z'}.$$

Therefore

$$H_{\text{diff,circ}}(\mu_x, \mu_y, \lambda) = U_0^2 \; \text{circ}\left[\frac{\mu_r}{\mu_c}\right] \otimes \text{circ}\left[\frac{\mu_r}{\mu_c}\right].$$

The auto-correlation can be performed by graphically calculating the overlap [10]. This yields the following normalised result,

$$H_{\text{diff,circ}}(\mu_r, \lambda) = \begin{cases} \dfrac{2}{\pi}\left(\cos^{-1}\left(\dfrac{\mu_r}{\mu_c}\right) - \dfrac{\mu_r}{\mu_c}\sqrt{1 - \left(\dfrac{\mu_r}{\mu_c}\right)^2}\right) & \text{for } \dfrac{\mu_r}{\mu_c} \leqslant 1 \\ 0 & \text{for } \dfrac{\mu_r}{\mu_c} > 1 \end{cases}. \tag{3.21}$$

This expression is equivalent to the FT of equation (3.19) normalised to unity at (0,0). Taking the modulus yields the MTF which is usually expressed as a percentage.

It can be seen that the incoherent diffraction OTF for a circular aperture drops to zero at the spatial frequency defined by μ_c. This value can be interpreted as the *cut-off frequency* due to diffraction in the presence of incoherent illumination. Any scene information requiring spatial frequencies above μ_c on the sensor plane will be lost due to the effects of diffraction.

If the surrounding medium is air and focus is set at infinity, $z' \to D_{xp}N$ and the cut-off frequency becomes

$$\boxed{\mu_c = \frac{1}{\lambda N}}. \tag{3.22}$$

Figure 3.16 illustrates how the cut-off frequency is lowered as N increases. This behaviour is consistent with the discussion of diffraction softening given in section 3.2.4.

3.2.6 Wavefront error

A lens which produces an image differing from a perfect image projected onto the sensor plane only due to the effects of diffraction is said to be *diffraction-limited*. In such a lens, the wavefront emerging from the exit pupil will be a perfect spherical wave converging towards the ideal Gaussian image point [10]. Departures from this ideal spherical wave are caused by residual lens *aberrations* which Gaussian optics

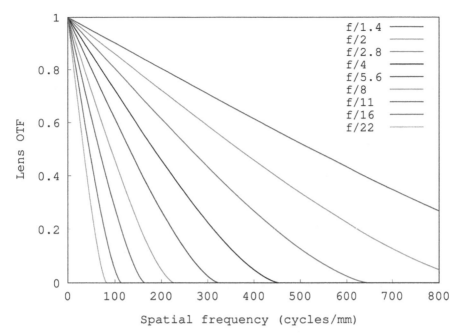

Figure 3.16. OTF or MTF for an ideal aberration-free lens with circular aperture as a function of f-number. The chosen wavelength is $\lambda = 550$ nm and so the cut-off frequency is $\mu_c = 1818/N$.

leaves out of consideration. Section 5.3 of chapter 5 gives a brief description of some basic photographic lens aberrations.

One way of modelling aberrations is to replace the aperture function with the *pupil function* $p(x, y)$,

$$p(x_{\mathrm{xp}}, y_{\mathrm{xp}}) = a(x_{\mathrm{xp}}, y_{\mathrm{xp}})\,\mathrm{e}^{\mathrm{i}2\pi W(x_{\mathrm{xp}}, y_{\mathrm{xp}})}.$$

A description of the wavefront error as a function of position on the exit pupil plane is specified by the *aberration function* or *wavefront error function* $W(x_{\mathrm{xp}}, y_{\mathrm{xp}})$. For the lens design under consideration, this must be obtained numerically using lens design software.

Figure 3.17 shows the geometry for defining the wavefront error [10]. A *Gaussian reference sphere* is constructed which intersects the exit pupil at the optical axis. This reference sphere describes the shape of the ideal spherical wave as it emerges from the exit pupil and converges towards the ideal Gaussian image point defined by the paraxial chief ray. For a real ray emerging from the exit pupil at position $(x_{\mathrm{xp}}, y_{\mathrm{xp}})$, the wavefront error $W(x_{\mathrm{xp}}, y_{\mathrm{xp}})$ describes the distance along the ray between the reference sphere and the actual emerging wavefront which intersects the exit pupil at the optical axis. The wavefront error is measured in units of wavelength and is related to the *optical path difference* (OPD) [13, 15],

$$W(x_{\mathrm{xp}}, y_{\mathrm{xp}}) = \frac{\mathrm{OPD}(x_{\mathrm{xp}}, y_{\mathrm{xp}})}{\lambda}.$$

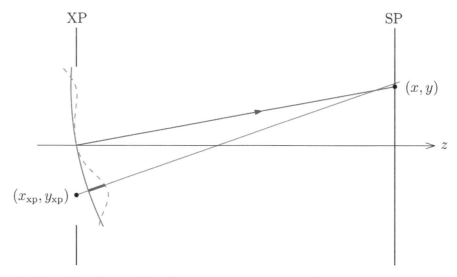

Figure 3.17. Gaussian reference sphere (blue arc) and example real wavefront (green curve) at the exit pupil. The blue ray is the paraxial chief ray. The red line indicates the optical path difference OPD(x_{xp}, y_{xp}) for the example green ray.

Multiplying the wavefront error function by 2π gives the phase difference [13, 15]. For example, if the OPD $= \lambda/4$ at a given position (x_{xp}, y_{xp}) then $W = 1/4$ at the same position. The peak-to-peak wavefront error W_{PP} is the maximum OPD value over all points on the reference sphere. The *Rayleigh quarter-wave limit* [16] specifies $W_{PP} = 1/4$ as an aberration allowance for a lens to be sensibly classed as perfect or diffraction-limited [17].

A useful measure for the overall effect of aberrations is the root-mean-square (RMS) wavefront error W_{RMS}. This is defined in terms of the mean of the squared wavefront error over the reference sphere coordinates minus the square of the mean wavefront error,

$$W_{RMS} = \sqrt{\langle W^2 \rangle - \langle W \rangle^2}.$$

A small aberration content is classed as an **RMS** wavefront error up to 0.07, medium between 0.07 and 0.25, and large above 0.25 [13]. Geometrical optics provides a good approximation to the MTF in the large aberration region, $W_{RMS} > 0.25$.

The *Strehl ratio* is the ratio of the irradiance at the centre of the PSF for an aberrated system compared to the irradiance at the centre of the PSF for a diffraction-limited system. According to the *Marechal criterion*, a lens can be considered essentially diffraction-limited if the Strehl ratio is at least 80%. For *defocus aberration* where the plane of best focus no longer corresponds with the sensor plane, the Merechal criterion is identical to the Rayleigh quarter-wave limit because there is an exact relationship between the peak-to-peak and RMS wavefront error in this case, $W_{PP} = 3.5 \, W_{RMS}$.

Since the wavefront error generally becomes worse for light rays that are further from the optical axis, the system PSF will no longer be isoplanatic over the entire sensor plane. In other words, the system can no longer be treated as LSI once a description of aberrations is included. In practice, a way forward is to treat the system as a group of subsystems which are LSI over specific regions of the sensor plane [2, 3].

3.2.7 Polarisation

Light consists of transverse waves with oscillations perpendicular to the direction of propagation. If an incoming beam of light is visualised travelling along the z-axis towards an observer, the oscillations at any instant in time will appear to the observer to lie in a plane oriented at an angle θ with the z-axis. In *unpolarised* light, this angle fluctuates randomly as a function of time and so any oriented plane is equally likely. This is illustrated in figure 3.18(b). Direct natural light is unpolarised.

Mathematically, the electric field vector **E** defines the orientation of the oscillations. It is useful to resolve **E** into x and y components where A is the amplitude,

$$E_x = A \cos \theta$$
$$E_y = A \sin \theta.$$

In the case of unpolarised light, θ fluctuates randomly. Since all values are equally probable, symmetry is restored on the average. Equivalently, each component has the same amplitude but there is no phase coherence between these components as a function of time. This description is a simplified picture of the physical reality, nevertheless it is mathematically equivalent [18].

Linearly polarised or *plane-polarised* light arises when θ takes a fixed value which does not fluctuate. In other words, the oscillations are always confined to one plane. An example is illustrated in figure 3.19.

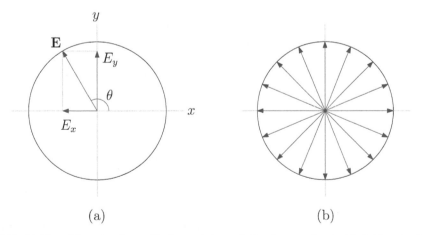

(a) (b)

Figure 3.18. (a) Viewed from head-on with the z-axis towards the observer, the electric-field vector **E** can be resolved into x and y components. (b) For unpolarised light, the electric-field vector can take any value at random.

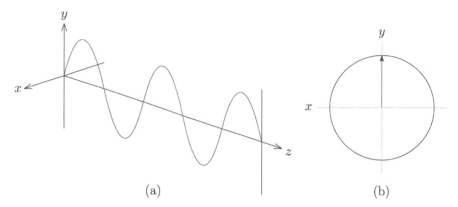

Figure 3.19. (a) Linear polarisation. In this example, the wave is confined to lie parallel to the *y*-axis. (b) The corresponding vector **E** is fixed in the direction of the *y*-axis.

Plane-polarised light is important in photography because a *polarising filter* can be used to reduce or block plane-polarised light from entering the lens. By selectively reducing the plane-polarised light, image appearance can be improved. In particular:

- Unwanted surface reflections and glare can be eliminated.
- Blue skies can be darkened.

These applications are discussed below, along with the functioning of the polarising filter.

Surface reflections

When an unpolarised light beam is incident upon a dielectric surface such as glass, refraction and reflection will take place. The incident ray, the normal to the surface, and the reflected ray all lie in the same plane referred to as the *plane of incidence*. This is shown in figure 3.20(a).

The reflected beam arises from re-radiation due to the vibration of atoms in the dielectric material. Vibrations due to the refracted beam will contribute to generating the reflected beam, and these vibrations have components both in the plane of incidence (p-vibrations) and perpendicular to the plane of incidence (s-vibrations). Generally, a greater proportion of s-vibrations will contribute, and so the reflected beam will be *partially plane-polarised*. This means that light approaching the photographic lens which has been directly reflected from dielectric scene objects such as glass, leaves, wood, paint, and water will be partially plane-polarised.

There is in fact a situation where the reflected light will be completely plane-polarised as illustrated in figure 3.20(b). If it so happens that the angle between the refracted and reflected beams is 90°, then only the s-vibrations can contribute to generating the reflected beam [18]. In this case, the reflected beam will be completely plane-polarised by s-vibrations, and the reflected light is said to be *s-polarised*. This happens when the angle of incidence ϕ takes a particular value known as *Brewster's*

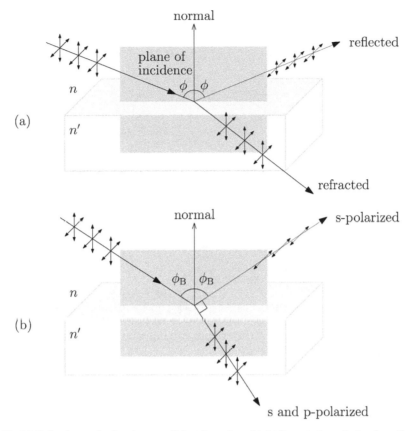

Figure 3.20. (a) Reflection and refraction at a dielectric surface. (b) At Brewster's angle ϕ_B, the reflected beam is completely polarised perpendicular to the plane of incidence.

angle, ϕ_B. Significantly, ϕ_B depends only on the refractive indices of the materials, n (usually air) and n'. Simple trigonometry shows that

$$\boxed{\tan \phi_B = \frac{n'}{n}}.$$

For a beam of light in air ($n = 1$) incident on a glass dielectric surface ($n' = 1.5$), Brewster's angle $\phi_B \approx 57°$ and about 15% of the incident light is reflected. If the beam is incident on water ($n' = 1.33$) then $\phi_B \approx 53°$.

If the light beam is incident on a stack of a sufficient number of glass plates, all s-polarised light will eventually be reflected from the incident beam, leaving only p-polarised light in the refracted beam [18].

Blue skies
Non-direct sunlight reaches an observer on the ground by scattering from particles in the atmosphere. According to the Rayleigh theory, the scattering is proportional

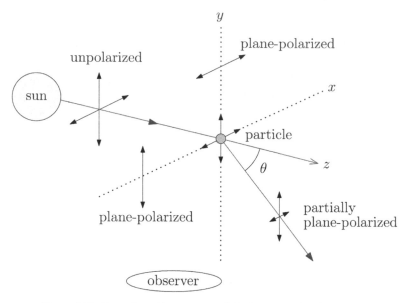

Figure 3.21. Scattering of incoming sunlight from a particle in the sky.

to $1/\lambda^4$. Since shorter wavelengths experience greater scattering, the overall colour of the sky is a light blue [18].

The incoming light from the direction of the Sun is unpolarised. Light which scatters in the plane perpendicular to the direction of the incoming light will be completely plane-polarized. If the incoming light is propagating in the z-direction, light which scatters at an angle θ with the z-axis will only be partially plane-polarized, and the light parallel to the z-axis will be unpolarised. This is illustrated in figure 3.21.

For an observer on the ground, light scattered from the strip of sky parallel with the observer and forming a right angle to the direction of the Sun will be most strongly reduced by using a polarising filter. Since light from clouds will be unpolarised due to repeated scatterings, blue skies can be selectively darkened. Figure 3.22 shows how excessive use of a polarising filter at very wide angles can reveal the graduated darkening with respect to angle θ.

Polarising filters
A *polarising filter* only allows light to be transmitted in one plane. When *unpolarised* light passes through a polarising filter, the appearance of the resulting image will be unaffected. However, the power per unit area or irradiance will be reduced by half. For example, if the E_y component is eliminated then only the $E_x = A \cos \theta$ component remains in the beam. Because θ continues to fluctuate randomly, the time-averaged irradiance E_e is reduced from A^2 to

$$E_e = \langle |E_x|^2 \rangle = A^2 \langle \cos^2 \theta \rangle = \frac{A^2}{2} .$$

Figure 3.22. Sky polarisation gradient from use of a polarising filter at a wide angle.

An ideal polarising filter therefore acts as a 1-stop neutral density filter when the transmitted light is unpolarised.

On the other hand, completely *plane-polarised* light has a *fixed* angle θ which defines the *plane of polarisation*. This angle may be defined relative to a convenient choice of x and y coordinate axes which are perpendicular to the direction of propagation. The polarising filter itself transmits light only in a plane defined by the angle of rotation of the filter. This plane is referred to as the *plane of transmission*. When a beam of plane-polarised light passes through a polarising filter, the axes defining the angle θ can be aligned with the plane of transmission. In this way, θ defines the angle between the plane of polarisation and the plane of transmission. The filter eliminates the perpendicular E_y component, and only the E_x component remains in the beam. Since the angle θ is fixed and does not fluctuate, the irradiance is reduced to

$$\boxed{E_e = |E_x|^2 = A^2 \cos^2 \theta}.$$

This is known as *Malus' law* [18]. When the plane of polarisation and the plane of transmission are aligned, $\theta = 0°$ and so 100% transmission is achieved in principle. When $\theta = 90°$, no light is transmitted. In practice, polarising filters are not ideal and so the transmission never quite reaches these 100% and 0% extremes. When plane-polarised light is mixed with unpolarised light, the 100% transmission figure will not be achieved even with an ideal filter. The utility of the polarising filter is that the ratio between the unpolarised light and plane-polarised light entering the lens can be altered.

Modern nanoparticle polarising filters used on photographic lenses belong to the class of dichroic polarisers. A *circular* polarising filter (CPL) rather than a linear polarising filter should be used with cameras that utilise a beamsplitter for autofocus and exposure determination. Beamsplitters themselves function using polarisation, and so the additional use of a polarising filter can cause metering issues in such cameras [19]. A CPL is composed of a linear polariser and a quarter-wave retarding plate. The retarding plate induces a phase difference between the electric field components resolved along the 'fast' and 'slow' axes of the plate. This causes the light to become circularly polarised so that the electric-field vector viewed from head-on traces out a helix as a function of time. Use of a CPL produces exactly the same image as a linear polarising filter, however the metering issues are avoided.

3.3 Sensor

The PSF due to diffraction derived in the previous section is straightforward to visualise; light from a point object spreads out over an area surrounding the ideal image point. For a circular aperture, the central part of this area forms the Airy disk.

The imaging sensor also causes light to spread out from the ideal image point. A significant blurring effect arises from the fact that a photosensitive *area* for receiving light exists at each photosite. In other words, each photosite is not a point object. The radiant flux arising from the irradiance distribution over each photosensitive area is mixed together when generating the charge signal representing the photosite. This blurring effect can be described by a spatial *detector-aperture* PSF, which is commonly referred to simply as the detector PSF or pixel PSF.

Although many contributions to the overall sensor PSF can be defined [6, 7], in this chapter only the spatial detector–aperture PSF will be considered.

3.3.1 Irradiance spatial integration

Consider the input function defined as a convolution of the ideal irradiance distribution at the sensor plane with the lens diffraction PSF,

$$f(x, y) = E_{\lambda,\text{ideal}}(x, y) * h_{\text{diff}}(x, y, \lambda). \tag{3.23}$$

Sensor photosites have an area of order microns (µm) squared. However, not all of this area is available for receiving light. Photosites in charge-coupled device (CCD) sensors typically have rectangular photosensitive areas, whereas photosites in complimentary metal-oxide semiconductor (CMOS) sensors typically have notched-rectangular or L-shaped photosensitive areas in order to accommodate circuitry [7]. An example of these types of areas viewed from above is shown in figure 3.23.

A *microlens* is normally fitted above each photosite in order to further increase the area available for receiving light. The effective photosensitive area of a photosite with a microlens fitted will be referred to in this chapter as the *flux detection area* and labelled as A_{det}. In a CCD sensor, A_{det} will typically be an enlarged rectangle. In CMOS sensors, A_{det} is less well-defined due to the presence of circuitry obstructing the light path [7].

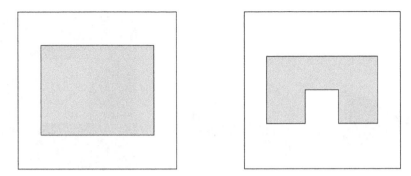

Figure 3.23. Example rectangular (left) and notched-rectangular (right) photosensitive areas shown in blue.

The ratio of the flux detection area to the photosite area A_p specifies the fill-factor (FF),

$$\boxed{\text{FF} = \frac{A_{\text{det}}}{A_p}}.$$ (3.24)

Since the irradiance at all parts of A_{det} contributes to generating the charge signal for the photosite, mathematically the irradiance must be *integrated* over A_{det} to yield the radiant flux responsible for photoconversion. Significantly, integrating the irradiance over A_{det} is proportional to *averaging* over the same area,

$$\int_{A_{\text{det}}} f(x, y)\mathrm{d}A = A_{\text{det}}\langle f(x, y)\rangle_{A_{\text{det}}}.$$

This averaging leads to a *blurring* of the corresponding scene detail. As mentioned in the introduction to this section, this blurring can be considered a form of point-spread and can equivalently be expressed in terms of a spatial detector–aperture PSF. The generation of the charge signal itself will be discussed in section 3.6 later.

3.3.2 Detector–aperture PSF

Recall from section 3.1.4 that the convolution operation slides the flipped PSF over the input function, and integrates all point spread *towards* the point at which the PSF is centred. This has direct analogy with the irradiance spatial integration over the flux detection area described above. It will be shown below that the point at which the integration is centred is the associated *sampling* point.

A rectangular detection area $A_{\text{det}} = d_x d_y$ associated with a CCD sensor can be represented by a 2D rectangle function,

$$\text{rect}\left[\frac{x}{d_x}, \frac{y}{d_y}\right] = \text{rect}\left[\frac{x}{d_x}\right]\text{rect}\left[\frac{y}{d_y}\right].$$

Figure 3.24. Spatial detector–aperture PSF.

The 1D rectangle function was defined in section 3.1.4 and illustrated in figure 3.4(b),

$$\text{rect}\left[\frac{x}{d}\right] = \begin{cases} 1 & |x| < d/2 \\ \frac{1}{2} & |x| = d/2 \\ 0 & |x| > d/2. \end{cases}$$

The PSF which represents the averaging over A_{det} is referred to as the *detector–aperture* PSF [2, 6, 7],

$$h_{\text{det–ap}}(x, y) = \frac{1}{A_{\text{det}}} \text{rect}\left[\frac{x}{d_x}\right] \text{rect}\left[\frac{y}{d_y}\right]. \tag{3.25}$$

The aperture area is defined by A_{det}, and the $1/A_{\text{det}}$ factor ensures that the convolution operation performs an averaging rather than an integration. The integration itself will be required when deriving the sensor signal in section 3.6. Detector–aperture PSFs for a variety of aperture shapes can be found in the literature [20, 21].

Consider the input function $f(x, y)$ defined by equation (3.23). At the centre of the aperture area, the convolution operation will output the averaged value of $f(x, y)$ over the extent of the aperture as it slides over $f(x, y)$. This will occur as the centre passes over *every* spatial coordinate on the sensor plane. The output function will be the following continuous function of position,

$$g(x, y) = f(x, y) * h_{\text{det–ap}}(x, y). \tag{3.26}$$

However, only *one* output value associated with each photosite is required. This means that the detector–aperture PSF must be accompanied by a *sampling* operation which restricts the output of the convolution operation to the appropriate grid of sampling positions.

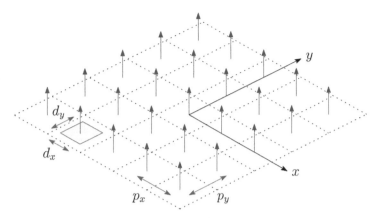

Figure 3.25. Detector sampling represented by a Dirac comb function. Each upward arrow is a delta function.

Mathematically, the sampling of a function can be achieved by multiplying with the *Dirac comb* function illustrated in figure 3.25,

$$\text{comb}\left[\frac{x}{p_x}, \frac{y}{p_y}\right] = \sum_{m=-\infty}^{\infty} \sum_{n=-\infty}^{\infty} \delta(x - mp_x)\delta(y - np_y).$$

The Dirac comb function is a 2D array of delta functions. Points on the output grid of sampling positions are separated by integer multiples of the *pixel pitch* in the x and y directions, denoted as p_x and p_y. The pixel pitch in a given direction is equal to the reciprocal of the number of photosites per unit area in that direction.

Multiplying equation (3.26) by the Dirac comb yields the following sampled output function denoted with a tilde symbol,

$$\tilde{g}(x, y) = \left(f(x, y) * h_{\text{det-ap}}(x, y)\right) \text{comb}\left[\frac{x}{p_x}, \frac{y}{p_y}\right]. \tag{3.27}$$

Sampling can introduce an unwanted effect known as aliasing which can be minimised by using an OLPF. Sampling and aliasing will be explained further in section 3.4.

3.3.3 Detector–aperture MTF

For a rectangular detector aperture, the MTF is defined by the modulus of the FT of equation (3.25). The FT of the 1D rectangle function is given by

$$\text{FT}\left\{\text{rect}\left[\frac{x}{d}\right]\right\} = |d|\,\text{sinc}(d\mu_x).$$

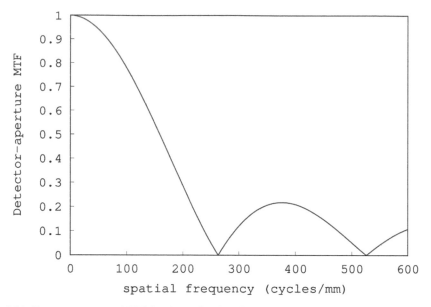

Figure 3.26. Detector–aperture MTF in the x-direction for a rectangular detector. In this example the detection area width d_x is 3.8 µm for a 4 µm pixel pitch p_x. The detector cut-off frequency is 263 cycles/mm.

Since $|d_x d_y| = A_{\text{det}}$, it follows that

$$
\begin{aligned}
\text{MTF}_{\text{det-ap}}(\mu_x, \mu_y) &= \left| \text{sinc}(d_x \mu_x, d_y \mu_y) \right| \\
&= \left| \frac{\sin(\pi \, d_x \mu_x)}{\pi \, d_x \mu_x} \frac{\sin(\pi \, d_y \mu_y)}{\pi \, d_y \mu_y} \right| .
\end{aligned}
\tag{3.28}
$$

The extent of the detection areas in each direction denoted by d_x and d_y will be less than the pixel pitches p_x and p_y in general.

Figure 3.26 and 3.27 illustrate the MTF for a square detector with $d_x = 3.8$ µm and $p_x = 4$ µm. In analogy with the lens aperture diffraction MTF, the detector–aperture MTF also has a cut-off frequency. This is defined as the frequency where the MTF first drops to zero. In the present example, the cut-off frequency is $(3.8 \text{ µm})^{-1} = 263$ cycles/mm.

The *sensor Nyquist frequency* μ_{sensor} to be introduced in the next section is the maximum cut-off frequency required to prevent aliasing. If $d_x = p_x$ then the detector–aperture cut-off frequency will be double the sensor Nyquist frequency. In the present example, $\mu_{\text{sensor}} = 125$ cycles/mm. The detector cut-off frequency is slightly more than $2 \times \mu_{\text{sensor}}$ because the FF is less than 100%. Although a higher FF increases QE, a higher FF also increases the width of the detector–aperture PSF which in turn increases point spread and lowers the detector cut-off frequency.

Figure 3.27. Detector–aperture MTF for a square detector.

3.4 Optical low-pass filter

An *optical low-pass filter* (OLPF) is commonly fitted above the imaging sensor in order to eliminate an unwanted effect known as *aliasing*. For 2D images, aliasing manifests itself as *moiré* patterns. Aliasing is a consequence of the *sampling* of the irradiance distribution at the sensor plane modelled by equation (3.27). The OLPF can reduce aliasing to an acceptable level by modifying the flow of light *before* it reaches the sensor plane.

By design, the OLPF is another source of blurring which can be modelled by a PSF. This section begins with a brief introduction to sampling theory and the causes of aliasing. Subsequently, it is shown that the introduction of an OLPF can minimise aliasing, and an expression for the PSF due to the OLPF is given which can be included as part of the system PSF.

3.4.1 Sampling theorem

The function to be sampled is the real irradiance distribution at the sensor plane $g(x, y)$ modelled by the ideal irradiance distribution $f(x, y)$ convolved with the diffraction PSF and detector–aperture PSF,

$$g(x, y) = f(x, y) * h_{\text{diff}}(x, y) * h_{\text{det–ap}}(x, y).\qquad(3.29)$$

In order to discuss the consequences of sampling a function, for clarity it is convenient to consider the sampling of a 1D function denoted by $f(x)$. This 1D function is related to its FT via the following FT pair,

$$\boxed{\begin{aligned} f(x) &= \int_{-\infty}^{\infty} F(\mu_x)e^{i2\pi\mu_x x}\,d\mu_x \\ F(\mu_x) &= \int_{-\infty}^{\infty} f(x)e^{-i2\pi\mu_x x}dx \end{aligned}}.$$

Function sampling

A function with a FT that is zero everywhere outside some region or band is said to be *band-limited* [22, 23]. In the present context, the input function defined by equation (3.29) is band-limited because the diffraction OTF has a finite-valued cut-off frequency μ_c.

In analogy with section 3.3.2, the sampling of a continuous input function $f(x)$ which is band-limited to the region $[-\mu_{x,\max}, \mu_{x,\max}]$ can be achieved by multiplying with a Dirac comb function,

$$\tilde{f}(x) = f(x)\,\mathrm{comb}\left[\frac{x}{\Delta x}\right]. \tag{3.31}$$

The tilde symbol indicates that the function is a sampled function. The *spatial period* Δx is the spacing of the discrete sampling intervals. The Dirac comb in 1D is defined by

$$\mathrm{comb}\left[\frac{x}{\Delta x}\right] = \sum_{n=-\infty}^{\infty} \delta(x - n\Delta x).$$

The *value* of an arbitrary sample at location x_n can be obtained by integration in analogy with equation (3.6),

$$f(x_n) = \int_{-\infty}^{\infty} f(x)\,\delta(x - n\Delta x)\,\mathrm{d}x = f(n\Delta x).$$

Replicated spectra

Apart from a scaling factor, the FT of the Dirac comb function is also a Dirac comb function,

$$\mathrm{FT}\left\{\mathrm{comb}\left[\frac{x}{\Delta x}\right]\right\} = \Delta\mu_x\,\mathrm{comb}\left[\frac{\mu_x}{\Delta\mu_x}\right].$$

However, the spatial period is given by

$$\Delta\mu_x = \frac{1}{\Delta x}.$$

The *convolution theorem* was introduced in section 3.1.5 where it was seen that the convolution operation in the real domain is equivalent to a simple multiplication in the Fourier domain. Conversely, the multiplication operation in the real domain is equivalent to a *convolution* operation in the Fourier domain. The FT of the sampled function $\tilde{f}(x)$ defined by equation (3.31) is therefore given by

$$\boxed{\tilde{F}(\mu_x) = F(\mu_x) * \left(\Delta\mu_x\,\mathrm{comb}\left[\frac{\mu_x}{\Delta\mu_x}\right]\right).}$$

Significantly, the convolution of the continuous function $F(\mu_x)$ with a Dirac comb function of infinite extent and period $\Delta\mu_x$ yields a periodic sequence of *copies* of $F(\mu_x)$ with period $\Delta\mu_x$. This important result is illustrated in figure 3.28(a) and (b). Unlike the sampled function $\tilde{f}(x)$, the FT $\tilde{F}(\mu_x)$ is a *continuous* function.

The high-frequency harmonic copies of $F(\mu_x)$ are referred to as *replicated spectra* $F_{\text{high}}(\mu_x)$,

$$\tilde{F}(\mu_x) = F(\mu_x) + F_{\text{high}}(\mu_x).$$

The replicated spectra can be considered as undesirable high-frequency components which corrupt the original signal and are responsible for the discrete appearance of a sampled image. However, if $F_{\text{high}}(\mu_x)$ can be *removed* then only the *original continuous signal* $F(\mu_x)$ will remain [22, 23].

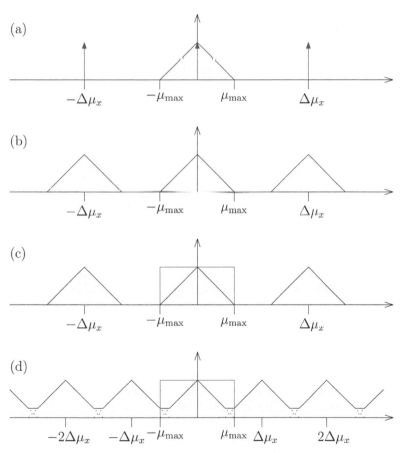

Figure 3.28. (a) FT $F(\mu_x)$ shown by the triangle function (yellow) along with the Dirac sampling comb (green arrows). (b) The convolution of $F(\mu_x)$ with the sampling comb yields copies of $F(\mu_x)$ with period $\Delta\mu_x$. (c) Ideal reconstruction filter in the Fourier domain (blue rectangle). (d) Aliasing caused by undersampling.

Reconstruction

In principle, the original function $f(x)$ can be recovered from its samples by multiplying $\tilde{F}(\mu_x)$ with an *ideal reconstruction filter* or *ideal low-pass filter*. The ideal reconstruction filter in the Fourier domain is a rectangle function defined by

$$H_{\text{ideal}}(\mu_x) = \begin{cases} 1/\Delta\mu_x & -\mu_{\text{max}} \leqslant \mu \leqslant \mu_{\text{max}} \\ 0 & \text{otherwise} \end{cases}$$

This isolates the so-called *baseband* $F(\mu_x)$ as illustrated in figure 3.28(c). Subsequently, $f(x)$ can be recovered by taking the inverse FT of the baseband.

It is also instructive to show how $f(x)$ can be recovered from its samples in the real domain. The baseband can be written

$$F(\mu_x) = H(\mu_x)\tilde{F}(\mu_x).$$

Taking the inverse FT yields

$$f(x) = \text{FT}^{-1}\big\{H(\mu_x)\,\tilde{F}(\mu_x)\big\} = \tilde{f}(x) * h_{\text{ideal}}(x). \tag{3.32}$$

The function $h_{\text{ideal}}(x)$ is the inverse FT of the rectangle function $H_{\text{ideal}}(\mu_x)$,

$$h_{\text{ideal}}(x) = \text{sinc}(x) = \frac{\sin(\pi x)}{\pi x}.$$

This reveals that the ideal reconstruction filter in the real domain is the *sinc function*. Equation (3.32) may be rewritten in the following way,

$$\boxed{f(x) = \sum_{n=-\infty}^{\infty} f(n\Delta x)\ \text{sinc}\left[\frac{x - n\Delta x}{n\Delta x}\right].}$$

The reconstructed function $f(x)$ is equal to the sample values at the sample locations. Between samples, $f(x)$ is given by an exact interpolation defined by an infinite sum of sinc functions.

In practice, a signal can only be reconstructed in an approximate way because the infinite sum of sinc functions is not physically realisable. Digital image display relies on low-pass filtering by the display medium and the HVS [6, 7]. At normal viewing distances, the cut-off frequency of the HVS will bandlimit the spectrum and the digital image will appear to be continuous.

Aliasing

Up to this point in the discussion it has been assumed that exact reconstruction is always possible. However, this is not the case. Two conditions are required [22, 23]:

- The signal must be band-limited. This prevents replicated spectra of infinite extent that are impossible to separate.
- The sampling frequency must be greater than twice the maximum frequency present in the signal. This ensures that the replicated spectra do not overlap and corrupt the baseband.

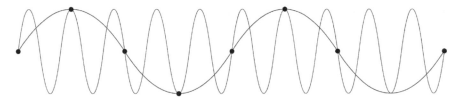

Figure 3.29. Illustration of aliasing. In this example the sampling indicated by the black circles is insufficient for reconstruction of the continuous signal shown in green. Consequently, the signal shown in green incorrectly appears as the signal shown in magenta upon reconstruction.

The first of these conditions is always satisfied for a camera system because the signal sampled at the sensor plane will be band-limited by the PSF due to aperture diffraction, $h_{\mathrm{diff}}(x, y)$. However, the second of these conditions depends upon a number of variables. Notably, the sampling frequency is fixed by the pixel pitch. Whether or not this sampling frequency is greater than twice the maximum frequency present in the signal depends upon the extent of the low-pass filtering by the camera components. The most important of these is the cut-off frequency defined by the PSF due to diffraction, $h_{\mathrm{diff}}(x, y)$, and this depends upon the lens f-number used to take the photograph. It will be shown later in this section that an OLPF can be fitted above the sensor to ensure that the second condition is always satisfied irrespective of the lens f-number.

The second condition above is a statement of the Shannon–Whittaker *sampling theorem* [24]. If the sampling theorem is not satisfied, a perfect copy of $F(\mu_x)$ cannot be isolated and so the original function will not be correctly recovered. This issue is known as *aliasing* because higher spatial frequencies will incorrectly appear as lower spatial frequencies in the reconstructed signal. A simple example is shown in figure 3.29. Expressed mathematically, aliasing can be avoided by sampling at a rate $\mu_{x,\mathrm{Nyq}}$ which must satisfy

$$\mu_{x,\mathrm{Nyq}} = \frac{1}{\Delta x} > 2\mu_{x,\mathrm{max}}.$$

(3.33)

Here $\mu_{x,\mathrm{max}}$ is the highest spatial frequency content of the function, and $\mu_{x,\mathrm{Nyq}}$ is known as the *Nyquist rate*. Figure 3.28(d) shows an example of aliasing by sampling at a rate which fails to satisfy the above condition. This is known as *undersampling*.

The sampling theorem applied to a function of two spatial variables $f(x, y)$ yields separate Nyquist rates in the x and y directions, $\mu_{x,\mathrm{Nyq}}$ and $\mu_{y,\mathrm{Nyq}}$.

3.4.2 Sensor Nyquist frequency

The imaging sensor in a camera has fixed photosites and so the sampling period is fixed in both the x and y directions. The sampling periods are $\Delta x = p_x$ and $\Delta y = p_y$, where p_x is the pixel pitch in the x direction, and p_y is the pixel pitch in the y direction. The sampling rates are therefore

$$\frac{1}{\Delta x} = \frac{1}{p_x}$$

$$\frac{1}{\Delta y} = \frac{1}{p_y}.$$

According to the sampling theorem expressed by equation (3.33), the highest frequency content that can be correctly reproduced in the x and y directions without aliasing is

$$\mu_{x,\text{sensor}} = \frac{1}{2p_x}$$

$$\mu_{y,\text{sensor}} = \frac{1}{2p_y}.$$

The frequencies $\mu_{x,\text{sensor}}$ and $\mu_{y,\text{sensor}}$ are defined as the *sensor Nyquist frequencies* in the x and y directions. Although the detection areas are usually rectangular or L-shaped, the photosites are typically square so that $p_x = p_y = p$. In this case it is usual practice to refer to a single sensor Nyquist frequency,

$$\boxed{\mu_{\text{sensor}} = \frac{1}{2p}}$$

Figure 3.30 shows square photosites in the presence of a Bayer CFA. The photosites belonging to the R and B mosaics are arranged separately with pixel pitch $2p$ in the x and y directions. The G mosaic contains twice as many photosites as R and B and is rotated at a 45 degree angle in relation to them. The pixel pitch for the G mosaic is therefore $\sqrt{2}p$ with the axes in the rotated direction. If the two green channels have different properties, the G mosaic can also be considered as two separate mosaics G_1 and G_2 with pixel pitch $2p$ in the x and y directions. Although uncommon, some cameras have non-square photosites. An interesting example is the Nikon® D1X which has a sensor with $p_y = 2p_x$.

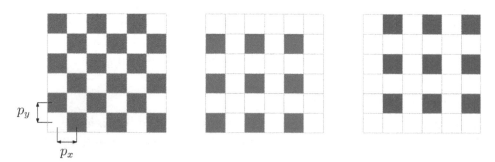

Figure 3.30. Bayer CFA showing the red, green, and blue mosaics.

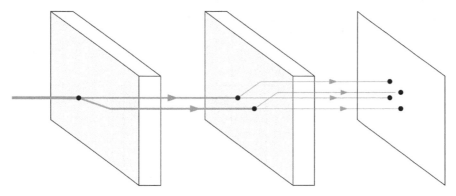

Figure 3.31. Four-spot OLPF. The first plate splits the light in the horizontal direction, and the second plate splits the light in the vertical direction.

3.4.3 Pre-filtering

Having illustrated the basic concept of sampling and aliasing in 1D, it is now appropriate to consider the real 2D irradiance distribution at the sensor plane modelled by equation (3.29),

$$g(x, y) = f(x, y) * h_{\text{diff}}(x, y) * h_{\text{det-ap}}(x, y).$$

If $g(x, y)$ is the continuous function to be sampled at the sensor plane and $G(\mu_x, \mu_y)$ is its FT, aliasing can only be minimised if all spatial frequency content in $G(\mu_x, \mu_y)$ present above the sensor Nyquist frequency μ_{sensor} is removed *before* $g(x, y)$ is sampled. In other words, $g(x, y)$ must be appropriately band-limited to the sensor Nyquist frequency by *pre-filtering* before sampling at the sensor plane. One solution is to fit an OLPF above the sensor. This strategy can reduce aliasing to a minimal level irrespective of the photographic conditions.

3.4.4 Four-spot filter PSF

Many cameras have a dedicated OLPF [25, 26] fitted above the sensor which acts as an anti-aliasing filter. An OLPF is made from a *birefringent* material such as quartz or lithium niobate which is capable of causing double refraction. The refractive index of birefringent materials depends upon the polarisation and direction of the light passing though, and so a ray of light entering the material can be split into two rays taking separate paths. A four-spot birefringent OLPF is made of two plates so that light from each point in the scene is spread over four points, the spot separation value being determined by the thickness of the plates.

The irradiance distribution which would have resulted in the absence of the OLPF is split into four distributions displaced slightly from each other. If the spot separation is chosen to be the pixel pitch, splitting the light in this way will reduce the modulation depth to zero at the sensor Nyquist frequency μ_{sensor}. Irradiance contributions from spatial frequencies above μ_{sensor} will be suppressed by the remaining contributions to the system PSF [26]. This combination of OLPF and system PSF effectively reduces aliasing to a minimal level. This will become clear when discussing the OLPF MTF.

The PSF for a four-spot birefringent OLPF can be modelled in terms of delta functions representing the four spots [26],

$$
h_{\mathrm{OLPF}}(x, y) = \frac{1}{4} \left\{ \begin{array}{l} \delta(x - a_0)\, \delta(y - b_0) \\ + \quad \delta(x - a_1)\, \delta(y - b_1) \\ + \quad \delta(x - a_2)\, \delta(y - b_2) \\ + \quad \delta(x - a_3)\, \delta(y - b_3) \end{array} \right\}. \tag{3.36}
$$

The constants define the point separation and hence the strength of the filter. A maximum strength filter is obtained by setting the point separation equal to the pixel pitch,

$$
\begin{aligned}
(a_0, b_0) &= (0, 0) \\
(a_1, b_1) &= (p_x, 0) \\
(a_2, b_2) &= (0, p_y) \\
(a_3, b_3) &= (p_x, p_y).
\end{aligned}
\tag{3.37}
$$

In this example, the spots are not situated symmetrically about the origin and so there will be a phase contribution to the OTF. It is preferable that OLPF filters be designed so that the spots are symmetrical about the origin. The use of a birefringent OLPF has other benefits such as reduction of colour interpolation error when demosaicing the raw data.

Objects containing fine repeated patterns are most susceptible to aliasing artefacts since these patterns are most likely to be associated with well-defined spatial frequencies above μ_{sensor}. The disadvantage of using an OLPF is that its PSF contributes to the system PSF at all times, even when other contributions to the system PSF such as lens aperture diffraction are already sufficiently band-limiting the signal to prevent aliasing. As discussed in chapter 5, this reduces the system MTF at spatial frequencies below μ_{sensor} and reduces perceived image sharpness.

Cameras with very high sensor pixel counts are less prone to aliasing. It is becoming more common for camera manufacturers to use a very weak OLPF or even completely remove it. Although aliased scene information corresponding to frequencies above μ_{sensor} cannot be recovered, the photographer can use image-processing software to reduce the prominence of the aliasing artefacts.

3.4.5 Four-spot filter MTF

The four-spot filter OTF is straightforwardly given by the FT of the PSF defined by equation (3.36),

$$H_{\mathrm{OLPF}}(\mu_x, \mu_y) = \frac{1}{4} \left\{ \begin{array}{l} \exp\left(-\mathrm{i}2\pi(a_0\mu_x + b_0\mu_y)\right) \\ + \ \exp\left(-\mathrm{i}2\pi(a_1\mu_x + b_1\mu_y)\right) \\ + \ \exp\left(-\mathrm{i}2\pi(a_2\mu_x + b_2\mu_y)\right) \\ + \ \exp\left(-\mathrm{i}2\pi(a_3\mu_x + b_3\mu_y)\right) \end{array} \right\}. \tag{3.38}$$

Selecting the constants corresponding to a maximum-strength filter, the OTF in the x-direction may be written in terms of its modulus and phase,

$$H_{\mathrm{OLPF}}(\mu_x) = \mathrm{MTF}(\mu_x)\mathrm{e}^{\mathrm{iPTF}(\mu_x)}.$$

The MTF and PTF are defined by

$$\begin{aligned} \mathrm{MTF}_{\mathrm{OLPF}}(\mu_x) &= |\cos(\pi p_x \mu_x)| \\ \mathrm{PTF}_{\mathrm{OLPF}}(\mu_x) &= -\pi p_x \mu_x \end{aligned}.$$

The PTF arises from the fact that the four spots defined by equation (3.37) are not symmetrical about the origin and so the overall image is shifted by half a pixel in the x and y directions. The PTF will vanish if the spots can be arranged symmetrically around the origin.

Figure 3.32 illustrates the maximum-strength four-spot MTF in the x-direction along with the detector–aperture MTF for the same model parameters used in section 3.3.3. The cut-off frequency for the detector–aperture MTF is 263 cycles/mm. Since the cut-off frequency for the four-spot filter is defined by the sensor Nyquist frequency $\mu_{\mathrm{sensor}} = 125$ cycles/mm, the combined MTF of the four-spot and detector–aperture MTFs taken at each spatial frequency similarly drops to 125 cycles/mm. The detector–aperture MTF suppresses the combined MTF above μ_{sensor}. Stronger suppression will occur when other contributions to the system MTF such as the optics MTF are included in the model, and this and will reduce aliasing to a minimal level.

3.5 Real image

Recall that for incoherent illumination, the ideal geometrical irradiance distribution at the sensor plane is defined by equation (3.2),

$$E_{\lambda,\mathrm{ideal}}(x, y) = \frac{\pi}{4} L_\lambda\left(\frac{x}{m}, \frac{y}{m}\right) \frac{1}{N_{\mathrm{w}}} T_{\mathrm{lens}} \cos^4 \varphi.$$

Here L_λ is the spectral scene radiance, m is the magnification, T_{lens} is the lens transmission factor, and N_{w} is the working f-number. The cosine fourth term can be replaced by the RI factor, $R(x, y, \lambda)$, which includes vignetting arising from a specific real lens design [3].

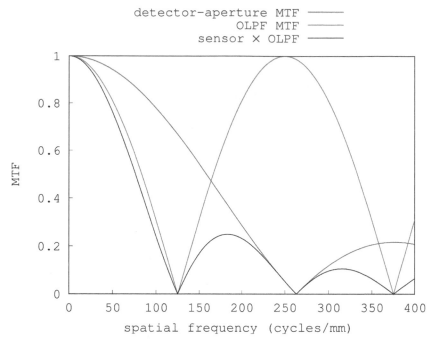

Figure 3.32. MTF for a maximum-strength four-spot OLPF in the x-direction (blue). The detector–aperture MTF corresponds to a pixel pitch $p_x = 4.0\ \mu\text{m}$ and detection area width $p_x = 3.8\ \mu\text{m}$ (magenta). The product of the OLPF and detector MTFs (black) drops to zero at $\mu_{\text{sensor}} = 125\ \text{cycles/mm}$.

The real irradiance distribution at the sensor plane, $E_\lambda(x, y)$, is described by a convolution of the ideal irradiance distribution with the system PSF,

$$E_\lambda(x, y) = h_{\text{system}}(x, y, \lambda) * E_{\text{ideal}}(x, y).$$

The sampling of this distribution by the imaging sensor can be modelled by restricting the output of the convolution operation to the appropriate grid of sampling positions. Mathematically, this is achieved via multiplication by a 2D array of delta functions defined by the photosite (sensor pixel) spacings p_x and p_y,

$$\tilde{E}_\lambda(x, y) = \left(h_{\text{system}}(x, y, \lambda) * E_{\lambda,\text{ideal}}(x, y)\right) \text{comb}\left[\frac{x}{p_x}, \frac{y}{p_y}\right]. \tag{3.39}$$

For the model camera system introduced in section 3.1.8, the contributions to the system PSF derived in this chapter can now be summarised, along with the corresponding contributions to the system MTF in the Fourier domain.

3.5.1 System PSF

The model camera system introduced in section 3.1.8 includes only the contribution to the lens PSF arising from lens aperture diffraction, the contribution to the sensor

PSF arising from the spatial detector–aperture, and the contribution from a four-spot OLPF,

$$\boxed{h_{\text{system}}(x, y, \lambda) = h_{\text{diff}}(x, y, \lambda) * h_{\text{OLPF}}(x, y) * h_{\text{det-ap}}(x, y)}. \qquad (3.40)$$

The irradiance PSF due to lens aperture diffraction for a circular aperture is defined by equation (3.19),

$$h_{\text{diff}}(x, y, \lambda) = \frac{U_0^2}{(\lambda z')^2} \left| \frac{\pi}{4} D_{\text{xp}}^2 \text{ jinc}\left(D_{\text{xp}}\sqrt{\left(\frac{x}{\lambda z'}\right)^2 + \left(\frac{y}{\lambda z'}\right)^2} \right) \right|^2.$$

Here z' is the distance from the exit pupil to the sensor plane, and D_{xp} is the diameter of the exit pupil.

The four-spot PSF for an OLPF is defined by equation (3.36),

$$h_{\text{OLPF}}(x, y) = \frac{1}{4}\left\{ \begin{array}{l} \delta(x - a_0)\,\delta(y - b_0) \\ + \quad \delta(x - a_1)\,\delta(y - b_1) \\ + \quad \delta(x - a_2)\,\delta(y - b_2) \\ | \quad \delta(x - a_3)\,\delta(y - b_3), \end{array} \right.$$

For a full-strength filter, the constants take the values $(a_0, b_0) = (0, 0)$, $(a_1, b_1) = (p_x, 0)$, $(a_2, b_2) = (0, p_y)$, and $(a_3, b_3) = (p_x, p_y)$.

Finally, the spatial detector–aperture PSF for a rectangular CCD detector is defined by equation (3.25),

$$h_{\text{det-ap}}(x, y) = \frac{1}{A_{\text{det}}} \text{rect}\left[\frac{x}{d_x}\right] \text{rect}\left[\frac{y}{d_y}\right].$$

The detection area $A_{\text{det}} = d_x\,d_y$, where d_x and d_y are the horizontal and vertical dimensions of the effective aperture area.

3.5.2 System MTF

The corresponding system MTF is defined by

$$\text{MTF}_{\text{system}}(\mu_x, \mu_y, \lambda) = \text{MTF}_{\text{diff}}(\mu_x, \mu_y, \lambda)\text{MTF}_{\text{OLPF}}(\mu_x, \mu_y)\text{MTF}_{\text{det-ap}}(\mu_x, \mu_y).$$

The MTF due to lens aperture diffraction for a circular aperture is defined by equation (3.21),

$$\text{MTF}_{\text{diff,circ}}(\mu_r, \lambda) = \left\{ \begin{array}{ll} \frac{2}{\pi}\left(\cos^{-1}\left(\frac{\mu_r}{\mu_c}\right) - \frac{\mu_r}{\mu_c}\sqrt{1 - \left(\frac{\mu_r}{\mu_c}\right)^2} \right) & \text{for } \frac{\mu_r}{\mu_c} \leqslant 1 \\ \\ 0 & \text{for } \frac{\mu_r}{\mu_c} > 1. \end{array} \right.$$

Here $\mu_r = \sqrt{\mu_x^2 + \mu_y^2}$ is the radial spatial frequency, and $\mu_c = 1/(\lambda N_w)$ is the cut-off frequency.

The MTF due to a four-spot OLPF is defined by equation (3.38),

$$H_{\text{OLPF}}(\mu_x, \mu_y) = \frac{1}{4} \left| \begin{array}{l} \exp\left(-i2\pi(a_0\mu_x+b_0\mu_y)\right) \\[6pt] + \exp\left(-i2\pi(a_1\mu_x+b_1\mu_y)\right) \\[6pt] + \exp\left(-i2\pi(a_2\mu_x+b_2\mu_y)\right) \\[6pt] + \exp\left(-i2\pi(a_3\mu_x+b_3\mu_y)\right) \end{array} \right|.$$

For a full-strength filter, the constants are the same as those for the PSF given above.

Finally, the spatial detector–aperture MTF for a rectangular CCD detector is defined by equation (3.28),

$$\begin{aligned} \text{MTF}_{\text{det-ap}}(\mu_x, \mu_y) &= \left| \, \text{sinc}(d_x\mu_x, d_y\mu_y) \right| \\[6pt] &= \left| \frac{\sin(\pi d_x\mu_x)}{\pi d_x\mu_x} \frac{\sin(\pi d_y\mu_y)}{\pi d_y\mu_y} \right|. \end{aligned}$$

Again, d_x and d_y are the horizontal and vertical dimensions of the effective aperture area.

3.6 Sensor signal

The expected charge signal generated at a given photosite during a camera exposure can be modelled in terms of the sampled irradiance distribution at the sensor plane summarised in the previous section, along with the photoconversion properties of the imaging sensor. The photoconversion properties can be expressed in terms of the spectral responsivity functions, also referred to as the camera response functions. These depend upon the QE of the sensor and the transmissive properties of the CFA.

The model charge signal derived in this section does not include signal noise. However, a signal noise estimate can be included based on the measurement procedures discussed in the final section of this chapter.

3.6.1 Charge collection

Although the physics of semiconductor devices is beyond the scope of this chapter, it is useful to very briefly outline how CCD and CMOS architectures utilise photo-elements to collect charge [27, 28, 29, 30, 31].

Photoelements
In a metal-oxide semiconductor (MOS) capacitor or *photogate* situated inside a photosite, a gate electrode situated above doped p-type silicon is held at a positive bias. This causes mobile positive holes to flow to the ground electrode, thus creating a *depletion region* capable of storing electrons. A photogate is illustrated in figure 3.33.

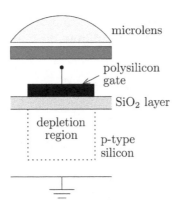

Figure 3.33. Simplified illustration of a MOS capacitor.

The radiant flux Φ_λ incident at the detection area A_{det} must be considered as a stream of *photons*. Each photon has electromagnetic energy hc/λ, where c is the speed of light and h is Plank's constant. Silicon has a band gap energy of 1.12 eV, which means that the depletion region can absorb photons with wavelengths shorter than 1100 nm [32].

The absorption of a photon creates an *electron–hole pair*. The gate voltage causes the holes created to flow to the ground electrode and prevents the electron–hole pairs from recombining. The electrons remain in the depletion region as stored charge. The *well capacity* is determined by factors such as gate electrode area, substrate doping, gate voltage, and oxide layer thickness.

Another type of photoelement is a *photodiode*. In a photodiode, the depletion region is formed at the junction between n-type and p-type silicon. A reverse bias is applied to the junction in order to increase the width of the depletion region. Overlaying electrodes are not required, and the well capacity is limited by the junction width.

CCD sensors typically use photogates and CMOS sensors typically use photo-diodes. If photodiodes are used with CCD architecture, the device may be referred to as a charge-coupled photodiode (CCPD) device [7]. In all cases, electrons generated in the depletion region itself contribute to the collected charge, however only a fraction of the electrons generated in the bulk neutral region will reach the depletion region through diffusion [32].

Charge signal

For incoherent illumination with spectral passband $\lambda_1 \rightarrow \lambda_2$, the spectral radiant flux incident at a given photosite is defined by

$$\Phi_\lambda = A_{\text{det}}\, \tilde{E}_\lambda(x, y).$$

Here $\tilde{E}_\lambda(x, y)$ is the real sampled irradiance distribution at the sensor plane expressed by equation (3.39), and (x, y) are the sampling coordinates associated with each flux detection area A_{det}.

Since each photon has energy hc/λ, the number of photons with wavelength λ incident at the flux detection area A_{det} during the camera exposure duration t_{exp} is given by

$$n_{\mathrm{ph}}(\lambda) = t_{\mathrm{exp}}\Phi_\lambda\frac{\lambda}{hc}.$$

Substituting for the flux Φ_λ yields

$$n_{\mathrm{ph}}(\lambda) = t_{\mathrm{exp}}\, A_{\mathrm{det}}\,\frac{\lambda}{hc}\,\tilde{E}_\lambda(x, y). \qquad (3.41)$$

Since only a fraction of these photons will be converted into stored electric charge, the average number of stored electrons generated per incident photon at wavelength λ can be expressed as

$$\boxed{n_e(\lambda) = n_{\mathrm{ph}}(\lambda)\, \mathrm{QE}(\lambda)}. \qquad (3.42)$$

The overall *external quantum efficiency*, or simply the *quantum efficiency* (QE), is defined by [32]

$$\boxed{\mathrm{QE}(\lambda) = T(\lambda)\, \eta(\lambda)\mathrm{FF}}.$$

The QE depends greatly upon the photoelement configuration and architecture of the sensor. Along with the FF, two major contributions to the QE can be isolated:

- The *charge collection efficiency* (CCE) or *internal QE* denoted by $\eta(\lambda)$ is a function of wavelength. The CCE describes the ratio of the charge generated through photoconversion to the charge that is successfully stored, and it can have a maximum value of unity. Although $\eta(\lambda) = 1$ when photoelectrons are generated in the depletion region, photoelectrons generated deep in the bulk neutral region may fail to successfully diffuse to the depletion region to be stored as charge. In this case, $\eta(\lambda) < 1$. This tends to occur at longer wavelengths because the flux $\Phi(\lambda)$ penetrates deeper into the bulk as λ increases. Ideally $\eta(\lambda)$ will remain high in the visible region below 780 nm. This is achieved by ensuring the material thickness and applied voltage are large enough to provide a depletion region with sufficient depth. Furthermore, the diffusion length can be increased by controlled doping.
- The transmission factor $T(\lambda)$ takes into account unwanted surface absorption and reflectance effects. Reflection at the SiO_2–Si interface can be reduced using anti-reflective films [32]. In front-illuminated devices with photogates, the polysilicon electrodes reduce sensitivity in the blue region below 600 nm and become opaque below 400 nm [7]. Back-illuminated devices do not suffer from reduced sensitivity in the blue region provided appropriate anti-reflective coating is applied and the wafer is thinned to minimise recombination [7].

Now using the definition of the QE and substituting equation (3.41) into (3.42) yields

$$n_e(\lambda) = t_{\mathrm{exp}}\, A_{\mathrm{p}}\, \mathrm{QE}(\lambda)\frac{\lambda}{hc}\,\tilde{E}_\lambda(x, y).$$

Recall that the photosite area A_p is related to the flux detection area A_{det} according to equation (3.24),

$$A_p = \frac{A_{det}}{FF}.$$

Since the FF has been included in the definition of the QE, the photosite area appears in the above expression for $n_e(\lambda)$ instead of the flux detection area.

Finally, the total number of stored electrons (electron count) can be modelled by integrating over the the spectral passband $\lambda_1 \rightarrow \lambda_2$,

$$n_e = t_{exp} A_p \int_{\lambda_1}^{\lambda_2} QE(\lambda) \frac{\lambda}{hc} \tilde{E}_\lambda(x, y) d\lambda.$$ (3.43)

Denoting the charge of an electron by e, the charge signal Q is defined as

$$Q = n_e e.$$

3.6.2 Colour filter array

The electron count defined by equation (3.43) is valid for a monochrome sensor. When a CFA is present, the spectral composition of the flux reaching the detection areas will be altered by the spectral transmission properties of the CFA. The response will be different for photosites belonging to each colour mosaic.

The electron count in the presence of the CFA can be obtained simply by multiplying the QE by the CFA *transmission function* $T_{CFA,i}(\lambda)$ [32]. This describes the spectral transmission of the colour filter for mosaic i. For example, i can denote the red, green, or blue mosaic for a Bayer CFA. In principle, the CFA should be designed so that the overall response is a linear combination of the eye response functions which describe human colour vision. The overall response is described by the spectral responsivity functions defined below, and this topic will be discussed further in chapter 4.

Sometimes the definition of the QE is generalised to include the CFA transmission function,

$$QE_i(\lambda) = QE(\lambda) T_{CFA,i}(\lambda).$$

In this case the QE has a different functional form for each mosaic i. The electron count defined by equation (3.43) similarly depends on mosaic,

$$n_{e,i} = t_{exp} A_p \int_{\lambda_1}^{\lambda_2} QE_i(\lambda) \frac{\lambda}{hc} \tilde{E}_\lambda(x, y) d\lambda.$$ (3.44)

3.6.3 Spectral responsivity

An alternative way of expressing equation (3.44) is in terms of the *spectral responsivity*. This can be defined as the weighting factor $R(\lambda)$ such that

$$\int R(\lambda) \Phi_\lambda \, d\lambda = I,$$ (3.45)

where I is the total generated photocurrent measured in amperes,

$$I = \frac{n_{e,i}\, e}{t_{\exp}}.$$

Here e is the charge of an electron, and spectral responsivity has been expressed in units of amperes per watt (A/W).

In the absence of a CFA, equations (3.43) and (3.45) can be combined to yield the following alternative definition,

$$R(\lambda) = \mathrm{QE}(\lambda)\,\frac{e\lambda}{hc}.$$

If a CFA is present, the CFA transmission for each colour channel i can be included in the definition,

$$\boxed{R_i(\lambda) = \mathrm{QE}_i(\lambda)\,\frac{e\lambda}{hc}}.$$

Although the set of spectral responsivity functions are highly non-linear with respect to wavelength, they should ideally be linear functions with respect to input spectral flux Φ_λ and hence *linear functions of radiant exposure* below saturation exposure. Figure 3.34 illustrates an example set of spectral responsivity functions [33].

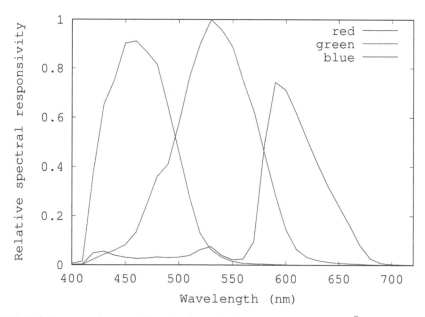

Figure 3.34. Relative spectral responsivity $R_i(\lambda)$ for each colour channel of the Nikon® D700 as a function of wavelength. The curves have been normalised by the peak response.

The photosite electron count in the presence of a CFA can now be expressed in the final form

$$\boxed{n_{e,i} = \frac{t_{\exp} A_{\mathrm{p}}}{e} \int_{\lambda_1}^{\lambda_2} R_i(\lambda)\tilde{E}_\lambda(x, y)\, \mathrm{d}\lambda}.$$ (3.46)

This is equivalent to equation (3.44). The set of spectral responsivity functions are also referred to as the photoconversion response functions or *camera response functions*. In order for the camera to correctly reproduce scene colour, the camera response functions should in principle be a linear transformation of the eye response functions. This topic will be discussed in chapter 4.

3.6.4 Polychromatic PSF and MTF

The component PSFs convolved together to define the incoherent system PSF used to model the sensor signal are generally functions of wavelength λ. When the sensor signal was derived above, the polychromatic effects of incoherent light were taken into account by integrating all relevant wavelength-dependent quantities over the spectral passband. This is not always possible, in which case polychromatic effects can be approximated by using the average wavelength instead, which is typically around 550 nm [7].

In some circumstances it is possible to define polychromatic PSFs. Such functions are valid only for the spectral conditions under which they were calculated. In other words, the monochromatic system PSF must be weighted with respect to the spectral characteristics of the sensor and illumination source,

$$h_{\mathrm{poly}}(x, y) = \frac{\int_{\lambda_1}^{\lambda_2} R_i(\lambda)L_\lambda\, h_{\mathrm{system}}(x, y, \lambda)\, \mathrm{d}\lambda}{\int_{\lambda_1}^{\lambda_2} R_i(\lambda)L_\lambda\, \mathrm{d}\lambda}.$$

Here $R_i(\lambda)$ is the spectral responsivity, and L_λ is the spectral radiance of the illumination source. More generally, L_λ can take the form of a spectral power distribution (SPD) which will be encountered in chapter 4. The magnitude of L_λ is removed through normalisation because only the spectral characteristics of L_λ are relevant [2, 34]. The corresponding OTF is defined by

$$H_{\mathrm{poly}}(\mu_x, \mu_y) = \frac{\int_{\lambda_1}^{\lambda_2} R_i(\lambda)L_\lambda\, H_{\mathrm{system}}(\mu_x, \mu_y, \lambda)\, \mathrm{d}\lambda}{\int_{\lambda_1}^{\lambda_2} R_i(\lambda)L_\lambda\, \mathrm{d}\lambda}.$$

Analogous expressions can be written for individual system components. For example, the polychromatic lens MTF can be extracted after replacing the system OTF with the lens OTF in the above expression.

If the polychromatic system PSF is known for a given set of spectral conditions, the electron count under the same conditions can be modelled in the following way,

$$n_{e,i} = \frac{t_{\exp} A_p}{e} \int_{\lambda_1}^{\lambda_2} R_i(\lambda) \{E_{\lambda,\mathrm{ideal}}(x, y) * h_{\mathrm{poly}}(x, y)\} \; \mathrm{comb}\left[\frac{x}{p_x}, \frac{y}{p_y}\right] \mathrm{d}\lambda.$$

3.7 Analog-to-digital conversion

A major difference between CCD and CMOS architecture lies in the strategy used for reading out the charge. A CCD photosite typically contains between two and four photogates. The corresponding depletion regions overlap, and adjusting the gate voltage through clocking in a systematic manner allows charge to be quickly transferred from one gate to another. At the end of the columns, a horizontal pixel register transports the charge packets of each column to the output amplifier in a serial fashion [7]. In contrast, charge readout occurs inside a photosite in CMOS sensors, and photosites can be addressed individually.

After charge collection and readout, the charge needs to be *detected* in order to generate a voltage signal. Although the charge detection process occurs at the end of the horizontal shift register in CCD sensors and inside a photosite in CMOS sensors, it is similar in both cases [32]. After charge detection, the output voltage is amplified and converted into raw data by an ADC. A simple model for analog-to-digital conversion is developed in this section.

3.7.1 Charge detection

Recall that for a photosite belonging to mosaic i, the charge signal Q_i can be modelled as

$$Q_i = n_{e,i} \, e = t_{\exp} A_p \int_{\lambda_1}^{\lambda_2} R_i(\lambda) \tilde{E}_\lambda(x, y) \, \mathrm{d}\lambda.$$

Here $n_{e,i}$ is the electron count for a photosite belonging to mosaic i as defined by equation (3.46), e is the charge of an electron, $t_{\exp}$ is the camera exposure duration, A_p is the photosite area, $R_i(\lambda)$ is the spectral responsivity, $\tilde{E}_\lambda(x, y)$ is the real sampled irradiance distribution at the sensor plane defined by equation (3.39), and the sampling coordinates (x, y) specify the location of the photosite on the sensor plane. The spectral responsivity $R_i(\lambda)$ includes the CCE, FF, and CFA transmission. For clarity, the mosaic label i will be dropped in this section.

The charge signal from the photosite is converted into a voltage by the sense node capacitance C,

$$V_p = Q \frac{G_p}{C}.$$

The source follower amplifier gain G_p is near unity [7]. The maximum voltage V_{FWC} occurs at FWC,

$$V_{\mathrm{FWC}} = Q_{\mathrm{FWC}} \frac{G_p}{C}.$$

The value Q_{FWC} is the maximum charge that the photosite can hold.

A characteristic related to charge detection is the output-referred *conversion gain* [32]. This describes the output voltage change per electron in $\mu V/e^-$ units and is defined as

$$G_{\mathrm{CG}} = \frac{V_{\mathrm{p}}}{n_e}.$$

3.7.2 ISO gain

The voltage from the sense node capacitance, V_{p}, is subsequently amplified by a programmable gain amplifier (PGA) to a useful level V which lies within the input range of the ADC,

$$V = GV_{\mathrm{p}}. \tag{3.47}$$

For a CCD sensor, the PGA will be off-chip. The programmable gain G is controlled by the camera ISO setting S. Doubling the ISO setting doubles G. In the simplest case, the ISO setting controls a single analog PGA. Some cameras use a second-stage PGA for intermediate ISO settings. As detailed in chapter 2, the *value* of S is based upon the JPEG output at the selected gain setting G and must be determined using the SOS or REI methods.

The maximum output voltage V_{max} occurs when the raw output saturates or clips. The ISO setting which uses the *least analog amplification* to saturate the raw output is defined as the *base ISO setting*, S_{base}. This typically occurs either when FWC is utilised or the ADC saturates. Assuming that FWC is utilised, the corresponding gain value $G = G_{\mathrm{base}}$ satisfies

$$V_{\mathrm{max}} = G_{\mathrm{base}} \, V_{\mathrm{FWC}}. \tag{3.48}$$

It is useful to express the programmable gain G as the product of the base value G_{base} and an *ISO gain* G_{ISO},

$$G = G_{\mathrm{base}} \, G_{\mathrm{ISO}}. \tag{3.49}$$

At the base ISO setting S_{base}, the ISO gain takes a value of unity, $G_{\mathrm{ISO}} = 1$. Substituting equation (3.49) into (3.47) yields

$$V = G_{\mathrm{base}} \, G_{\mathrm{ISO}} \, V_{\mathrm{p}}. \tag{3.50}$$

Each time the ISO setting is doubled from the base value, the exposure H is halved. In turn, half as many signal electrons n_e are generated, and the signal voltage V_{p} will halve. However, the output voltage level V which is fed to the ADC will remain unchanged because doubling the ISO setting doubles the ISO gain G_{ISO}.

By comparing equation (3.50) with (3.48) and utilising the fact that $V_{\mathrm{p}} \leqslant V_{\mathrm{FWC}}$, the following relation is seen to always hold,

$$\boxed{V G_{\mathrm{ISO}} \leqslant V_{\mathrm{max}}}.$$

At ISO settings higher than the base value, FWC will not be utilised because $G_{ISO} > 1$ and so $V < V_{max}$. For example, $V \leqslant V_{max}/2$ when $G_{ISO} = 2$. This might correspond to a doubling of the ISO setting from say ISO 200 ($G_{ISO} = 1$) to ISO 400 ($G_{ISO} = 2$). Notably, this means that one stop of *raw exposure headroom* below the raw clipping point at the highlight end of the raw histogram will be lost. In fact, a stop will be lost for each subsequent doubling of the ISO setting. This leads to a loss of dynamic range (DR) and also affects the signal-to-noise ratio (SNR). These topics will be discussed further in chapter 5.

The equations for charge detection and the programmable gain can be combined into a simple summary of the charge detection and signal amplification processes,

$$V = Q \, \frac{G_p}{C} \, G \qquad (3.51a)$$

$$V_{max} = Q_{FWC} \, \frac{G_p}{C} \, G_{base} \,. \qquad (3.51b)$$

3.7.3 Digital numbers

The ADC can be modelled by converting the fraction VG_{ISO}/V_{max} into a pixel *raw value* to be stored in the raw data file. The value output by a perfectly linear ADC in *digital numbers* (DNs) or *analog-to-digital units* (ADU) can be modelled as

$$n_{DN} = \text{INT}\left[\frac{VG_{ISO}}{V_{max}} \, k(2^M - 1) \right]. \qquad (3.52)$$

The INT operation returns the integer part. The position of the pixel in relation to the associated photosite on the sensor plane is indicated by the sampling coordinates and mosaic label defined by equation (3.46). The maximum possible raw value is obtained when $V_{max} = VG_{ISO}$,

$$n_{DN,max} = k(2^M - 1).$$

Here M is the bit-depth of the ADC, and the constant k has been included to take into account situations where the raw clipping point is reached without utilising the maximum number of levels available given the bit-depth of the ADC. Therefore $k \leqslant 1$. On the other hand, a value $k = 1$ does not necessarily imply that FWC is utilised because in rare cases the raw clipping point may be limited by the bit-depth of the ADC If $k = 1$ then $n_{DN,max} = 1023$, 4095, or 16 383 for 10, 12, or 14-bit output, respectively.

3.7.4 Conversion factor

Since the voltages are proportional to electron counts, it is possible to substitute the voltages appearing in equation (3.52) by electron counts. Inserting equations (3.51a) and (3.51b) into (3.52) and utilising the fact that $Q = n_e e$ yields the following result,

$$n_{DN} = \mathrm{INT}\left[\frac{n_e}{g}\right] \qquad (3.53a)$$

$$g = \frac{U}{G_{ISO}} \qquad (3.53b)$$

$$U = \frac{n_{e,FWC}}{k(2^M - 1)} . \qquad (3.53c)$$

In scientific photography and astrophotography, g is conventionally referred to simply as the *gain* [35]. Although g derives from a succession of gains, it is actually a *conversion factor* [35, 36] between electron counts and raw values and has units e$^-$/DN. Under typical photographic conditions at the base ISO setting, the electron count is larger than $2^M - 1$ and so $g \geqslant 1$. For example, 10 000 electron counts converted to 1000 DN implies that $g = 10$e$^-$/DN. In this respect, the behaviour of g is more characteristic of an inverse gain. Indeed the gain is sometimes defined in DN/e$^-$ units in which case g should be replaced by g^{-1}. For generality, the mosaic index i should be included in the above equations because the gain g may not be identical for different mosaics.

If the ISO setting and associated ISO gain are doubled, the exposure H will be halved and so half as many signal electrons n_e will be generated. However, it is evident from equations (3.53a) and (3.53b) that g will also be halved and so the raw value n_{DN} will remain unchanged. As discussed in chapter 2, this can be useful when needing to freeze the appearance of moving action or when an exposure time short enough to counteract camera-shake in low-light conditions is needed. The impact upon IQ due to the change in SNR will be discussed in chapter 5.

When the ISO gain is adjusted such that $G_{ISO} = U$, the gain will have value $g = 1$ and so each electron count will be converted into an individual raw value. The quantity U is known as the *unity gain*. Because U depends on factors such as the bit-depth of the ADC, FWC, and the constant k, unity gain U and its corresponding *unity ISO setting* will differ between camera models. In principle, there is no advantage to increasing the ISO gain above unity gain in comparison with increasing the brightness of the image digitally via simple multiplication of the raw values. Furthermore, the fact that usable DR goes down each time the ISO setting is raised because fewer electron counts will saturate the ADC suggests that ISO settings above the unity ISO setting should be avoided. In practice, a more useful upper limit is defined by the so-called *ISO-less* setting which takes into account SNR. These concepts will be discussed further in chapter 5.

3.7.5 Bias offset

If a bias offset voltage V_{bias} is added to the voltage signal before it is digitised by the ADC, a bias offset digital number $bias_{DN}$ will be added to every raw value n_{DN},

$$n_{DN} \rightarrow n_{DN} + bias_{DN}.$$

Some camera manufacturers subtract off this value before writing the output to the raw data file. In the case that $bias_{DN}$ is not subtracted, the constant k now takes into account situations where the raw clipping point is reached without utilising the maximum number of levels available given the bit-depth of the ADC minus the bias offset,

$$n_{DN,max} \rightarrow k(2^M - 1 - bias_{DN}).$$

The maximum possible raw value can be re-expressed in the form

$$max_{DN} = n_{DN,max} + bias_{DN}$$
$$= k(2^M - 1 - bias_{DN}) + bias_{DN}.$$

Equations (3.53a–c) become

$$n_{DN} + bias_{DN} = INT\left[\frac{n_e}{g}\right] + bias_{DN}$$

$$g = \frac{U}{G_{ISO}}$$

$$U = \frac{n_{e,FWC}}{k(2^M - 1 - bias_{DN})}.$$

The bias offset has minimal impact on the maximum achievable DR because it is an offset rather than a factor. For example, a linear 12-bit ADC with a bias offset $bias_{DN} = 256$ can encode a maximum luminance ratio (4096-256):1 or a maximum representable DR equal to $\log_2 3840 \approx 11.9$ stops in the absence of read noise, a loss of only 0.1 stops from the maximum linear 12-bit value.

3.8 Noise

Unfortunately, a variety of noise sources exist which will appear as unwanted variations in the signal. Noise sources will affect the output image in various different ways [37, 38]. Noise can be broadly classified into two main types, *fixed-pattern noise* (FPN) and *temporal noise*. Forms of FPN will display a fixed pattern from image to image, whereas temporal noise will vary in appearance from image to image in a statistical manner.

This section gives a brief introduction to some of the major noise sources in digital photography. Practical approaches for measuring noise are described. The measured noise can be added to the model charge signal defined by equation (3.46).

3.8.1 Temporal noise

The electron count defined by equation (3.46) multiplied by the electron charge e yields the mean or expected charge signal. In fact, the signal fluctuates randomly over time with the fluctuations appearing as *temporal noise*. The mean signal is considered to be stationary so that the time average over a period long compared to the time scale over which the fluctuations occur can be replaced by the ensemble average over all possible fluctuation configurations. The noise can then be measured by the standard deviation σ from the mean value of its statistical distribution. *Noise power* is defined by the variance σ^2 and so independent temporal noise sources add in quadrature,

$$\sigma_{\text{total}} = \sqrt{\sum_{m=1}^{M} \sigma_m^2}.$$

A characteristic of temporal noise to be discussed in chapter 5 is that it can be reduced by *frame-averaging*. The main temporal noise sources affecting the signal of a digital camera are photon shot noise, dark-current shot noise, and read noise.

Photon shot noise

For a constant scene radiance, the number of photons arriving at the sensor plane fluctuates randomly over short time scales. Nevertheless, the *mean* rate at which photons arrive at the sensor plane is constant. The mean signal is a valid measure because an exposure duration over which the signal is measured is extremely long compared to the time scale over which photons are absorbed by the sensor. Unfortunately, the random fluctuations about the mean signal during the exposure will manifest themselves as *photon shot noise* appearing in the resulting image. Photon shot noise is an unavoidable consequence of the quantum nature of light.

In terms of photoelectron counts, photon shot noise is denoted by $\sigma_{e,\text{ph}}$. Photons obey Poisson statistics and so form a Poisson distribution about the mean or expected signal. An important characteristic of the Poisson distribution is that its variance is equal to the mean value itself [11],

$$\boxed{\sigma_{e,\text{ph}}^2 = n_e}. \tag{3.55}$$

Although photon shot noise is a dominant source of noise at high exposure levels, it increases in proportion with the square root of the charge signal and so becomes *relatively* less significant as the exposure level increases. In other words, the SNR increases with exposure. This is the primary motivation for the expose-to-the-right (ETTR) strategy discussed in chapter 5.

Dark-current shot noise

A charge signal $Q_{\text{dark}} = n_{e,\text{dark}}\, e$ referred to as the *dark signal* is generated due to thermal agitation of electrons even in the absence of irradiance at the sensor plane [32]. The corresponding dark current is defined as

$$I_{\text{dark}} = \frac{n_{e,\text{dark}}\, e}{t}.$$

The exposure duration t is more generally referred to as the *integration time*. This term applies both in the presence and absence of irradiance.

Dark signal is dependent upon temperature. Although it only provides a minor contribution to the total noise at short integration times, dark signal can become a dominant noise source at long integration times such as those used in long-exposure photography. Dark signal reduces the effective FWC and therefore reduces usable DR [32].

Dark signal is typically deducted before the raw data is written. A typical method for measuring the dark signal is to shield photosites around the edge of the sensor from light. In principle, the average value of these so-called *optical black* pixels provides an appropriate dark signal value which can be subtracted from every active photosite. More sophisticated methods will compensate for shading gradients with respect to row or column as a function of the operating temperature [32].

Since the dark signal is a temporal noise source, it is the average value of an associated dark-current shot noise distribution. Unfortunately, subtracting the dark signal will not eliminate all of the dark-current shot noise distribution.

Read noise

Read noise $\sigma_{e,\mathrm{read}}$ mainly arises from voltage fluctuations in the readout circuitry. It will be present whenever charge readout occurs even in the absence of sensor-plane irradiance. Read noise defines the *noise floor*. The readout circuitry includes the charge detection circuitry and PGA. Dark signal and dark-current shot noise are generated inside a photon well and are not included in the definition of the read noise [32]. Forms of read noise include the following:

- Thermal (Johnson–Nyquist) noise: this occurs due to thermal agitation of electrons.
- Flicker (1/f) noise: a circuit resistance fluctuation which appears at low frequencies.
- Reset or kTC noise: a type of thermal noise due to reset of the photon-well capacitance after a camera exposure.

The *correlated double-sampling* (CDS) technique is very important for eliminating reset noise in CMOS sensors through subtraction by sampling both the reset-hold voltage and the output voltage.

A level of read noise will already be present in the signal before it reaches the PGA. This part of the read noise will be amplified when the ISO gain is increased. Read noise due to circuitry downstream from the PGA is independent of the ISO gain. This is an important consideration which influences SNR as a function of ISO setting.

3.8.2 Fixed pattern noise

Unlike temporal noise, FPN has a fixed pattern associated with it which does not change from frame to frame. Because of the ability of the HVS to detect patterns, FPN it is often the most visually unpleasant type of noise [39].

Dark-signal non-uniformity (DSNU) refers to FPN present in the absence of irradiance at the sensor plane. The major contribution to DSNU for long integration times is dark-current non-uniformity (DCNU) which arises from variations in photosite response to thermally induced dark current over the sensor plane.

Pixel response non-uniformity (PRNU) refers to FPN in the presence of irradiance at the sensor plane. This again arises from the variation in photosite response over the sensor plane, however PRNU increases in proportion with exposure. FPN is discussed further in section 5.8.2 of chapter 5.

3.8.3 Noise measurement

When measuring noise, it is important to analyse the original linear raw data without performing a colour demosaic or further image processing. Available software with such capability includes the freeware astrophotography program *iris*[1] which can analyse the CFA channels by utilising *dcraw*[2] to read the raw data.

The measurement of FPN is described in section 5.8.2 of chapter 5, and only the measurement of temporal noise is described below.

Photon shot noise is already known in terms of *input-referred* units (electron count). According to equation (3.55), it is simply the square root of the electron count itself,

$$\sigma_{e,\mathrm{ph}} = \sqrt{n_e}.$$

The QE of the sensor reveals itself through the SNR at a given ISO setting, as discussed in chapter 5.

All other noise contributions obtained by analysing the raw data will be in *output-referred* units (DN or ADU). Output-referred units can be converted into input-referred units by using the conversion factor or gain g defined by equation (3.53a-b). Therefore g needs to be determined as a function of ISO setting. A useful technique for determining g is to carry out a temporal noise measurement on the raw data. Effectively, the photon shot noise measured in DN is used as a signal which provides useful information [32, 36, 35].

Conversion factor measurement

The conversion factor g emerges from the temporal noise measurement procedure detailed below [35, 36]. Ideally, each CFA channel should be measured individually. Only the green channel is considered here.

1. Take two successive frames of a uniformly-illuminated surface such as a neutral grey card. The two frames must be of equal duration so that they will be identical apart from the statistical variation in temporal noise.

---

[1] The freeware astrophotography software *iris* by C Buil is available at http://www.astrosurf.com/buil/us/iris/iris.htm.
[2] The freeware raw converter *dcraw* by D. Coffin is available at https://www.cybercom.net/~dcoffin/dcraw.

2. Add the two frames together and measure the mean green-channel raw value in a fixed area at the centre of the image. Dividing by two gives the mean green-channel raw value in the fixed area for the two frames.

3. Subtract one frame from the other and divide the result by 2. This removes the FPN through cancellation and averages the temporal noise. Now measure the standard deviation in the fixed area. Since the temporal noise adds in quadrature, the measured noise is given by $\frac{1}{2}\sqrt{\sigma^2 + (-\sigma)^2} = \sigma/\sqrt{2}$, where σ is the noise of either of the original images. The temporal noise will now have been reduced by a factor of $\sqrt{2}$. Multiplying by $\sqrt{2}$ yields the temporal noise σ for either of the original images in the absence of FPN.

4. Repeat the procedure a number of times for a given ISO setting, each for a different integration time, starting from the minimum available in manual mode (e.g. 1/8000 s) and finishing with a duration just below raw saturation.

5. Plot a graph of $\sigma_{DN,temp}^2$ along the vertical axis versus mean green-channel raw value n_{DN} along the horizontal axis and fit the result to a straight line. Since the dark-current shot noise will be negligible at the minimum available integration time, the intercept with the y-axis will be the square of the read noise, $\sigma_{DN,read}^2$, measured in DN or ADU. The square of the photon shot noise, $\sigma_{DN,ph}^2$, is given by subtracting $\sigma_{DN,read}^2$ from the graph value.

Figure 3.35 shows temporal noise measurement for the Olympus® E-M1 at ISO 1600. The fitted straight line is shown near the origin.

The value of the conversion factor g emerges as part of the above measurement. The first step is to utilise equation (3.55) which states that the square of the photon shot noise yields the expected signal itself measured in electron counts,

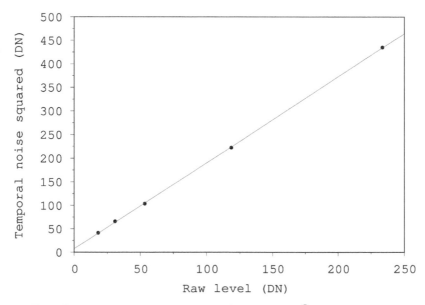

Figure 3.35. Temporal noise measurement for the Olympus® E-M1 at ISO 1600.

$$\sigma^2_{e,\mathrm{ph}} = n_e.$$

The second step is to divide both sides of this equation by g to obtain the following result,

$$\sigma^2_{\mathrm{DN,ph}} = n_{\mathrm{DN}}.$$

Since $n_{\mathrm{DN}} = n_e/g$, it follows that the value of g at the selected ISO setting is given by the inverse of the gradient of the fitted straight line [32, 35, 36].

Read noise measurement

Although a read noise estimate will emerge when performing the temporal noise measurement described above, alternative methods can be used to determine the read noise more accurately.

A camera exposure in the absence of irradiance at the sensor plane is known as a *dark frame*, and a dark frame with zero integration time is known as a *bias frame*. The dark current will be absent when the integration time is zero, and so a bias frame only contains read noise. A practical option for photographers is to obtain an approximate bias frame by taking a photo in a dark room with the lens cap fitted and selecting the minimum shutter duration available in manual mode (e.g. 1/8000 s).

Some camera manufacturers leave a bias offset in the raw data. In this case, the mean of the read noise distribution in a bias frame will be the bias offset value defined in section 3.7.5 earlier, and the standard deviation of the distribution can be measured accurately. For example, read noise distributions for the Olympus® E-M1 are shown in figure 3.36 at several high-ISO settings. This camera includes a bias offset centred at DN = 256. Unfortunately, if a bias offset is not present in the raw data then the mean will be zero. In this case, half of the distribution will be clipped to zero which makes analysis more difficult [35, 40].

The read noise distribution may differ from its ideal Gaussian form, primarily because of undesirable periodic pattern components arising from circuit interference. The character of the read noise can be analysed by taking the FT of a bias frame.

3.8.4 Noise models

Once the conversion factor g is known at each ISO setting, noise measured in DNs can be converted into electron units. Importantly, this includes the read noise even though this was not part of the original detected charge.

Figure 3.37 shows read noise measured in DN, the gain, and the calculated read noise measured in electrons for the Olympus® E-M1 as a function of ISO setting. As perhaps expected, the read noise in DN increases as the ISO setting is raised from its base value at ISO 200 through to ISO 25600. The conversion factor data appears to indicate the presence of a single-stage PGA for all ISO settings. Furthermore, the same analog gain is used for ISO 100 and ISO 200, indicating that these ISO settings are defined through application of different tone curves.

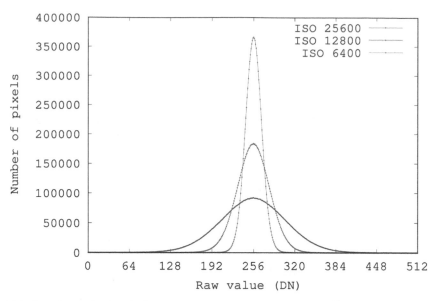

Figure 3.36. Gaussian read noise distribution measured in DNs for the Olympus® E-M1 at a selection of high ISO settings. The distribution is centred at the DN = 256 offset present in the raw file.

It is often assumed that higher ISO settings are noisier, and this assertion appears to be suggested by the above data. In fact, the opposite is true. Higher ISO settings are typically used when insufficient exposure is available at the sensor plane. SNR decreases as exposure is lowered, and it is the lack of exposure which is responsible for the higher noise. This can be illustrated by examining the read noise data converted into electron units using *g*. In electron units, the read noise *decreases* as the ISO setting is raised from ISO 200 through to ISO 25600. In other words, for a *fixed* exposure at the sensor plane, the higher ISO settings are less noisy. The explanation for this lies in the fact that part of the read noise arises from circuitry downstream from the PGA, and this contribution is not amplified by raising the ISO setting. Nevertheless, higher ISO settings bring disadvantages such as reduced available DR, as mentioned in section 3.7.4 earlier. The section on SNR in chapter 5 will discuss this topic in detail.

It is straightforward to develop temporal noise models for cameras that use a single-stage PGA. The read noise component can be modelled as [35]

$$\sigma_{\mathrm{DN,read}}^2 = (S\sigma_0)^2 + \sigma_1^2.$$

Here S is the ISO setting which is proportional to the PGA gain defined by equation (3.49) of section 3.7. The read-noise term σ_0 describes the contribution to the total read noise arising from electronics upstream from the PGA, and the read-noise term σ_1 describes the contribution from electronics downstream from the PGA [35]. Since these terms describe temporal noise, they must be added in quadrature. This model can be fitted to the data of figure 3.37.

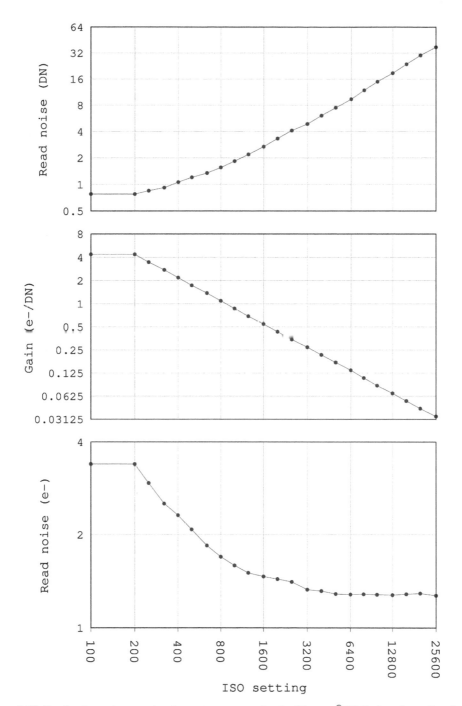

Figure 3.37. Read noise and conversion factor measurement for the Olympus® E-M1 plotted as a function of ISO setting using base 2 logarithmic axes. (Top) Output-referred read noise measured in DNs. Data measured by the author. (Middle) Conversion factor or gain measured in electrons/DN. Data courtesy of W J Claff [41]. (Bottom) Calculated input-referred read noise measured in electrons.

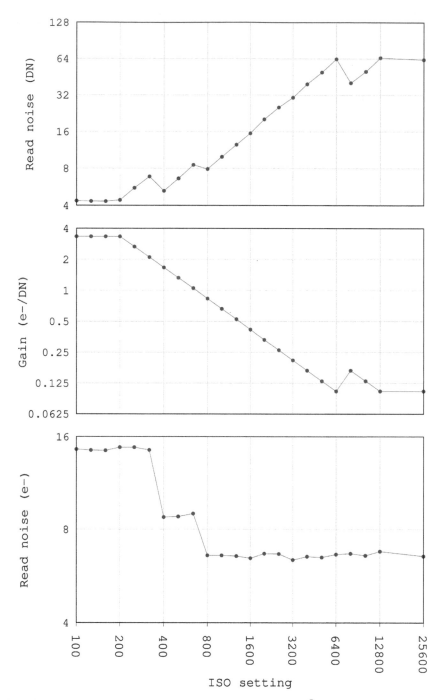

Figure 3.38. Read noise and conversion factor measurement for the Nikon® D700 plotted as a function of ISO setting using base 2 logarithmic axes. Data courtesy of W J Claff [41]. (Top) Output-referred read noise measured in DNs. (Middle) Conversion factor or gain measured in electrons/DN. (Bottom) Calculated input-referred read noise measured in electrons.

As a second example, figure 3.38 shows measured data for the Nikon® D700. The behaviour of the conversion factor suggests that all ISO settings below ISO 200 use different levels of digital gain. Furthermore, the read noise data appears to indicate the use of a second-stage PGA for certain ISO settings. A more sophisticated noise model is required for a two-stage PGA, for example [35]

$$\sigma^2_{\mathrm{DN,read}} = m^2\big\{(S\sigma_0)^2 + \sigma_1^2\big\}^2 + \sigma_2^2.$$

Here σ_0 is the noise upstream from the PGA at the main ISO setting S, and σ_1 is the noise contribution from the first-stage amplifier. For an intermediate ISO setting, the multiplier m for the second-stage amplifier takes a value of 1.25 or 1.6 rather than 1, in which case all noise present is amplified. The final term σ_2 is the noise contribution from the second-stage amplifier along with the read noise downstream from the PGA.

Bibliography

[1] Gaskill J D 1978 *Linear Systems, Fourier Transforms, and Optics* (New York: Wiley)

[2] Fiete R D 2010 *Modeling the Imaging Chain of Digital Cameras* (Bellingham, WA: SPIE) (*SPIE Tutorial Texts in Optical Engineering* vol TT92)

[3] Maeda P, Catrysse P and Wandell B 2005 Integrating lens design with digital camera simulation *Proc. SPIE* **5678** 48

[4] Farrell J E, Xiao F, Catrysse P B and Wandell B A 2003 A simulation tool for evaluating digital camera image quality *Proc. SPIE* **5294** 124

[5] Farrell J E, Catrysse P B and Wandell B A 2012 Digital camera simulation *Appl. Opt.* **51** A80

[6] Holst G C 1998 *CCD Arrays, Cameras, and Displays* 2nd edn (Oviedo, FL: JCD)

[7] Holst G C and Lomheim T S 2011 CMOS/CCD Sensors and Camera Systems 2nd edn (Oviedo, FL: JCD)

[8] ISO 2006 Photography–Digital still cameras–Determination of exposure index, ISO speed ratings, standard output sensitivity, and recommended exposure index, ISO 12232:2006

[9] Palmer J M and Grant B G 2008 *The Art of Radiometry* (Bellingham, WA: SPIE) (*SPIE Press Monograph* vol 184)

[10] Goodman J 2004 *Introduction to Fourier Optics* 3rd edn (Englewood, CO: Roberts)

[11] Saleh B E A and Teich M C 2007 *Fundamentals of Photonics* 2nd edn (New York: Wiley)

[12] Nasse H H 2008 *How to Read MTF Curves Carl Zeiss Camera Lens Division* http://lenspire.zeiss.com/en/overview-technical-articles

[13] Shannon R R 1997 *The Art and Science of Optical Design* (Cambridge: Cambridge University Press)

[14] Boreman G D 2001 *Modulation Transfer Function in Optical and Electro-Optical Systems* (Bellingham, WA: SPIE) (*SPIE Tutorial Texts in Optical Engineering* vol TT52)

[15] Shannon R R 1994 Optical specifications *Handbook of Optics* (New York: McGraw-Hill) chapter 35

[16] Born M and Wolf E 1999 *Principles of Optics: Electromagnetic Theory of Propagation Interference and Diffraction of Light* 7th edn (Cambridge: Cambridge University Press)

[17] Smith W J 2007 *Modern Optical Engineering* 4th edn (New York: McGraw-Hill)

[18] Jenkins F A and White H E 1976 *Fundamentals of Optics* 4th edn (New York: McGraw-Hill)

[19] Goldberg N 1992 *Camera Technology: The Dark Side of the Lens* (New York: Academic)

[20] Yadid-Pecht O 2000 Geometrical modulation transfer function for different pixel active area shapes *Opt. Eng.* **39** 859

[21] Fliegel K 2004 Modeling and measurement of image sensor characteristics *Radioengineering* **13** 27

[22] Wolberg G 1990 *Digital Image Warping* 1st edn (New York: Wiley/IEEE Computer Society Press)

[23] Gonzalez R C and Woods R E 2007 *Digital Image Processing* 3rd edn (Englewood Cliffs, NJ: Prentice Hall)

[24] Shannon C E 1949 Communication in the presence of noise *Proc. Inst. Radio Eng* **37** 10

[25] Greivenkamp J E 1990 Color dependent optical prefilter for the suppression of aliasing artifacts *Appl. Opt.* **29** 676

[26] Palum R 2009 *Single-Sensor Imaging: Methods and Applications for Digital* ed R Lukac (Boca RAton, FL: CRC Press)

[27] Theuwissen A J P 1995 *Solid-State Imaging with Charge-Coupled Devices* (Dordrecht: Kluwer)

[28] Sze S M and Ng K K 2006 *Physics of Semiconductor Devices* 3rd edn (New York: Wiley)

[29] Sze S M and Lee M-K 2012 *Semiconductor Devices: Physics and Technology* 3rd edn (New York: Wiley)

[30] Yamada T 2006 *Image Sensors and Signal Processing for Digital Still Cameras* ed J Nakamura (Boca Raton, FL/London: CRC Press/Taylor and Francis)

[31] Takayanagi I 2006 *Image Sensors and Signal Processing for Digital Still Cameras* ed J Nakamura (Boca Raton, FL/London: CRC Press/Taylor and Francis)

[32] Nakamura J 2006 *Image Sensors and Signal Processing for Digital Still Cameras* ed J Nakamura (Boca Raton, FL/London: CRC Press/Taylor and Francis)

[33] Jiang J, Liu D, Gu J and Susstrunk S 2013 What is the space of spectral sensitivity functions for digital color cameras? *IEEE Workshop on the Applications of Computer Vision* pp 168–79

[34] Subbarao M 1990 Optical transfer function of a diffraction-limited system for polychromatic illumination *Appl. Opt.* **29** 554

[35] Martinec E 2008 Noise, dynamic range and bit depth in digital SLRs http://theory.uchicago.edu/~ejm/pix/20d/tests/noise/ and http://www.photonstophotos.net/Emil%20Martinec/noise.html

[36] Mizoguchi T 2006 *Image Sensors and Signal Processing for Digital Still Cameras* ed J Nakamura (Boca Raton, FL/London: CRC Press/Taylor and Francis)

[37] Butler R 2015 What's that noise? Part one: Shedding some light on the sources of noise http://www.dpreview.com/articles/8189925268

[38] Butler R and Sanyal R 2015 Sources of noise part two: electronic noise http://www.dpreview.com/articles/0388507676

[39] Sato K 2006 *Image Sensors and Signal Processing for Digital Still Cameras* ed J Nakamura (Boca Raton, FL/London: CRC Press/Taylor and Francis)

[40] Claff W J 2009 Sensor analysis primer—Engineering and photographic dynamic range http://www.photonstophotos.net/

[41] Claff W J 2017 http://www.photonstophotos.net/

IOP Publishing

Physics of Digital Photography

Andy Rowlands

Chapter 4

Raw conversion

Numerous procedures are involved in the conversion of the recorded raw file into a viewable output image. Some basic steps in the raw conversion process include:

1. Linearisation: The raw data may be stored in a compressed form which needs to be uncompressed for processing, for example by using a look-up table (LUT).
2. Dark frame subtraction: This can vary in sophistication from subtraction of an average optical black pixel through to a full dark frame.
3. White balance (WB): This is performed by raw channel equalisation in conjunction with a matrix transformation to a standard output-referred colour space. Raw channel equalisation is achieved by direct application of multipliers to the raw channels in order that equal raw values correspond to a neutral subject.
4. Colour demosaic: Raw data obtained from a sensor with a colour filter array (CFA) contains incomplete colour information. The missing data needs to be determined through interpolation.
5. Transformation matrix: The demosaiced raw data resides in the internal camera raw space and needs to be transformed into a standard device-independent colour space such as sRGB for viewing on a display. This is achieved through application of a colour rotation matrix in combination with the raw WB multipliers. The matrix can be derived after having characterised the camera by mapping the internal camera raw space to a reference colour space such as CIE XYZ.
6. Tone curve: Bit-depth reduction can be achieved while preserving image quality (IQ) through nonlinear encoding of the digital output levels (DOLs). For preferred tone reproduction, a tone curve which goes beyond the gamma encoding or compression curve of the output-referred colour space will be applied, typically through the use of a LUT. Compensating gamma decoding or expansion will be performed by the display device, as described in chapter 2.
7. Image processing: Various proprietary image-processing techniques will be applied by the in-camera image-processing engine.

doi:10.1088/978-0-7503-1242-4ch4

8. JPEG encoding: For JPEG output, the output-referred RGB colour space will be converted into the $Y'C_bC_r$ colour space, where Y' is luma (gamma-encoded luminance Y) and C_b, C_r are chroma components.

Many of the techniques used by in-camera image-processing engines are proprietary. Nevertheless, external open-source raw converters such as *dcraw*[1] include code containing valid computational strategies and details which may be freely examined.

This chapter discusses the underlying physical principles behind several of the important steps involved in producing a viewable output image from the recorded raw file. Colour theory [1, 2, 3] will be central to this description.

4.1 Reference colour spaces

A colour space is a specific range of colours in which a colour can be specified by an associated colour model. For example, the RGB colour model uses a Cartesian coordinate system. *Reference* colour spaces contain all possible colours. Examples of reference colour spaces include LMS, CIE XYZ, and CIE LAB.

Similarly, a camera has its own internal *camera raw space* which should in principle contain all possible colours albeit organised in a non-standard manner. Camera raw spaces differ considerably between different camera models and need to be characterised by establishing a linear mapping to a reference colour space such as CIE XYZ. However, camera raw spaces do not contain all possible colours in practice because this mapping can only be defined in an approximate way.

This section introduces the CIE XYZ reference colour space which will be used for camera colour characterisation later in this chapter. Reference colour spaces can be used to translate colours from one colour space to another. The reference colour space specified by the International Color Consortium (ICC) is known as the Profile Connection Space (PCS) and this can be based on either CIE LAB or CIE XYZ encodings.

4.1.1 Physics of colour

Colour is a perceived human physiological sensation to electromagnetic waves with wavelengths in the visible region, which ranges from approximately 380 nm to 780 nm. A common way to categorise colour is in terms of *hue, saturation*, and *luminance* descriptors. Hue and saturation together describe the *chromaticity* of a colour.

Electromagnetic waves with wavelengths in the visible region can be divided into six main colour regions: red, orange, yellow, green, blue, and violet. These *hues* or *pure spectrum colours* are the colours seen in a rainbow. There is a smooth transition from one colour region to the next, as illustrated in figure 4.1. This means that the term 'red' does not define any specific colour; any of the hues corresponding to the first colour region may be described as being red. The same reasoning applies to the other colour regions. Colours which are not pure spectrum colours have been diluted with white light, which is a mixture of all possible hues. Adding white light to

---

[1] The freeware raw converter *dcraw* by D Coffin is available at https://www.cybercom.net/~dcoffin/dcraw.

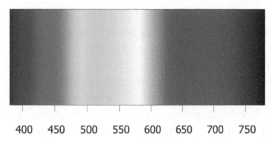

400   450   500   550   600   650   700   750

Figure 4.1. Pure spectrum colours as a function of wavelength λ in nanometres.

a hue decreases the *saturation* of the colour. Pure spectrum colours are fully saturated. An example of a colour with reduced saturation is pink, obtained from mixing a red hue with white light. Colours which can only be described on a grey scale have zero saturation and are said to be fully desaturated or *achromatic*. The term *monochrome* is used to describe an image which contains colours which may vary in luminance but not in chromaticity. A monochrome image is not necessarily achromatic.

Metamerism

Light incident upon the retina of the eye is generally composed of a mixture of electromagnetic waves of various wavelengths. The mixture can be characterised by its *spectral power distribution* (SPD). In principle this function describes the 'amount' of light in terms of power contribution at each wavelength.

SPDs can be used to characterise direct light sources. Another form of SPD is spectral radiance L_λ which was first encountered in chapter 3. This is commonly used to characterise light reflected from surfaces. Spectral radiance is the power emitted from a surface per unit area, unit solid angle, and unit wavelength. In the current context, the solid angle is that subtended from the scene by the pupil of the human eye.

There may be many different SPDs which appear to have the same colour to a human observer. For example, different SPDs may be found which appear to have the same colour as a pure monochromatic spectrum colour. This concept is known as the principle of *metamerism*, and a group of SPDs that yield the same colour response under identical viewing conditions are known as *metamers*. The principle of metamerism is fundamental to the theory discussed in the following sections.

4.1.2 Standard colourimetric observer

Given three linearly independent monochromatic light sources, it is known from experiments that almost *any* desired colour can be matched by an SPD containing a mixture or linear combination of these three light sources only. However, it must be stipulated that 'negative amounts' of the source colours are allowed, as described below.

This combination of linear systems theory with the principle of metamerism is known as *trichromatic matching*. Trichromatic matching follows from *Grassman's laws* which infer that colour can be treated in a similar way to a mathematical vector space. The set of three monochromatic light sources which represent the unit vectors are known as primary light sources or *primaries*, and the colours spanned by the choice of primaries define a *colour space*. (However, it should be noted that colour spaces are not true vector spaces in a mathematical sense.) In principle, any set of three linearly independent monochromatic sources can be chosen as primaries, although sources with wavelengths in each of the red, green, and blue regions of the pure spectrum are most useful in practice. This is because a large range of colours can be matched by such a choice when only positive linear combinations of the primaries are allowed.

In 1931 the *Commission Internationale de l'Eclairage* (CIE) (translating as 'International Commission on Illumination') considered a set of data that had been obtained experimentally by Wright (1928–9) and Guild (1931) in which the following fixed primaries were chosen,

$$\lambda_R = 700 \text{ nm}$$

$$\lambda_G = 546.1 \text{ nm}$$

$$\lambda_B = 435.8 \text{ nm}.$$

Human observers had been asked to visually match the colour of a target monochromatic light source of wavelength λ within a viewing angle of 2° by mixing any amounts of the three primaries.

The aim of the experiments was to define a set of *colour-matching functions* representative of normal human colour vision which could be used to perform trichromatic matching. These functions define the CIE 2° *standard colourimetric observer*. Colour-matching functions obtained using a 10° viewing angle were later defined in 1964. These define the CIE 10° standard colourimetric observer.

Units

It is important to understand the units that were defined by the CIE when analysing the experimental data of Wright and Guild. The units for the primaries were defined such that one unit of each would match the colour of a hypothetical *polychromatic* equi-energy source which has constant power at all wavelengths. This SPD is known as *illuminant E*. The relationship between the units can be expressed in the following way,

$$\boxed{[E] \equiv [R] + [G] + [B]} \,. \tag{4.1}$$

Here [E] is the unit of the equi-energy source, and [R], [G], [B] are the units of the red, blue and green primaries, respectively. These units each represent their own individual quantities of power and can be treated as dimensionless. Consequently, it is important to keep track of the luminance and radiance ratios implied by the units. The luminance ratio between [E], [R], [G], and [B], respectively, is given by

$$1 : 0.17697 : 0.81240 : 0.01603. \tag{4.2}$$

This implies that 0.17697 cd m^{-2} of red primary, 0.81240 cd m^{-2} of green primary, and 0.01063 cd m^{-2} of blue primary would be needed to match 1 cd m^{-2} of illuminant E. The corresponding radiance ratio is given by [2]

$$1 : 0.96805 : 0.01852 : 0.01343.$$

This ratio can be obtained by using $V(\lambda_R)$, $V(\lambda_G)$, and $V(\lambda_B)$, where $V(\lambda)$ is the 1924 CIE standard luminosity function introduced in section 3.1.1 of chapter 3.

Colour-matching functions
The results of the experiments can be summarised by the following expression,

$$[E(\lambda)] \equiv \bar{r}(\lambda)[R] + \bar{g}(\lambda)[G] + \bar{b}(\lambda)[B]. \tag{4.3}$$

Here $[E(\lambda)]$ is one unit of *monochromatic target colour* such that

$$1[E] = \int_{380}^{780} 1[E(\lambda)] \, d\lambda.$$

The *colour-matching functions* $\bar{r}[\lambda]$, $\bar{g}[\lambda]$, and $\bar{b}[\lambda]$ describe the 'amounts' of the primaries needed to achieve a colour match at each value of monochromatic target wavelength λ, each measured in their own units. The colour-matching functions are shown in figure 4.2. Because the units of the primaries are defined according to equation (4.1), the area under each curve is the same. Notice that the curves define *negative* values at some wavelengths. In these cases it was found that the primary needed to be added to the target colour to obtain a colour match instead of being mixed with the other primaries.

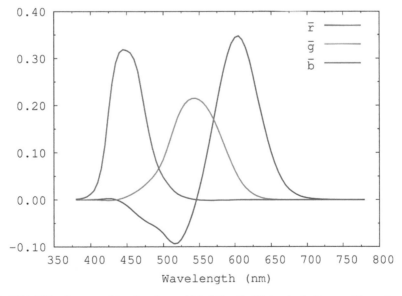

Figure 4.2. 1931 CIE colour-matching functions which define the 2° standard observer. The units are defined according to equation (4.1).

Relationship with $V(\lambda)$

The normalisation of the colour-matching functions is revealed by the relationship with the 1924 standard luminosity function, $V(\lambda)$.

When a colour-match is obtained at a given λ, the total luminance on both sides of equation (4.3) must be equal. This follows from the fact that luminance is one of the defining characteristics of colour, along with chromaticity. Since luminance is obtained from radiance at a given wavelength via the function $V(\lambda)$, the relationship between the colour-matching functions and $V(\lambda)$ must satisfy the luminance ratio between the units defined by equation (4.2),

$$V(\lambda) = c\big(0.17697\ \bar{r}(\lambda) + 0.81240\ \bar{g}(\lambda) + 0.01063\ \bar{b}(\lambda)\big).$$

Here c is a normalisation constant. At $\lambda = 700$ nm where $\lambda = \lambda_R$, it can be seen in figure 4.2 that the functions $\bar{g}(\lambda)$ and $\bar{b}(\lambda)$ are zero but $\bar{r}(\lambda)$ remains non-zero. Therefore

$$V(\lambda_R) = c(0.17697\ \bar{r}(\lambda_R)).$$

This reveals the value for the normalisation constant,

$$c = 5.6508. \tag{4.4}$$

It now follows that

$$\boxed{V(\lambda) = 1.0000\ \bar{r}(\lambda) + 4.5907\ \bar{g}(\lambda) + 0.0601\ \bar{b}(\lambda)}. \tag{4.5}$$

The relationship between $V(\lambda)$ and each term on the right-hand side of this equation is illustrated in figure 4.3. The area under each of the colour-matching functions shown in figure 4.2 will be 1/5.6508 of the area under $V(\lambda)$.

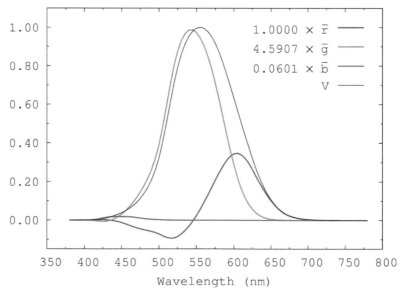

Figure 4.3. The colour-matching functions $\bar{r}(\lambda)$, $\bar{g}(\lambda)$, $\bar{b}(\lambda)$ each multiplied according to the luminance ratio between their respective dimensionless units illustrates the relationship with the 1924 CIE standard luminosity function $V(\lambda)$.

4.1.3 CIE RGB colour space

After having defined the colour-matching functions over the visible range of unit monochromatic target wavelengths, it is possible to use them to obtain a colour match between amounts of the three primaries and a general polychromatic SPD.

Denoting the SPD by P and the component at wavelength λ by $P(\lambda)$, both sides of equation (4.3) can be multiplied by $P(\lambda)$ in order to match the colour at wavelength λ,

$$P(\lambda)[E(\lambda)] \equiv P(\lambda)\bar{r}(\lambda)[R] + P(\lambda)\bar{g}(\lambda)[G] + P(\lambda)\bar{b}(\lambda)[B].$$

The colour of the SPD itself can then be matched by integrating over all visible wavelengths,

$$P \equiv \int_{380}^{780} P(\lambda)[E(\lambda)] \, d\lambda.$$

This means that

$$P \equiv \int_{380}^{780} P(\lambda)\bar{r}(\lambda)[R] \, d\lambda + \int_{380}^{780} P(\lambda)\bar{g}(\lambda)[G] \, d\lambda + \int_{380}^{780} P(\lambda)\bar{b}(\lambda)[B] \, d\lambda.$$

This can be written more compactly in the form

$$P \equiv R\,[R] + G\,[G] + B\,[B].$$

Here R, G, B are the CIE RGB *tristimulus values* measured in $[R]$, $[G]$, $[B]$ units,

$$R = \int_{380}^{780} P(\lambda)\bar{r}(\lambda)d\lambda, \qquad G = \int_{380}^{780} P(\lambda)\bar{g}(\lambda)d\lambda, \qquad B = \int_{380}^{780} P(\lambda)\bar{b}(\lambda)d\lambda \,.$$

The CIE RGB tristimulus values are a set of numbers which represent a colour in the CIE RGB *colour space*. Under identical viewing conditions, different SPDs which lead to the same tristimulus values will appear the same colour.

SPDs are commonly expressed in spectral radiance units, $\mathrm{W\,sr^{-1}\,m^{-2}\,nm^{-1}}$, and the numerical values of $\bar{r}(\lambda)$, $\bar{g}(\lambda)$, $\bar{b}(\lambda)$ are defined according to equation (4.5). This means that the CIE RGB tristimulus values can be negative. Depending on the normalisation, tristimulus values can be absolute or relative. This will be discussed in section 4.1.7 later.

The CIE RGB colour space contains all colours visible to the 2° standard colourimetric observer. The following section discusses the *rg chromaticity diagram* which provides a straightforward way to visualise the CIE RGB colour space. The CIE RGB colour space is rarely used as a reference space in practice. However, it provides the foundation for the widely used CIE XYZ reference colour space to be discussed later.

4.1.4 Chromaticity diagram (*rg*)

Colour spaces can be visualised by using a colour model to specify the tristimulus values. For example, a three-dimensional Cartesian coordinate system is often used to represent output-referred RGB colour spaces such as sRGB and Adobe® RGB to be discussed later. Although the CIE RGB colour space can also be represented by a 3D coordinate system by regarding the units $[R]$, $[G]$, and $[B]$ as vector components, all possible colours are included and the construction is difficult to visualise.

Instead, it is convenient to separate the chromaticity information from the luminance information by introducing the *rg chromaticity diagram*. This describes the relative *proportion* of the R, G, and B tristimulus values defining a colour [4]. The *rg* chromaticity coordinates are defined as

$$r = \frac{R}{R + G + B}, \quad g = \frac{G}{R + G + B}, \quad b = \frac{B}{R + G + B}.$$

Since $b = 1 - r - g$, the *rg* chromaticity diagram illustrated in figure 4.4 uses (r,g) chromaticity coordinates in two dimensions.

In figure 4.7, the chromaticity coordinates corresponding to all colours that are visible to the human visual system (HVS) represented by the 2° standard colourimetric observer are shown by the grey horseshoe-shaped area. The *rg* chromaticity

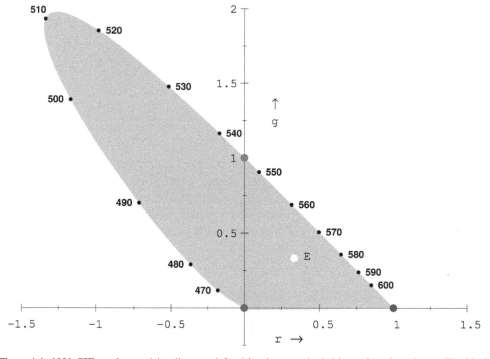

Figure 4.4. 1931 CIE *rg* chromaticity diagram defined by the grey shaded horseshoe-shaped area. The black circles on the boundary indicate a selection of pure spectrum colours and their associated wavelengths. The point corresponding to illuminant E is shown in white. The red, green, and blue circles mark the primaries of the 1931 CIE RGB colour space.

coordinates of the primaries defining the CIE RGB colour space are (0,0), (0,1), and (1,0) by definition. The usefulness of chromaticity diagrams will become apparent in section 4.1.6 which introduces the xy chromaticity diagram.

The horseshoe-shaped area has been shown in grey because the range of colours that can be displayed correctly on a computer display depends upon the gamut of the display and the viewing conditions. For reference, figure 4.13 of section 4.4 displays the chromaticities of the smaller sRGB colour space since these can be viewed correctly on a standard-gamut monitor.

4.1.5 CIE XYZ colour space

The choice of primaries made when defining a reference colour space is not unique. The requirement is that the primaries are linearly independent so that one primary cannot be obtained as a linear combination (mixture) of the other two. Mathematically this means that colour-matching functions $\bar{x}(\lambda)$, $\bar{y}(\lambda)$, $\bar{z}(\lambda)$ could be defined for an arbitrary set of linearly independent primaries, and these colour-matching functions would be related to $\bar{r}(\lambda)$, $\bar{g}(\lambda)$, $\bar{b}(\lambda)$ via a simple *linear transformation*,

$$\begin{bmatrix} \bar{x}(\lambda) \\ \bar{y}(\lambda) \\ \bar{z}(\lambda) \end{bmatrix} = \underline{T} \begin{bmatrix} \bar{r}(\lambda) \\ \bar{g}(\lambda) \\ \bar{b}(\lambda) \end{bmatrix}.$$

Here $\underline{T}$ is a 3 × 3 transformation matrix,

$$\underline{T} = \begin{bmatrix} T_{11} & T_{12} & T_{13} \\ T_{21} & T_{22} & T_{23} \\ T_{31} & T_{32} & T_{33} \end{bmatrix}.$$

When the CIE RGB colour space was defined in 1931, the CIE also introduced the CIE XYZ colour space as a linear transformation from CIE RGB. This colour space was defined by a new set of colour-matching functions $\bar{x}(\lambda)$, $\bar{y}(\lambda)$, $\bar{z}(\lambda)$ according to the following transformation matrix,

$$\underline{T} = c \begin{bmatrix} 0.49 & 0.31 & 0.20 \\ 0.17697 & 0.81240 & 0.01063 \\ 0.00 & 0.01 & 0.99 \end{bmatrix}.$$

Here $c = 5.6508$ is the normalisation constant defined by equation (4.4). Written more explicitly,

$$\bar{x}(\lambda) = c \left(0.49\, \bar{r}(\lambda) + 0.31\, \bar{g}(\lambda) + 0.20\, \bar{b}(\lambda) \right) \tag{4.6a}$$

$$\bar{y}(\lambda) = c \left(0.17697\, \bar{r}(\lambda) + 0.81240\, \bar{g}(\lambda) + 0.01063\, \bar{b}(\lambda) \right) \tag{4.6b}$$

$$\bar{z}(\lambda) = c \left(0.01\, \bar{g}(\lambda) + 0.99\, \bar{b}(\lambda) \right). \tag{4.6c}$$

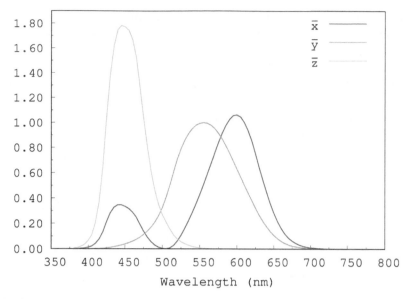

Figure 4.5. 1931 CIE colour-matching functions $\bar{x}(\lambda)$, $\bar{y}(\lambda)$, $\bar{z}(\lambda)$. Arbitrary colours have been used for the curves.

The colour-matching functions $\bar{x}(\lambda)$, $\bar{y}(\lambda)$, $\bar{z}(\lambda)$ are plotted in figure 4.5. The differences in height compared with $\bar{r}(\lambda)$, $\bar{g}(\lambda)$, $\bar{b}(\lambda)$ arise from the presence of the normalisation constant [5]. In analogy with section 4.1.3, the following colour match holds for an SPD,

$$P\,[E] = \int_{380}^{780} P(\lambda)[E_\lambda]\,\mathrm{d}\lambda = X[X] + Y[Y] + Z[Z].$$

The *CIE XYZ tristimulus values* are defined by the following relations,

$$X = k \int_{380}^{780} P(\lambda)\bar{x}(\lambda)\mathrm{d}\lambda, \qquad Y = k \int_{380}^{780} P(\lambda)\bar{y}(\lambda)\mathrm{d}\lambda,$$
$$Z = k \int_{380}^{780} P(\lambda)\bar{z}(\lambda)\mathrm{d}\lambda. \tag{4.7}$$

Here k is a normalisation factor which determines whether the values are *absolute* or *relative* as discussed in sections 4.1.7 and 4.1.8 later.

The above choice of linear transformation has several useful mathematical properties. Firstly, $\bar{x}(\lambda)$, $\bar{y}(\lambda)$, $\bar{z}(\lambda)$ remain non-negative for all λ so that the XYZ tristimulus values will always be be *non-negative*. Nevertheless, all visible colours are described. This apparent contradiction is resolved by the fact that the primaries have been chosen to correspond with non-visible chromaticities. Such primaries are referred to as *imaginary*. The location of the XYZ primaries on the *rg* chromaticity diagram is shown in figure 4.6.

A second useful property of the XYZ colour space is that the function $\bar{y}(\lambda)$ has adopted the luminance ratio of the units [R], [G], [B] defined by equation (4.2).

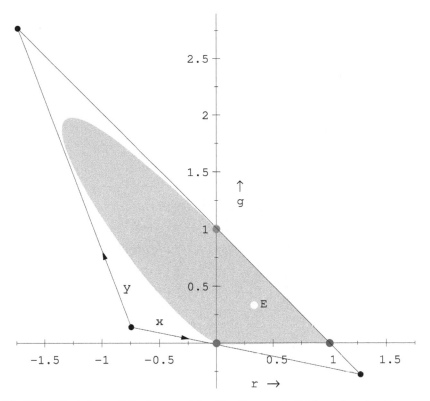

Figure 4.6. 1931 CIE *rg* chromaticity diagram defined by the grey shaded horseshoe-shaped area. The red, green, and blue points mark the primaries of the 1931 CIE RGB colour space. The black points mark the primaries of the XYZ space.

Furthermore, $\bar{x}(\lambda)$ and $\bar{z}(\lambda)$ have been cleverly defined to yield zero luminance. Since the normalisation constant $c = 5.6508$ is the same as that defined by equation (4.4), comparison of equation (4.6*b*) with equation (4.5) reveals that

$$\boxed{\bar{y}(\lambda) = V(\lambda)}.$$
(4.8)

This means that *the tristimulus value Y will be proportional to the luminance of the target SPD being colour-matched.*

4.1.6 Chromaticity diagram (*xy*)

The *xy* chromaticity diagram can be defined in analogy with the *rg* chromaticity diagram introduced in section 4.1.4. The *xy* chromaticity coordinates are defined as

$$x = \frac{X}{X + Y + Z}, \quad y = \frac{Y}{X + Y + Z}, \quad z = \frac{Z}{X + Y + Z}.$$
(4.9)

Similarly, the *xyz* chromaticity coordinates represent relative *proportions* of the *XYZ* tristimulus values [4]. Since $z = 1 - x - y$, the *xy* chromaticity diagram illustrated in figure 4.7 uses (x,y) chromaticity coordinates in two dimensions.

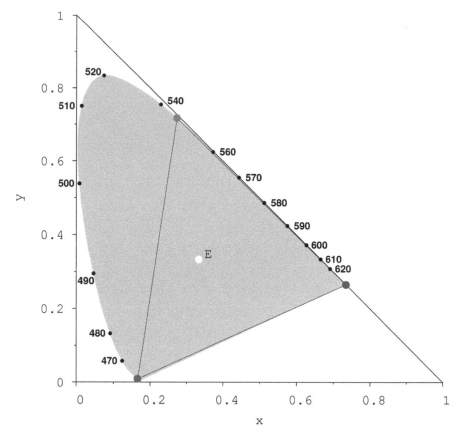

Figure 4.7. 1931 CIE *xy* chromaticity diagram defined by the grey shaded horseshoe-shaped area. The black circles on the boundary indicate a selection of pure spectrum colours and their associated wavelengths. The point corresponding to illuminant E is shown in white. The red, green, and blue circles mark the primaries of the 1931 CIE RGB colour space.

Equivalently, this is a projection of the *rg* chromaticity diagram shown in figure 4.6 onto the indicated *x* and *y* chromaticity axes. The *xy* chromaticity coordinates of the primaries defining the XYZ colour space are (0,0), (0,1), and (1,0) by definition.

The shaded horseshoe-shaped area shows all chromaticities that are visible to the HVS represented by the 2° standard colourimetric observer. Again this area has been shown in grey because the range of colours that can be displayed correctly on a computer display depends upon the gamut of the display and the viewing conditions. For reference, figure 4.13 of section 4.4 displays the chromaticities of the smaller sRGB colour space since these can be viewed correctly on a standard-gamut monitor. With the exception of the line at the base of the horseshoe which corresponds to the non-spectral purples, the boundary of the horseshoe corresponds to pure spectrum colours or hues. Notably, *saturation decreases with distance from the boundary*.

Chromaticity diagrams have some useful properties. Consider adding two colours with chromaticities (x_1, y_1) and (x_2, y_2). The chromaticity coordinates of the resulting colour will lie on the straight line connecting (x_1, y_1) and (x_2, y_2). This explains why the line at the base of the horseshoe cannot represent pure spectrum colours. This also implies that the area enclosed by a triangle connecting a fixed set of primaries reveals the (x,y) chromaticities that can be obtained by *additive* mixtures of those primaries. This is illustrated in figure 4.7 for the primaries of the CIE RGB colour space indicated by the red, green, and blue circles. This triangular area does not enclose the entire horseshoe because negative tristimulus values cannot be obtained from additive mixtures. The entire horseshoe is filled when the appropriate negative CIE RGB tristimulus values are included.

It will be shown in section 4.3 later that the area defining all visible chromaticities takes the form of a horseshoe because there is overlap in the spectral response curves of the human eye. If only non-negative colour-matching functions and tristimulus values are allowed when defining a reference colour space, the primaries must lie outside of the horseshoe. This is the only way that a triangle connecting the primaries can enclose all visible chromaticities. In other words, additive mixtures of three fixed real primaries cannot reproduce all real chromaticities. All chromaticity coordinates outside of the horseshoe correspond to non-visible chromaticities which are mathematically more saturated than pure spectrum colours, and consequently the primaries are referred to as *imaginary*.

4.1.7 Absolute colourimetry

The xy chromaticity diagram only describes relative amounts of the XYZ tristimulus values and knowledge of their *magnitude* is lost. If the magnitude of Y is known, then X and Z can be recovered using the following formulae,

$$X = \frac{xY}{y}, \quad Z = \frac{(1 - x - y)Y}{y}. \tag{4.10}$$

The magnitude of Y can be either *absolute* or *relative*, depending on the nature of the normalisation constant k appearing in equation (4.7).

Absolute colorimetry is used for self-luminous SPD sources such as lamps or colour monitors. The normalisation constant k is set equal to the *luminous efficacy K* defined in section 3.1.1 of chapter 3,

$$\boxed{k = K = 683 \text{ lm W}^{-1}} \, .$$

Consequently the magnitude of Y is given by

$$Y_{\text{abs}} = K \int_{380}^{780} P(\lambda)\bar{y}(\lambda)\mathrm{d}\lambda.$$

The subscript has been added to indicate that this is the *absolute* luminance in cd m^{-2}, assuming the SPD $P(\lambda)$ is specified to be spectral radiance $L_{e,\lambda}$ in units of Wsr^{-1} m^{-2} nm^{-1}. This follows because $\bar{y}(\lambda) = V(\lambda)$ according to equation (4.8), and so the above equation is equivalent to equation (3.1) of chapter 3 which defines *absolute* luminance L_v,

$$Y_{abs} \equiv L_v = K \int_{\lambda_1}^{\lambda_2} L_{e,\lambda} V(\lambda) d\lambda.$$

4.1.8 Relative colourimetry

Relative colourimetry is typically used when the source SPD is not self-luminous but instead describes the light reflected from objects in the scene.

Consider a scene *uniformly* illuminated by a source SPD denoted by $S(\lambda)$. Scene objects can be described by their reflectance $R(\lambda)$ which can take values in the range [0,1]. The reflected SPD denoted by $P(\lambda)$ is given by

$$P(\lambda) = S(\lambda)R(\lambda).$$

A reflectance $R(\lambda) = 1.0$ describes a perfect diffuse reflector. In this case $P(\lambda)$ is equivalent to $S(\lambda)$. Relative colourimetry generally specifies the normalisation constant k to be

$$k = \frac{100}{\int_{380}^{780} P(\lambda)\bar{y}(\lambda)d\lambda}.$$

This normalises the tristimulus values so that $Y = 100$ when $R(\lambda) = 1.0$. All *relative tristimulus values* will therefore have *relative luminance* Y in the range [0,100].

In digital imaging, the normalisation constant k is commonly defined to be

$$\boxed{k = \frac{1}{\int_{380}^{780} P(\lambda)\bar{y}(\lambda)d\lambda}.} \qquad (4.11)$$

Here relative luminance Y can take values in the range [0,1]. Visible colours do not form a cube in a 3D representation of the XYZ colour space and so only $Y \leqslant 1$.

The normalisation of equation (4.11) is useful when transforming digital image data between different colour spaces and will be used in the remainder of this chapter. It is useful to express relative tristimulus values in the form of a vector,

$$\begin{bmatrix} X \\ Y \\ Z \end{bmatrix}.$$

4.1.9 Reference white

The native white or *reference white* of a colour space is the colour stimulus to which the tristimulus values are normalised. Using relative colourimetry with Y normalised to the range [0,1], the reference white of a colour space is defined by the unit vector in that colour space. For example, the reference white of the XYZ colour space itself is illuminant E,

$$\begin{bmatrix} X \\ Y \\ Z \end{bmatrix}_E = \begin{bmatrix} 1 \\ 1 \\ 1 \end{bmatrix}.$$

Reference whites of several other standard colour spaces will be considered in section 4.4. Reference whites are significant because all other greyscale colours will similarly have equal vector components but with a lower relative luminance.

The reference white of a colour space depends upon its primaries and their units. Although the unit vector specifying the reference white has equal components, this does not imply that those components are equal in a photometric or radiometric sense. For example, in the case of the CIE RGB colour space the photometric and radiometric ratios between the components of the unit vector were given in section 4.1.2 as 1:4.5907:0.0601 and 72.09:1.38:1, respectively.

4.2 Illumination

4.2.1 Colour temperature

A *black body* is an ideal object which absorbs all incident electromagnetic radiation [6]. A black body in thermal equilibrium with its surroundings at constant temperature T emits electromagnetic radiation specified by an SPD which is a function of temperature only. This is known as *Planck's law*. If the SPD is specified in terms of spectral radiance $L_{e,\lambda}$, Planck's law can be expressed by the formula

$$L_{e,\lambda}(T) = \frac{2hc^2}{\lambda^5} \frac{1}{\exp\left(\dfrac{hc}{\lambda k_B T}\right) - 1}.$$

Here h is Planck's constant, k_B is the Boltzmann constant, and c is the speed of light in the medium. The temperature T measured in kelvins (K) is known as the *colour temperature* of the black body because its colour ranges from red at low temperatures through to blue at high temperatures.

The *Planckian locus* is the locus formed on a chromaticity diagram by a black-body radiator as a function of temperature. In the case of the XYZ colour space, the chromaticity coordinates of the Planckian locus can be obtained by substituting the above equation into equation (4.7) to calculate the XYZ tristimulus values, and then substituting these into equation (4.9) to calculate $(x(T), y(T))$. In practice it is convenient to use an approximate formula such as a cubic spline [7]. The Planckian locus for the 1931 CIE xy chromaticity diagram is shown in figure 4.8.

4.2.2 Correlated colour temperature

Sources of everyday illumination are typically *incandescent*, meaning the electromagnetic radiation emitted derives from a heated object. Although such sources are not true black-body radiators, the colour of the illumination can often be closely

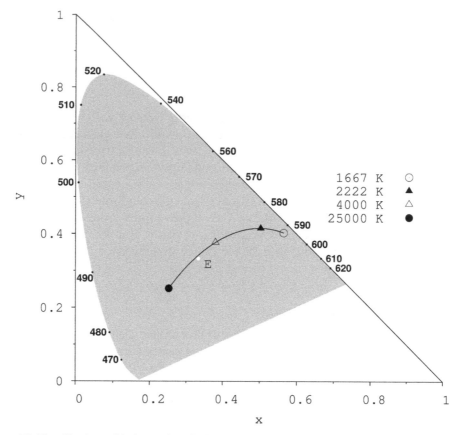

Figure 4.8. Planckian locus (black curve) on the 1931 CIE *xy* chromaticity diagram calculated using the cubic spline approximation. A selection of colour temperatures are indicated.

matched to the colour of the SPD emitted by a black body at a given temperature T. Provided this colour match is within a specified perceptual difference, the source of illumination can be associated with a *correlated colour temperature* (CCT) which is the colour temperature of the closest-matching black-body radiator.

The *xy* chromaticity diagram is unsuitable for determining the CCT associated with given chromaticity coordinates (x,y). This is because the XYZ colour space is not perceptually uniform, meaning distances do not correlate uniformly with colour perception. Instead, the *xy* chromaticities can be transformed into the *uv* chromaticities of the CIE 1960 uniform chromaticity scale (UCS) colour space,

$$u = \frac{4x}{12y - 2x + 3}, \quad v = \frac{6y}{12y - 2x + 3}. \tag{4.12}$$

The *uv* chromaticity diagram is known as MacAdam's diagram. Although now superseded by the CIE 1976 UCS colour space, an important feature of MacAdam's diagram is that lines with the same CCT or *isotherms* are normal to the Planckian locus. This enables the CCT associated with given chromaticity coordinates to be straightforwardly computed using numerical schemes such as Robertson's method [8]. Approximate formulae have also been developed [9, 10].

There are many possible chromaticities that map to the same CCT. If only the illumination CCT is known, the corresponding chromaticities can be distinguished by defining a *colour tint* value. For a given pair of chromaticity coordinates (u,v), the colour tint describes the distance along the isotherm in uv space between (u,v) and the Planckian locus. According to the CIE, the concept of CCT is only valid for distances up to a value ± 0.05 from the Planckian locus in uv space. The colour tint will be magenta or red below the Planckian locus and green or amber above the Planckian locus.

4.2.3 White point

The *white point* of a source SPD is defined by the chromaticity coordinates (x,y) of a 100% diffuse reflector illuminated by that SPD. The white point can also be expressed in terms of relative tristimulus values. In this chapter, the following notation will be used to indicate the specific vector corresponding to the white point with Y normalised to the range $[0,1]$,

$$\begin{bmatrix} X(\text{WP}) \\ Y(\text{WP}) \\ Z(\text{WP}) \end{bmatrix}.$$

Here $Y(\text{WP}) = 1$. The values for $X(\text{WP})$ and $Z(\text{WP})$ can be calculated using equation (4.10).

The terms 'white point' and 'reference white' are often used interchangeably. In this chapter, 'white point' will be used only to describe the above property of the *illumination*. The term 'reference white' will be used to describe the white reference of a colour space defined by the unit vector in that colour space.

4.2.4 Standard illuminants

The CIE have defined a set of standard illuminants which are useful for theoretical work, including camera colour characterisation [2]. Figure 4.9 illustrates the SPDs which define some common standard illuminants. Table 4.1 gives the white point for a selection of standard illuminants in terms of chromaticity coordinates and relative tristimulus values together with the corresponding CCTs.

If the illumination under consideration is a standard illuminant, this can be indicated at the lower-right hand corner of the vector. For example, the white point of D65 illumination in the XYZ colour space can be indicated in the following way,

$$\begin{bmatrix} X(\text{WP}) \\ Y(\text{WP}) \\ Z(\text{WP}) \end{bmatrix}_{\text{D65}} = \begin{bmatrix} 0.9504 \\ 1 \\ 1.0888 \end{bmatrix}.$$

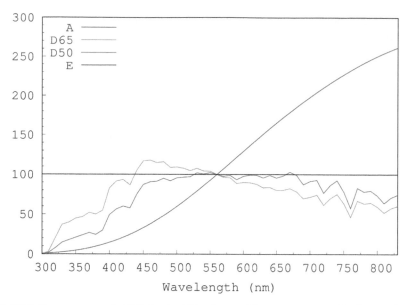

Figure 4.9. SPDs for some example CIE standard illuminants. All curves are normalised to a value of 100 at 560 nm.

Table 4.1. XYZ colour space data for a selection of CIE standard illuminants. The D series all represent natural daylight.

Illuminant	White point (x,y)	CIE standard illuminants White point $(Y = 1)$	CCT (K)	Description
A	(0.4476, 0.4074)	$X = 1.0985, Z = 0.3558$	2856	Incandescent bulb
D50	(0.3457, 0.3586)	$X = 0.9642, Z = 0.8252$	5003	Horizon
D55	(0.3324, 0.3475)	$X = 0.9568, Z = 0.9214$	5503	Mid-morning
D65	(0.3127, 0.3291)	$X = 0.9504, Z = 1.0888$	6504	Noon
D75	(0.2990, 0.3150)	$X = 0.9497, Z = 1.2261$	7504	North sky
E	(1/3,1/3)	$X = 1, Z = 1$	5454	Equi-energy

4.3 Camera raw space

4.3.1 Eye response functions

The legitimacy of trichromatic colour-matching and Grassman's laws is related to the fact that most humans are *trichromats*. This means that the human eye has three types of cone cells which act as light receptors. According to the *Young–Helmholtz theory*, the physiological sensation of colour arises from differences in these cone responses in terms of absorption of photons as a function of wavelength. The three types of cone cells are known as long (L), medium (M), and short (S) since they respond to a range of wavelengths which can broadly be classified in this way.

Mathematically, the responses can be described by *eye response functions* $\bar{l}(\lambda)$, $\bar{m}(\lambda)$, $\bar{s}(\lambda)$.

In analogy with the colour-matching functions $\bar{r}(\lambda)$, $\bar{g}(\lambda)$, $\bar{b}(\lambda)$ which generate the CIE RGB reference colour space using Grassman's laws, the eye response functions define the so-called LMS colour space which by definition must be a reference colour space containing all visible colours. The LMS tristimulus values are defined as

$$L = \int_{380}^{780} P(\lambda)\bar{l}(\lambda)d\lambda, \quad M = \int_{380}^{780} P(\lambda)\bar{m}(\lambda)d\lambda, \quad S = \int_{380}^{780} P(\lambda)\bar{s}(\lambda)d\lambda.$$

The LMS colour space is unsuitable for use as a general colour space in digital photography. Nevertheless, it is widely used in scientific research when information is required about the extent to which particular cone cells are being stimulated.

In the same way that the colour-matching functions of the CIE RGB and XYZ colour spaces are related via a linear matrix transformation, the eye-response functions must also be related to these colour-matching functions via a linear matrix transformation. Figure 4.10 shows an example set of eye response functions derived from more recent colour-matching data [11].

Since the eye response functions shown in figure 4.10 have considerable overlap, it is not possible to stimulate each type of cone cell independently. This explains why it is not possible to find a colour match between a pure spectrum colour and a linear combination of real primaries with coefficients that are all positive when performing colour-matching experiments. For example, the colour-matching functions $\bar{r}(\lambda)$, $\bar{g}(\lambda)$, $\bar{b}(\lambda)$ have negative values over certain wavelength ranges as shown previously in figure 4.2. However, the eye-response curves always have positive values since

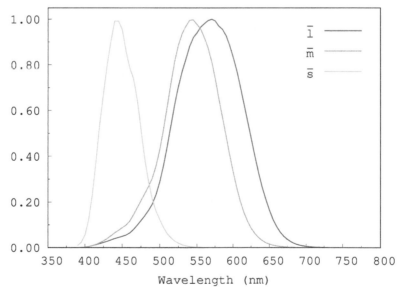

Figure 4.10. Normalised eye response curves based on the Stiles and Burch 10° colour-matching functions adjusted to 2°. Arbitrary colours have been used for the curves.

negative values would not be physically possible. The LMS colour space is therefore defined by a set of *imaginary* primaries which are located outside the horseshoe-shaped spectral locus of the *xy* chromaticity diagram in analogy with the XYZ colour space.

4.3.2 Camera response functions

The most common approach for capturing colour information used in consumer cameras is to place one of three or four different types of colour filter above each sensor photosite. The pattern of colour filters forms a CFA over the sensor. For example, a Bayer CFA uses a pattern of red, green, and blue filters [12]. The pattern can be separated into three or four different mosaics according to filter type. The filter properties contribute to defining the *camera raw space* in which raw values specify a 'colour'. The camera raw space cannot be interpreted as a true colour space unless the *Luther–Ives condition* is satisfied. Furthermore, colour information is incomplete when the raw data is obtained because only one type of filter can be associated with each photosite. Interpolation or *demosaicing* is used to fill in the missing colour information. The Luther–Ives condition and colour demosaicing are both described later in this section.

It was shown in the previous section that *eye response functions* $\bar{l}(\lambda)$, $\bar{m}(\lambda)$, $\bar{s}(\lambda)$ can be defined which describe the response of each type of eye cone cell as a function of wavelength, and the corresponding primaries define the LMS colour space. Similarly, *camera response functions* can be defined for an imaging sensor. According to section 3.6 of chapter 3, the camera response functions are defined by the set of spectral responsivity functions

$$R_i(\lambda) = \lambda.\mathrm{QE}_i(\lambda).$$

Here i is the mosaic label and $\mathrm{QE}_i(\lambda)$ is the external QE defined as

$$\mathrm{QE}_i(\lambda) = T_{\mathrm{CFA},i}(\lambda)\eta(\lambda)T(\lambda)\mathrm{FF}.$$

In this expression, $\eta(\lambda)$ is the charge-collection efficiency (CCE), $T(\lambda)$ is a transmission factor which takes into account unwanted absorption or reflectance effects such as the reflection at the SiO$_2$/Si interface, FF is the fill-factor, and $T_{\mathrm{CFA},i}(\lambda)$ is the CFA transmission function. These camera response functions can be interpreted as specifying 'amounts' of the *raw primaries* at each given wavelength. Since the camera response functions are defined by physical filters, their values will always be non-negative. This means that the tristimulus values of the camera raw space will also be non-negative and so the camera raw space is *additive*.

In order to specify tristimulus values in the camera raw space, first recall from chapter 3 that the signal at a photosite belonging to mosaic i expressed in terms of photoelectron count can be modelled by equation (3.46),

$$n_{e,i} = \frac{A_p t}{e} \int_{\lambda_1}^{\lambda_2} R_i(\lambda)\tilde{E}_\lambda(x, y)\mathrm{d}\lambda.$$

The constants A_p, t, and e are the photosite area, shutter speed or exposure duration, and charge of an electron, respectively. The sampled sensor-plane irradiance function $\tilde{E}_\lambda(x, y)$ incorporates the working f-number N_w and can be modelled using linear systems theory. The integration limits λ_1 and λ_2 depend on the range of wavelengths over which the spectral responsivity functions remain non-zero.

Next, recall that the photoelectron count generates a voltage which is quantised by the analog-to-digital converter (ADC). Mathematically, the digital number (DN) which represents a raw level can be modelled directly in terms of photoelectron count,

$$n_{DN,i} = INT\left[\frac{n_{e,i}}{g_i}\right].$$

The gain g_i is a direct conversion factor between photoelectron count and raw level. Its value depends upon the raw clipping point and the ISO gain G_{ISO}, and camera manufacturers may apply further processing so that g_i is not necessarily the same for each mosaic. Combining the above equations yields

$$n_{DN,i} = INT\left[\left(\frac{A_p\, t}{g_i\, e}\right)\int_{\lambda_1}^{\lambda_2} R_i(\lambda)\tilde{E}_\lambda(x, y)d\lambda\right].$$

This expression has direct analogy with the defining expressions for tristimulus values in the CIE RGB and XYZ colour spaces. The raw levels can therefore be interpreted as relative tristimulus values in the camera raw space normalised to the maximum raw level.

In this chapter, the presence of a Bayer CFA will be assumed. The raw levels for photosites belonging to mosaic i will be denoted using the following notation,

$$n_{DN,i} = \mathcal{R}, \ \mathcal{G}_1, \ \mathcal{G}_2, \ \text{or } \mathcal{B}.$$

Calligraphic symbols have been used in order to distinguish Bayer raw levels from tristimulus values of standard RGB colour spaces. The colour responses of the two green photosites in a 2×2 Bayer block are not necessarily the same and so they should be treated separately for generality. In this chapter, only three components $\mathcal{R}, \mathcal{G}, \mathcal{B}$ will be used for simplicity.

Although the camera raw space is defined by the sensor primaries, the $\mathcal{R}, \mathcal{G}, \mathcal{B}$ raw levels defined above belong to different photosites in a Bayer block. The set of all raw levels belonging to a given mosaic is referred to as a *raw channel*. After the colour demosaic has been performed so that $\mathcal{R}, \mathcal{G}, \mathcal{B}$ raw levels are known at every photosite, a *raw pixel vector* can then be defined for a given photosite. The $\mathcal{R}, \mathcal{G}, \mathcal{B}$ raw levels defining a pixel vector are referred to as *raw pixel components*. A linear transformation from the camera raw space to a reference colour space can be applied to pixel vectors but not mosaiced raw data.

The camera raw space for a given camera model has its own reference white. By definition this is the white point of the illumination which produces equal raw levels for a neutral diffuse object. Using relative colourimetry with the raw levels normalised to the range [0,1], the reference white can be labelled using the following notation,

$$\begin{bmatrix} \mathcal{R} \\ \mathcal{G} \\ \mathcal{B} \end{bmatrix}_{\text{reference}} = \begin{bmatrix} 1 \\ 1 \\ 1 \end{bmatrix}.$$

However, this cannot be interpreted as a raw pixel vector until the colour demosaic has been performed.

4.3.3 Luther–Ives condition

Recall that the CIE RGB and XYZ are both reference colour spaces and their respective colour matching functions are related through a linear transformation. The LMS colour space is a reference colour space defined by the eye response functions which must also be related to the colour matching functions through a linear transformation.

Recall from section 4.1.1 that a group of SPDs that yield the same colour response under identical viewing conditions are known as metamers. *Metameric error* occurs when the principle of metamerism is violated so that SPDs that should be metamers lead to different tristimulus values being recorded and therefore different colour responses. Unlike reference colour spaces, the camera raw space is not guaranteed to be free from metameric error. It can be inferred from the *Luther–Ives condition* [13] that the camera raw space will be free from metameric error if and only if the camera response functions are related to the colour-matching functions through a linear transformation.

The CIE RGB colour space uses real primaries and requires negative tristimulus values to be included in order to describe all visible colours. On the other hand, the CIE XYZ and LMS colour spaces are *additive*. This means that linear combinations of the primaries with non-negative coefficients can generate all visible colours, and so the primaries must be *imaginary*. This is the only way that a triangle formed by the primaries can enclose the entire horseshoe-shaped spectral locus of the xy chromaticity diagram. The camera response functions along with the raw levels can only be non-negative, and so the camera raw space must likewise be additive. Furthermore, imaging sensors are sensitive to all wavelengths over the visible spectrum. These two characteristics imply that if the Luther–Ives condition were to be satisfied exactly, the raw primaries would be imaginary, the triangle defined by the primaries would enclose the entire horseshoe-shaped spectral locus of the xy chromaticity diagram, and the camera raw space would correctly describe all visible colours without any metameric error.

In practice, restrictions on filter design along with image noise considerations dictate that sensors do not satisfy the Luther–Ives condition exactly, and so there will be a degree of residual metameric error. This means that a linear transformation from the camera raw space to the XYZ colour space can only be defined in an approximate way [14]. The details of this transformation will be given in section 4.3.5. The camera raw space cannot be interpreted as a true colour space unless the Luther–Ives condition is satisfied exactly. The approximate linear transformation from the XYZ space to the camera raw space defines an approximate *raw colour space* with a warped spectral locus [15]. The warped spectral locus may not encompass all of the horseshoe-shaped area defined by the *xy* spectral locus. This in turn reduces the range of visible chromaticities which can be estimated by the camera [15].

4.3.4 Demosaicing methods

A linear transformation can be applied only to *raw pixel vectors* which typically have three or four colour components per photosite. The raw data therefore needs to be demosaiced before an approximate linear transformation can be defined from the camera raw space to a reference colour space such as XYZ.

Conceptually the very simplest demosaicing method is nearest-neighbour bilinear interpolation as illustrated in figure 4.11. In the diagram on the left, only the green pixel component is known at site *i*. The red and blue pixel components R_i and B_i can be calculated in the following way,

$$R_i = (R_1 + R_2)/2$$
$$B_i = (B_1 + B_2)/2.$$

In the diagram in the centre, only the blue pixel component is known at site *j*. The red and green pixel components R_j and G_j can be calculated as

$$R_j = (R_1 + R_2 + R_3 + R_4)/4$$
$$G_j = (G_1 + G_2 + G_3 + G_4)/4.$$

Finally, only the red pixel component is known at site *k* in the diagram on the right. The blue and green pixel components can be calculated as

$$B_k = (B_1 + B_2 + B_3 + B_4)/4$$
$$G_k = (G_1 + G_2 + G_3 + G_4)/4.$$

In other words, the mosaics are treated as three independent images. However, bilinear interpolation generates cyclic pattern noise and zipper patterns along edges because of the cyclic change of direction of the interpolation filter [16, 17].

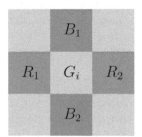 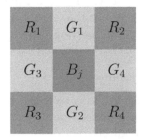 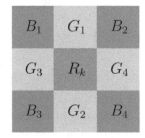

Figure 4.11. Colour demosaicing using nearest-neighbour bilinear interpolation.

Although the demosaicing algorithms used by in-camera image-processing engines are proprietary, a variety of sophisticated demosaicing algorithms have been published in the literature [18]. The freeware raw converter *dcraw* offers the following [17]:

- Halfsize: This method does not carry out an interpolation but instead produces a halfsize image by combining each 2×2 Bayer block into a single raw pixel vector. Because the red and blue photosites are physically separated, this method causes colour fringes to appear along diagonal edges [17].
- Bilinear interpolation: This is used mainly as a first step when applying the variable number of gradients (VNG) algorithm.
- Threshold-based VNG algorithm [19]: This method measures the colour gradients in each of the eight directions around each pixel. Only the gradients closest to zero are used to calculate the missing colour components in order to avoid averaging over sharp edges. Although this method is slow and produces zipper patterns at orthogonal edges, it excels for shapes that do not have well-defined edges such as leaves and feathers [17].
- Patterned pixel grouping (PPG) [20]: This method first fills in the green mosaic using gradients and pattern matching before filling in the red and blue mosaics based on the green. Whenever two interpolation directions are possible, the preferred direction is calculated based on the gradients [17].
- Adaptive homogeneity-directed (AHD) method [21]: This method generates two separate interpolated images which are then combined together. The first image is generated by interpolating the green channel in the horizontal direction and then interpolating the red and blue based on the green, resulting in perfect horizontal edges but ragged vertical edges. Conversely, the second image is generated by interpolating the green channel in the vertical direction and then interpolating the red and blue based on the green, resulting in perfect vertical edges but ragged horizontal edges. The combined image is generated by choosing the most homogeneous image at each pixel location. The homogeneity is measured by converting to the CIE LAB colour space which is perceptually uniform [17].

The AHD method yields the best quality output overall. The only weakness of the AHD method occurs at 45° edges where horizontal and vertical interpolation can fail simultaneously. This is problematic for Fuji® raw files produced by cameras which use the Fuji® X-Trans® CFA. This non-Bayer type of CFA is designed to eliminate the need for an OLPF. Since the raw data contain many 45° edges, *dcraw* instead defaults to the PPG method for Fuji® raw files [17].

4.3.5 Camera colour characterisation

The demosaiced raw data needs to be converted from the camera raw space to a standard output-referred colour space so that an image can be viewed on a standard display. The aim of camera colour characterisation is to determine an approximate linear matrix transformation from the camera raw space to a reference colour space such as XYZ. Conversion from the reference space to an output-referred colour space can similarly be achieved via a matrix transformation as described for sRGB in section 4.4 later.

The transformation from the camera raw space to XYZ can be specified by a transformation matrix $\underline{M}$ applied to every raw pixel vector,

$$\begin{bmatrix} X \\ Y \\ Z \end{bmatrix} = \underline{M} \begin{bmatrix} \mathcal{R} \\ \mathcal{G} \\ \mathcal{B} \end{bmatrix}.$$

As described earlier, if the set of camera response functions satisfy the Luther–Ives condition, this transformation can be defined exactly and the resulting colours will be free from metameric error. Since the Luther–Ives condition is rarely satisfied in practice, the transformation matrix can only be defined in an approximate way.

The ISO 17321-1 standard [22] provides two methods for camera colour characterisation. Method A involves use of a monochromator to directly measure the sensor spectral responsivity functions. Method B involves the use of a standard colour target such as that shown in figure 4.12 and is a practical option for photographers who wish to obtain their own transformation matrix for use with external raw converters. The method described in ISO 17321-1 requires experimental determination of the opto-electronic conversion function (OECF) [23] which defines the nonlinear relationship between sensor-plane irradiance and the output image DOLs. A variation of method B is described below which bypasses determination of the OECF by using non-commercial raw conversion software to obtain a linear demosaiced image in the camera raw space.

Figure 4.12. A typical colour chart which can be used for camera colour characterisation.

Characterisation methodology

1. Take a photograph of a suitable colour chart illuminated by a known standard illuminant according to the conditions detailed in the ISO 17321-1 standard. Since the raw values scale linearly, only their relative values are important. Nevertheless, it is recommended that the f-number and shutter duration are chosen to provide an exposure level within 50%–90% of saturation.

2. Calculate relative XYZ tristimulus values for each patch of the colour chart by normalising Y to the range [0,1] using the white patch as a white reference.

3. Obtain a linear ($\gamma_{\mathrm{E}} = 1$) demosaiced image from the raw data in the *camera raw space* without converting to a standard colour space. Gamma encoding, tone curves and WB must all be *disabled*. (If WB is not disabled, the calculated transformation matrix $\underline{M}$ will incorporate raw WB multipliers. These will be discussed in section 4.5.) Some non-commercial raw converters such as *dcraw* are capable of providing this type of output.

   Next, measure average $\mathcal{R}$, $\mathcal{G}$, $\mathcal{B}$ values for each patch. In particular, the block of pixels over which the average is taken should be at least 64×64 pixels in size. Each patch can then be associated with an appropriate average raw pixel vector.

4. Build a $3 \times n$ matrix $\underline{A}$ which contains the XYZ tristimulus vectors for each patch 1, ..., n as columns,

$$\underline{A} = \begin{bmatrix} X_1 & X_2 & \cdots & X_n \\ Y_1 & Y_2 & \cdots & Y_n \\ Z_1 & Z_2 & \cdots & Z_n \end{bmatrix}.$$

Similarly build a $3 \times n$ matrix $\underline{B}$ which contains the corresponding raw pixel vectors as columns,

$$\underline{B} = \begin{bmatrix} \mathcal{R}_1 & \mathcal{R}_2 & \cdots & \mathcal{R}_n \\ \mathcal{G}_1 & \mathcal{G}_2 & \cdots & \mathcal{G}_n \\ \mathcal{B}_1 & \mathcal{B}_2 & \cdots & \mathcal{B}_n \end{bmatrix}.$$

5. Calculate the 3×3 colour transformation matrix $\underline{M}$ which transforms $\underline{B}$ to $\underline{A}$. Unless the Luther–Ives condition is satisfied exactly, the matrix $\underline{M}$ will only be an approximation,

$$\underline{A} \approx \underline{M}\underline{B}.$$

The simplest method for minimising the error is to use linear least-squares minimisation [24, 25]. This yields the following solution where T denotes the matrix transpose,

$$\underline{M} = \underline{A}\,\underline{B}^T(\underline{B}\,\underline{B}^T)^{-1}.$$

6. Optionally, transform into the perceptually uniform CIE LAB reference colour space and calculate the colour difference ΔE_i between the estimated tristimulus values X_i, Y_i, Z_i and real tristimulus values for each patch. The average digital still camera *sensitivity metamerism index* (DSC/SMI) can be calculated from the set of $\{\Delta E_i\}$. This is a colour error score where 100 corresponds to the Luther–Ives condition being satisfied exactly. Starting with $\underline{M}$ from the previous step, $\{\Delta E_i\}$ can be minimised using a nonlinear optimisation technique. The potential colour error for the final improved $\underline{M}$ is defined by the final DSC/SMI. Full details of this step are described in the ISO 17321-1 standard [22, 24].

7. Scale $\underline{M}$ according to the normalisation required for its practical implementation.

Example normalisations for $\underline{M}$ will be described in sections 4.6 and 4.7. Provided WB was disabled in step 3, $\underline{M}$ can be used with arbitrary scene illumination. However, optimum results will be obtained for scene illumination matching the characterisation illuminant.

4.4 sRGB colour space

Now that a linear transformation has been defined between the camera raw space and the XYZ colour space, a further transformation is needed from XYZ to an output-referred colour space designed for viewing images. The gamut of the sRGB colour space is comparable with that of a standard CRT monitor, and sRGB is the colour space used by the internet. Other output-referred colour spaces such as Adobe® RGB and ProPhoto RGB will be discussed in section 4.8.

Output-referred colour spaces include a type of gamma curve so that the encoded DOLs are nonlinearly related to luminance. As described in chapter 2, the gamma encoding will be compensated for by the display gamma, however the gamma encoding and decoding will prevent posterisation when reducing the bit-depth down to 8 from the greater bit-depth of the raw data.

4.4.1 sRGB gamut

The sRGB colour space standardised by IEC 61966-2-1:1999 [26] is defined by the ITU-R BT.709 primaries which are also used by high-definition television. The xy chromaticity coordinates of the primaries are

$$R: \ (x, y) = (0.64, 0.33)$$
$$G: \ (x, y) = (0.30, 0.60)$$
$$B: \ (x, y) = (0.15, 0.06).$$

These primaries are not pure spectrum colours, and figure 4.13 shows their location on the xy chromaticity diagram. The sRGB colour space is additive with non-negative tristimulus values and so contains the set of chromaticites defined by the coloured triangular region in figure 4.13. Unlike the remainder of the horseshoe area which has been shown in grey, these chromaticities have been shown in colour

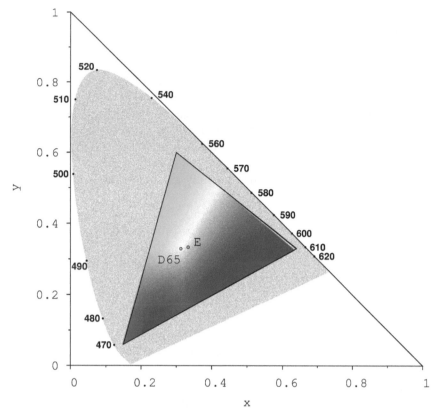

Figure 4.13. The coloured region defined by the ITU-R BT.709 primaries shows the chromaticities represented by the sRGB colour space.

because they can be displayed correctly on a standard-gamut monitor. When transforming to the sRGB colour space, out-of-gamut source colours will be clipped to the edge of the sRGB gamut.

The definition of the sRGB colour space includes a *nonlinear* relationship between the tristimulus values and DOLs in the form of a gamma curve. However, the linear form of the sRGB colour space needs to be defined first.

The linear transformation from XYZ to linear sRGB is specified as

$$
\begin{bmatrix} R_L \\ G_L \\ B_L \end{bmatrix}_{D65} = \underline{M}_{sRGB}^{-1} \begin{bmatrix} X \\ Y \\ Z \end{bmatrix}_{D65}
$$

where

$$
\underline{M}_{sRGB}^{-1} = \begin{bmatrix} 3.2406 & -1.5372 & -0.4986 \\ -0.9689 & 1.8758 & 0.0415 \\ 0.0557 & -0.2040 & 1.0570 \end{bmatrix}.
$$

Relative luminance Y is normalised to the range $[0,1]$, and any resulting R_L, G_L, B_L values lying outside the range $[0,1]$ are clipped to 0 or 1. The reverse transformation is defined by

$$\begin{bmatrix} X \\ Y \\ Z \end{bmatrix}_{D65} = \underline{M}_{sRGB} \begin{bmatrix} R_L \\ G_L \\ B_L \end{bmatrix}_{D65} \tag{4.13}$$

with

$$\underline{M}_{sRGB} = \begin{bmatrix} 0.4124 & 0.3576 & 0.1805 \\ 0.2126 & 0.7152 & 0.0722 \\ 0.0193 & 0.1192 & 0.9565 \end{bmatrix}.$$

The reference white of the sRGB colour space has a chromaticity equivalent to that of D65 illumination. For illumination with a D65 white point, the following unit vector specifies the relative tristimulus values corresponding to a 100% diffuse reflector,

$$\begin{bmatrix} R_L = 1 \\ G_L = 1 \\ B_L = 1 \end{bmatrix}_{D65} = \underline{M}_{sRGB}^{-1} \begin{bmatrix} X(\text{WP}) = & 0.9504 \\ Y(\text{WP}) = & 1 \\ Z(\text{WP}) = & 1.0888 \end{bmatrix}_{D65}.$$

The sRGB colour space is designed to be viewed under D65 illumination, and so colour data obtained under scene illumination with a different white point may not be correctly interpreted by the HVS when transformed from XYZ into sRGB. One way to solve this issue is to first *adapt* the white point of the illumination represented in XYZ to a D65 white point by using a chromatic adaptation transform (CAT), and then applying the transformation $\underline{M}_{sRGB}$. White-balancing and CATs will be described in section 4.5.

4.4.2 sRGB gamma

The final form of the sRGB colour space includes a nonlinear gamma curve applied to the linear tristimulus values. When plotted on standard axes, the curve appears almost identical to the $\gamma_E = 1/2.2$ power law curve shown in figure 2.4 of chapter 2. In fact, there are subtle differences because the γ_E value is not constant. A piecewise gamma curve is applied in the following way:

For R_L, G_L, B_L values $\leqslant 0.0031308$,

$$\begin{aligned} R' &= 12.92 \, R_L \\ G' &= 12.92 \, G_L \\ B' &= 12.92 \, B_L. \end{aligned} \tag{4.14}$$

For R_L, G_L, B_L values > 0.0031308,

$$R' = 1.055 \, R_L^{1/2.4} - 0.055$$
$$G' = 1.055 \, G_L^{1/2.4} - 0.055 \qquad (4.15)$$
$$B' = 1.055 \, B_L^{1/2.4} - 0.055.$$

The R_L, G_L, B_L values must be normalised to the range [0,1] before applying the above transformations. The resulting nonlinear R', G', B' values can be scaled to the range required by the bit-depth of the output file using the scale factor $2^M - 1$, where M is the required bit-depth. For example, an 8-bit JPEG or TIFF file requires scaling of all R', G', B' values to the range [0,255]. This is achieved by multiplying all R', G', B' values by 255 and then quantising to the nearest integer.

The above piecewise gamma curve has a linear portion with constant $\gamma_E = 1$ below 0.0031308 which is present in order to avoid numerical issues close to zero. It is possible to see the differences between the sRGB curve and a standard $\gamma_E = 1/2.2$ curve more clearly by plotting the curves using logarithmic axes. Data plotted on logarithmic axes are not altered numerically but the spacing between axis values changes in a logarithmic fashion. A power law plotted on linear axes appears as a straight line when plotted on logarithmic axes with the gradient of the line equal to the exponent of the power law. Unlike the sRGB curve, the standard $\gamma_E = 1/2.2$ curve appears as a straight line with gradient equal to 1/2.2 as shown in figure 4.14.

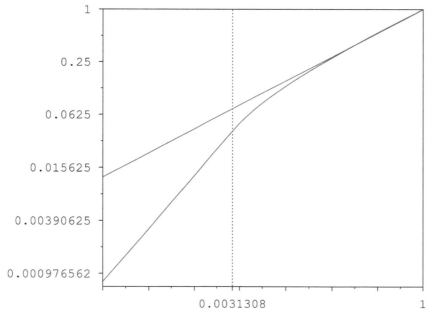

Figure 4.14. A power law gamma curve appears as a straight line when plotted on logarithmic axes. The blue line shows a gamma curve defined by $\gamma_E = 1/2.2$. The digital levels on the x and y axes have been normalised to a maximum value of unity. The standard sRGB curve shown in red has constant gamma only below the value indicated by the vertical dotted line.

In terms of how easily the HVS discerns relative luminance levels, the above nonlinear conversion can be considered an efficient use of 8-bit DOLs to encode the data. As discussed in chapter 2, the effect of the encoding gamma curve must be compensated for by the display gamma γ_D so that the overall input–output luminance relationship is linear. In practice, the overall gamma will be slightly higher than unity in order to compensate for environmental viewing factors such as flare.

4.4.3 sRGB dynamic range

The maximum dynamic range (DR) that can be represented by an output image file with DOLs encoded using the sRGB colour space is generally higher than that from DOLs that are linearly related to luminance. Following the procedure previously described in section 2.1.7 of chapter 2, the maximum representable DR can be calculated by taking the ratio of the highest to lowest non-zero representable relative luminance. For 8-bit output, these are represented by DOL = 255 and 1, where DOL can be R', G', or B'. If the linear data is normalised to the range [0,1] and 8-bit output is obtained by multiplying by 255 and taking the integer part, the relationship between DOL and relative luminance is

$$\frac{1}{255 \times 12.92} \rightarrow \text{DOL} = 1$$
$$1 \rightarrow \text{DOL} = 255.$$

The sRGB gamma curve can therefore encode $\log_2(255 \times 12.92) \approx 11.7$ stops of DR. This may differ depending on the rounding strategy used.

In analogy with the calculation presented in section 2.1.7 of chapter 2, the calculation above assumes that there is negligible spacing between the available input raw levels on a relative luminance axis, in other words an unlimited bit-depth. Nevertheless, 11.7 stops is achievable for 14-bit input data. The figure reduces to 11 and 8 stops for 12-bit and 8-bit input data, respectively, assuming that the integer part is taken when rounding.

If an additional tone curve beyond the gamma curve is applied to the linear data, the representable DR will be altered as discussed in the tone curves section of chapter 2.

4.4.4 sRGB colour cube

The *RGB colour model* uses a three-dimensional Cartesian coordinate system to represent additive RGB colour spaces. The Cartesian axes are defined by the chosen primaries and therefore the RGB vector components,

$$\begin{bmatrix} R \\ G \\ B \end{bmatrix}_{\text{reference}}.$$

When normalised to the range [0,1], the primaries themselves are specified by setting one RGB component to unity and the other two to zero.

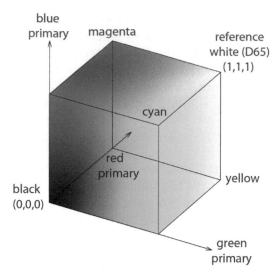

Figure 4.15. sRGB colour cube with DOLs normalised to the range [0,1].

Since the sRGB colour space is additive with non-negative tristimulus values and the vector components clip at the same value, the representable colours take the form of a cube in the RGB colour model. Figure 4.15 shows the sRGB colour cube with DOLs normalised to the range [0,1]. All greyscale colours lie along the diagonal between the origin and the reference white at (1,1,1) which corresponds to the chromaticity of D65 illumination defined by the following unit vector,

$$\begin{bmatrix} R'(\mathrm{WP}) = 1 \\ G'(\mathrm{WP}) = 1 \\ B'(\mathrm{WP}) = 1 \end{bmatrix}_{\mathrm{D65}}.$$

Here R', G', B' are the are DOLs defined by equations (4.14) and (4.15) and are nonlinear *gamma-encoded* values. All colours on the faces of the cube are fully saturated. The red, green, and blue sRGB primaries defined in section 4.4.1 correspond to (0,1,0), (1,0,0), and (0,0,1).

The sRGB triangle on the xy chromaticity diagram shown in figure 4.13 can obtained from the colour cube by inverting the gamma curves applied to the R', G', B' values, converting from linear sRGB to XYZ, and then calculating the xy chromaticity coordinates.

4.5 White balance

Recall that the imaging sensor and the HVS both have their own set of response functions which are in principle related by a linear transformation, as required by the Luther–Ives condition. Unlike the imaging sensor, the HVS naturally *adjusts* its response functions depending on the ambient lighting conditions. Such remarkable characteristics of the HVS include light adaptation, dark adaptation, and chromatic adaptation. Advanced *colour appearance models* aim to describe such characteristics [27]. In photography the most important of these is *chromatic adaptation*.

Chromatic adaptation is a mechanism used by the HVS to adapt to the chromatic conditions so that the chromaticity of any given object appears to remain constant under varying types of illumination. Chromatic adaptation involves an adjustment of the eye cone responses so that the HVS can adjust its perception of the illumination white point. Although the mechanisms for colour constancy are not fully understood, an overly simplistic but useful way of thinking about chromatic adaptation is to assume that the HVS will aim to discount the chromaticity of the illuminant. For example, consider a perfect diffuse reflecting object placed in the scene. Rather than appearing to have the chromaticity of the illumination white point, the object is likely to appear as neutral white. This object may continue to be recognised as being neutral white even if the colour temperature of the ambient illumination changes. The colour stimulus which an observer adapted to the ambient conditions considers to be neutral white (perfectly achromatic with 100% relative luminance) is referred to as the *adapted white* [28].

Since the camera does not naturally adjust its response functions according to the lighting conditions, issues arise when the photographic scene illumination and the viewing illumination do not have the same white point. For example, the photographic scene could be illuminated by candle-light, while the image viewing environment could be daylight. Unless this difference is accounted for, the image will appear to have incorrect *white balance* (WB) because the HVS will discount the chromaticity of the viewing illumination rather than the photographic scene illumination.

The strategy for achieving correct WB in practice is to remove the scene illumination from the image and replace it with the viewing illumination. This is equivalent to adjusting the illumination white point from that of the scene to that of the viewing environment. This can be achieved by using a chromatic adaptation transform (CAT) which is a computational technique for adjusting the white point of a given SPD. It achieves this goal by mimicking the chromatic adaptation mechanism used by the HVS. In the present context, knowledge of both the photographic scene and viewing illumination white points is required. In practice, these are estimated in the following way:

- The photographer can specify the white point of the scene illumination by using a preset WB corresponding to the ambient lighting conditions. A more accurate method is to take a photograph of a diffuse reflecting card under the scene illumination to determine the white point, although this is not always practical. Alternatively, the camera can estimate the scene illumination white point if the auto-WB function is selected. In all cases, the camera estimate for the scene illumination white point is known as the *adopted white* (AW). The AW will be discussed in the section below.

- A standard viewing illumination white point is chosen which is considered to be most generally representative of actual image viewing conditions. This typically corresponds to the reference white of the output colour space.

The situation is complicated by the fact that the raw data is represented using the camera raw space, whereas the viewed output image is represented by the output colour space. White-balancing is therefore an integral part of the linear transformation of colours from the camera raw space to the output colour space, and must be performed before gamma-encoding or any other nonlinear transformations are applied.

An example of incorrect WB is shown in figure 4.16. Remembering that a black body appears red at *low* colour temperatures and blue at *high* colour temperatures, the upper image assumes a scene-illumination CCT lower than the true value. Consequently, the image appears to be bluer or colder than expected. Conversely, the lower image assumes a scene-illumination CCT higher than the true value, and so the image appears to be redder or warmer than expected.

Before discussing practical strategies for white-balancing, it is useful to first discuss the AW along with some important types of CAT.

4.5.1 Adopted white

The adopted white (AW) [28] or *camera neutral* [29] is the colour in the photographic scene that the camera considers to be neutral white (perfectly achromatic with 100% relative luminance). Assuming that this is identical to the scene illumination white point, the simplest approach for determining the AW would be to estimate the colour of the light reflected from a 100% diffuse reflecting object in the scene.

As mentioned above, the photographer can manually specify an AW by selecting a camera manual WB setting or by taking a photo of a diffuse reflecting card placed in the photographic scene. If the camera auto-WB function is enabled, proprietary methods will be used to automatically determine an appropriate AW, typically by analysing the raw data. The simplest approach is the 'grey world' method which assumes that the average of the scene colours will turn out to be achromatic, however practical algorithms are much more sophisticated. The outcome will be three (or four) values labelled here as $\mathcal{R}(AW)$, $\mathcal{G}(AW)$, $\mathcal{B}(AW)$. Since the green channel contains the majority of the luminance information and is typically the first to saturate, the AW is usually normalised so that $\mathcal{G}(AW) = 1$ with $\mathcal{R}(AW)$, $\mathcal{B}(AW) < 1$.

Mathematically, the AW can be represented by a vector derived from the above values. Note that this is not a true raw pixel vector since the colour demosaic has not yet been performed at this stage. Nevertheless, the colour transformation matrix $\underline{M}$ obtained through camera colour characterisation can be used to express the AW in the XYZ colour space,

$$\begin{bmatrix} X(AW) \\ Y(AW) \\ Z(AW) \end{bmatrix}_{\text{scene}} = \underline{M} \begin{bmatrix} \mathcal{R}(AW) \\ \mathcal{G}(AW) \\ \mathcal{B}(AW). \end{bmatrix}_{\text{scene}}$$

The corresponding chromaticity coordinates (x,y) can be related to a CCT and tint according to the methods described in section 4.2.2 earlier.

Figure 4.16. Due to the abundance of white objects in the scene, the camera has been able to accurately determine correct WB by analysing the raw data, as shown in the middle image. The upper and lower images show raw conversions using lower and higher scene colour temperatures, respectively.

4.5.2 Chromatic adaptation transforms

Before discussing practical strategies for white-balancing, this section introduces some important CATs. A simple adjustment of the illumination white point in the XYZ colour space is demonstrated. The example chosen is for an illumination white point adjustment from that of D50 illumination to that of D65 illumination.

(1) von-Kries transform

Back in 1902, von-Kries postulated that the chromatic adaptation mechanism of the HVS could be modelled as an automatic gain control of the eye cone responses. In other words, the responses of the three types of cone receptors are simply scaled in order to minimise the effect of any chromatic changes in viewing illumination. Moreover, the magnitude of the scaling factors for each type of cone are assumed to be *independent*. This means that LMS tristimulus values will scale independently according to the chromatic properties of the illumination, and the scale factors can be represented as a diagonal matrix in LMS space.

The von-Kries hypothesis can be used as a basis for a CAT which can in principle be used to adapt the illumination white point from one value to another. As an illustrative example, consider the use of a von-Kries transform to adapt the white point of illumination represented in the XYZ colour space from that of D50 to that of D65 illumination. This can be accomplished in the following way,

$$
\begin{bmatrix} X \\ Y \\ Z \end{bmatrix}_{D65} = M_{vK}^{-1} \begin{bmatrix} \dfrac{L(D65)}{L(D50)} & 0 & 0 \\ 0 & \dfrac{M(D65)}{M(D50)} & 0 \\ 0 & 0 & \dfrac{S(D65)}{S(D50)} \end{bmatrix} M_{vK} \begin{bmatrix} X \\ Y \\ Z \end{bmatrix}_{D50}.
$$

First, the matrix M_{vK} transforms each pixel specified by a vector in XYZ space into LMS cone space. Its modern form is the Hunt–Pointer–Estevez transformation matrix [27] defined as

$$
M_{vK} = \begin{bmatrix} 0.38971 & 0.68898 & -0.07868 \\ -0.22981 & 1.18340 & 0.04641 \\ 0.00000 & 0.00000 & 1.00000 \end{bmatrix}.
$$

Subsequently a diagonal matrix divides out the chromaticity of D50 illumination assuming $Y = 1$, and multiplies in the chromaticity of D65 illumination. Then the inverse of M_{vK} transforms from the LMS cone space back into XYZ. The diagonal components of the scaling matrix can be obtained from the XYZ vectors for D50 and D65 illumination listed in table 4.1 expressed in LMS cone space,

$$\begin{bmatrix} L(\text{D50}) \\ M(\text{D50}) \\ S(\text{D50}) \end{bmatrix}_{\text{D50}} = \underline{M}_{\text{vK}} \begin{bmatrix} X(\text{D50}) = 0.9642 \\ Y(\text{D50}) = 1.0000 \\ Z(\text{D50}) = 0.8252 \end{bmatrix}_{\text{D50}} \qquad (4.16a)$$

$$\begin{bmatrix} L(\text{D65}) \\ M(\text{D65}) \\ S(\text{D65}) \end{bmatrix}_{\text{D65}} = \underline{M}_{\text{vK}} \begin{bmatrix} X(\text{D65}) = 0.9504 \\ Y(\text{D65}) = 1.0000 \\ Z(\text{D65}) = 1.0888 \end{bmatrix}_{\text{D65}} . \qquad (4.16b)$$

(2) Bradford transform

The Bradford CAT [30] uses a narrow or 'sharpened' $\rho\gamma\beta$ cone space which does not match that of the HVS but yields improved results compared to the von-Kries transform. The model is able to account for partial adaptation and includes a small nonlinearity. A simplified and linearised version of the Bradford CAT is recommended by the ICC [31]. This can be viewed as a modified von-Kries transform with transformation matrix defined by

$$\underline{M}_{\text{BFD}} = \begin{bmatrix} 0.8951 & 0.2664 & -0.1614 \\ -0.7502 & 1.7135 & 0.0367 \\ 0.0389 & -0.0685 & 1.0296 \end{bmatrix}.$$

The example D50 to D65 white-point adaptation in the **XYZ** colour space is defined as

$$\begin{bmatrix} X \\ Y \\ Z \end{bmatrix}_{\text{D65}} = \underline{M}_{\text{BFD}}^{-1} \begin{bmatrix} \dfrac{\rho(\text{D65})}{\rho(\text{D50})} & 0 & 0 \\ 0 & \dfrac{\gamma(\text{D65})}{\gamma(\text{D50})} & 0 \\ 0 & 0 & \dfrac{\beta(\text{D65})}{\beta(\text{D50})} \end{bmatrix} \underline{M}_{\text{BFD}} \begin{bmatrix} X \\ Y \\ Z \end{bmatrix}_{\text{D50}} . \qquad (4.17)$$

Here ρ, γ, β denote values in the sharpened cone space. The diagonal components of the scaling matrix are obtained in a similar fashion to equation (4.16) with $\underline{M}_{\text{BFD}}$ replacing $\underline{M}_{\text{vK}}$,

$$\begin{bmatrix} \rho(\text{D50}) \\ \gamma(\text{D50}) \\ \beta(\text{D50}) \end{bmatrix}_{\text{D50}} = \underline{M}_{\text{BFD}} \begin{bmatrix} X(\text{D50}) = 0.9642 \\ Y(\text{D50}) = 1.0000 \\ Z(\text{D50}) = 0.8249 \end{bmatrix}_{\text{D50}}$$

$$\begin{bmatrix} \rho(\text{D65}) \\ \gamma(\text{D65}) \\ \beta(\text{D65}) \end{bmatrix}_{\text{D65}} = \underline{M}_{\text{BFD}} \begin{bmatrix} X(\text{D65}) = 0.9504 \\ Y(\text{D65}) = 1.0000 \\ Z(\text{D65}) = 1.0888 \end{bmatrix}_{\text{D65}} .$$

(3) XYZ scaling

Although less effective in practice, a simplified CAT can be defined by scaling the XYZ components directly in the XYZ colour space without transforming into an intermediate cone space.

Using the same example as above, the chromaticity of D50 illumination can be divided out in the following way:

$$
\begin{bmatrix} X \\ Y \\ Z \end{bmatrix}_{\text{reference}} = \begin{bmatrix} \dfrac{1}{X(\text{D50})} & 0 & 0 \\ 0 & \dfrac{1}{Y(\text{D50})} & 0 \\ 0 & 0 & \dfrac{1}{Z(\text{D50})} \end{bmatrix} \begin{bmatrix} X \\ Y \\ Z \end{bmatrix}_{\text{D50}}. \tag{4.18}
$$

Here the diagonal multipliers are obtained from the D50 white point vector,

$$
\begin{bmatrix} X(\text{D50}) \\ Y(\text{D50}) \\ Z(\text{D50}) \end{bmatrix}_{\text{D50}} = \begin{bmatrix} 0.9642 \\ 1 \\ 0.8252 \end{bmatrix}.
$$

More precisely, a diagonal matrix can be formed from the vector components. The diagonal multipliers are the diagonal elements of the inverse of this matrix. This changes the illumination white point from that of D50 illumination to that of the *reference white* of the XYZ colour space specified by the unit vector. This becomes clear when equation (4.18) is applied to the D50 white-point vector itself,

$$
\begin{bmatrix} X = 1 \\ Y = 1 \\ Z = 1 \end{bmatrix}_{\text{reference}} = \begin{bmatrix} \dfrac{1}{X(\text{D50})} & 0 & 0 \\ 0 & \dfrac{1}{Y(\text{D50})} & 0 \\ 0 & 0 & \dfrac{1}{Z(\text{D50})} \end{bmatrix} \begin{bmatrix} X(\text{D50}) \\ Y(\text{D50}) \\ Z(\text{D50}) \end{bmatrix}_{\text{D50}}.
$$

The reference white of the XYZ colour space is illuminant E.

The chromaticity of D50 illumination can now be multiplied in by using the following diagonal matrix:

$$
\begin{bmatrix} X \\ Y \\ Z \end{bmatrix}_{\text{D65}} = \begin{bmatrix} X(\text{D65}) & 0 & 0 \\ 0 & Y(\text{D65}) & 0 \\ 0 & 0 & Z(\text{D65}) \end{bmatrix} \begin{bmatrix} X \\ Y \\ Z \end{bmatrix}_{\text{reference}}. \tag{4.19}
$$

The diagonal scaling components are obtained from the D65 white point vector,

$$\begin{bmatrix} X(\text{D65}) \\ Y(\text{D65}) \\ Z(\text{D65}) \end{bmatrix}_{\text{D65}} = \begin{bmatrix} 0.9504 \\ 1 \\ 1.0888 \end{bmatrix}.$$

The full CAT can be specified by substituting equation (4.18) into equation (4.19),

$$\begin{bmatrix} X \\ Y \\ Z \end{bmatrix}_{\text{D65}} = \begin{bmatrix} \dfrac{X(\text{D65})}{X(\text{D50})} & 0 & 0 \\ 0 & \dfrac{Y(\text{D65})}{Y(\text{D50})} & 0 \\ 0 & 0 & \dfrac{Z(\text{D65})}{Z(\text{D50})} \end{bmatrix} \begin{bmatrix} X \\ Y \\ Z \end{bmatrix}_{\text{D50}}. \tag{4.20}$$

Chromatic adaptation through XYZ scaling is not as effective as the von-Kries or Bradford methods in practice. A likely explanation is that the latter methods perform scaling in an intermediate space based on physical eye cones and their associated reference white. On the other hand, the reference white of the XYZ colour space is illuminant E and this is purely a mathematical construct [17].

4.5.3 White balance strategies

The introduction to this section described how the white-balancing operation requires an illumination white-point adjustment from that of the photographic scene illumination in the camera raw space to that of the image viewing illumination in the output colour space. In practice, white-balancing is an integral part of the overall colour conversion from the camera raw space into a device-independent colour space such as XYZ or sRGB. Two possible example approaches to the problem are described in this section.

The first approach involves use of a conventional colour transformation matrix and a CAT, and is the type of approach typically described in academic literature. The second approach involves the use of so-called *raw WB multipliers* together with a *colour rotation matrix*. This is the type of approach often used by in-camera image-processing engines. It is also used by the raw converter *dcraw*.

(a) Transformation matrix + CAT
First, a colour transformation matrix is used to convert the demosaiced raw colours from the camera raw space into XYZ,

$$\begin{bmatrix} X \\ Y \\ Z \end{bmatrix}_{\text{scene}} = \underline{M} \begin{bmatrix} \mathcal{R} \\ \mathcal{G} \\ \mathcal{B} \end{bmatrix}_{\text{scene}}. \tag{4.21}$$

Subsequently, a CAT is used to move into an intermediate cone space where the chromaticity of the scene illumination is divided out and the chromaticity of the image viewing illumination is multiplied in. The vector is then transformed back into XYZ. Mathematically,

$$\begin{bmatrix} X \\ Y \\ Z \end{bmatrix}_{\text{D65}} = M_{\text{BFD}}^{-1} \begin{bmatrix} \dfrac{\rho(\text{D65})}{\rho(\text{AW})} & 0 & 0 \\ 0 & \dfrac{\gamma(\text{D65})}{\gamma(\text{AW})} & 0 \\ 0 & 0 & \dfrac{\beta(\text{D65})}{\beta(\text{AW})} \end{bmatrix} M_{\text{BFD}} \begin{bmatrix} X \\ Y \\ Z \end{bmatrix}_{\text{scene}}.$$

The Bradford CAT has been used in this example, and it has been assumed that the image viewing illumination has a D65 white point. The diagonal components of the scaling matrix in the sharpened cone space are obtained from the following vectors,

$$\begin{bmatrix} \rho(\text{D65}) \\ \gamma(\text{D65}) \\ \beta(\text{D65}) \end{bmatrix}_{\text{D65}} = M_{\text{BFD}} \begin{bmatrix} X(\text{D65}) = 0.9504 \\ Y(\text{D65}) = 1.0000 \\ Z(\text{D65}) = 1.0888 \end{bmatrix}_{\text{D65}}$$

$$\begin{bmatrix} \rho(\text{AW}) \\ \gamma(\text{AW}) \\ \beta(\text{AW}) \end{bmatrix}_{\text{scene}} = M_{\text{BFD}} \begin{bmatrix} X(\text{AW}) \\ Y(\text{AW}) \\ Z(\text{AW}) \end{bmatrix}_{\text{scene}}.$$

The AW is the estimate of the scene illumination white point provided by the camera. If the AW is specified in terms of chromaticity coordinates (x, y), the above vector assumes $Y(\text{AW}) = 1$.

A practical example of the above type of approach is Method 1 of the Digital Negative (DNG) open-source raw format developed by Adobe®. Full details are given in section 4.6.1.

(b) Raw WB multipliers + rotation/forward matrix
A type of CAT similar in principle to XYZ scaling can be defined that is only applicable to the camera raw space. This can be used to divide out the chromaticity of the scene illumination from the raw data,

$$\begin{bmatrix} \mathcal{R} \\ \mathcal{G} \\ \mathcal{B} \end{bmatrix}_{\text{reference}} = \begin{bmatrix} \dfrac{1}{\mathcal{R}(\text{AW})} & 0 & 0 \\ 0 & \dfrac{1}{\mathcal{G}(\text{AW})} & 0 \\ 0 & 0 & \dfrac{1}{\mathcal{B}(\text{AW})} \end{bmatrix} \begin{bmatrix} \mathcal{R} \\ \mathcal{G} \\ \mathcal{B} \end{bmatrix}_{\text{scene}}. \tag{4.22}$$

The diagonal multipliers are known as *raw WB multipliers* and these can be obtained from the AW calculated by the camera. The raw WB multipliers adapt the illumination white point to that of the *camera raw space reference white*. This becomes clear when considering the above equation for the specific case of the AW vector itself,

$$
\begin{bmatrix} \mathcal{R} = 1 \\ \mathcal{G} = 1 \\ \mathcal{B} = 1 \end{bmatrix}_{\text{reference}} = \begin{bmatrix} \dfrac{1}{\mathcal{R}(\text{AW})} & 0 & 0 \\[2mm] 0 & \dfrac{1}{\mathcal{G}(\text{AW})} & 0 \\[2mm] 0 & 0 & \dfrac{1}{\mathcal{B}(\text{AW})} \end{bmatrix} \begin{bmatrix} \mathcal{R}(\text{AW}) \\ \mathcal{G}(\text{AW}) \\ \mathcal{B}(\text{AW}) \end{bmatrix}_{\text{scene}} . \tag{4.23}
$$

The raw WB multipliers can be applied directly to the raw channels *before* the colour demosaic. This is known as *raw channel equalisation* and it results in a demosaic of better quality [17]. The multipliers can be stored in the raw metadata for use by the camera image-processing engine or by an external raw converter. The components of the 'vectors' above denote pixel values belonging to a given mosaic and are not true raw pixel vectors.

After raw channel equalisation, the colour demosaic can be performed. However, only the initial part of the overall white-balancing operation has been achieved because the chromaticity of the viewing illumination has not yet been included. The viewing illumination is *not* included by applying further multipliers in the camera raw space. Instead, the viewing illumination is included as part of a direct matrix transformation from the camera raw space to the output colour space. Clearly, this matrix is not a standard colour transformation matrix such as that used by equation (4.21) of approach (a) above. Two possibilities are *rotation* and *forward* matrices:

1. Many in-camera image-processing engines, along with the raw converter *dcraw*, use a *colour rotation matrix*. Typically this matrix will transform from the camera raw space directly to the linear form of the output RGB colour space. A rotation matrix has the property that each row sums to unity. This means that a rotation matrix can map the reference white of the camera raw space directly to the *reference white* of the output colour space. For example, the sRGB colour space has a D65 reference white, in which case the rotation matrix $\underline{M}_{\text{R}}$ performs the following mapping,

$$
\begin{bmatrix} R_{\text{L}} = 1 \\ G_{\text{L}} = 1 \\ B_{\text{L}} = 1 \end{bmatrix}_{\text{D65}} = \underline{M}_{\text{R}} \begin{bmatrix} \mathcal{R} = 1 \\ \mathcal{G} = 1 \\ \mathcal{B} = 1 \end{bmatrix}_{\text{reference}} . \tag{4.24}
$$

Here R_{L}, G_{L}, B_{L} denote the tristimulus values of the linear sRGB colour space. The combination of the appropriate raw WB multipliers together with the rotation matrix applied to the raw data ensures overall WB for D65 viewing illumination in this example. Mathematically, this can be seen by combining equations (4.23) and (4.24),

$$
\begin{bmatrix} R_{\text{L}} = 1 \\ G_{\text{L}} = 1 \\ B_{\text{L}} = 1 \end{bmatrix}_{\text{D65}} = \underline{M}_{\text{R}} \begin{bmatrix} \dfrac{1}{\mathcal{R}(\text{AW})} & 0 & 0 \\[2mm] 0 & \dfrac{1}{\mathcal{G}(\text{AW})} & 0 \\[2mm] 0 & 0 & \dfrac{1}{\mathcal{B}(\text{AW})} \end{bmatrix} \begin{bmatrix} \mathcal{R}(\text{AW}) \\ \mathcal{G}(\text{AW}) \\ \mathcal{B}(\text{AW}) \end{bmatrix}_{\text{scene}} .
$$

This approach to white-balancing is computationally efficient, and furthermore is found to work better in practice compared to approach (a). Further details of this approach are given in section 4.7 in the context of the *dcraw* raw converter.

2. Adobe® have defined a *forward matrix* for use with Method 2 of the DNG open raw image format [29]. The DNG format uses the PCS as its output colour space, which is based on the XYZ colour space with a D50 white point. The PCS is not an output-referred colour space intended for viewing images, and D50 is not the reference white (which is illuminant E). Consequently, the required matrix will not have rows which sum to unity and so a rotation matrix cannot perform the required mapping. Instead, a forward matrix is introduced which maps directly from the camera raw space reference white to the PCS. Full details of this approach are given in section 4.6.2.

4.6 Example 1: Adobe® DNG (raw to XYZ D50)

The DNG file format is an open-source raw format developed by Adobe® [29]. The freely available Adobe® DNG Converter is not a raw converter which produces an output image, but rather it is provided to enable raw files to be converted into the open source DNG raw format. As such, the colour-processing model used by the DNG Converter must provide appropriate transformation matrices along with a strategy for white-balancing. In fact, the Adobe® DNG specification [29] provides two different methods, referred to here as method 1 and method 2. In both cases, the colour-processing model outputs to the PCS based on the XYZ reference colour space with a D50 illumination white point.

This section provides detailed derivations of the two methods provided by the DNG specification. The following notation will be used:

M	Colour transformation matrix as defined in section 4.3.5
ColorMatrix1	Colour transformation matrix by Adobe® for low-temperature characterisation illuminant (maps in opposite direction to M)
ColorMatrix2	Colour transformation matrix by Adobe® for high-temperature characterisation illuminant (maps in opposite direction to M)
C	Colour transformation matrix interpolated from ColorMatrix1 and ColorMatrix2
ForwardMatrix1	Forward matrix by Adobe® for low-temperature characterisation illuminant
ForwardMatrix2	Forward matrix by Adobe® for high-temperature characterisation illuminant
F	Forward matrix interpolated from ForwardMatrix1 and ForwardMatrix2
D	Diagonal WB matrix containing raw WB multipliers
$\begin{bmatrix} \mathcal{R} \\ \mathcal{G} \\ \mathcal{B} \end{bmatrix}$	Camera raw space vector

Although not considered in this section, the DNG specification provides tags to take into account cases where part of the white-balancing operation is achieved through *analog* adjustment of channel gains prior to analog-to-digital conversion.

The values in the linear camera raw space ($\mathcal{RGB}$) are scaled to the range [0,1] after subtracting the black level on a per-pixel basis. Similarly, the XYZ vectors are based on relative colourimetry with Y normalised to the range [0,1].

4.6.1 Method 1 (transformation matrix + CAT)

Tags are provided for two colour transformation matrices ColorMatrix1 and ColorMatrix2. The first should be obtained by characterisation using a low colour-temperature illuminant such as illuminant A, and the second is for a high colour-temperature illuminant such as D65. Both of these matrices are obtained with the camera digital WB *disabled* and map colours from the XYZ colour space directly to the camera raw space,

$$
\begin{bmatrix} \mathcal{R} \\ \mathcal{G} \\ \mathcal{B} \end{bmatrix}_{(1)} = \underline{\text{ColorMatrix1}} \begin{bmatrix} X \\ Y \\ Z \end{bmatrix}_{(1)}
$$
$$
\begin{bmatrix} \mathcal{R} \\ \mathcal{G} \\ \mathcal{B} \end{bmatrix}_{(2)} = \underline{\text{ColorMatrix2}} \begin{bmatrix} X \\ Y \\ Z \end{bmatrix}_{(2)} .
$$

$$(4.25)$$

Here (1) and (2) denote the first and second characterisation illuminants, respectively. The mapping is in the reverse direction to the mapping defined by the transformation matrix of section 4.3.5. This allows the clipping points to be determined for highlight recovery logic based on the white point [29].

(i) Characterisation interpolation
It is only necessary to include one of ColorMatrix1 and ColorMatrix2. However, if only one matrix is included then the transformation from the camera raw space to the XYZ colour space will be *optimum* only if the CCT of the scene illumination happens to match that of characterisation illuminant (1) or (2), respectively.

If both ColorMatrix1 and ColorMatrix2 are available, a third matrix $\underline{C}$ can be calculated which is optimised for use with arbitrary scene illumination. In particular, $\underline{C}$ can be optimised for scene illumination with a white-point estimate given by the AW. This matrix can be calculated by interpolating between ColorMatrix1 and ColorMatrix2 based on the scene illumination CCT estimate denoted by CCT(AW), together with the CCTs associated with each of the two characterisation illuminants denoted by CCT(1) and CCT(2), respectively, with CCT(1) < CCT(2).

After the interpolation has been performed, the transformation from XYZ to the camera raw space can be written

$$\begin{bmatrix} \mathcal{R} \\ \mathcal{G} \\ \mathcal{B} \end{bmatrix}_{\text{scene}} = \underline{C} \begin{bmatrix} X \\ Y \\ Z \end{bmatrix}_{\text{scene}}. \qquad (4.26)$$

For completeness, the interpolation algorithm is described below.

(ii) Interpolation algorithm
The interpolation procedure for determining $\underline{C}$ is complicated by the fact that the AW is known in terms of raw values provided by the camera rather than XYZ values,

$$\begin{bmatrix} \mathcal{R}(\text{AW}) \\ \mathcal{G}(\text{AW}) \\ \mathcal{B}(\text{AW}) \end{bmatrix}_{\text{scene}}. \qquad (4.27)$$

Finding the corresponding CCT(AW) requires converting to XYZ and then to the 1960 UCS colour space via a matrix transformation $\underline{C}$ which itself depends upon the unknown CCT(AW). This problem can be solved using a self-consistent iteration procedure:

1. Make a guess for the AW chromaticity, $(x(\text{AW}), y(\text{AW}))$. For example, the chromaticity corresponding to one of the characterisation illuminants could be used.
2. Convert the xy chromaticity coordinates $(x(\text{AW}), y(\text{AW}))$ to the corresponding uv coordinates $(u(\text{AW}), v(\text{AW}))$ of the 1960 UCS colour space using equation (4.12) of section 4.2.2.
3. Use Robertson's method [8] or an approximate formula [9, 10] as described previously in section 4.2.2 to determine a guess for CCT(AW).
4. Calculate the interpolation weighting factor g according to

$$g = \frac{\dfrac{1}{\text{CCT(AW)}} - \dfrac{1}{\text{CCT(2)}}}{\dfrac{1}{\text{CCT(1)}} - \dfrac{1}{\text{CCT(2)}}}. \qquad (4.28)$$

5. Calculate the interpolated colour transformation matrix $\underline{C}$ according to

$$\underline{C} = g \text{ ColorMatrix1} + (1 - g)\text{ColorMatrix2}. \qquad (4.29)$$

6. Use the inverse of $\underline{C}$ to transform the raw vector (4.27) to XYZ, and then calculate a new guess for $(x(\text{AW}), y(\text{AW}))$ by applying equation (4.9).
7. Repeat the procedure until $(x(\text{AW}), y(\text{AW}))$ and CCT(AW) converge to a stable solution.

If CCT(AW) < CCT(1) or if only ColorMatrix1 is provided, then $\underline{C}$ is set equal to ColorMatrix1. Similarly, if CCT(AW) > CCT(2) or if only ColorMatrix2 is provided, then $\underline{C}$ is set equal to ColorMatrix2.

(iii) White-point adaptation

In order to achieve overall WB, the white point needs to be adapted from the AW in the camera raw space to the white point of the assumed viewing illumination in the output colour space. Recall that method 1 outputs to the PCS, which is based on the XYZ colour space with a D50 illumination white point.

Since the mapping is in the reverse direction, the PCS white point first needs to be adapted to the AW value expressed as an XYZ vector. This can be achieved by using a CAT,

$$
\begin{bmatrix} X \\ Y \\ Z \end{bmatrix}_{\text{scene}} = \underline{\text{CAT}} \begin{bmatrix} X \\ Y \\ Z \end{bmatrix}_{\text{D50}} . \tag{4.30}
$$

The Bradford CAT is recommended by the ICC,

$$
\underline{\text{CAT}} = \underline{M}_{\text{BFD}}^{-1} \begin{bmatrix} \dfrac{\rho(\text{AW})}{\rho(\text{D50})} & 0 & 0 \\[2ex] 0 & \dfrac{\gamma(\text{AW})}{\gamma(\text{D50})} & 0 \\[2ex] 0 & 0 & \dfrac{\beta(\text{AW})}{\beta(\text{D50})} \end{bmatrix} \underline{M}_{\text{BFD}} \tag{4.31}
$$

where

$$
\begin{bmatrix} \rho(\text{D50}) \\ \gamma(\text{D50}) \\ \beta(\text{D50}) \end{bmatrix} = \underline{M}_{\text{BFD}} \begin{bmatrix} X(\text{WP}) = 0.9642 \\ Y(\text{WP}) = 1.0000 \\ Z(\text{WP}) = 0.8249 \end{bmatrix}_{\text{D50}}
$$
$$
\begin{bmatrix} \rho(\text{AW}) \\ \gamma(\text{AW}) \\ \beta(\text{AW}) \end{bmatrix} = \underline{M}_{\text{BFD}} \begin{bmatrix} X(\text{AW}) \\ Y(\text{AW}) \\ Z(\text{AW}) \end{bmatrix}_{\text{scene}} . \tag{4.32}
$$

Subsequently, the transformation from the PCS to the camera raw space with the AW as the illumination white point is given by substituting equation (4.30) into equation (4.26),

$$
\begin{bmatrix} \mathcal{R} \\ \mathcal{G} \\ \mathcal{B} \end{bmatrix}_{\text{scene}} = \underline{C} \, \underline{\text{CAT}} \begin{bmatrix} X \\ Y \\ Z \end{bmatrix}_{\text{D50}} . \tag{4.33}
$$

Finally, this transformation needs to be normalised in order to be applied in practice.

(iv) Normalisation

Consider equation (4.33) for the specific case of the D50 white-point vector in the PCS transformed to the AW vector in the camera raw space,

$$\begin{bmatrix} \mathcal{R}(\mathrm{AW}) \\ \mathcal{G}(\mathrm{AW}) \\ \mathcal{B}(\mathrm{AW}) \end{bmatrix}_{\mathrm{scene}} = \underline{C} \ \underline{\mathrm{CAT}} \begin{bmatrix} X(\mathrm{WP}) \\ Y(\mathrm{WP}) \\ Z(\mathrm{WP}) \end{bmatrix}_{\mathrm{D50}} . \tag{4.34}$$

Let the maximum entry of the resulting AW vector be denoted by s,

$$s = \max \left\{ \underline{C} \ \underline{\mathrm{CAT}} \begin{bmatrix} X(\mathrm{WP}) \\ Y(\mathrm{WP}) \\ Z(\mathrm{WP}) \end{bmatrix}_{\mathrm{D50}} \right\} .$$

Now dividing equation (4.33) by s normalises the maximum of $\mathcal{R}(\mathrm{AW})$, $\mathcal{G}(\mathrm{AW})$, $\mathcal{B}(\mathrm{AW})$ to unity. Since the green channel is usually the first to saturate, this typically yields the following normalisation,

$$\begin{bmatrix} \mathcal{R}(\mathrm{AW}) \\ 1 \\ \mathcal{B}(\mathrm{AW}) \end{bmatrix}_{\mathrm{scene}} = \frac{1}{s} \ \underline{C} \ \underline{\mathrm{CAT}} \begin{bmatrix} X(\mathrm{WP}) \\ Y(\mathrm{WP}) \\ Z(\mathrm{WP}) \end{bmatrix}_{\mathrm{D50}} .$$

This ensures that the PCS white-point vector is mapped to the raw saturation point under the scene illumination. Equation (4.33) can now be replaced so that the normalisation is applied to every pixel,

$$\boxed{ \begin{bmatrix} \mathcal{R} \\ \mathcal{G} \\ \mathcal{B} \end{bmatrix}_{\mathrm{scene}} = \frac{1}{s} \ \underline{C} \ \underline{\mathrm{CAT}} \begin{bmatrix} X \\ Y \\ Z \end{bmatrix}_{\mathrm{D50}} . } \tag{4.35}$$

Summary

In conclusion, it should be evident that the full method 1 transformation in the forward direction from the camera raw space to the PCS can be expressed by inverting the mapping defined by equation (4.35),

$$\boxed{ \begin{bmatrix} X \\ Y \\ Z \end{bmatrix}_{\mathrm{D50}} = s \ \underline{\mathrm{CAT}}^{-1} \underline{C}^{-1} \begin{bmatrix} \mathcal{R} \\ \mathcal{G} \\ \mathcal{B} \end{bmatrix}_{\mathrm{scene}} . }$$

1. The interpolated transformation matrix inverse $\underline{C}^{-1}$ transforms from the camera raw space to XYZ. This transformation is optimised according to the nature of the scene illumination.
2. The CAT inverse $\underline{\mathrm{CAT}}^{-1}$ obtained from equation (4.31) adapts the illumination white point from the AW to D50 in XYZ space.

3. The normalisation factor s ensures that the raw saturation point is mapped to the PCS white-point vector under the scene illumination.

4.6.2 Method 2 (raw WB multipliers + forward matrix)

Method 2 uses raw WB multipliers together with two so-called *forward matrices* labelled ForwardMatrix1 and ForwardMatrix2. These matrices are obtained from low and high CCT camera characterisations, respectively. However, they differ from ColorMatrix1 and ColorMatrix2 in several ways:

1. The forward matrices map in the direction from the camera raw space to the XYZ colour space. This is in the opposite direction to the mapping defined by ColorMatrix1 and ColorMatrix2.
2. The forward matrices are colour transformation matrices obtained from camera characterisation performed with the appropriate in-camera WB *enabled*.
3. The forward matrices additionally have a CAT built into them in order to map the illumination white point in the XYZ colour space from that of the characterisation illuminant to that of D50 illumination.

Although the derivation of method 2 is much more complex than method 1, the final equations are straightforward and easier to apply in practice.

(i) Raw WB multipliers
Since the characterisation is performed with the appropriate camera WB setting enabled, the camera applies a diagonal WB matrix $\underline{D}$ directly to the raw channels to divide out the chromaticity of the calibration illuminant. This adapts the white point of the illumination to the reference white of the camera raw space,

$$\begin{bmatrix} \mathcal{R} \\ \mathcal{G} \\ \mathcal{B} \end{bmatrix}_{\text{reference}} = \underline{D}_{(1)} \begin{bmatrix} \mathcal{R} \\ \mathcal{G} \\ \mathcal{B} \end{bmatrix}_{(1)} \tag{4.36a}$$

$$\begin{bmatrix} \mathcal{R} \\ \mathcal{G} \\ \mathcal{B} \end{bmatrix}_{\text{reference}} = \underline{D}_{(2)} \begin{bmatrix} \mathcal{R} \\ \mathcal{G} \\ \mathcal{B} \end{bmatrix}_{(2)} . \tag{4.36b}$$

The diagonal elements of the WB matrix are the raw WB multipliers calculated by the camera,

$$\underline{D}_{(1)} = \begin{bmatrix} \dfrac{1}{\mathcal{R}(\text{AW})} & 0 & 0 \\ 0 & \dfrac{1}{\mathcal{G}(\text{AW})} & 0 \\ 0 & 0 & \dfrac{1}{\mathcal{B}(\text{AW})} \end{bmatrix}_{(1)} \tag{4.37a}$$

$$\underline{D}_{(2)} = \begin{bmatrix} \dfrac{1}{\mathcal{R}(\text{AW})} & 0 & 0 \\[2ex] 0 & \dfrac{1}{\mathcal{G}(\text{AW})} & 0 \\[2ex] 0 & 0 & \dfrac{1}{\mathcal{B}(\text{AW})} \end{bmatrix}_{(2)}. \tag{4.37b}$$

The AW in the present case should be equal to the white point of either illuminant (1) or (2). In other words, application of the appropriate raw WB multipliers to the AW vector itself yields the unit vector of the camera raw space,

$$\begin{bmatrix} \mathcal{R} = 1 \\ \mathcal{G} = 1 \\ \mathcal{B} = 1 \end{bmatrix}_{\text{reference}} = \underline{D}_{(1)} \begin{bmatrix} \mathcal{R}(\text{AW}) \\ \mathcal{G}(\text{AW}) \\ \mathcal{B}(\text{AW}) \end{bmatrix}_{(1)} \tag{4.38a}$$

$$\begin{bmatrix} \mathcal{R} = 1 \\ \mathcal{G} = 1 \\ \mathcal{B} = 1 \end{bmatrix}_{\text{reference}} = \underline{D}_{(2)} \begin{bmatrix} \mathcal{R}(\text{AW}) \\ \mathcal{G}(\text{AW}) \\ \mathcal{B}(\text{AW}) \end{bmatrix}_{(2)}. \tag{4.38b}$$

(ii) Characterisation

The relative XYZ tristimulus values for the colour target used for the characterisation are known under the scene illumination, which in the present case will be either the first or second characterisation illuminant, (1) or (2). The characterisation can be described by a transformation matrix $\underline{T}_{(1)}$ or $\underline{T}_{(2)}$.

Since the characterisation is performed with the appropriate camera WB setting enabled, the transformation matrix must be applied to raw values which have already been scaled by the raw WB multipliers applied by the camera. In other words, the transformation matrix must be applied to the raw vectors defined by equation (4.36).

Consider again the specific case of the AW vector itself, which is equal to the white point of either characterisation illuminant (1) or (2). In both cases the transformation matrix will map from the unit vector in the camera raw space defined by equation (4.38) to the characterisation illuminant white point in the XYZ space,

$$\begin{bmatrix} X(\text{WP}) \\ Y(\text{WP}) \\ Z(\text{WP}) \end{bmatrix}_{(1)} = \underline{T}_{(1)} \begin{bmatrix} \mathcal{R} = 1 \\ \mathcal{G} = 1 \\ \mathcal{B} = 1 \end{bmatrix}_{\text{reference}} \tag{4.39a}$$

$$\begin{bmatrix} X(\text{WP}) \\ Y(\text{WP}) \\ Z(\text{WP}) \end{bmatrix}_{(2)} = \underline{T}_{(2)} \begin{bmatrix} \mathcal{R} = 1 \\ \mathcal{G} = 1 \\ \mathcal{B} = 1 \end{bmatrix}_{\text{reference}}. \tag{4.39b}$$

Now combining equations (4.38) and (4.39) yields

$$\begin{bmatrix} X(\text{WP}) \\ Y(\text{WP}) \\ Z(\text{WP}) \end{bmatrix}_{(1)} = \underline{T}_{(1)}\underline{D}_{(1)} \begin{bmatrix} \mathcal{R}(\text{AW}) \\ \mathcal{G}(\text{AW}) \\ \mathcal{B}(\text{AW}) \end{bmatrix}_{(1)} \tag{4.40a}$$

$$\begin{bmatrix} X(\text{WP}) \\ Y(\text{WP}) \\ Z(\text{WP}) \end{bmatrix}_{(2)} = \underline{T}_{(2)}\underline{D}_{(2)} \begin{bmatrix} \mathcal{R}(\text{AW}) \\ \mathcal{G}(\text{AW}) \\ \mathcal{B}(\text{AW}) \end{bmatrix}_{(2)} . \tag{4.40b}$$

These equations are valid for scene illumination which matches the characterisation illuminant (1) or (2) and describe the transformation from the camera raw space to XYZ without any adjustment of the illumination white point.

(iii) Forward matrices
Ultimately the white point of the illumination needs to be adapted to that of the PCS (D50). For characterisation illuminants (1) and (2), this adaptation can be achieved by using a CAT. The ICC recommends the linear Bradford CAT,

$$\begin{bmatrix} X(\text{WP}) \\ Y(\text{WP}) \\ Z(\text{WP}) \end{bmatrix}_{\text{D50}} = \underline{\text{CAT}}_{(1)} \begin{bmatrix} X(\text{WP}) \\ Y(\text{WP}) \\ Z(\text{WP}) \end{bmatrix}_{(1)} \tag{4.41a}$$

$$\begin{bmatrix} X(\text{WP}) \\ Y(\text{WP}) \\ Z(\text{WP}) \end{bmatrix}_{\text{D50}} = \underline{\text{CAT}}_{(2)} \begin{bmatrix} X(\text{WP}) \\ Y(\text{WP}) \\ Z(\text{WP}) \end{bmatrix}_{(2)} . \tag{4.41b}$$

Here the CAT matrices are defined by

$$\begin{aligned}
\underline{\text{CAT}}_{(1)} &= \underline{M}_{\text{BFD}}^{-1} \begin{bmatrix} \dfrac{\rho(\text{D50})}{\rho(1)} & 0 & 0 \\ 0 & \dfrac{\gamma(\text{D50})}{\gamma(1)} & 0 \\ 0 & 0 & \dfrac{\beta(\text{D50})}{\beta(1)} \end{bmatrix} \underline{M}_{\text{BFD}} \\[2em]
\underline{\text{CAT}}_{(2)} &= \underline{M}_{\text{BFD}}^{-1} \begin{bmatrix} \dfrac{\rho(\text{D50})}{\rho(2)} & 0 & 0 \\ 0 & \dfrac{\gamma(\text{D50})}{\gamma(2)} & 0 \\ 0 & 0 & \dfrac{\beta(\text{D50})}{\beta(2)} \end{bmatrix} \underline{M}_{\text{BFD}}
\end{aligned} \tag{4.42}$$

where

$$\begin{bmatrix} \rho(\text{D}50) \\ \gamma(\text{D}50) \\ \beta(\text{D}50) \end{bmatrix} = \underline{M}_{\text{BFD}} \begin{bmatrix} X(\text{WP}) = 0.9642 \\ Y(\text{WP}) = 1.0000 \\ Z(\text{WP}) = 0.8249 \end{bmatrix}_{\text{D}50}$$

$$\begin{bmatrix} \rho(1) \\ \gamma(1) \\ \beta(1) \end{bmatrix} = \underline{M}_{\text{BFD}} \begin{bmatrix} X(\text{AW}) \\ Y(\text{AW}) \\ Z(\text{AW}) \end{bmatrix}_{(1)} \tag{4.43}$$

$$\begin{bmatrix} \rho(2) \\ \gamma(2) \\ \beta(2) \end{bmatrix} = \underline{M}_{\text{BFD}} \begin{bmatrix} X(\text{AW}) \\ Y(\text{AW}) \\ Z(\text{AW}) \end{bmatrix}_{(2)} .$$

Now substituting equation (4.40) into equation (4.41) yields

$$\begin{bmatrix} X(\text{WP}) \\ Y(\text{WP}) \\ Z(\text{WP}) \end{bmatrix}_{\text{D}50} = \underline{\text{ForwardMatrix1}} \; \underline{D}_{(1)} \begin{bmatrix} \mathcal{R}(\text{AW}) \\ \mathcal{G}(\text{AW}) \\ \mathcal{B}(\text{AW}) \end{bmatrix}_{(1)}$$

$$\begin{bmatrix} X(\text{WP}) \\ Y(\text{WP}) \\ Z(\text{WP}) \end{bmatrix}_{\text{D}50} = \underline{\text{ForwardMatrix2}} \; \underline{D}_{(2)} \begin{bmatrix} \mathcal{R}(\text{AW}) \\ \mathcal{G}(\text{AW}) \\ \mathcal{B}(\text{AW}) \end{bmatrix}_{(2)} . \tag{4.44}$$

Here the *forward matrices* have been defined as

$$\boxed{\begin{aligned} \underline{\text{ForwardMatrix1}} &= \underline{\text{CAT}}_{(1)} \underline{T}_{(1)} \\ \underline{\text{ForwardMatrix2}} &= \underline{\text{CAT}}_{(2)} \underline{T}_{(2)} \end{aligned}} . \tag{4.45}$$

These map the unit vector in the camera raw space directly to the PCS white point vector (D50) under characterisation illuminants (1) or (2), respectively,

$$\boxed{\begin{bmatrix} X(\text{WP}) \\ Y(\text{WP}) \\ Z(\text{WP}) \end{bmatrix}_{\text{D}50} = \underline{\text{ForwardMatrix1}} \begin{bmatrix} \mathcal{R} = 1 \\ \mathcal{G} = 1 \\ \mathcal{B} = 1 \end{bmatrix}_{\text{reference}}} \tag{4.46a}$$

$$\boxed{\begin{bmatrix} X(\text{WP}) \\ Y(\text{WP}) \\ Z(\text{WP}) \end{bmatrix}_{\text{D}50} = \underline{\text{ForwardMatrix2}} \begin{bmatrix} \mathcal{R} = 1 \\ \mathcal{G} = 1 \\ \mathcal{B} = 1 \end{bmatrix}_{\text{reference}}} . \tag{4.46b}$$

The forward matrices will differ numerically because of characterisation differences between illuminants (1) and (2).

To summarise the derivation up to this point,

- The camera applies raw WB multipliers to the raw data according to equation (4.36). In particular, this adjusts the camera raw space AW vector to the camera raw space reference white as described by equation (4.38).
- Subsequently, the forward matrices transform from the camera raw space to XYZ, and at the same time adapt the white point to D50. Equation (4.46) describes this transformation for the specific case of the camera raw space reference white.

At this stage the forward matrices are optimised only for scene illumination which matches illuminants (1) or (2). However, the forward matrices can be optimised for arbitrary scene illumination through interpolation.

(iv) Forward matrix interpolation

The forward matrices ForwardMatrix1 and ForwardMatrix2 are both valid for use with arbitrary scene illumination provided the diagonal WB matrix $\underline{D}$ appropriate for the scene illumination is first applied. However, ForwardMatrix1 and ForwardMatrix2 are *optimised* for use with the characterisation illuminants (1) and (2) and not for arbitrary scene illumination.

If both ForwardMatrix1 and ForwardMatrix2 are available, a third matrix $\underline{F}$ can be calculated which is optimised for use with arbitrary scene illumination. The same iterative procedure detailed in section 4.6.1 of method 1 can be used to determine the CCT corresponding to the AW, CCT(AW). This procedure requires use of the colour transformation matrices ColorMatrix1 and ColorMatrix2 from method 1. After performing the iteration procedure to determine CCT(AW), the interpolation is defined by

$$\underline{F} = g \ \underline{\text{ForwardMatrix1}} + (1 - g)\underline{\text{ForwardMatrix2}}.$$

Again g is defined by equation (4.28),

$$g = \frac{\dfrac{1}{\text{CCT(AW)}} - \dfrac{1}{\text{CCT(2)}}}{\dfrac{1}{\text{CCT(1)}} - \dfrac{1}{\text{CCT(2)}}}.$$

If CCT(AW) < CCT(1) or if only ForwardMatrix1 is provided, then $\underline{F}$ is set equal to ForwardMatrix1. Similarly, if CCT(AW) > CCT(2) or if only ForwardMatrix2 is provided, then $\underline{F}$ is set equal to ForwardMatrix2.

Since ForwardMatrix1 and ForwardMatrix 2 both have a CAT built into them which adapts the illumination white point in the XYZ space to D50, the interpolated forward matrix $\underline{F}$ will naturally adapt the illumination white point from the AW to D50.

The complete white-point adaptation process can be summarised by substituting equation (4.38) into equation (4.46),

$$
\begin{bmatrix} X(\text{WP}) \\ Y(\text{WP}) \\ Z(\text{WP}) \end{bmatrix}_{\text{D50}} = \underline{F}\,\underline{D} \begin{bmatrix} \mathcal{R}(\text{AW}) \\ \mathcal{G}(\text{AW}) \\ \mathcal{B}(\text{AW}) \end{bmatrix}_{\text{scene}} .
\tag{4.47}
$$

Here $\underline{F}$ replaces ForwardMatrix1 or ForwardMatrix2, and $\underline{D}$ is the raw WB matrix appropriate for the scene illumination.

Summary

By considering equation (4.47) for an arbitrary pixel, the complete transformation from the camera raw space to **XYZ** is defined as

$$
\begin{bmatrix} X \\ Y \\ Z \end{bmatrix}_{\text{D50}} = \underline{F}\,\underline{D} \begin{bmatrix} \mathcal{R} \\ \mathcal{G} \\ \mathcal{B} \end{bmatrix}_{\text{scene}} .
$$

- The diagonal WB matrix $\underline{D}$ applies WB multipliers to the raw channels in order to adapt the illumination white point from that of the scene illumination estimate (AW) to the reference white of the camera raw space.
- The forward matrix $\underline{F}$ subsequently transforms from the camera raw space to **XYZ** and at the same time adapts the illumination white point to that of D50 illumination.

Method 2 is found to work better in extreme cases than method 1, and so method 2 is the default if the forward matrices are available [29].

Note that it is not possible to obtain the forward matrix from the colour matrix. These matrices are obtained from characterisations with different starting points; the forward matrix is obtained through characterisation with WB enabled, whereas the colour matrix is obtained through characterisation with WB disabled. It is possible to algebraically re-express method 1 in the form of method 2, however the 'forward matrix' obtained in this way will be of a different nature to that obtained through a characterisation with WB enabled.

4.7 Example 2: *dcraw* (raw to sRGB D65)

The widely used freeware raw converter *dcraw* by default outputs directly to the sRGB colour space with a D65 illumination white point. The colour-processing model is slightly different to that used by the Adobe® DNG specification and is the type of model often used by in-camera image-processing engines. Nevertheless, *dcraw* utilises the colour transformation matrices from Adobe® DNG method 1 in combination with raw WB multipliers from method 2 as part of its colour-processing model. In this section the following notation will be used:

$\underline{M}$	Colour transformation matrix as defined in section 4.3.5
$\underline{\text{ColorMatrix1}}$	Colour transformation matrix by Adobe® for low-temperature characterisation illuminant (maps in opposite direction to $\underline{M}$)
$\underline{\text{ColorMatrix2}}$	Colour transformation matrix by Adobe® for high-temperature characterisation illuminant (maps in opposite direction to $\underline{M}$)
$\underline{C}$	Colour transformation matrix interpolated from $\underline{\text{ColorMatrix1}}$ and $\underline{\text{ColorMatrix2}}$
$\underline{M}_\text{R}$	Colour rotation matrix
$\underline{D}$	Diagonal WB matrix containing raw WB multipliers
$\underline{D}_\text{D65}$	Diagonal WB matrix containing D65 raw WB multipliers
$\begin{bmatrix} R_\text{L} \\ G_\text{L} \\ B_\text{L} \end{bmatrix}$	Linear sRGB colour-space vector
$\begin{bmatrix} \mathcal{R} \\ \mathcal{G} \\ \mathcal{B} \end{bmatrix}$	Camera raw space vector

(i) Normalisation

Only one colour transformation matrix from method 1 of the Adobe® DNG colour-processing model is retained by *dcraw*, specifically ColorMatrix2 which corresponds to a characterisation using D65 illumination,

$$
\begin{bmatrix} \mathcal{R} \\ \mathcal{G} \\ \mathcal{B} \end{bmatrix}_\text{D65} = \frac{1}{s} \underline{C} \begin{bmatrix} X \\ Y \\ Z \end{bmatrix}_\text{D65} .
\tag{4.48}
$$

Here $\underline{C}$ = ColorMatrix2 and s is a normalisation constant. Any *characterisation* differences compared with characterisations performed at other colour temperatures are therefore neglected. Nevertheless, correct WB can be achieved through a reformulation of the problem described later in this section.

Recall that method 1 by default normalises the colour matrices so that their middle rows map the PCS white point (D50) to the raw green channel saturation point,

$$
\begin{bmatrix} \mathcal{R} \\ 1 \\ \mathcal{B} \end{bmatrix}_\text{D50} = \underline{C} \begin{bmatrix} X(\text{WP}) = & 0.9641 \\ Y(\text{WP}) = & 1 \\ Z(\text{WP}) = & 0.8249 \end{bmatrix}_\text{D50} .
$$

In *dcraw*, the default sRGB output colour space has a D65 reference white, and the viewing illumination is assumed to have a D65 white point. Ultimately $\underline{C}$ must be rescaled by a factor $1/s$ so that its middle row maps the D65 white point in XYZ to raw green channel saturation. This means that the normalisation constant s appearing in equation (4.48) can be determined from

$$\begin{bmatrix} \mathcal{R} \\ 1 \\ \mathcal{B} \end{bmatrix}_{\text{D65}} = \frac{1}{s}\, \underline{C} \begin{bmatrix} X(\text{WP}) = & 0.9504 \\ Y(\text{WP}) = & 1 \\ Z(\text{WP}) = & 1.0888 \end{bmatrix}_{\text{D65}}. \tag{4.49}$$

This is simply a linear scaling of the matrix entries and no attempt at chromatic adaptation is being made.

Normalisation example
The colour matrix for the Olympus® E-M1 is stored in the following form by *dcraw*,

$$7687,\ -1984,\ -606,\ -4327,\ 11\,928,\ 2721,\ -1381,\ 2339,\ 6452.$$

Dividing by 10 000 and rearranging in matrix form yields

$$\underline{C} = \begin{bmatrix} 0.7687 & -0.1984 & -0.0606 \\ -0.4327 & 1.1928 & 0.2721 \\ -0.1381 & 0.2339 & 0.6452 \end{bmatrix}. \tag{4.50}$$

Substituting this matrix into equation (4.49) confirms that $\underline{C}$ is indeed currently normalised so that its middle rows map the PCS white point to raw green channel saturation. In the new normalisation, the required scale factor in this example is $s = 1.0778$,

$$\begin{bmatrix} \mathcal{R} \\ 1 \\ \mathcal{B} \end{bmatrix}_{\text{D65}} = \frac{1}{s} \begin{bmatrix} 0.7687 & -0.1984 & -0.0606 \\ -0.4327 & 1.1928 & 0.2721 \\ -0.1381 & 0.2339 & 0.6452 \end{bmatrix} \begin{bmatrix} X(\text{WP}) = & 0.9504 \\ Y(\text{WP}) = & 1 \\ Z(\text{WP}) = & 1.0888 \end{bmatrix}_{\text{D65}}.$$

(ii) sRGB to raw
The transformation which maps D65 illumination from the linear form of the sRGB colour space to XYZ was defined by equation (4.13) of section 4.4,

$$\begin{bmatrix} X \\ Y \\ Z \end{bmatrix}_{\text{D65}} = \underline{M}_{\text{sRGB}} \begin{bmatrix} R_{\text{L}} \\ G_{\text{L}} \\ B_{\text{L}} \end{bmatrix}_{\text{D65}}$$

where

$$\underline{M}_{\text{sRGB}} = \begin{bmatrix} 0.4124 & 0.3576 & 0.1805 \\ 0.2126 & 0.7152 & 0.0722 \\ 0.0193 & 0.1192 & 0.9505 \end{bmatrix}.$$

Here R_L, G_L, B_L denote tristimulus values in the *linear* form of the sRGB colour space before gamma encoding. Combining the above with equation (4.48) yields

$$\begin{bmatrix} \mathcal{R} \\ \mathcal{G} \\ \mathcal{B} \end{bmatrix}_{D65} = \frac{1}{s} \underline{C} \underline{M}_{sRGB} \begin{bmatrix} R_L \\ G_L \\ B_L \end{bmatrix}_{D65} . \tag{4.51}$$

This relation maps illumination with D65 white point in the sRGB colour space directly to the camera raw space. Unfortunately, WB will be correctly achieved only for scene illumination with a matching D65 white point. In order to achieve WB for arbitrary scene illumination, a reformulation of the problem is required [17].

(iii) Reformulation: raw WB multipliers + rotation matrix
A way forward is to extract out raw WB multipliers appropriate for D65 illumination from equation (4.51), and replace them with the raw WB multipliers appropriate for the scene illumination [17].

Consider equation (4.51) for the specific the case of the D65 reference white represented by the unit vector. Since both $\underline{M}_{sRGB}$ and $\underline{C}$ preserve the D65 white point, this equation defines the corresponding D65 white-point vector in the camera raw space,

$$\begin{bmatrix} \mathcal{R}(WP) \\ \mathcal{G}(WP) \\ \mathcal{B}(WP) \end{bmatrix}_{D65} = \frac{1}{s} \underline{C} \underline{M}_{sRGB} \begin{bmatrix} R_L = 1 \\ G_L = 1 \\ B_L = 1 \end{bmatrix}_{D65} . \tag{4.52}$$

This vector can be transformed into a diagonal matrix and then inverted,

$$\underline{D}_{D65} = \begin{bmatrix} \dfrac{1}{\mathcal{R}(WP)} & 0 & 0 \\ 0 & \dfrac{1}{\mathcal{G}(WP)} & 0 \\ 0 & 0 & \dfrac{1}{\mathcal{B}(WP)} \end{bmatrix}_{D65} . \tag{4.53}$$

The diagonal elements of $\underline{D}_{D65}$ are simply the raw WB multipliers for D65 illumination and have been extracted here from the row sums of the matrix product $\underline{C}\underline{M}_{sRGB}$. The normalisation constant s ensures that

$$\frac{1}{\mathcal{G}(WP)} = 1.$$

It follows that the product of $\underline{D}_{D65}$ with $(1/s)\underline{C}\underline{M}_{sRGB}$ yields a matrix with the property that each of its rows sums to unity,

$$\underline{M}_R^{-1} = \underline{D}_{D65} \left(\frac{1}{s} \underline{C} \right) \underline{M}_{sRGB}. \tag{4.54}$$

This is an example of a colour *rotation matrix*. Since the rotation matrix and its inverse both have rows which sum to unity, the inverse has been used in the above definition because the mapping direction is from the output space to the input space. In the forward direction the rotation matrix is defined as

$$\boxed{\underline{M}_R = \underline{M}_{sRGB}^{-1}(s\,\underline{C}^{-1})\underline{D}_{D65}^{-1}}\,. \tag{4.55}$$

Substituting equation (4.54) into equation (4.51) yields

$$\boxed{\begin{bmatrix} \mathcal{R} \\ \mathcal{G} \\ \mathcal{B} \end{bmatrix}_{D65} = \underline{D}_{D65}^{-1}\,\underline{M}_R^{-1} \begin{bmatrix} R_L \\ G_L \\ B_L \end{bmatrix}_{D65}}\,. \tag{4.56}$$

Equations (4.51) and (4.56) are equivalent. However, the reformulation in terms of the rotation matrix provides a method for white-balancing with arbitrary scene illumination.

To see this, consider scene illumination with an arbitrary white point. In this case the matrix $\underline{D}_{D65}$ can simply be replaced by the appropriate raw WB matrix defined by equation (4.37),

$$\underline{D} = \begin{bmatrix} \dfrac{1}{\mathcal{R}(AW)} & 0 & 0 \\[2ex] 0 & \dfrac{1}{\mathcal{G}(AW)} & 0 \\[2ex] 0 & 0 & \dfrac{1}{\mathcal{B}(AW)} \end{bmatrix}_{scene}\,.$$

In this general case equation (4.56) becomes

$$\begin{bmatrix} \mathcal{R} \\ \mathcal{G} \\ \mathcal{B} \end{bmatrix}_{scene} = \underline{D}^{-1}\underline{M}_R^{-1} \begin{bmatrix} R_L \\ G_L \\ B_L \end{bmatrix}_{D65}\,.$$

In the forward direction this may be written

$$\boxed{\begin{bmatrix} R_L \\ G_L \\ B_L \end{bmatrix}_{D65} = \underline{M}_R\underline{D} \begin{bmatrix} \mathcal{R} \\ \mathcal{G} \\ \mathcal{B} \end{bmatrix}_{scene}}\,. \tag{4.57}$$

Summary

Given the AW estimated by the camera, WB is achieved according to equation (4.57) in two steps:

1. The WB matrix $\underline{D}$ containing the appropriate raw WB multipliers divides out the chromaticity of the scene illumination by adjusting the AW vector to the reference white of the camera raw space,

$$\begin{bmatrix} \mathcal{R} = 1 \\ \mathcal{G} = 1 \\ \mathcal{B} = 1 \end{bmatrix}_{\text{reference}} = \underline{D} \begin{bmatrix} \mathcal{R}(\text{AW}) \\ \mathcal{G}(\text{AW}) \\ \mathcal{B}(\text{AW}) \end{bmatrix}_{\text{scene}} .$$

2. Since the rotation matrix $\underline{M}_R$ has rows which each sum to unity, $\underline{M}_R$ maps the unit vector of the camera raw space directly to the unit vector of the sRGB colour space,

$$\begin{bmatrix} R_L = 1 \\ G_L = 1 \\ B_L = 1 \end{bmatrix}_{\text{D65}} = \underline{M}_R \begin{bmatrix} \mathcal{R} = 1 \\ \mathcal{G} = 1 \\ \mathcal{B} = 1 \end{bmatrix}_{\text{reference}} .$$

In other words, equation (4.57) transforms from the camera raw space directly to the linear form of the sRGB colour space and at the same time adjusts the estimated white point of the scene illumination to that of D65 illumination in the sRGB colour space. This ensures overall WB for arbitrary scene illumination and assumed D65 viewing illumination. Gamma encoding can subsequently be applied to transform to the final nonlinear form of the sRGB colour space.

Example: Olympus® E-M1
The colour transformation matrix $\underline{C} = \text{ColorMatrix2}$ used by *dcraw* for the Olympus® E-M1 was defined by equation (4.50),

$$\underline{C} = \begin{bmatrix} 0.7687 & -0.1984 & -0.0606 \\ -0.4327 & 1.1928 & 0.2721 \\ -0.1381 & 0.2339 & 0.6452 \end{bmatrix} .$$

This is obtained from a characterisation using D65 illumination. Application of equation (4.52) with normalisation constant $s = 1.0778$ yields

$$\frac{1}{s} \underline{C} \underline{M}_{\text{sRGB}} \begin{bmatrix} R_L = 1 \\ G_L = 1 \\ B_L = 1 \end{bmatrix}_{\text{D65}} = \begin{bmatrix} \mathcal{R}(\text{WP}) = 0.4325 \\ \mathcal{G}(\text{WP}) = 1.0000 \\ \mathcal{B}(\text{WP}) = 0.7471 \end{bmatrix}_{\text{D65}} .$$

This enables the raw WB multipliers for D65 illumination to be extracted according to equation (4.53),

$$\underline{D}_{\text{D65}} = \begin{bmatrix} 2.3117 & 0 & 0 \\ 0 & 1 & 0 \\ 0 & 0 & 1.3385 \end{bmatrix}_{\text{D65}} .$$

The raw-to-sRGB rotation matrix calculated according to equation (4.55) is

$$M_R = \begin{bmatrix} 1.7901 & -0.6689 & -0.1212 \\ -0.2167 & 1.7522 & -0.5354 \\ 0.0543 & -0.5582 & 1.5039 \end{bmatrix}.$$

Although this matrix is optimised for use with D65 illumination, *dcraw* uses the same matrix with arbitrary illumination in combination with the appropriate raw WB multipliers.

The Olympus® E-M1 raw metadata also provides its own raw WB multipliers and a rotation matrix for use by the camera JPEG image-processing engine. The raw WB multipliers along with the rotation matrix listed in the metadata are dependent on factors such as:

- Which of the sRGB or Adobe® RGB colour spaces is selected in-camera.
- The colour temperature of the scene illumination estimated by the AW.
- The lens model used to take the raw photo.
- The camera used to take the raw photo. Due to sensor calibration differences between different examples of the same camera model, the listed matrix may differ even if the same settings are selected on different examples and the same firmware is installed.

In contrast to *dcraw*, the Olympus® rotation matrices and associated raw WB multipliers are obtained from characterisations performed at a range of different colour temperatures and so provide better accuracy over a range of CCTs. This is analogous to the interpolation based on the scene CCT employed by the Adobe® DNG methods. Table 4.2 lists example raw WB multipliers and rotation matrices for preset WB settings found in the raw metadata. The listed values are 8-bit fixed point numbers used by the internal processor and so need to be divided by 256. For comparison with *dcraw*, the custom preset has been set to 6400 K which

Table 4.2. Raw WB multipliers and raw-to-sRGB colour rotation matrices corresponding to in-camera preset CCTs for the Olympus® E-M1 with 12-40 f/2.8 lens and v4.1 firmware. These raw metadata values are 8-bit fixed-point numbers used by the internal processor.

CCT	Description	Raw WB multipliers	Rotation matrix
3000 K	Tungsten	296 760 256 256	324 −40 −28 −68 308 16 16 −248 488
4000 K	Cool fluorescent	492 602 256 256	430 −168 −6 −50 300 6 12 −132 376
5300 K	Fine weather	504 434 256 256	368 −92 −20 −42 340 −42 10 −140 386
6000 K	Cloudy	544 396 256 256	380 −104 −20 −40 348 −52 10 −128 374
7500 K	Fine weather, shade	588 344 256 256	394 −116 −22 −38 360 −66 8 −112 360
5500 K	Flash	598 384 256 256	368 −92 −20 −42 340 −42 10 −140 386
6400 K	Custom	556 382 256 256	380 −104 −20 −40 348 −52 10 −128 374

is close to the CCT of D65 illumination. In this case the raw WB multipliers are seen to be

$$D_{6400\,K} = \begin{bmatrix} 2.1719 & 0 & 0 \\ 0 & 1 & 0 \\ 0 & 0 & 1.4922 \end{bmatrix}_{6400\,K}.$$

The rotation matrix is seen to be

$$\frac{1}{256}\begin{bmatrix} 380 & -104 & -20 \\ -40 & 348 & -52 \\ 10 & -128 & 374 \end{bmatrix} = \begin{bmatrix} 1.4844 & -0.4063 & -0.0781 \\ -0.1563 & 1.3594 & -0.2031 \\ 0.0391 & -0.5000 & 1.4609 \end{bmatrix}.$$

Clearly the Olympus® rotation matrix takes the same general form as the *dcraw* rotation matrix, however there are numerical differences. Although characterisation differences are possible since the *dcraw* matrix originates from the Adobe® ColorMatrix2, the differences are likely to arise from preferred colour rendering applied by the Olympus® matrix. For example, it is known that increasing the main diagonal values produces richer colours [16].

The above analysis reveals that the *dcraw* raw WB multipliers are in general not identical with those used by the camera manufacturer. Therefore when performing a raw conversion using *dcraw*, it is preferable to instruct *dcraw* to calculate its own raw WB multipliers by analysing the raw data rather than choosing the option to use the values stored in the raw metadata.

4.8 Image editing

This chapter has described some of the main physical principles underlying raw conversion in the context of accurate tone reproduction. In practice, the in-camera image-processing engine will apply its own preferred tone and colour rendering. However, the use of an external raw converter provides the photographer with considerable control over the appearance of the output image, and further editing can be carried out using image-editing software. Colour management and image resizing are two technical aspects of image editing discussed in this final section.

4.8.1 Colour management

The sRGB colour space [26] is a suitable output-referred colour space for photographers following a colour strategy with minimal requirements. The in-camera image-processing engine can produce output JPEG images encoded in sRGB that are suitable for viewing on the internet and on standard-gamut displays. The sRGB colour space is also the most suitable choice of encoding for images viewed on devices which do not have appropriate colour management in place.

On the other hand, an *optimal* colour strategy aims to preserve as much of the colour information captured by the camera as possible at each stage of the processing chain before the final output image encoding is chosen. For example, the input camera raw space can be transformed into a *working space* for editing the image that is much larger than sRGB. The final output image encoding can utilise a large colour space suitable for printing or for display on a wide-gamut monitor. Even when sRGB is the intended output colour space, colour clipping can be minimised by performing the editing in a larger working space prior to the output sRGB encoding. An optimal colour strategy requires a wide-gamut monitor/display and appropriate colour management in place.

An essential prerequisite for successful colour management is that the monitor or display be calibrated and profiled by an external hardware device to produce an ICC monitor/display profile. Calibration will set the display to its optimum state. Profiling will characterise the colour response of the calibrated display so that a mapping can be determined between the display gamut and the PCS. This is analogous to the way that the Adobe® DNG specification described in section 4.6 maps the camera raw space to the PCS. In recent versions of Microsoft® Windows®, the display profile created by the profiling software will be stored in the C:\Windows \System32\spool\drivers\color directory. Colour-managed applications such as raw converters and image-editing software will automatically utilise this profile. The translation of colours between devices that have an ICC profile is carried out by the Color Matching Module (CMM).

Photographers following an *optimal* colour strategy who wish to work only with camera JPEG output files can select Adobe® RGB as the in-camera output colour space rather than sRGB. Standard output-referred colour spaces have associated ICC profiles, and so the camera will add an exchangeable image file (EXIF) format colour space *tag* to the image file to associate the Adobe® RGB ICC profile with the image encoding. If the option is given, it is good practice to *embed* the ICC profile in the image file instead for the benefit of users who do not have the relevant ICC profile installed on their viewing device. If the image is to be viewed or edited on a display, it is essential to install an appropriate ICC monitor/display profile and use a colour-managed viewing or editing application. If Adobe® Photoshop® is used to edit the image, it is advisable to set Adobe® RGB as the working space, as discussed below. If printing the image directly, the printer software will appropriately handle the translation of colours from the Adobe® RGB gamut to the printer gamut provided an appropriate ICC printer profile is installed.

The output colour space that can be selected in-camera, typically sRGB or Adobe® RGB, only applies to JPEG images and does not affect the raw data. Photographers who choose to process the raw file using a raw converter can perform editing in the working space utilised by the raw converter, which ideally will correspond to a camera raw-space ICC profile or a reference colour space. When exporting the image from the raw converter, an output encoding can be chosen such as sRGB, Adobe® RGB, or an even larger colour space such as ProPhoto RGB. The gamuts of these colour spaces are illustrated in figure 4.17. ProPhoto RGB has a gamut comparable with that of camera raw spaces and can therefore preserve more of the scene colours captured by the camera [15]. These colours may fall within the gamut of multi-ink printers, but may not be viewable on a wide-gamut display. If using ProPhoto RGB, it is advisable to save the image as a 16-bit TIFF to prevent posterisation. If necessary, further editing of the output image should be performed

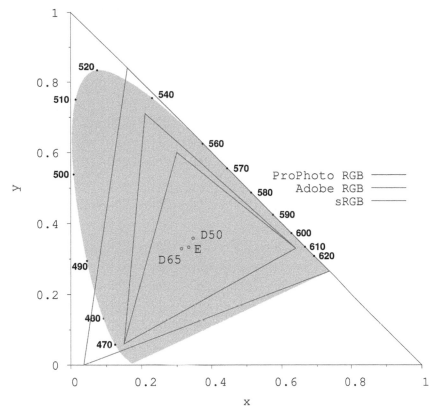

Figure 4.17. sRGB, Adobe® RGB, and ProPhoto RGB gamuts on the *xy* chromaticity diagram. The sRGB and Adobe® RGB colour spaces have a D65 reference white, and ProPhoto RGB has a D50 reference white. Two of the ProPhoto RGB primaries lie outside the visible gamut represented by the grey horseshoe-shaped area.

using a colour-managed application. The colour settings for Adobe® Photoshop® are discussed below.

4.8.2 Adobe® Photoshop® colour settings

The 'Color Settings' menu option allows default colour settings to be specified. These options are discussed in more detail in this section. For reference, the colour settings box is shown in figure 4.18. The monitor/display profile name currently in use should be listed as 'Monitor RGB—*profile name*' in the RGB 'Working Spaces' tab.

Working spaces
The *working space* is the colour space used for editing the image. Generally, this will be the colour space associated with the ICC profile of the imported image, although other options are available as discussed in the colour management policies section below. Adobe® RGB is a sensible choice because it is much larger than sRGB and

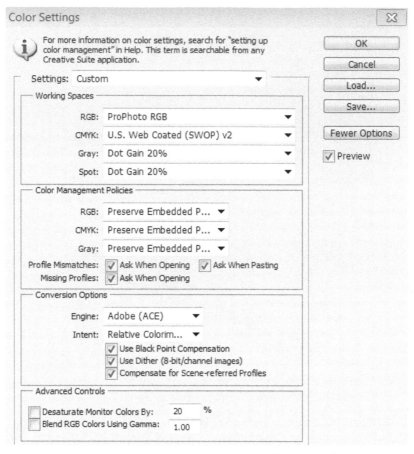

Figure 4.18. 'Color Settings' box in Adobe® Photoshop®.

contains many additional colours which fall within the gamut of typical printers. Furthermore, Adobe® RGB is defined by real primaries and can therefore be shown in its entirety on wide-gamut displays in principle.

When following an optimal colour strategy, another popular working space is ProPhoto RGB. If the image exported from the raw converter has been encoded using ProPhoto RGB, more of the scene colours can be retained which fall within the printing gamut of high-quality printers. Even if the image will ultimately be converted into sRGB for displaying online as described in the conversion options section below, a major advantage of working in ProPhoto RGB is that colour clipping can be minimised when editing the image. However, ProPhoto RGB requires the use of 16-bit TIFF files to prevent posterisation, and extreme editing should be avoided in order to prevent colours unrelated to the captured scene from appearing.

When the intention is to print the image, a drawback of using ProPhoto RGB as the working space is that its gamut cannot be shown in its entirety on wide-gamut displays, and so the photographer cannot be certain that the image will print as intended. Recall from sections 4.1 and 4.3 that non-negative linear combinations of three real primaries cannot reproduce all visible chromaticities. This is because the three types of eye cones cannot be stimulated independently, and so the visible gamut appears as a horseshoe shape rather than a triangle on the xy chromaticity diagram. The primaries associated with response functions of capture devices can be imaginary. However, the primaries of a display device must be physically realisable and therefore cannot lie outside of the visible gamut. Since non-negative linear combinations of primaries lie within a triangle defined by the primaries on the chromaticity diagram, it follows that *no display device can reproduce all visible colours using only three real primaries*. Modern wide-gamut displays can show many colours outside both the sRGB and Adobe® RGB gamuts, although some regions of these gamuts may not be covered. ProPhoto RGB includes many additional colours which can be shown on wide-gamut displays, but ultimately the entire colour space cannot be shown because two of the primaries are imaginary. These primaries are illustrated in figure 4.17.

When exporting an image from a raw converter, the selected output colour space should ideally be the smallest which retains the scene colours, assuming all scene colours can be captured to begin with. Provided editing time is available, this can be chosen on an image-by-image basis by examining the nature of the image histogram [32], and then setting the working space in Adobe® Photoshop® to match this colour space.

Colour management policies

The DOLs of digital images will be interpreted differently depending on the associated colour space. JPEG output files produced by the camera will be tagged as sRGB or Adobe® RGB or will have embedded ICC profiles. This enables an imaging application to correctly interpret the RGB values when opening the image.

However, an *embedded profile mismatch* will occur when opening an image if the colour space associated with the embedded ICC profile differs from the working space, or if the embedded ICC profile or tag is missing. In this case, the photographer is provided with control over handling of the profile mismatch via the dialogue box shown in figure 4.19. The options are:

(A) Use the embedded profile (instead of the working space).
(B) Convert document's colors to the working space.
(C) Discard the embedded profile (don't color manage).

In most cases it is advisable to choose option A. The working space will temporarily be set to that associated with the embedded profile instead of the default chosen in 'Color Settings'. For example, the working space might be ProPhoto RGB and the embedded profile might be sRGB or Adobe® RGB. When opening multiple image files simultaneously, the embedded profile associated with each image will be used as the temporary working space for the appropriate image window.

Provided the working space is larger than the image ICC profile colour space, it is also perfectly acceptable to choose option B in the above instance and convert the colours to the working space. Although the additional colours available in the

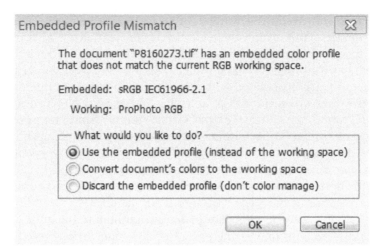

Figure 4.19. 'Embedded Profile Mismatch' dialogue box upon importing an image in Adobe® Photoshop®.

working space will not be utilised upon conversion, the entire gamut of the working space can subsequently be utilised when editing the image. In some cases this can be undesirable, as noted in the above discussion of working spaces. If the image ICC profile colour space is larger than the working space, choosing option **B** may lead to unnecessary clipping of the scene colours. If the photographer does not wish to change the working space and selects option **B**, the *rendering intent* default in the colour options will be applied. Rendering intent is discussed in the conversion options section below.

If the embedded profile is missing, a colour profile can be assigned to the image. In order to test different profiles, choose 'Leave as is (don't color manage)' and then assign a profile using the 'Assign Profile' menu option. The appearance of the image will suggest the most suitable profile. Most likely, the RGB values will correspond to the sRGB colour space.

Conversion options
This option defines defaults when converting between ICC profiles upon opening an image, for example when converting the image colours to the working space when option **B** above is selected. Converting between profiles will transform the image colours to a destination gamut by *altering the DOLs*.

Converting between ICC profiles can also be performed at any time using the 'Convert to Profile' menu option. For example, consider the situation where the embedded profile of the imported image is ProPhoto RGB. After using the embedded profile as the working space and editing the image, the photographer may wish to create a version converted to sRGB for displaying on a standard-gamut monitor or online.

Since the source and destination colour spaces have different gamuts, the ICC have defined several *rendering intents* which can be applied by the CMM when performing the conversion. In photography, the two most useful rendering intents are *relative colorimetric* and *perceptual*. Relative colorimetric intent clips out-of-gamut colours to the edge of the destination gamut, and leaves in-gamut colours unchanged. It is generally advisable to enable *black point compression* when using relative colorimetric intent. Perceptual intent also clips out-of-gamut colours to the edge of the destination gamut, but at the same time shifts in-gamut colours to preserve colour gradations. This can be viewed as a compression of the source gamut into the destination gamut. Relative colorimetric intent with black-point compression should be used when the source image colours all lie inside the gamut of the destination colour space. Perceptual intent may be preferable when source image colours lie outside of the destination gamut. If the preview option is selected, the photographer can choose the most suitable rendering intent on a case-by-case basis.

The 'Proof Colors' menu option allows the effects of conversion to destination profiles to be simulated. The destination profile can be selected via 'Proof Setup'. Note that the 'Monitor RGB' option simulates the appearance of colours on the monitor *without* the monitor profile applied, in other words an uncalibrated monitor.

4.8.3 Image resizing

It is useful to define the following terminology:

- The *pixel count* of a digital image is the total number of pixels. The pixel count n is often specified in terms of the *pixel dimensions*, $n = n(h) \times n(v)$, where $n(h)$ is the number of pixels in the horizontal direction and $n(v)$ is the number of pixels in the vertical direction.
- *Image resolution* specifies the number of displayed image pixels per unit distance, most commonly in terms of *pixels per inch* (ppi). This can equally refer to an image displayed on a computer screen or to a printed image. A more precise term is *image display resolution* because it should be remembered that this describes the way that the image is displayed and it is not a property of the image itself. The relevant image attribute is the pixel count.
- The *display size* is determined by the pixel count together with the image display resolution,

$$\text{display size} = \frac{\text{pixel count}}{\text{image display resolution}}.$$

The display size may refer to the *image display size* when an image is displayed on a monitor or the *image print size* when an image is printed.
- The *monitor resolution* is the monitor ppi value. The monitor resolution defines the image display resolution when the image is displayed on the monitor.
- The *printer resolution* is a measure of the number of ink dots per unit distance used by a printer to print an image, and is commonly measured in *dots per inch* (dpi). A higher dpi generally results in better print quality. Unlike monitor resolution when displaying an image on a monitor, printer resolution in dpi is independent from image display resolution when printing an image.

The image display resolution in ppi is defined by the image print size together with the pixel count,

$$\text{image display resolution} = \frac{\text{pixel count}}{\text{image print size}}.$$

For high-quality prints, 300 ppi is typically considered to be sufficient for a standard enlargement viewed at a standard distance. Unfortunately, ppi and dpi are often incorrectly used interchangeably.

For example, a 720×480 pixel image will appear with an image display size equal to 10 by 6.66 inches on a computer monitor set at 72 ppi. The same image will appear with an image print size equal to 2.4 by 1.6 inches when printed with the image display resolution set to 300 ppi, and is independent from the printer resolution in dpi.

Clients or commercial printers often request images to be 'saved at 300 dpi' or similar. Such phrases are not meaningful because, unlike pixel count, neither print resolution nor image display resolution are properties of an image. Nevertheless, it is possible to add a ppi *resolution tag* to an image. This does not alter the image pixels in any way and is simply a number stored in the image metadata which is read by the printing software. In any case, the printing software will allow this value to be overridden by providing image display resolution and image print size options.

It is likely that the client or commercial printer intends to print the image with a 300 ppi image display resolution. In the absence of any further information such as the final print size, it is advisable to leave the pixel count unchanged, add a 300 ppi resolution tag to the image, and rely on the printing software used by the client to

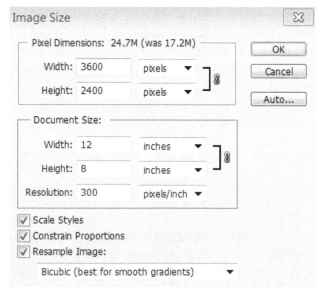

Figure 4.20. 'Image Size' option available in Adobe® Photoshop®.

take care of any resizing. However, if the final print size is already known then quality can be optimised by resizing the image in advance using more specialised software before sending to the client. This *will* change the pixel count according to the following formula,

required pixel count = image print size × image display resolution.

For example, if the image print size will be 12 × 8 inches and the image display resolution is required to be 300 ppi, then the required pixel count is 3600 × 2400. If the image pixel count is currently say 3000 × 2000, then the pixel count needs to be increased through resampling.

Adobe® Photoshop® provides the 'Image Size' option shown in figure 4.20. For the present example, one way of using this feature is to set the required width and height to be 3600 pixels and 2400 pixels in 'Pixel Dimensions' with 'Resolution' set to 300 ppi. In this case the 'Document Size' will automatically change to 12 × 8 inches. Alternatively, the width and height in 'Document Size' can be set to 12 inches and 8 inches, respectively. In this case the 'Pixel Dimensions' will automatically change to 3600 × 2400. Selecting 'OK' will perform the resampling.

Bibliography

[1] Wyszecki G and Stiles W S 2000 *Color Science: Concepts and Methods, Quantitative Data and Formulae (Wiley Series in Pure and Applied Optics)* 2nd revised edn (New York: Wiley-Blackwell)

[2] Ohta N and Robertson A R 2005 *Colorimetry: Fundamentals and Applications, (Wiley-IS & T Series in Imaging Science and Technology)* (New York: Wiley)

[3] Schanda J (ed) 2007 *Colorimetry: Understanding the CIE system* (New York: Wiley)

[4] Hunt R W G and Pointer M R 2011 *Measuring Colour* 4th edn (New York: Wiley)

[5] Hunt R W G 1997 The heights of the CIE colour-matching functions *Color Res. Appl.* **22** 355

[6] Stewart S M and Johnson R B 2016 *Blackbody Radiation: A History of Thermal Radiation Computational Aids and Numerical Methods (Optical Sciences and Applications of Light)* (Boca Raton, FL: CRC Press)

[7] Kim Y-S, Cho B-H, Kang B-S, and Hong D-I 2006 Color temperature conversion system and method using the same *US patent* 7024034

[8] Robertson A R 1968 Computation of correlated color temperature and distribution temperature *J. Opt. Soc. Am.* **58** 1528

[9] McCamy C S 1992 Correlated color temperature as an explicit function of chromaticity coordinates *Color Res. Appl.* **17** 142

[10] Hernández-Andrés J, Lee R L and Romero J 1999 Calculating correlated color temperatures across the entire gamut of daylight and skylight chromaticities *Appl. Opt.* **38** 5703

[11] CIE 2006 *Fundamental Chromaticity Diagram with Physiological Axes–Part 1 (Vienna: Commission Internationale de l'Eclairage)* CIE 170-1:2006

[12] Bayer B E 1976 3971065 Color imaging array *US Patent* 3971065

[13] Luther R 1927 Aus dem Gebiet der Farbreizmetrik (On color stimulus metrics) *Z. Tech. Phys.* **8** 540

[14] Hung P-C 2006 *Image Sensors and Signal Processing for Digital Still Cameras* ed J Nakamura (Boca Raton, FL/London: CRC Press/Taylor and Francis)

[15] Holm J 2006 Capture color analysis gamuts *Proc. 14th Color and Imaging Conf. IS&T* p 108

[16] Sato K 2006 *Image Sensors and Signal Processing for Digital Still Cameras* ed J Nakamura (Boca Raton, FL/London: CRC Press/Taylor and Francis)

[17] Coffin D 2015 private communication

[18] Li X, Gunturk B and Zhang L 2008 Image demosaicing: a systematic survey *SPIE. Proc* **6822** 68221J

[19] Chang E, Cheung S and Pan D Y 1999 Color filter array recovery using a threshold-based variable number of gradients *Proc. SPIE* **3650** 36

[20] Chuan-kai Lin 2003 *Pixel Grouping Interpolator Reference Implementation* https://sites.google.com/site/chklin/demosaic

[21] Hirakawa K and Parks T W 2005 Adaptive homogeneity-directed demosaicing algorithm *IEEE Trans. Image Process* **14** 360

[22] ISO 2012 Graphic technology and photography—Colour target and procedures for the colour characterisation of digital still cameras (DCSs), ISO 17321-1:2012

[23] ISO 2009 Photography—Electronic still-picture cameras—Methods for measuring opto-electronic conversion functions (OECFs), ISO 14524:2009

[24] Hung P-C 2002 Sensitivity metamerism index for digital still camera *Proc. SPIE* **4922** 1–14

[25] Balasubramanian R 2003 *Digital Colour Imaging Handbook* ed G Sharma (Boca Raton, FL: CRC Press)

[26] IEC 1999 Multimedia systems and equipment—Colour measurement and management—Part 2-1: Colour management—Default RGB colour space—sRGB, IEC 61966-2-1:1999

[27] Fairchild M D 2013 *Color Appearance Models* 3rd edn (New York: Wiley)

[28] ISO 2012 Photography—Electronic still picture imaging–Vocabulary, ISO 12231:2012

[29] Adobe 2012 Digital negative (DNG) specification, version 1.4

[30] Lam K M 1985 Metamerism and colour constancy *PhD thesis* University of Bradford

[31] ICC 2004 Image technology colour management—Architecture, profile format, and data structure *ICC.* 1: 2004–10 (Profile version 4.2.0.0)

[32] Rodney A 2006 *The role of working spaces in Adobe applications*

Chapter 5

Image quality

This chapter discusses image quality (IQ) with two main objectives in mind. The first is to provide background information for interpreting several of the important IQ metrics that are used by online reviewers and sources of camera data. The second is to discuss IQ in relation to photographic practice, and in particular some of the methods that can be used to help utilise the full IQ potential of a camera.

Many aspects of IQ are subjective in that different observers will value a given aspect of IQ differently. For example, image noise deemed unacceptable by one observer may even be judged to be aesthetically pleasing by another. Furthermore, photographers may judge the relative importance of the various aspects of IQ differently.

Nevertheless, objective IQ metrics can be helpful when determining the suitability of a given camera system for a given application. An important distinction must be made between two types of IQ metrics:

(1) System IQ metrics: these describe aspects of system capability. Examples include camera system resolving power, signal-to-noise ratio (SNR), engineering dynamic range (DR), and camera system MTF. In some cases, component IQ metrics can be defined for individual system components.

(2) Perceived IQ metrics: these describe IQ as perceived by an observer of the displayed output image. Ideally the image size and viewing distance will be taken into account along with relevant properties of the human visual system (HVS). Examples include sharpness and photographic DR.

In photography, system IQ metrics are not necessarily the most useful in practice. A simple example is that of camera system resolving power, which is often confused with image sharpness. Camera system resolving power is defined as the highest spatial frequency which the camera and lens combination can resolve. However, this spatial frequency will not be observed in an output image displayed at a standard size and viewed from a normal distance. In this case, contrast reproduction at lower spatial frequencies will have a much greater impact upon perceived image sharpness. A camera with lower system resolving power could produce images which appear sharper provided it has superior MTF performance over the range of spatial frequencies that are most relevant.

Furthermore, system IQ metrics can be misleading when comparing different camera models. A simple example is SNR per photosite (sensor pixel). If the cameras being compared have sensors with different pixel counts, the comparison would be biased because the photosite areas are not the same. In this case, SNR per unit sensor area would be a more suitable metric provided the sensors themselves are the same size. The comparison is complicated further if the sensor formats are different, in which case the metric should normalise for the different sensor sizes in an appropriate manner. This could be achieved by normalising according to the ratio between the enlargement factors required to produce a displayed image of the same size. For example, either SNR per percentage frame height or SNR per circle of confusion (CoC) would appropriately normalise for photosite area in conjunction with sensor size.

Another factor to consider when performing cross-format comparisons is that the cameras involved will not be used in the same way in practice. For example, an identical combination of f-number, focal length, and ISO setting used on different formats will not lead to an output image with the same appearance in terms of angular field of view (AFoV) and depth of field (DoF). A solution is to specify the characteristics which define an 'equivalent image'. Once this has been accomplished, a different but 'equivalent' combination of f-number, focal length, and ISO setting is required on each format to produce equivalent images.

If IQ metric comparisons are based on equivalent images, then these 'equivalent' camera settings (including an equivalent ISO setting) should be used when comparing IQ. However, the larger format offers additional photographic capability when the combination of f-number, focal length, and ISO setting is such that the smaller format cannot provide an equivalent image. This additional photographic capability also potentially offers higher IQ.

On the other hand, *perceived* IQ metrics are based upon the viewed output image, and therefore sensor format and sensor pixel count are automatically taken into account. Ideally, perceived IQ metrics will involve observer resolving power and contrast sensitivity in conjunction with relevant aspects of system capability. Observer resolving power is defined as the highest spatial frequency which a human observer can resolve when viewing the output image at a specified image size and viewing distance, and can be specified in terms of the prescribed CoC.

The CoC was introduced in chapter 1. Due to its fundamental role in the definition of IQ metrics, this chapter begins with a detailed discussion of observer resolving power and the CoC. This is followed by a detailed derivation of equivalence theory for performing cross-format comparisons. Subsequently, some important system and perceived IQ metrics are described. The final part of the chapter discusses IQ in relation to photographic practice.

5.1 Perceived resolution

Camera system resolving power places an upper bound on the level of scene detail which can be captured by the camera. In turn, this serves as an upper bound on the potential detail that can be resolved by a human observer when viewing the output image on a screen or print. The actual detail resolved by the observer depends upon several factors. These include those listed in chapter 1:

- The resolving power or acuity of the observer's visual system.
- The image viewing distance and ambient conditions.
- The degree of enlargement from the sensor dimensions to the viewed output image dimensions.

Given a photographic scene with a high level of detail, consider camera systems A and B, where system B has a greater resolving power than system A. If an observer moves closer to a print obtained from system A or if the print is enlarged, a limiting situation will eventually be reached where the observer is unable to resolve any further detail in the print. However, the observer may continue to resolve detail in the print from system B upon moving closer or upon further enlargement. In other words, the main advantage of a higher system resolving power is that the output image can be viewed under stricter conditions before perceived quality begins to deteriorate. A higher system resolving power also has other advantages which will be discussed later in this chapter.

Observer resolving power can be related to the CoC which was introduced in chapter 1 when deriving the DoF equations. Under the viewing conditions which specify the CoC, details separated by a distance less than the CoC diameter will not be resolved by the observer of the output image. In other words, the CoC defines the *defocus blur afforded by the observer of the output image*. The defocus blur can be quantified by the allowable *depth of focus* at the sensor plane.

5.1.1 Observer resolving power

The retina of the eye has a granular structure. Its ability to resolve detail differs depending on the criterion used, for example point discrimination, point separation, isolated line discrimination, or line pattern separation [1]. In photography, the ability of the eye to resolve detail is defined using a pattern of *line pairs*. Each line pair consists of a vertical black stripe and vertical white stripe of equal width. As the width of the lines decreases, the stripes eventually become indistinguishable from a grey block. Observer *resolution* is then defined as the *least resolvable separation* (LRS) in millimetres per line pair, which is the minimum distance between the centres of neighbouring white stripes or neighbouring black stripes when the pattern can still just be resolved by the eye. Observer *resolving power* is the reciprocal of the observer resolution [1] and is measured in line pairs per millimetre,

$$\mathrm{RP} = \frac{1}{\mathrm{LRS}}.$$

The term 'high resolution' should be interpreted as referring to a high resolving power and a small LRS.

Observer resolving power depends upon the viewing distance. The distance where resolving power is considered to be at its optimum is known as the *least distance of distinct vision* D_v and is generally taken to be 250 mm or 10 inches [2, 3]. However, observer resolving power varies considerably depending upon the visual acuity of the individual and the ambient conditions. At D_v, camera and lens manufacturers typically assume a value of around 5 lp mm^{-1} when defining DoF scales [3].

Note that a resolving power of 5 lp mm^{-1} corresponds to 127 lp inch^{-1}, or equivalently 254 ppi (pixels per inch) for a digital image. This is the reason that 300 ppi is considered a sufficient image display resolution for a high quality print viewed at D_v.

5.1.2 Circle of confusion specification

As mentioned in the introduction to this section, observer resolving power can be specified in terms of the CoC introduced in chapter 1 when deriving the DoF equations. Camera and lens manufacturers base their CoC values on an assumed set of conditions under which the output image will be viewed by an observer. Photographers can use their own CoC values when the intended viewing conditions are known.

CoC specification by manufacturer
The output image viewed by the observer will typically have been enlarged from the sensor dimensions. The 60° *cone of vision* defines the limits of near peripheral vision. At the least distance of distinct vision $D_v = 250$ mm, the cone of vision roughly forms a circle of diameter $D_v \tan 30° = 288$ mm. If it is assumed that the width of the viewed image corresponds with this diameter, the enlargement factor from a 35 mm full-frame sensor will be 8. This is shown in figure 5.1 where the full-frame sensor dimensions (36 × 24 mm) have been enlarged by a factor of 8. The closest paper size which accommodates a print of this size is A4.

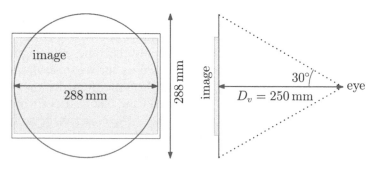

Figure 5.1. A viewing circle of approximately 60° diameter defines the limits of near peripheral vision. This is shown in relation to a 3 × 2 image (green) printed on A4 (210 × 297 mm) paper (black border) viewed at the least distance of distinct vision D_v.

If the observer can resolve 5 lp mm^{-1} when viewing the output image at D_v and the enlargement factor is 8, then the observer resolving power projected down to the sensor dimensions becomes 40 lp mm^{-1} [3]. Mathematically,

$$\text{RP(sensor dimensions)} = \text{RP(print viewed at } D_v) \times \text{enlargement} \qquad (5.1)$$

where

$$\text{RP(print viewed at } D_v) = 5 \text{ lp mm}^{-1}.$$

Here 'print' refers to an image either printed or viewed on a display. The value RP (sensor dimensions) does not refer to the actual capability or resolving power of the *camera system* itself. Nevertheless using the 35 mm full-frame format as an example, it is clear that the camera system does not need to resolve a line pair of width less than the value RP(sensor dimensions) = 40 lp mm^{-1}. This detail cannot be resolved by the observer of the output image when it has been enlarged by a factor of 8 and viewed at the least distance of distinct vision, $D_v = 250$ mm. These are typical viewing conditions assumed by the camera or lens manufacturer [3].

An equivalent viewpoint is that the value RP(sensor dimensions) affords a certain amount of defocus blur to be present in the output image which is assumed to be undetectable to the observer. The allowed defocus blur can be treated rigorously by calculating the defocus PSF using wave optics. However, this is not convenient for simple photographic calculations. Instead, photographic calculations treat defocus blur in a purely geometrical manner by using geometrical optics. In this description, the blur will be *uniform* over a circle which approximates the shape of the lens aperture. This is defined as the CoC. The CoC describes the amount of defocus blur which can be tolerated before the output image begins to appear 'out of focus' to the observer.

The relationship between the value RP(sensor dimensions) and the corresponding CoC diameter c is given by

$$\boxed{c = \frac{1.22}{\text{RP(sensor dimensions)}}}. \qquad (5.2)$$

This is illustrated graphically in figure 5.2. Derivation of this relationship requires treating the CoC as a geometrical PSF and then calculating the cut-off frequency. These concepts were introduced in chapter 3. For completeness, the derivation is given at the end of the present section.

For a 35 mm full-frame camera, RP(sensor dimensions) = 40 lp mm^{-1} and so the CoC diameter will be $c = 0.030$ mm according to equation (5.2). Smaller or larger sensors require a smaller or larger diameter c, respectively, because the enlargement factor in equation (5.1) will change accordingly. Figure 1.2 in chapter 1 lists example CoC diameters for various sensor formats.

Custom CoC

In practice, the output image will not necessarily be viewed under the conditions assumed by the camera or lens manufacturer. The required CoC diameter for any

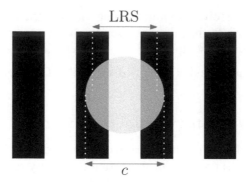

Figure 5.2. The required CoC diameter on the sensor is slightly wider than the LRS between neighbouring like stripes. A convolution of the CoC with the line pattern renders the stripes unresolvable to an observer of the output image under the specified viewing conditions.

desired enlargement and viewing distance can be calculated using the following formula,

$$c = \frac{1.22 \times \text{viewing distance}}{\text{RP(print viewed at } D_\text{v}) \times \text{enlargement} \times D_\text{v}}.$$

The value RP(print viewed at D_v) = 5 lp mm^{-1} assumed by the manufacturer can be adjusted. For example, the photographer may consider 5 lp mm^{-1} as underestimating the capability of the HVS. Ideally, the value will be adjusted according to the actual visual acuity of the observer and the ambient conditions, if known.

The CoC diameter c is proportional to the viewing distance and inversely proportional to the enlargement factor. If these scale in the same manner, then c will remain constant. If only the viewing distance increases, then the value for c will increase and more defocus blur can be tolerated.

Moreover, there is no requirement that the viewed image must fit within a comfortable viewing circle. For example, a poster-sized print situated close to the observer may be much larger than the circle of vision. In this case, the required CoC diameter will be very small. For a camera fitted with a CFA, observed IQ will certainly deteriorate if the required CoC size is smaller than a 2 × 2 block of sensor photosites. Sensors with a smaller pixel pitch have the advantage that a smaller CoC can be utilised if necessary. An image viewed at 100% on a computer display is an extreme enlargement that is beyond this practical CoC limit [4].

Depth of focus
It is straightforward to obtain the relationship between the prescribed CoC and the tolerable depth of focus within geometrical optics. The depth of focus is the image-space equivalent of the DoF. From figure 5.3, the CoC diameter c is related to the allowed depth of focus W by

$$c = \frac{W}{2} \frac{D_\text{xp}}{s' - s'_\text{xp}}.$$

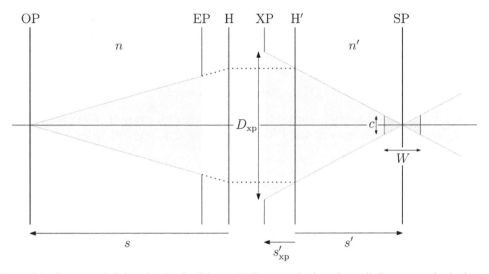

Figure 5.3. Geometry defining the depth of focus W. Here D_{xp} is the exit pupil diameter, s' is the image distance measured from the second principal plane, s'_{xp} is the distance from the second principal plane to the exit pupil, m is the Gaussian magnification, m_p is the pupil magnification, and f'_R is the rear effective focal length.

The exit pupil diameter D_{xp} is related to the entrance pupil diameter D by the pupil magnification,

$$D_{xp} = m_p D.$$

The distances s' and s'_{xp} were obtained when deriving the FoV equations in chapter 1,

$$s' = (1 + |m|)f'_R$$

$$s'_{xp} = (1 - m_p)f'_R.$$

Combining the above equations leads to the following result,

$$\boxed{W = \left(\frac{n'}{n}\right)2cN_w}.$$

Derivation of the CoC MTF
Equation (5.2) defined the following relationship,

$$c = \frac{1.22}{\text{RP(sensor dimensions)}}.$$

Here c is the diameter of the geometrical CoC, and RP(sensor dimensions) is the observer resolving power projected down to the sensor dimensions. Given a line pattern on the sensor plane with spatial frequency equal to RP(sensor dimensions), a *convolution* with the CoC will render the pattern unresolvable.

In order to derive the above relationship, the CoC needs to be treated mathematically as a circle function such as that used to describe the lens exit pupil in section 3.2.4 of chapter 3. There it was found that the OTF corresponding to a circle function is a jinc function. The OTF for the CoC is analogously given by

$$\text{OTF}_{\text{CoC}}(\pi c \mu_r) = \text{jinc}(\pi c \mu_r).$$

Here μ_r is the radial spatial frequency. The OTF for an example CoC is plotted in figure 5.4. If the first zero of the OTF defines the CoC cut-off frequency μ_c, then $\pi c \mu_c = 1.22\pi$ and so

$$\mu_c = \frac{1}{(c/1.22)}.$$

In the present context, μ_c is equal to RP(sensor dimensions) if it is assumed that an MTF value of 0% corresponds with the observer resolving power projected down to the sensor dimensions, where MTF = |OTF|. Equation (5.2) then follows.

According to the above analysis, the required CoC diameter is slightly wider than the narrowest line pair which needs to be resolved at the sensor-plane dimensions. This is illustrated graphically in figure 5.2. However, there is latitude in the value of the numerator depending on the criterion used for the cut-off frequency. For example, the 1.22 factor in the numerator can be dropped if RP (sensor dimensions) is instead defined as the spatial frequency where the MTF value drops to 20% rather than by the stricter 0% criterion. In this case, μ_c would become

$$\mu_c = \frac{1}{c}.$$

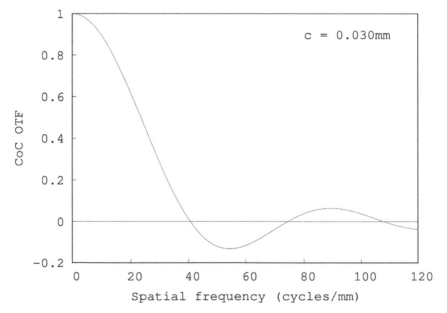

Figure 5.4. OTF for the CoC with diameter $c = 0.030$ mm.

In fact, both definitions are approximate because observer resolving power is measured using a solid line pattern rather than a sinusoidal line pattern. The contrast transfer function (CTF) describes the frequency response of a square wave pattern, and this can be related to the MTF of a sinusoidal pattern through Coltman's formula [5],

$$\text{CTF}(\mu) = \frac{4}{\pi}\left(\text{MTF}(\mu) - \frac{\text{MTF}(3\mu)}{3} + \frac{\text{MTF}(5\mu)}{5} + \cdots\right).$$

In this chapter, equation (5.2) will be used to define the CoC diameter. In practice, the criterion used for the cut-off frequency is much less significant than the value assumed for the visual acuity of the HVS. The *relative* size of the CoC is the most important factor when comparing different sensor formats.

5.2 Cross-format comparisons

Many factors need to be considered when choosing a camera system, one of which is the sensor format. This is an important consideration because camera systems based on larger formats can offer additional photographic capability such as extremely shallow DoF and higher peak SNR, but this generally comes at the cost of a higher total *system* size and weight when the camera and all required lenses are considered.

For example, a landscape photographer may prefer to use a large format in order to take advantage of the higher peak SNR on offer when a tripod can be used to maximise exposure duration. On the other hand, a smaller format may be preferred by a travel photographer due to practical restrictions on weight and the need to appear unobtrusive or inconspicuous. Generally, if the additional photographic capability of a larger format will rarely be utilised in practice, a smaller format may be a more sensible option.

All modern digital cameras produce good IQ, and other factors such as autofocus speed and accuracy, operation, controls and ergonomics are equally if not more important when choosing a camera system. Nevertheless, a framework needs to be established for comparing the IQ output from camera systems which use different sensor formats so that IQ metrics can be correctly interpreted. Such a framework is necessary because photos taken using different sensor formats naturally have different characteristics which are independent from the underlying camera and lens technology.

For a given object distance s and a typical scene with 18% average luminance metered using average photometry, an identical combination of focal length f, f-number N, and ISO setting S used on different formats will lead to the following:

- The same exposure duration (or 'shutter speed') t.
- The same average exposure $\langle H \rangle$ at the sensor plane.
- An image with the same standard brightness.
- An image with the same perspective.
- An image with the same magnification, $m = f/(s - f)$.

However, the following aspects of the image appearance will be different:

- AFoV.
- DoF.

This is because the AFoV depends upon sensor dimension d, and the DoF depends upon the CoC diameter c which is format-dependent for the same image display dimensions. Furthermore, the sensor area of the smaller format will collect a smaller total amount of light compared with the larger format. Assuming the sensors are equally efficient in terms of QE and signal processing, this will result in higher total image noise for the smaller format.

In order to place cross-format IQ comparisons on an equal footing, reference [6] provides a useful definition of *equivalent photos*. These are defined as photos taken on different formats with:

(1) The same perspective.
(2) The same framing (AFoV).
(3) The same DoF.
(4) The same shutter speed.
(5) The same brightness.
(6) The same display dimensions.

These are image attributes which depend only upon sensor format and are independent from the underlying camera and lens technology [6].

This section discusses each of the above attributes in detail. The end result will be that equivalent photos can be taken on different formats provided an *equivalent* combination of focal length, f-number, and ISO setting is used on each respective format. The equivalence relationship turns out to be very simple when focus is set at infinity.

An important result from equivalence theory is that *equivalent* photos turn out to have the *same total image noise* provided the sensors are equally efficient in terms of QE and signal processing [6]. In other words, a smaller format will in principle provide the same IQ performance as a larger format when equivalent photos are taken. This follows because equivalent photos are produced using the *same total amount of light* and therefore the same total signal.

However, the larger format offers *additional photographic capability* when the smaller format is unable to match the larger format by providing an equivalent photo. When the extra photographic capability of the larger format is utilised, the image IQ will in principle be higher. The total signal can be increased beyond the maximum defined by the equivalence overlap of the two systems, and this offers a higher SNR.

5.2.1 Equivalence ratio

In order to facilitate comparison of different sensor formats, it is useful to define a ratio between the lengths of the sensor diagonals,

$$ R = \frac{d_1}{d_2} . $$

Here d_1 is the length of the larger sensor diagonal, and d_2 is the length of the smaller sensor diagonal. This can be referred to as the *equivalence ratio* [6]. For example, if $d_1 = d$, then $d_2 = d/R$.

For the special case that the larger format is 35 mm full-frame, the equivalence ratio is equal to the focal-length multiplier m_f defined in chapter 1.

5.2.2 Equivalence at infinity focus

This section follows the logical discussion given in reference [6]. Mathematical proofs are included based upon the specification of the CoC from section 5.1.2 along with the photographic formulae derived in chapters 1 and 2.

1. The same perspective

The same perspective requires the same object-plane distance s. Recall that s is measured from the first principal plane of the lens to the object plane. The first principal plane will generally be located away from the aperture stop. The first and second principal planes will both coincide with the aperture stop only for the special case of a thin lens with the aperture stop at the lens.

2. The same framing

The same framing requires the same AFoV. Recall that the AFoV at infinity focus is defined by equation (1.27),

$$\alpha = 2 \tan^{-1} \frac{d}{2f}.$$

Here d is the sensor dimension in the required direction, and f is the effective focal length in air, hereafter referred to simply as the focal length.

Let the AFoV be measured in the diagonal direction. Consider camera system 1 with a sensor diagonal d and effective focal length f_1 focused at an object distance s. The AFoV is

$$\alpha_1 = 2 \tan^{-1} \frac{d}{2f_1}.$$

Now consider camera system 2 with a smaller sensor diagonal d/R and effective focal length f_2 focused at the same object distance s in order to achieve the same perspective. The AFoV is

$$\alpha_2 = 2 \tan^{-1} \frac{d}{2Rf_2}.$$

If $\alpha_1 = \alpha_2$ then

$$\boxed{f_2 = \frac{f_1}{R}}. \tag{5.3}$$

Equivalent focal lengths for the two systems focused at infinity are seen to be related by the equivalence ratio R.

Example The following focal lengths yield the same perspective and framing on their respective formats:

35 mm full frame:	24 mm
APS-C:	18 mm
Micro Four Thirds:	12 mm
2/3":	6 mm
1/2.5":	4 mm

3. The same depth of field

Consider camera system 1 with sensor diagonal d, focal length f_1, f-number N_1, and entrance pupil diameter D_1. Additionally consider camera system 2 with a smaller sensor diagonal d/R, focal length f_2, f-number N_2, and entrance pupil diameter D_2.

Assume the focal lengths are related according to equation (5.3) in order to achieve the same perspective and framing. This requires the focal lengths to be *equivalent*,

$$f_2 = \frac{f_1}{R}.$$

Both systems will have the same DoF provided the entrance pupil diameters of both systems are *equal*,

$$D_2 = D_1. \tag{5.4}$$

The proof of this requirement is given in section 5.2.3 which deals with arbitrary focus distances. It now follows from the two equations above that the f-numbers for the two systems must be *equivalent* and therefore must be related through the equivalence ratio R,

$$\boxed{N_2 = \frac{N_1}{R}}. \tag{5.5}$$

This equation holds at infinity focus but requires correction at closer focus distances.

Example The following focal length and f-number combinations yield the same perspective, framing and DoF on their respective formats:

35 mm full frame:	24 mm	$N = 2.8$
APS-C:	18 mm	$N = 2$
Micro Four Thirds:	12 mm	$N = 1.4$
2/3":	6 mm	$N = 0.7$

The 1/2.5" and smaller formats are unable to provide equivalent photos.

4. The same shutter speed

Equivalent photos taken by cameras with different sensor formats must contain the same degree of *subject motion blur*. This is defined as blur that occurs due to objects moving in the scene. Since equivalent photos have the same perspective and framing, it follows that equivalent photos must be taken using the same exposure duration or shutter speed.

Note that this requirement does not specify an appropriate shutter speed, but merely states that it must be the same. As discussed below, the shutter speed depends upon the chosen image brightness.

5. The same brightness

Consider camera system 1 with a sensor diagonal d, and camera system 2 with a smaller sensor diagonal d/R. Let A_1 be the area of sensor 1, and A_2 be the area of sensor 2.

For the same perspective, framing, DoF and shutter speed t, the total electromagnetic energy $Q = \Phi t$ entering the lens of each system will be *equal*. In other words, the same energy will be spread over different-sized sensor areas. In terms of exposure, this means that

$$\Phi t = \int_{A_1} H_1 \, dA_1 = \int_{A_2} H_2 \, dA_2. \tag{5.6}$$

Here Φ is the total flux, t is the shutter speed or exposure duration, H_1 is the exposure at an infinitesimal area element dA_1 on sensor 1, and H_2 is the exposure at the corresponding infinitesimal area element dA_2 on sensor 2.

In order to prove equation (5.6), consider any position on the object plane. The exposure at the corresponding position on the sensor plane for the two systems focused at infinity will be

$$H_1 = \frac{\pi}{4} LT \frac{t}{N_1^2} \cos^4 \varphi \tag{5.7a}$$

$$H_2 = \frac{\pi}{4} LT \frac{t}{N_2^2} \cos^4 \varphi. \tag{5.7b}$$

Here φ defines the object-space angle that the object position subtends with the optical axis, L is the scene luminance, and T is the lens transmission factor which is assumed to be the same for both systems. The luminance and cosine fourth terms will be the same for both systems at the same perspective and framing. Now combining these two equations and substituting equation (5.5) yields

$$\boxed{H_2 = R^2 H_1}. \tag{5.8}$$

The exposure at the area element on sensor 2 corresponding to the chosen object position is therefore a factor R^2 greater than the exposure at the corresponding area

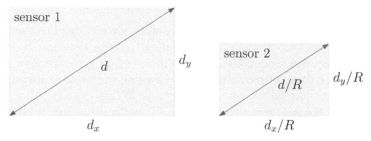

Figure 5.5. The area of sensor 1 is $d_x d_y$ and the area of sensor 2 is $(d_x/R)(d_y/R)$. Sensor 2 is therefore a factor R^2 smaller than sensor 1.

element on sensor 1 for the same object position. Now from figure 5.5, it is evident that the sensor area A_2 is smaller than A_1 by a factor R^2,

$$A_2 = \frac{A_1}{R^2}.$$

Therefore the infinitesimal area elements on the two sensors are related by

$$dA_2 = \frac{dA_1}{R^2}. \tag{5.9}$$

The proof of equation (5.6) is completed by using equations (5.8) and (5.9) to project the exposure distribution over A_1 onto A_2,

$$\int_{A_1} H_1 \, dA_1 = \int_{A_2} H_1 R^2 \, dA_2 = \int_{A_2} H_2 \, dA_2.$$

According to equation (5.6), the total electromagnetic energy Q that enters the lens of each system during the exposure duration is the same. Therefore equation (5.8) implies that

$$\langle H_2 \rangle = R^2 \langle H_1 \rangle. \tag{5.10}$$

Here $\langle H_1 \rangle$ and $\langle H_2 \rangle$ are the arithmetic average exposures for systems 1 and 2, respectively. Section 2.2.2 of chapter 2 showed that the product of the arithmetic average exposure with the exposure index S defines a photographic *constant P*. Therefore

$$\langle H_1 \rangle S_1 = \langle H_2 \rangle S_2. \tag{5.11}$$

Now combining equations (5.10) and (5.11) yields the following result,

$$\boxed{S_2 = \frac{S_1}{R^2}}. \tag{5.12}$$

The required ISO setting for the smaller sensor format is therefore a factor R^2 lower than the required ISO setting for the larger sensor format. If the ISO setting is defined using SOS and the metering is performed using average photometry, the images from the two systems will have the same JPEG brightness. In other words, *smaller sensors require less ISO gain to produce an image with the same JPEG brightness.*

In the following examples, the shutter speed has been chosen arbitrarily. In practice, an appropriate shutter speed will be recommended by the metering system and is dependent upon the nature of the scene luminance distribution.

Example 1 The following equivalent systems yield equivalent photos:

35 mm full frame:	24 mm	$N = 2.8$	1/100	ISO 800
APS-C:	18 mm	$N = 2$	1/100	ISO 400
Micro Four Thirds:	12 mm	$N = 1.4$	1/100	ISO 200
2/3″:	6 mm	$N = 0.7$	1/100	ISO 50

Example 2 The following equivalent systems yield equivalent photos:

35 mm full frame:	200 mm	$N = 8$	1/200	ISO 3200
APS-C:	133 mm	$N = 5.6$	1/200	ISO 1600
Micro Four Thirds:	100 mm	$N = 4$	1/200	ISO 800

6. The same display dimensions

Provided equivalent photos are viewed at the *same display dimensions*, the relationship between the CoCs for the respective formats being compared is defined by the equivalence ratio R,

$$c_2 = \frac{c_1}{R}.$$

Naturally, the viewing distance and ambient conditions must also be the same. The above relation is of fundamental importance for the mathematical proof of equivalence theory.

An additional factor which needs to be taken into consideration when comparing equivalent photos is differing pixel count. Ideally, equivalent images should both be upsampled to a common pixel count in order to place IQ comparisons on an equal footing [6]. This topic is discussed further in sections 5.5.2 and 5.6.4.

5.2.3 Equivalence at arbitrary focus

Existing descriptions of equivalence theory all assume that the equivalence scenario at infinity focus described in the previous section remains unchanged at closer focus distances. However this is not the case; equations (5.3) and (5.5) both require correction at closer focus distances. This correction is required because equivalent focal lengths related by the equivalence ratio R do not have the same *refractive power*. Consequently, the magnification m and associated bellows factor b do not vary as a function of object distance in the same manner for systems with different sensor sizes.

In order to force the same perspective at closer focus distances, a correction to both the focal length and f-number is required. In practice, this correction is negligible for typical object distances but can become noticeable at macro object distances. For completeness, an extension of the existing equivalence theory is derived below. This generalised theory additionally serves to prove the validity of equation (5.4).

It will be shown that the equivalence ratio R only requires correction at closer focus distances when relating equivalent focal lengths and f-numbers in order to achieve the same perspective and framing. The requirement that equivalent photos have the same image brightness at closer focus distances is satisfied provided the equivalent *working* f-numbers replace the equivalent f-numbers. Equivalent ISO settings then remain directly related through R^2.

1. Focal-length correction
Recall that the general expression for the AFoV was given in chapter 1,

$$\alpha = 2 \tan^{-1} \frac{d}{2\,bf}.$$

Here d is the sensor dimension in the required direction, f is the focal length (referring to the effective focal length in air), and b is the bellows factor defined by equation (1.26),

$$b = 1 + \frac{|m|}{m_p}.$$

At closer focus distances, the bellows factor b is no longer unity. Significantly, systems with different albeit equivalent focal lengths have *different* bellows factors at the same perspective or object distance s. This is explained by the following expression for the magnification obtained by combining the Gaussian conjugate and magnification equations,

$$|m| = \frac{f}{s - f}.$$

The pupil magnification must also be taken into consideration. Exact equivalence between two camera systems with different sensor formats is possible if the lens designs have the same symmetry and therefore the *same* pupil magnification m_p.

Consider camera system 1 with a sensor diagonal d and focal length f_1 focused at an object distance s_1 measured from the first principal plane. The AFoV is

$$\alpha_1 = 2 \tan^{-1} \frac{d}{2\,b_1 f_1}$$

with bellows factor

$$b_1 = 1 + \frac{|m_1|}{m_p}.$$

Now consider camera system 2 with a smaller sensor diagonal d/R and focal length f_2 focused on the same object plane positioned a distance s_2 from the first principal plane. In this case the AFoV is

$$\alpha_2 = 2 \tan^{-1} \frac{d}{2R b_2 f_2}$$

with bellows factor

$$b_2 = 1 + \frac{|m_2|}{m_p}.$$

The requirement that $\alpha_1 = \alpha_2$ yields the following equivalence condition,

$$\boxed{b_1 f_1 = R\, b_2 f_2}\,. \qquad (5.13)$$

By making use of the Gaussian conjugate equation along with the expression for the Gaussian magnification in the form $|m| = f/(s - f)$, algebraic manipulation similar to that carried out when deriving the bellows factor in chapter 1 shows that

$$b_1 = \frac{s_1 - s_{ep,1}}{s_1 - f_1}$$

$$b_2 = \frac{s_2 - s_{ep,2}}{s_2 - f_2}.$$

The terms $s_{ep,1}$ and $s_{ep,2}$ are the distances between the first principal plane and entrance pupil for systems 1 and 2, respectively,

$$s_{ep,1} = \left(\frac{m_p - 1}{m_p} \right) f_1$$

$$s_{ep,2} = \left(\frac{m_p - 1}{m_p} \right) f_2 .$$

Since these distances are not equal when the pupil magnification differs from unity, the object plane distances s_1 and s_2 measured from the first principal plane of systems 1 and 2 will also be different. This is because the total distance from the *entrance pupil* to the object plane must be the same for both systems in order that the AFoV and perspective be the same. Mathematically, this demands that

$$s_1 - s_{ep,1} = s_2 - s_{ep,2}. \qquad (5.14)$$

This requirement is illustrated graphically in figure 5.6. Now combining this result with the bellows factors above and substituting into equation (5.13) yields the following equivalence condition,

$$\boxed{f_2 = \frac{f_1}{R_w}}\,. \qquad (5.15)$$

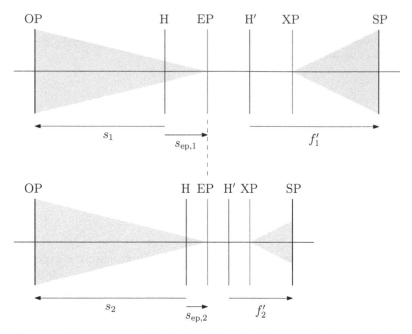

Figure 5.6. The vector distance $s_1 - s_{ep,1}$ for the larger format and $s_2 - s_{ep,2}$ for the smaller format must be equal in order to achieve the same perspective and framing.

The *working equivalence ratio* R_w is defined by

$$R_w = \left(\frac{b_2}{b_1}\right)R = \left(\frac{s_1 - f_1}{s_2 - f_2}\right)R. \tag{5.16}$$

If the lens focal length of the *larger* format is known (system 1) and the equivalent lens focal length of the *smaller* format is required (system 2), then the system 2 terms s_2 and f_2 need to be eliminated from equation (5.16) in order to obtain a usable expression for R_w. With the help of equation (5.14), algebraic manipulation leads to the following result,

$$R_w = R\left(1 - \frac{m_{c,1}}{p_{c,1}}\right). \tag{5.17}$$

The correction $m_{c,1}$ arises due to the differing magnifications, and the correction $p_{c,1}$ arises for a non-unity pupil magnification. These corrections are defined by

$$m_{c,1} = \left(\frac{R-1}{R}\right)\frac{f_1}{s_1}$$
$$p_{c,1} = m_p + (1 - m_p)\frac{f_1}{s_1}. \tag{5.18}$$

Alternatively, if the lens focal length of the *smaller* format is known (system 2) and the equivalent lens focal length of the *larger* format is required (system 1), then the system 1 terms s_1 and f_1 need to be eliminated from equation (5.16) in order to obtain a usable expression for R_w. Again with the help of equation (5.14), algebraic manipulation leads to the following result,

$$R_w = \frac{R}{1 + \left(\dfrac{m_{c,2}}{p_{c,2}}\right)R} . \tag{5.19}$$

In analogy with above, the corrections $m_{c,2}$ and $p_{c,2}$ due to differing magnifications and a non-unity pupil magnification are defined by

$$m_{c,2} = \left(\frac{R-1}{R}\right)\frac{f_2}{s_2}$$
$$p_{c,2} = m_p + (1 - m_p)\frac{f_2}{s_2} .$$

For the purposes of determining equivalent focal lengths, the working equivalence ratio R_w provides a correction to R when focus is set closer than infinity. The correction vanishes when $R = 1$ or when s_1, $s_2 \to \infty$ in which case R_w reduces to R. For the special case that $m_p = 1$, the terms $p_{c,1}$ and $p_{c,2}$ are both unity. In this case, the object distances measured from the first principal plane of each system will be equal, $s_1 = s_2 = s$.

Example 1

Object distance $s = 1000$ mm, $m_p - 1$

35 mm full frame:	$f_1 = 200$ mm
APS-C:	$f_2 = 143$ mm
Micro Four Thirds:	$f_2 = 111$ mm

According to equation (5.15) with R_w specified by equation (5.17), a lens marked 200 mm on a 35 mm full-frame system, a lens marked 143 mm on APS-C, and a lens marked 111 mm on a Micro Four Thirds[TM] system will yield the same perspective and framing when focused at an object distance $s = 1000$ mm.

Example 2

Object distance $s = 1000$ mm, $m_p = 1$

Micro Four Thirds:	$f_2 = 100$ mm
APS-C:	$f_1 = 129$ mm
35 mm full frame:	$f_1 = 182$ mm

According to equation (5.15) with R_w given by equation (5.19), a lens marked 100 mm on a Micro Four Thirds^{TM} system, a lens marked 129 mm on APS-C, and a lens marked 182 mm on a 35 mm full-frame system will yield the same perspective and framing when focused at an object distance $s = 1000$ mm.

2. f-number correction

Recall from chapter 1 that the total DoF is defined by

$$\text{total DoF} = \frac{2h(s - f)(s - s_{ep})}{h^2 - (s - f)^2}$$

where

$$h = \frac{Df}{c}.$$

Here D is the entrance pupil diameter and c is the CoC diameter. This equation is strictly valid only for $s \leqslant H$ where $H = h + f$ is the hyperfocal distance. When $s = H$, the rear DoF extends to infinity.

Consider camera system 1 with sensor diagonal d, focal length f_1, entrance pupil diameter D_1, CoC diameter c_1, and consider an object plane positioned a distance s_1 from the first principal plane. The total DoF is given by

$$\text{DoF}_1 = \frac{2 h_1(s_1 - f_1)(s_1 - s_{ep,1})}{h_1^2 - (s_1 - f_1)^2}$$

where

$$h_1 = \frac{D_1 f_1}{c_1}.$$

Now consider camera system 2 with a smaller sensor diagonal d/R, focal length f_2, entrance pupil diameter D_2, CoC diameter c_2, and consider the same object plane positioned a distance s_2 from the first principal plane. The total DoF is given by

$$\text{DoF}_2 = \frac{2 h_2(s_2 - f_2)(s_2 - s_{ep,2})}{h_2^2 - (s_2 - f_2)^2} \tag{5.21}$$

where

$$h_2 = \frac{D_2 f_2}{c_2}. \tag{5.22}$$

Larger sensor formats have a larger CoC because the enlargement factor from the image projected onto the sensor to the viewed output image is less for larger sensors, as described in section 5.1.2. The relationship between the CoC diameters is always defined by the equivalence ratio provided the display dimensions are the same,

$$\boxed{c_2 = \frac{c_1}{R}}.$$

Since the same perspective and framing are required at an arbitrary focus distance, the relationship between f_2 and f_1 must satisfy the *working* equivalence ratio defined by equation (5.15),

$$f_2 = \frac{f_1}{R_w}.$$

Substituting these expressions for c_2 and f_2 into equation (5.22) yields

$$h_2 = \frac{R D_2 f_1}{R_w c_1}.$$

Finally, substituting f_2 and h_2 into equation (5.21) and working through the algebra leads to the following result,

$$\text{DoF}_2 = \text{DoF}_1$$

provided that the following condition is satisfied,

$$D_2 = D_1.$$

Since $N = f/D$, it follows that

$$\boxed{N_2 = \frac{N_1}{R_w}}.$$

(5.23)

This shows that the equivalence ratio R must be replaced by the working equivalence ratio R_w when relating equivalent focal lengths *and* relating equivalent f-numbers when focus is set closer than infinity.

Example 1

Object distance $s = 1000$ mm, $m_p = 1$

35 mm full frame:	$f_1 = 200$ mm	$N_1 = 4$
APS-C:	$f_2 = 143$ mm	$N_2 = 2.86$
Micro Four Thirds:	$f_2 = 111$ mm	$N_2 = 2.22$

According to equation (5.15) with R_w specified by equation (5.17), a lens marked 200 mm and $f/4$ on a 35 mm full-frame system, a lens marked 143 mm and $f/2.86$ on APS-C, and a lens marked 111 mm and $f/2.22$ on a Micro Four Thirds[TM] system will yield the same perspective, framing, and DoF when focused at an object distance $s = 1000$ mm.

Example 2

Object distance $s = 1000$ mm, $m_p = 1$

Micro Four Thirds:	$f_2 = 100$ mm	$N_2 = 2$
APS-C:	$f_1 = 129$ mm	$N_1 = 2.58$
35 mm full frame:	$f_1 = 182$ mm	$N_1 = 3.64$

According to equation (5.15) with R_w specified by equation (5.19), a lens marked 100 mm and $f/2$ on a Micro Four Thirds™ system, a lens marked 129 mm and $f/2.58$ on APS-C, and a lens marked 182 mm and $f/3.64$ on a 35 mm full-frame system will yield the same perspective and framing when focused at an object distance $s = 1000$ mm.

3. Working f-number equivalence

Part 5 of section 5.2.2 showed that the total light projected onto different sensor formats will be the same for equivalent photos taken at infinity focus. Equation (5.23) may lead to the incorrect conclusion that this property no longer holds when equivalent photos are taken at closer focus distances. In fact, this property always holds when equivalent photos are taken because it is the *working* f-number N_w which determines the illuminance or irradiance at the sensor plane when focus is set closer than infinity.

To see this mathematically, consider system 1 which corresponds to the larger format and system 2 which corresponds to the smaller format. The working f-numbers $N_{w,1}$ and $N_{w,2}$ are defined by

$$N_{w,1} = b_1 N_1$$
$$N_{w,2} = b_2 N_2.$$

Substituting these into equation (5.23) yields

$$N_{w,2} = \left(\frac{b_2}{b_1} \right) \frac{N_{w,1}}{R_w}.$$

Now substituting equation (5.16) leads to the following result,

$$\boxed{N_{w,2} = \frac{N_{w,1}}{R}}. \tag{5.24}$$

Therefore the *working* f-numbers are always directly related through the equivalence ratio R.

The proof given in part 5 of section 5.2.2 which showed that the total light projected onto different sensor formats will be the same when equivalent photos are taken at infinity focus can be generalised to hold at any focus distance simply by replacing the f-numbers with the working f-numbers. Equations (5.7a) and (5.7b) must be replaced by

$$H_1 = \frac{\pi}{4} L T \frac{t}{N_{w,1}^2} \cos^4 \varphi$$

$$H_2 = \frac{\pi}{4} L T \frac{t}{N_{w,2}^2} \cos^4 \varphi.$$

Now following the same argument leads to the result expressed by equation (5.6),

$$\Phi t = \int_{A_1} H_1 \, dA_1 = \int_{A_2} H_2 \, dA_2.$$

Therefore the relationship between the ISO settings for the two systems is *independent of the focus distance* and so equation (5.12) always holds,

$$\boxed{S_2 = \frac{S_1}{R^2}}.\qquad(5.25)$$

The following conclusions can now be made:
- The total light projected onto different sensor formats will be *identical* for equivalent photos taken at *any* focus distance.
- The ISO settings for different sensor formats will always be directly related though the square of the equivalence ratio R^2 when equivalent photos are taken at *any* focus distance.
- The shutter speeds will always be *identical* when equivalent photos are taken.

Example 1

Object distance $s = 1000$ mm, $m_p = 1$				
35 mm full frame:	$f_1 = 200$ mm	$N_1 = 4$	1/100	ISO 800
APS-C:	$f_2 = 143$ mm	$N_2 = 2.86$	1/100	ISO 400
Micro Four Thirds:	$f_2 = 111$ mm	$N_2 = 2.22$	1/100	ISO 200

The above systems yield equivalent photos. The focal lengths and f-numbers correspond to those marked on the lens, and the shutter speed has been chosen arbitrarily.

Example 2

Object distance $s = 1000$ mm, $m_p = 1$				
Micro Four Thirds:	$f_2 = 100$ mm	$N_2 = 2$	1/200	ISO 400
APS-C:	$f_1 = 129$ mm	$N_1 = 2.58$	1/200	ISO 800
35 mm full frame:	$f_1 = 182$ mm	$N_1 = 3.64$	1/200	ISO 1600

The above systems yield equivalent photos. The focal lengths and f-numbers correspond to those marked on the lens, and the shutter speed has been chosen arbitrarily.

5.2.4 Summary of equivalence

- Equivalent photos are defined as photos produced by different formats which have the same perspective, framing, DoF, shutter speed, brightness, and display dimensions [6].

- Equivalent camera exposures (*equivalent* combinations of focal length f, f-number N, and ISO setting S) are required on different formats in order to produce equivalent photos.
- At infinity focus, equivalent focal lengths and f-numbers are related through the equivalence ratio R, which is the ratio of the sensor diagonals, and equivalent ISO settings are related through R^2. For example, $R = 2$ if the larger format is 35 mm full-frame and the smaller format is Micro Four Thirds^{TM}. In this case, a 12 mm $f/1.4$ lens mounted on a Micro Four Thirds^{TM} camera set at ISO 200 and a 24 mm $f/2.8$ lens mounted on a 35 mm full-frame camera set at ISO 800 will produce equivalent photos.
- The effect of diffraction softening will be the same for equivalent photos viewed at the same display dimensions. This will be discussed further in section 5.5.3.
- Equivalent photos are produced using the same total amount of light, and therefore have the *same* IQ in principle (see below).
- A larger format offers *additional photographic capability* over a smaller format when the camera exposure is such that the smaller format cannot provide an equivalent photo.
- When a larger format *utilises* its additional photographic capability to take a photo, a greater amount of light can be used to produce the image. Such images therefore potentially have higher IQ.

The above framework can be used as a basis for performing cross-format IQ comparisons on an equal footing. The framework is independent from the underlying camera and lens technology, and so equivalent photos have the same IQ in principle [6]. Departures from this ideal scenario are a useful measure of real-life IQ differences between different camera systems.

Real-life IQ differences will occur in an enormous variety of ways. For example, sensors which do not use exactly the same technology will have different noise floors and QEs, and this will affect SNR. IQ differences will also arise from differing sensor pixel counts, and equivalent images should ideally be upsampled to a common pixel count in order to fairly take these IQ differences into account when performing comparisons [6]. Furthermore, the quality of the optics will have a huge effect on final image IQ. Even for lenses designed for the same format, the nature of the residual aberrations can vary enormously between lens designs. Perceived image sharpness depends upon the nature of MTF curves over a range of spatial frequencies, and MTF curves should be compared at *equivalent spatial frequencies* related through the equivalence ratio R. For example, 20 lp mm^{-1} on a 35 mm full-frame sensor should be compared with 30 lp mm^{-1} on APS-C and 40 lp mm^{-1} on Micro Four Thirds^{TM}. This will be discussed further in section 5.3.2.

Finally, it has been shown that an equivalence correction should in principle be introduced into the equivalence framework when focusing on an object plane positioned closer than infinity. The correction can be applied by replacing R with the working equivalence ratio, R_w. This correction only applies to focal lengths and f-numbers, and not to the shutter speed or ISO setting. However, the difference between R and R_w is negligible at normal object distances, and the correction is not required beyond macro object distances in practice. For zoom lenses, the focus breathing properties of the lens design actually oppose the bellows factor and will have a much greater impact than the equivalence correction.

5.3 Lens MTF

The point-spread function (PSF) and its Fourier transform (FT), the optical transfer function (OTF), were described in chapter 3. The modulation transfer function (MTF) and phase transfer function (PTF) are the modulus of the OTF and the phase of the OTF, respectively.

Recall that the PSF can be thought of as a blur filter. The convolution operation is analogous to sliding the PSF over the ideal image to produce the real output image. The shape of the PSF determines the level of blur present in the output, and most of the blur strength is concentrated in the region close to the ideal image point. However, the PSF is difficult to describe in simple numerical terms.

For incoherent lighting, the image at the sensor plane can be interpreted as a linear combination of sinusoidal irradiance waveforms of varying spatial frequency. This suggests that aspects of IQ can be described by the imaging of sinusoidal target objects such as stripe patterns. Significantly, the real image of a sinusoid will always be another sinusoid, irrespective of the shape of the PSF. Furthermore, the direction and spatial frequency of the real sinusoidal image will remain unchanged [2]. However, its contrast or *modulation* will be reduced compared to that of the ideal image formed in the absence of the PSF. Since the MTF is the modulus of the FT of the PSF, the MTF precisely describes how the modulation is attenuated as a function of spatial frequency.

The MTF provides a useful quantitative description of IQ. As well as lenses, various other components of the camera system can be described by their own MTF, and the system MTF can be straightforwardly calculated by multiplying these individual component MTFs together. The system MTF can be used to define system resolving power, along with other metrics such as perceived image sharpness.

This section begins with a very brief description of lens aberrations which profoundly affect the nature of the lens PSF and various aspects of the corresponding lens MTF. This is followed by an introduction to lens MTF plots. Based on the lens MTF, the final section discusses lens resolving power. System MTF and system resolving power will be discussed in section 5.4.

5.3.1 Aberrations

Residual lens aberrations lead to image defects which Gaussian optics leaves out of consideration [5, 7–9]. Seven basic forms of aberration can be described:

- *Axial chromatic aberration* (axial CA): In a lens with residual CA, light rays from an object point will be brought to a focus at different positions *along* the optical axis. The position is wavelength-dependent and arises due to variation of the lens material refractive index with wavelength. Axial CA improves upon closing the lens aperture ('stopping down' the lens).
- *Spherical aberration* (SA): In a lens with residual SA, light rays from an object point will again be brought to focus at different positions along the optical

axis. However, the positional dependence arises because refraction from the outer zone of a spherical surface is greater than the central zone, as illustrated in figure 1.2 of chapter 1. Spherical aberration can be controlled through the balancing of positive and negative elements, and it is reduced upon stopping down the lens. Modern photographic lenses increasingly use aspherical elements to minimise spherical aberration.

- *Lateral chromatic aberration* (CA): In a lens with residual lateral CA, light rays from an object point will be brought to a focus at different *heights* above the ideal image point. The height is wavelength-dependent and introduces coloured fringes. Stopping down the lens has no effect on lateral CA.

- *Comatic aberration* (coma): In a lens with residual coma, light rays from an object point will again be brought to a focus at different heights above the optical axis. However, coma arises due to variation of magnification with lens zone height. This causes a one-sided radial blurring of the ideal point image which resembles the shape of a comet.

Spherical aberration and axial CA are present at the optical axis and will therefore occur over the entire lens field. On the other hand, coma and lateral CA are oblique aberrations which do not appear at the optical axis, but increase in severity with radial distance outwards. The following aberrations are also oblique:

- *Astigmatism*. Astigmatism occurs because rays which lie in the plane containing the optical axis (meridional plane) and rays which lie in the plane perpendicular to the optical axis (sagittal plane) do not come to a focus at the same point. The image of an off-axis object point forms two small focal lines that are perpendicular to each other. Astigmatism improves upon stopping down the lens.

- *Field curvature*. Residual field curvature is considered to be present if the image of an object plane positioned perpendicular to the optical axis does not lie in the corresponding image plane positioned perpendicular to the optical axis. Although correctable, field curvature is a natural effect which is noticeable because the sensor plane is flat.

- *Distortion*. Distortion arises from variation in magnification with obliquity, which means that magnification varies across the image field. Distortion only affects image shape and does not change upon adjusting the lens aperture. Distortion does not introduce blur, however blur may be introduced by digital image-processing techniques applied to correct distortion.

5.3.2 Lens MTF plots

Lens MTF data published by lens manufacturers will originate either from calculations using lens design software, or preferably from direct measurements using specialist devices. Since lens MTF varies with spatial position over the optical image field, the most useful way to present lens MTF data is by choosing a set of important spatial frequencies, and then plotting MTF *as a function of image height* at each of these spatial frequencies. Image refers to the optical image and *image*

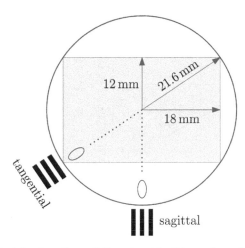

Figure 5.7. Image height is defined as the radially symmetric distance from the image centre and can be measured out to the lens circle. The short and long edges of a full-frame 36 × 24 mm sensor occur at image heights or radial positions 18 mm and 12 mm, respectively.

height refers to the radially symmetric field position between the optical axis and the lens circle [2, 4]. This is illustrated in figure 5.7 for the 35 mm full-frame format.

The spatial frequencies chosen are considered to be the most relevant to lens performance when a *human observer views the output image* from the camera under *standard viewing conditions*. These viewing conditions have been described in section 5.1. The output image viewing distance is taken to be the least distance of distinct vision $D_v = 250$ mm, the enlargement factor from the sensor dimensions to the viewed output image dimensions is such that the image fits within a comfortable viewing circle, and a standard value for the visual acuity of the observer at distance D_v is assumed. Higher spatial frequencies are not relevant unless the image is viewed more critically. In particular, the enlargement would need to be such that the entire image would not fit within a comfortable viewing circle.

Figure 5.8 shows the relationship between the MTF when plotted as a function of spatial frequency at specified image heights, and when plotted as a function of image height for a set of spatial frequencies. For a lens circle covering a 35 mm full-frame sensor, a typical set of spatial frequencies may include 10 lp mm^{-1}, 20 lp mm^{-1}, and 40 lp mm^{-1}. For a smaller lens circle, the relevant frequencies will be proportionally higher according to the equivalence ratio R. When comparing with 35 mm full-frame, the equivalence ratio is equal to the focal-length multiplier m_f. For example, the frequencies just mentioned would increase to 15 lp mm^{-1}, 30 lp mm^{-1}, and 60 lp mm^{-1} for a lens circle covering an APS-C sensor with $R = 1.5$. This follows because an image projected onto a smaller sensor needs a greater enlargement to match the dimensions of the viewed output image, as described in section 5.1 earlier.

PSFs are generally not circular, however the rotational symmetry of the lens dictates that the shortest or longest elongations of the PSF will always be parallel or perpendicular to the radius of the lens circle [2]. Different MTF curves will be obtained depending on whether the line pattern used to measure MTF is perpendicular or

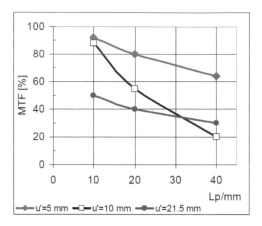 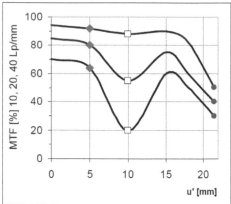

Figure 5.8. (Left) Spatial frequency representation of lens MTF for three selected image heights. (Right) Image height representation of lens MTF for three selected spatial frequencies. The example points indicated by circles, squares, and diamonds show identical data plotted in the two different representations. (Figure reproduced from reference [4] with kind permission.)

parallel to the radius of the lens circle. These are known as the *tangential* (or meridional) and the *sagittal* (or radial) directions, respectively. These directions are indicated in figure 5.7, and both of these types of curve are normally shown in lens MTF data. Typically the longest elongation of the PSF is parallel to the sagittal direction, in which case the sagittal MTF curve will have the higher MTF. Tangential and sagittal curves that are similar in appearance are indicative of a circular PSF.

The ideal Gaussian image position for the lens may not coincide precisely with the sensor plane of the camera. For example, field curvature may be present along with focus shift to balance aberrations. Lens MTF curves are sensitive to the plane of focus chosen because different parts of the image field will be affected differently as the image plane is shifted [2]. Moreover, lens MTF data is dependent upon the nature of the light used for the calculation or used to take the measurement. Data representing a single wavelength can be dramatically different from data representing polychromatic white light [2].

Ideal MTF curves will have high values which remain constant as the image height or radial field position changes. Such ideal curves are rarely seen in practice, particularly at the maximum aperture or lowest f-number due to the presence of residual aberrations and other optical phenomena. Experience is required to fully interpret the information present in lens MTF curves. Figure 5.9, which has been reproduced from reference [2], shows curves for the Zeiss Planar 1.4/50 ZF lens along with the type of information which can be extracted. References [2, 4] provide useful guidance for interpreting MTF curves of real lenses.

Limitations of MTF curves

It should also be pointed out that there is information about the imaging properties of lenses which cannot be represented by MTF curves. For example, MTF curves cannot describe *veiling glare*. This arises from unwanted reflections between the

Good contrast and very acceptable sharpness in the centre

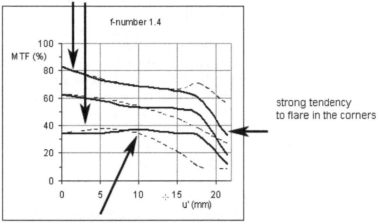

strong tendency
to flare in the corners

Good edge sharpness, moderate micro contrast,
high contrast edges with flare in the outer parts of the frame

MTF at 10Lp/mm in nearly the whole frame above 90%,
above 50% at 40 Lp/mm, that means images in rich contrast,
well defined, excellent image quality

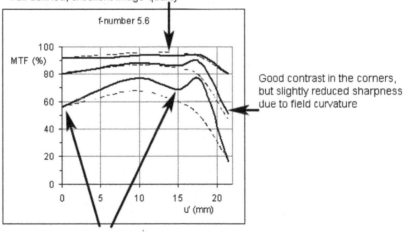

Good contrast in the corners,
but slightly reduced sharpness
due to field curvature

curve for 40Lp/mm varies a little, while 10Lp/mm remains flat,
this points to small focus shift and residual field curvature

Figure 5.9. Lens MTF for the Zeiss Planar 1.4/50 ZF as a function of 35 mm full-frame image height for white light. The spatial frequencies shown are 10, 20, and 40 lp mm^{-1}. The dashed curves are the tangential orientation and the lens is focused at infinity. (Figure reproduced from reference [2] with kind permission.)

optical surfaces and from light scattering from the interior barrel components, all of which cause light rays to reach the sensor plane a great distance from their intended target. Such phenomena are described by the *macro contrast* of the lens, rather than the *micro contrast* described by lens MTF curves [2].

Another example is the information contained in skewed PSFs. Although the separate tangential and sagittal MTF curves describe the *elongation* of the PSF in the tangential and sagittal directions as shown in figure 5.7, the MTF cannot describe any *asymmetry* in these directions. Such asymmetry arises from aberrations such as coma. Coma produces a PSF with a comet-shaped tail in the sagittal (radial) direction, and such information is contained in the PTF. As described in section 3.1.7 of chapter 3, the PTF describes the change in phase or *shifting* of the real sinusoids relative to the ideal sinusoids as a function of spatial frequency. The PTF can have a systematic effect on the nature of the image. In particular, a skewed PSF will affect an edge in the image differently depending on its relative orientation [2].

A final example is that of *bokeh*, which describes the aesthetic quality of the out-of-focus blur produced by a lens. A PSF of circular shape near the sensor plane is desirable, and this is indicated by the presence of similar tangential and sagittal MTF curves. However, this is no guarantee that the lens will produce bokeh of high aesthetic quality. Out-of-focus blur arises from the defocused PSF defined far from the sensor plane, whereas MTF curves are derived from the PSF present in the immediate vicinity of the sensor plane. For example, a circular PSF near the sensor plane can arise from over-corrected spherical aberration. This leads to annular defocused PSFs which produce a nervous or restless blurred background [2]. Some of the best lenses are characterised by the nature of the pleasing bokeh that they produce along with other special aesthetic character which cannot be derived from MTF curves.

5.3.3 Lens MTF and sensor format

Recall that the important spatial frequencies for lens MTF curves are typically between 10 and 40 lp mm^{-1} for the 35 mm full-frame format, and that the important spatial frequencies for other formats will scale in proportion with the focal-length multiplier. More generally, the important spatial frequencies scale in proportion with the equivalence ratio R between two different sensor formats, the reason being that an image projected onto a smaller sensor needs a greater enlargement to match the dimensions of the viewed output image. The relevant *enlargement factor* for any given sensor format is taken into account through the CoC diameter for that format, as described in section 5.1.2.

When using the spatial frequency representation for a selected radial field position, lens MTF data can be more generally interpreted by using a spatial frequency unit which is directly comparable between different sensor formats, namely *line pairs per picture height* (lp/ph). This unit is related to lp mm^{-1} as follows,

$$\text{lp/ph} = \text{lp mm}^{-1} \times \text{picture height(mm)}.$$

In the present context, *picture height* refers to the short edge of the sensor measured in mm and is therefore the same as the *image height* [4].

Picture height can also used to specify the print height, in which case the lp mm^{-1} value will downscale accordingly. In other words, lp/ph is a very general unit which is directly comparable between different sensor formats because picture height is proportional to CoC diameter.

5.3.4 Lens resolving power

Recall from section 5.1 that *observer* resolution is defined using a pattern of line pairs as the LRS in millimetre per line pair. This is the minimum distance between the centres of neighbouring white stripes or neighbouring black stripes when the alternating line pattern can still just be resolved by the eye. In other words, high resolution refers to a high density of resolvable lines or small LRS. Observer resolving power is defined as the reciprocal of the observer resolution [1],

$$RP = \frac{1}{LRS}.$$

Therefore resolving power is expressed in frequency units, in this case line pairs per millimetre. Unlike the resolving power of an imaging sensor which can in principle be made arbitrarily high by reducing pixel pitch as technological advances allow, diffraction places a fundamental restriction on *optical* resolution and resolving power referred to as the *diffraction limit*. Consequently, *the resolving power of the camera system as a whole cannot exceed the diffraction limit*.

The diffraction limit can be defined in a precise mathematical way in the Fourier domain as the spatial frequency where the diffraction component of the optics MTF drops to zero for a sinusoidal target waveform. The expression for the transfer function was derived in section 3.2 of chapter 3,

$$H_{\text{diff,circ}}(\mu_r, \lambda) = \begin{cases} \frac{2}{\pi}\left(\cos^{-1}\left(\frac{\mu_r}{\mu_c}\right) - \frac{\mu_r}{\mu_c}\sqrt{1 - \left(\frac{\mu_r}{\mu_c}\right)^2}\right) & \text{for } \frac{\mu_r}{\mu_c} \leqslant 1 \\ 0 & \text{for } \frac{\mu_r}{\mu_c} > 1 \end{cases}. \qquad (5.26)$$

The lighting has been assumed to be incoherent so that the PSF and sinusoidal target waveforms at the sensor plane are linear in terms of irradiance, and the aperture has been assumed to be circular. The MTF drops to zero at the *Abbe cut-off frequency* μ_c measured in cycles/mm. Spatial frequencies higher than μ_c *at the sensor plane* cannot be resolved by the lens. The Gaussian expression for μ_c is

$$\mu_c = \left(\frac{n}{n'}\right)\frac{1}{\lambda N_w}. \qquad (5.27)$$

This reduces to the following well-known expression when $n = n'$ and focus is set at infinity,

$$\boxed{\mu_c = \frac{1}{\lambda N}}.$$

In chapter 3, a lens free from aberrations was described as being *diffraction limited*. This means that the lens performance is limited only by diffraction and so its MTF obeys equation (5.26). For a lens with residual aberrations, the MTF value at any given spatial frequency cannot be greater than the diffraction-limited MTF at the same frequency, and generally will be lower. Even though the resolving power of an aberrated lens remains that of a diffraction-limited lens in principle, aberrations can reduce the MTF values at high spatial frequencies to such an extent that the effective cut-off is much lower [10].

A useful way to demonstrate this graphically is via the anticipated RMS wavefront error W_{RMS} introduced in chapter 3. This is a way of modelling the overall effect of aberrations as a statistical average of the wavefront error over the entire wavefront converging from the exit pupil to the image point. A small aberration content is classed as an RMS wavefront error up to 0.07, medium between 0.07 and 0.25, and large above 0.25 [11]. An empirical relationship due to Shannon [11, 12] for the transfer function corresponding to the RMS wavefront error is provided by the following formula,

$$H_{ATF}(\mu_n) = 1 - \left\{ (W_{RMS}/0.18)^2 \left[1 - 4(\mu_n - 0.5)^2 \right] \right\}.$$

Here $\mu_n = \mu_r/\mu_c$ is the normalised spatial frequency, and μ_c is the Abbe cut-off frequency defined above. This transfer function is referred to as the aberration transfer factor (ATF) [11] or optical quality factor (OQF) [13]. The approximate lens MTF is then defined as the product of the diffraction-limited transfer function and the ATF,

$$MTF_{lens} \approx H_{diff,circ}(\mu_r) H_{ATF}(\mu_r).$$

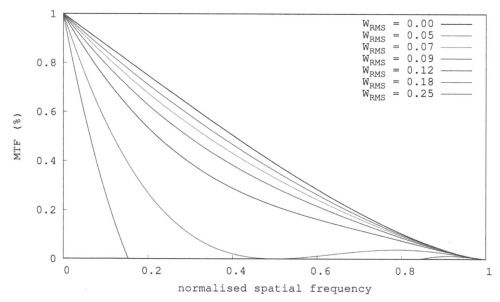

Figure 5.10. Approximate lens MTF as a function of normalised spatial frequency $\mu_n = \mu_r/\mu_c$ for a selection of RMS wavefront error values W_{RMS}. Aberrations are absent when $W_{RMS} = 0$.

This is plotted for several values of RMS wavefront error in figure 5.10. Since it is an empirical model, negative values are ignored [11]. The model is accurate up to $W_{\mathrm{RMS}} = 0.18$.

A practical value for an effective cut-off frequency therefore requires a less-stringent resolution criterion. For example, an effective cut-off frequency could be defined where the real aberrated lens MTF drops to a *small percentage value* instead of zero.

In order to establish an appropriate percentage value, it is useful to consider other resolution criteria. For example, the *Rayleigh two-point criterion* is based upon light from two isolated point sources in real space projected by the lens onto the sensor plane. As the points are brought closer together, a separation on the sensor plane is reached such that the points cannot be distinguished as separate objects due to the overlap of the diffraction PSF associated with each point. The Rayleigh criterion for the LRS on the sensor plane is defined as

$$1.22\left(\frac{n}{n'}\right)\lambda N_{\mathrm{w}}.$$

When $n = n'$ and focus is set at infinity, this becomes

$$\boxed{d_{\mathrm{Rayleigh}} = 1.22\,\lambda N}.\tag{5.28}$$

As illustrated in figure 5.11, each Airy disk is centred at the first zero ring of the other.

Now substituting a spatial frequency μ_r of order $1/d_{\mathrm{Rayleigh}}$ into the diffraction transfer function defined above reveals that the Rayleigh criterion corresponds to a diffraction-limited optics MTF value of approximately 9% [14]. In other words, MTF values between 0% and 9% do not provide useful detail according to the Rayleigh criterion. This suggests that an appropriate effective cut-off frequency for defining the resolving power of a real aberrated lens at a given f-number, wavelength, and field position is where the real aberrated lens MTF similarly drops to 9%.

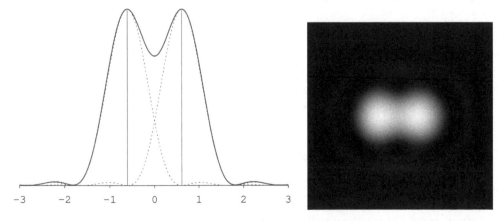

Figure 5.11. Rayleigh criterion for two-point resolution in units of λN. The distance between the centres of the Airy disks denoted by the pair of red vertical lines is the Airy disk radius itself, $d_{\mathrm{Rayleigh}} = 1.22\,\lambda N$.

When aberrations are present, this effective cut-off frequency will be smaller than the Abbe cut-off frequency. Depending on the application, other percentage criteria such as 5%, 10%, or 20% may be more suitable.

At the expense of a lower MTF at lower spatial frequencies, an inverse apodisation filter can be used to increase the resolving power of a lens [10, 14]. Nevertheless, it should be remembered that the resolving power of the camera system as a whole is the relevant metric for describing the smallest detail which can be reproduced in the output image. This may analogously be defined in terms of the spatial frequency where the *camera system* MTF drops to a small percentage value, as discussed in the next section. However, the system resolving power cannot be greater than the lens resolving power.

5.4 System MTF

The system MTF at a given spatial frequency is given by the product or cascade of the individual component MTFs at the same frequency,

$$\mathrm{MTF}_{\mathrm{sys}}(\mu_x, \mu_y) = \mathrm{MTF}_1(\mu_x, \mu_y)\mathrm{MTF}_2(\mu_x, \mu_y)\mathrm{MTF}_3(\mu_x, \mu_y) \cdots \mathrm{MTF}_n(\mu_x, \mu_y).$$

The ISO 12233 photographic standard provides a technique for measuring average system MTF based upon photographing a target edge of high contrast rather than target sinusoidal waveforms [15]. The edge is slanted and this enables the so-called average edge-spread function (ESF) to be determined from the output image file in a much greater resolution than the sampling pixel pitch. The system MTF can be derived from the ESF [16, 17].

Recall that the lens MTF will always be bounded from above by the diffraction MTF at any given spatial frequency. Furthermore, system resolving power cannot be greater than the lens resolving power. However, the in-camera image-processing engine may apply *sharpening* such as an unsharp mask (USM) filter to the output digital image, and the image-processing engine becomes part of the camera system. Because the MTF due to image sharpening can be greater than unity, the *system MTF can be higher than the lens MTF* at any given spatial frequency.

5.4.1 System MTF and sensor format

Recall that for equivalent output images from different sensor formats viewed at the same display dimensions, the spatial frequencies corresponding to the optical image at the sensor plane are related through the equivalence ratio R between the sensor formats. This follows because an optical image projected onto a smaller sensor needs a greater enlargement to match the dimensions of the viewed output image. The relevant *enlargement factor* for any given sensor format is taken into account through the CoC diameter, as described in section 5.1.2.

The sensor Nyquist frequency introduced in chapter 3 expressed in cycles/mm or lp mm^{-1} units depends upon the pixel pitch or photosite density. This is not directly comparable between systems with different sensor formats. The pixel pitch of the smaller format needs to be smaller than the pixel pitch of the larger format in order to produce an equivalent viewed output image when the different enlargement factors are taken into account. Furthermore, the comparison should ideally be between equivalent focal lengths and f-numbers for the two systems, as described in section 5.2.

In analogy with section 5.3.3 which introduced the *line pairs per picture height* (lp/ph) unit appropriate for comparing *lens* MTF curves associated with different sensor formats, the lp/ph unit is also commonly used for system MTF plots. This is a suitable unit when comparing system MTF plots associated with different sensor formats because picture height is proportional to CoC diameter. In particular, the sensor Nyquist frequency in lp/ph units depends only on photosite count rather than photosite density or pixel pitch. For example, a 12.1 MP APS-C sensor will have the same sensor Nyquist frequency as a 12.1 MP 35 mm full-frame sensor when expressed in lp/ph units. This is completely appropriate when equivalent images are being compared.

5.4.2 System resolving power

Camera system resolving power is defined as the spatial frequency where the camera system MTF drops to a small prescribed percentage value. This is referred to as the *system cut-off frequency*. The system cut-off frequency will ultimately be limited by the lowest system component cut-off frequency.

In order to illustrate how the resolving power of a real camera system may be influenced by some of the major contributions to the system MTF, it is useful to construct a very simple model consisting of the three MTF components derived in chapter 3. The relevant equations were summarised in section 3.5. Here the spatial frequency will be considered along one axis only. In this case the components are:

- Lens MTF which assumes that the lens is diffraction limited. This is defined by

$$\text{MTF}_{\text{diff,circ}}(\mu_x, \lambda) = \frac{2}{\pi}\left(\cos^{-1}(\mu_x/\mu_c) - (\mu_x/\mu_c)\sqrt{1 - (\mu_x/\mu_c)^2}\right).$$

This expression is valid when $\mu_x \leqslant \mu_c$. When $\mu_x > \mu_c$, $\text{MTF}_{\text{diff,circ}}(\mu_x, \lambda) = 0$. The model calculation can be performed at a single representative wavelength such as $\lambda = 550$ nm.

- Sensor MTF which includes only the spatial detector–aperture contribution,

$$\text{MTF}_{\text{det-ap}}(\mu_x) = \left|\frac{\sin(\pi d_x \mu_x)}{\pi d_x \mu_x}\right|.$$

The detection area width d_x can be varied up to the value of the pixel pitch p_x.

- Four-spot OLPF MTF,

$$\text{MTF}_{\text{OLPF}}(\mu_x) = |\cos(\pi s_x \mu_x)|.$$

The spot separation s_x between the two spots on a single axis can vary from the pixel pitch value p_x for a maximum strength filter down to zero for a non-existent filter.

The system MTF is calculated at each spatial frequency μ_x in the following way,

$$\boxed{\mathrm{MTF_{system}}(\mu_x, \lambda) = \mathrm{MTF_{diff,circ}}(\mu_x, \lambda)\mathrm{MTF_{det-ap}}(\mu_x)\,\mathrm{MTF_{OLPF}}(\mu_x)}\ .$$

As an example, consider a compact camera with a 1/1.7 inch sensor and a 12 MP pixel count. In this case the pixel pitch $p_x \approx 2\,\mu\mathrm{m}$. The sensor cut-off frequency is $1/0.002 = 500$ lp mm^{-1} assuming that the photosite detection area width $d_x = p_x$. The sensor Nyquist frequency is $0.5 \times (1/0.002) = 250$ lp mm^{-1}. For simplicity, assume that the system resolving power is defined by the frequency where the system MTF drops to zero.

Figure 5.12(a) shows the model results at $N = 2.8$ in the absence of the OLPF. The spatial frequencies have been expressed in lp mm^{-1} units. The system cut-off frequency corresponds with the sensor cut-off frequency at 500 lp mm^{-1} and so the system resolving power is limited by the sensor. Aliasing is present above the sensor Nyquist frequency.

When the f-number increases to $N = 8$, figure 5.12(b) shows that the system cut-off frequency has dropped to 228 lp mm^{-1} and so the system resolving power is limited by the lens. Furthermore, aliasing has been totally eliminated because the system cut-off frequency has dropped below the sensor Nyquist frequency at this f-number.

When a full-strength OLPF is included, aliasing can be minimised at any selected f-number. For example, figure 5.12(c) shows the system MTF at $N = 2.8$ when a full-strength OLPF is included. In this case the cut-off frequency corresponds with the sensor Nyquist frequency at 250 lp mm^{-1} and so the system resolving power is limited by the OLPF. The system MTF above the sensor Nyquist frequency is suppressed by the sensor MTF and lens MTF [18].

The above simple model illustrates that in order to increase system resolving power by reducing the sensor pixel pitch, diffraction needs to be accordingly reduced by lowering the f-number so that the lens cut-off frequency remains higher than the sensor Nyquist frequency. However, lenses at their lowest f-numbers or maximum apertures generally suffer from residual aberrations and are rarely diffraction limited in practice. Aberrations lower the effective lens cut-off frequency as described in section 5.3.4, particularly when measured at large radial field positions. This prevents achievable system resolving power from reaching the diffraction limit defined by the Abbe cut-off frequency. When diffraction dominates, sensor pixel pitch has negligible impact upon the system resolving power. However, reducing the pixel pitch will improve the detector–aperture component of the sensor MTF at low spatial frequencies and this can improve edge definition and perceived sharpness. Sharpness will be discussed in the next section.

5.5 Sharpness

Sharpness is a perceived physiological phenomenon which is influenced by factors such as edge definition in the recorded image along with properties of the HVS.

Although sharpness is synonymous with resolving power, the two are not necessarily correlated. A high resolving power corresponds to a high system cut-off

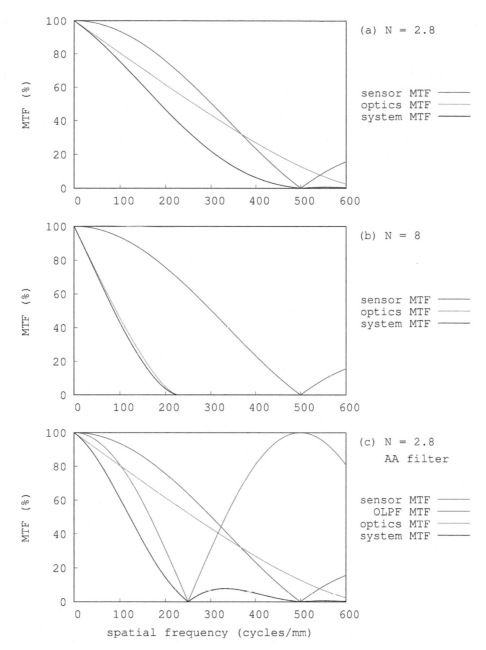

Figure 5.12. Illustration of system resolving power using a model system MTF.

frequency, whereas high perceived sharpness arises from a high MTF at spatial frequencies that are important to the HVS. The important spatial frequencies depend upon factors such as the viewing distance and the contrast sensitivity of the HVS.

For the same photographic scene and output image viewing conditions, one camera system could produce an image with high perceived sharpness but low resolution, whereas a different camera system could produce an image with low perceived sharpness but high resolution.

For a given lens and camera, the photographer plays an important role in influencing the system MTF and therefore perceived sharpness. An important example is *diffraction softening* described in chapter 3. This strongly affects system MTF and can be controlled by adjusting the lens f-number. Camera shake contributes a jitter component to the system MTF, and the resizing of the output digital image provides a resampling contribution to the system MTF [13]. Another example is digital image sharpening. This can *increase* overall system MTF, although care should be taken not to introduce sharpening artefacts. The fact that digital image sharpening can improve perceived sharpness but cannot improve resolution is evidence that sharpness and resolution are not necessarily correlated [2].

This section begins by introducing MTF50 and subjective quality factor (SQF), which are two perceived sharpness metrics that have found application in photography. The impact of image resampling and diffraction softening are subsequently described.

5.5.1 Sharpness metrics

Various metrics for perceived image sharpness have been developed. Examples include the *MTF area* (MTFA), *square root integral* (SQRI), and SQF [19]. *Heynacher numbers* are used by Zeiss [2]. Imatest® IQ evaluation software used by a number of camera reviewers includes *MTF50*, SQF, and *acutance* developed by the CPIQ initiative of the International Imaging Industry Association (I3A) [20]. DxO® Labs [21] have introduced a *perceptual megapixel* (MPix) score which aims to convey a measure of perceived sharpness that correlates with visual perception in terms of a single number familiar to photographers.

MTF50

System MTF50 is defined as the *spatial frequency* where the system MTF drops to 50% of the zero frequency value. The value is influenced by all contributions to the system MTF including optics, sensor, and image processing. A high MTF50 is associated with MTF curves which remain generally high over a wide range of important spatial frequencies and is therefore considered to be a reasonable indicator of perceived sharpness. MTF50P is a similar metric defined as the spatial frequency where the system MTF drops to 50% of the *peak* system MTF value. Since excessive sharpening improves MTF50 even when this leads to visible image artifacts such as halos at edges, MTF50P is designed to remove any influence that excessive sharpening may have on the result [22].

MTF50 is directly comparable between cameras with different sensor formats when expressed in the line pairs per picture height (lp/ph) units described in section 5.3.4. When the context is not clear, it is useful to refer to MTF50 as *system* MTF50 in order to avoid confusion with *lens* MTF50 which is sometimes used as a metric for lens sharpness. However, lens MTF50 it is not a particularly useful metric for assessing lens performance. Section 5.3.2 showed that evaluation of lens performance requires lens MTF data to be presented at several important spatial frequencies as a function of radial field position [2].

In order to relate MTF50 to an appropriate IQ level, MTF50 can be expressed in units related to the print dimensions such as line widths per inch on the print [22]. However, this rating of perceived sharpness does not take into account the viewing distance or the HVS.

Subjective quality factor

Subjective quality factor (SQF) [23] takes into account the viewed output image size, the viewing distance, and the contrast sensitivity of the HVS when evaluating perceived sharpness. It is defined as

$$\boxed{SQF = K \int_{\mu_1}^{\mu_2} MTF(\mu)CSF(\mu)d(\ln \mu)} .$$
(5.29)

It was found experimentally that there is a linear correlation between subjective IQ and just-noticeable differences. This suggests that the integration should be carried out on a logarithmic scale with respect to spatial frequency,

$$d(\ln \mu) = \frac{d\mu}{\mu}.$$

Furthermore, spatial frequency μ is expressed in *cycles/degree* units here. The *contrast sensitivity function* $CSF(\mu)$ describes the sensitivity of the HVS to contrast as a function of μ. The CSF used in the original definition of SQF was taken to be unity between 3 and 12 cycles/degree,

$$\mu_1 = 3$$
$$\mu_2 = 12.$$

This means that the SQF is simply the area under the camera system MTF curve calculated between 3 and 12 cycles/degree when the MTF is similarly expressed in cycles/degree units and plotted on a logarithmic scale. The constant K is a normalisation constant which ensures that a constant MTF with value unity will yield SQF = 100,

$$K = 100 \int_{\mu_1}^{\mu_2} CSF(\mu)d(\ln \mu).$$

In order to take into account the viewing distance, the cycles/degree units need to be related to the cycles/mm units used at the sensor plane. First consider the viewed output print. Denoting θ as the angle subtended by the eye with one spatial cycle p on the print, the spatial frequency μ(cycles/degree) at the eye and spatial frequency μ (cycles/mm) on the print are specified by $1/\theta$ and $1/p$, respectively. From figure 5.13,

$$p = 2l \tan(\theta/2) \approx l\theta \times \frac{\pi}{180},$$

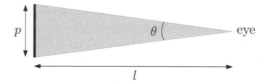

Figure 5.13. Geometry used to relate cycles/degree at the eye to cycles/mm on the print.

where l is the distance from the observer to the print, and the factor on the right-hand side converts radians into degrees. Therefore

$$\mu(\text{cycles/mm on print}) = \mu(\text{cycles/degree}) \times \frac{180}{l\pi}.$$

This can now be projected onto the sensor dimensions by using the enlargement factor,

$$\boxed{\mu(\text{cycles/mm on sensor}) = \mu(\text{cycles/degree}) \times \frac{180\,\text{PH}}{l\pi h}}.$$

Here PH is the picture height (print or monitor) in millimetres and h is the height of the short side of the sensor in millimetres. This formula can be used to relate the camera system MTF as a function of μ(cycles/mm) to the μ(cycles/degree) appearing in equation (5.29). An alternative spatial frequency unit used for system MTF calculation is cycles/pixel, where pixel refers to a photosite (sensor pixel) or pixel in a digital output image that has not been resampled. In this case the above formula becomes [22]

$$\boxed{\mu(\text{cycles/pixel}) = \mu(\text{cycles/degree}) \times \frac{180\,\text{PH}}{l\pi n_\text{h}}}.$$

Here n_h is the number of pixels on the short side of the sensor, and so the sensor height drops out of the equation. In practice, resampling will take place to satisfy a pixels per inch display resolution requirement on the print. As described later in this section, this will introduce a resampling MTF which will affect perceived sharpness.

Imatest®[22] have refined the original SQF calculation by introducing the CSF defined by reference [24] and extending the integration from zero up to the sensor Nyquist frequency expressed in cycles/degree units. The revised CSF is shown in figure 5.14. The revised integration limits are

$$\mu_1 = 0$$
$$\mu_2 = \mu_\text{Nyq}.$$

This CSF applies a refined weighting for how strongly the camera system MTF influences perceived sharpness at each spatial frequency.

SQF is a far superior metric for evaluating perceived sharpness compared with MTF50. A drawback of SQF is that *contour definition* is not taken into account [4].

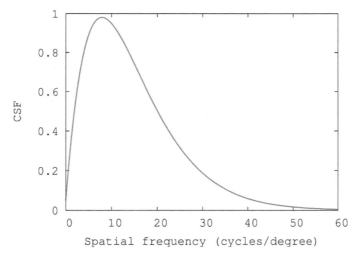

Figure 5.14. Contrast sensitivity function of the human eye.

Contour definition is higher for flatter MTF curves and this is associated with higher perceived sharpness in practice. In other words, further assessment is required to recognise special cases [4].

5.5.2 Image resampling

Digital image resampling is required when performing many common image-processing operations. Of particular relevance is the resizing of an image to satisfy a pixels per inch requirement on a monitor or print as described in section 4.8 of chapter 4.

The number of pixels in a digital image can be increased by *upsampling*. Although new scene information cannot be added, the aim is to preserve the appearance of the original image as closely as possible. Unfortunately, practical interpolation filters are not exact. Such filters will introduce undesirable artefacts and will affect perceived image sharpness.

The number of pixels can be reduced by *downsampling*. In this case, the signal will be smoothed and so detail will be lost which will again affect perceived image sharpness. The aim is to lose as little information as possible while minimising residual aliasing artefacts.

The optimum practical solution for image resampling varies depending upon the application and the nature of the image itself. Photographers typically devise their own image resizing strategies and learn through experience which methods work best in various circumstances. Nevertheless, it is useful to have a mathematical understanding of the basic idea of resampling. The sections below briefly discuss upsampling and downsampling based on the introduction to sampling theory given in chapter 3. In particular, it will be shown that the performance of resampling methods can be evaluated from the resampling MTF which can in principle be included as part of the system MTF.

Upsampling

It is useful to think of the digital image in terms of the sampled signal which ultimately arises from the optical image projected at the sensor plane. Aliasing may be present in the sampled signal depending on the value of the system cut-off frequency at the time of image capture in relation to the sensor Nyquist frequency. Nevertheless, the aim when upsampling is simply to increase the sampling rate without affecting the signal and image appearance.

For clarity, the following discussion will be restricted to resampling in 1D. Extension to 2D is straightforward. Upsampling in principle requires reconstruction of the continuous signal $f(x)$ from known sample values so that $f(x)$ can be resampled at a new and more densely spaced grid of positions [25]. In practice, the $f(x)$ values at the new sample positions can be directly calculated through convolution. The value of $f(x)$ at an arbitrary new sample location x can be reconstructed from the discrete input image samples $\tilde{f}(x)$ by convolving with a *reconstruction kernel* $h(x)$,

$$f(x) = \tilde{f}(x) * h(x) = \sum_i \tilde{f}(x_i)\, h(x - x_i).$$

This amounts to centring the kernel at the new sample location and then summing the products of the known discrete sample values with the kernel value at those positions. The sum over i runs over the number of known sample values within the range of the reconstruction kernel. The example shown in figure 5.15 extends over

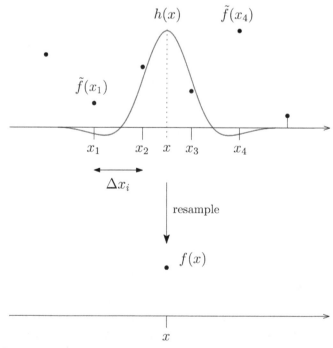

Figure 5.15. Image resampling in 1D. Here the non-ideal interpolation kernel $h(x)$ (green) centred at position x extends over four input samples located at x_1, x_2, x_3, and x_4. The output function value $f(x)$ at position x is shown in the lower diagram. The input image sample spacing is indicated by Δx_i.

four samples [25]. However, it was shown in chapter 3 that the ideal reconstruction filter is a sinc function which extends over all space,

$$h_{ideal}(x) = \text{sinc}(x) = \frac{\sin(\pi x)}{\pi(x)}.$$

Here x is normalised to the pixel sample spacing so that $\Delta x_i = 1$. The MTF corresponding to a sinc function is the rectangle function,

$$\text{MTF}_{ideal} = |\text{rect}(x)|.$$

This is plotted in figure 5.16. The horizontal axis in the figure represents cycles per pixel and the Nyquist frequency is located at 0.5 cycles per pixel. The region to the left of the Nyquist frequency is referred to as the *passband*, and the region to the right is referred to as the *stopband*. The rectangle function is equal to unity in the passband and zero in the stopband. This ensures that all frequencies below the Nyquist frequency are perfectly reconstructed and that all frequencies above the Nyquist frequency are completely suppressed.

Unfortunately, approximations must be made in practice because the sinc function extends over all space. The simplest reconstruction kernel is defined by nearest-neighbour interpolation,

$$h_{nn}(x) = \begin{cases} 1, & 0 \leqslant |x| < \dfrac{1}{2} \\[2mm] 0, & \dfrac{1}{2} \leqslant |x| \end{cases}$$

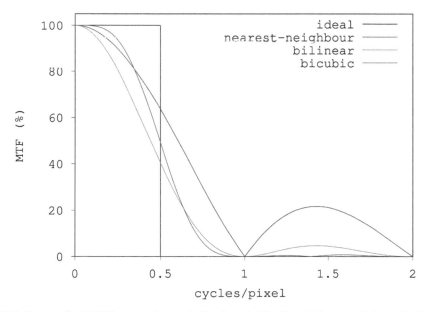

Figure 5.16. Resampling MTF for several example filter kernels. The Nyquist frequency is located at 0.5 cycles per pixel. When upsampling or downsampling, the pixel units are always defined by the image with the larger pixel sample spacing.

Again x is normalised to the pixel sample spacing. The performance of this reconstruction filter can be evaluated by comparing its transfer function with that of the ideal interpolation function. The nearest-neighbour interpolation MTF is given by

$$\text{MTF}_{nn}(\mu_x) = \left| \text{sinc}(\mu_x) \right|.$$

Figure 5.16 shows that the sharp transition between the passband and stopband is attenuated. The decay in the passband causes image blurring. Furthermore, there is considerable *frequency leakage* into the stopband. Unless the original replicated frequency spectra are sufficiently far apart, frequency leakage due to non-ideal reconstruction can cause spurious high frequencies to be introduced into the passband. This will cause undesirable jagged edges to appear in the image. Since the image is being resampled, these spurious high frequencies can be interpreted as aliasing artefacts because they will fall below the Nyquist frequency of the upsampled image [25]. Jagged edges can be improved by applying a low-pass filter to the upsampled image in order to bandlimit the signal down to the Nyquist frequency of the original image. This is essentially what happens upon stepping back when viewing the image [25].

An improvement on nearest-neighbour interpolation is *bilinear* interpolation,

$$h_{bl}(x) = \begin{cases} 1 - |x| & 0 \leqslant |x| < 1 \\ 0 & 1 \leqslant |x| \end{cases}.$$

Since x is normalised to the pixel sample spacing, the bilinear reconstruction kernel extends over two samples in 1D and four samples in 2D. The MTF is given by

$$\text{MTF}_{bl}(\mu_x) = \left| \text{sinc}^2(\mu_x) \right|.$$

Figure 5.16 shows that frequency leakage into the stopband is reduced when using bilinear interpolation compared with nearest-neighbour interpolation.

An even better approximation to the sinc function is provided by *bicubic convolution* [26],

$$h_{bc}(x) = \begin{cases} (\alpha + 2)|x|^3 - (\alpha + 3)|x|^2 + 1 & 0 \leqslant |x| < 1 \\ \alpha|x|^3 - 5\alpha|x|^2 + 8\alpha|x| - 4\alpha & 1 \leqslant |x| < 2 \\ 0 & 2 \leqslant |x| \end{cases}.$$

A commonly used value for α is -0.5. The reconstruction kernel extends over four samples in 1D and sixteen samples in 2D. The MTF is given by [27]

$$\text{MTF}_{bc}(\mu_x) = \left| \frac{3}{(\pi\mu_x)^2}(\text{sinc}^2(\mu_x) - \text{sinc}(2\mu_x)) \right|$$

$$+ \left| \frac{2\alpha}{(\pi\mu_x)^2}(3\,\text{sinc}^2(2\mu_x) - 2\,\text{sinc}(2\mu_x) - \text{sinc}(4\mu_x)) \right|.$$

Figure 5.16 shows that bicubic convolution with $\alpha = -0.5$ exhibits reduced attenuation in the passband and greatly reduced frequency leakage into the stopband. Bicubic convolution is the standard interpolation kernel used by Adobe® Photoshop. Many other interpolation methods exist such as Lanczos resampling which uses a kernel based on a windowed sinc function. Such methods can give superior results compared to bicubic convolution but may introduce other types of reconstruction artefacts [25].

In summary, the aim when upsampling an image is to leave the original signal and Nyquist frequency intact, $\mu'_{Nyq} = \mu_{Nyq}$, and simply increase the sampling rate $\mu'_s > \mu_s$ and associated pixel count. Unfortunately, non-ideal reconstruction will corrupt the signal and introduce a combination of image blurring and jagged edges. The image blurring will result from attenuation in the passband. Jagged edges may appear due to frequency leakage into the stopband. The latter will occur if the replicated spectra of the original image are sufficiently close together such that spurious high frequencies are retained which in turn raise the Nyquist frequency, $\mu'_{Nyq} > \mu_{Nyq}$.

Downsampling

Recall that when upsampling an image, the signal needs to be reconstructed in order to increase the sampling rate. In this case the interpolation filter acts as a reconstruction filter. The size of the reconstruction kernel $h(x)$ remains fixed because it depends upon the pixel sample spacing of the original image rather than the upsampled image.

However, the interpolation filter plays a different role when *downsampling* an image because information will be discarded. In contrast to upsampling which will increase the separation between the replicated frequency spectra, downsampling will decrease the separation. Signal information will be lost and aliasing will occur if the new sampling rate μ'_s drops below twice the Nyquist frequency μ_{Nyq} of the input image. This is because *undersampling* will cause the spectra to overlap and corrupt the passband. When undersampling, the interpolation filter must construct the output by acting as an *anti-aliasing filter* rather than a reconstruction filter and must bandlimit the image spectrum to the new Nyquist frequency $\mu'_{Nyq} < \mu_{Nyq}$. Although the new signal will naturally correspond to a smoothed lower-resolution representation of the original photographic scene, bandlimiting to μ'_{Nyq} will minimise aliasing.

A simple way to achieve the above is to increase the size of the interpolation kernel in accordance with the scale reduction factor used for downsampling [25, 28],

$$f(x) = \tilde{f}(x) * ah(ax) = a \sum_i \tilde{f}(x_i)h(ax - ax_i).$$

Here $a < 1$ is the scale reduction factor. In contrast to upsampling where $\Delta x_i = 1$ corresponds to the input image sample spacing as indicated in figure 5.15, here $\Delta ax_i = 1$ corresponds to the output image sample spacing. In other words, the sum over i covers a greater number of input pixels than the number used when upsampling. For example, the bicubic convolution kernel may extend over many input samples but only four and sixteen *output* samples in 1D and 2D, respectively. The filter frequency response will accordingly be narrower due to the reciprocal relationship between the spatial and frequency domains. This relationship is expressed by the following identity where H is the FT of h,

$$H\left(\frac{\mu_x}{a}\right) = \text{FT}\{ah(ax)\}.$$

The cut-off frequency where $H \to 0$ will be reached at a lower spatial frequency. Poorly implemented downsampling implementations are sometimes encountered which introduce aliasing by failing to include the scale reduction factor a in the interpolation filter kernel. In such cases, a blur filter can be applied *before* downsampling in order to reduce aliasing.

5.5.3 Diffraction softening

Diffraction softening introduced in chapter 3 strongly affects system MTF and therefore perceived sharpness. The impact of diffraction softening can be controlled by adjusting the lens f-number, however it cannot be eliminated.

The system MTF at frequencies below the Nyquist frequency will be lowered by diffraction, and so edge definition and perceived sharpness will be reduced. Although perceived sharpness may initially increase as the f-number is raised from its minimum value due to the lessening effect of lens aberrations on reducing the system MTF, the effects of diffraction will eventually begin to dominate. Such diffraction softening will be easily visible if viewing the output image at 100% on a computer display. For normal viewing distances and enlargements, a noticeable drop in perceived sharpness may not be expected until the Airy disk diameter approaches the CoC diameter,

$$2.44\lambda N \approx c.$$

For example, consider an output image from a 35 mm full-frame camera enlarged to A4 size and viewed from the least distance of distinct vision $D_v = 250$ mm. In this case the CoC diameter $c = 0.030$ mm. Rearranging the above equation indicates that a noticeable drop in perceived sharpness may occur around $N = 22$. For smaller sensor formats, the CoC value will be proportionally smaller. For example, corresponding estimates of $N = 16$ and $N = 11$ would be appropriate for APS-C and Micro Four Thirds[TM] formats, respectively. In practice, all these values can be reduced by about one stop since the estimate neglects all other contributions to the system MTF.

Diffraction and sensor format
The major factor in determining the onset of noticeable diffraction softening is the size of the Airy disk in relation to the CoC.

Since the CoC diameter takes into account the enlargement factor from the sensor dimensions to the viewed output image dimensions, diffraction softening will have the *same* impact on *equivalent* images produced by cameras with different sensor formats.

The relationship between the CoC diameters is always defined by the equivalence ratio R provided the display dimensions are the same,

$$c_2 = \frac{c_1}{R}.$$

Here c_1 and c_2 are the CoC diameters corresponding to the larger and smaller formats, respectively. Equivalent images require equivalent camera settings including equivalent f-numbers,

$$N_2 = \frac{N_1}{R}.$$

Here N_1 and N_2 are the f-numbers corresponding to the larger and smaller formats, respectively.

For example, a focal length $f_1 = 150$ mm and f-number $N = 11$ on a 35 mm full-frame system will produce an image with the same diffraction softening as $f_1 = 100$ mm and f-number $N = 8$ on APS-C in principle. Deviations from this ideal scenario will occur in practice due to differences between the underlying camera and lens technologies of the systems being compared.

Diffraction and pixel count

A smaller pixel pitch or higher sensor pixel count generally improves edge definition in the recorded image because the detector–aperture MTF will be improved below the system cut-off frequency. Nevertheless, there is only a weak correlation between pixel pitch and the onset of diffraction softening that will be noticeable to an observer of the output image at normal viewing distances and enlargements.

As explained above, the major factor in determining the onset of noticeable diffraction softening is the size of the Airy disk in relation to the CoC, and the prescribed CoC diameter depends upon sensor format rather than pixel pitch. In terms of IQ, it is advisable not to allow the CoC diameter to become smaller than a 2×2 block of photosites. An advantage of a smaller pixel pitch is that the CoC can be made smaller.

The above argument can be illustrated by calculating system MTF50 for two cameras with the same sensor format but different pixel counts. Here a very simple model for the system MTF will be constructed which includes the following components,

1. Optics MTF which assumes that the lens is diffraction limited.
2. Sensor MTF which includes only the spatial detector–aperture component and assumes a 100% FF.
3. OLPF MTF which assumes the presence of a full-strength 4-spot filter.

Using a representative wavelength $\lambda = 550$ nm, figure 5.17 illustrates system MTF50 plotted as a function of f-number for two 35 mm full-frame cameras. The first has a 12.1 MP sensor corresponding to a 8.45 μm pixel pitch, and the second has a 36.3 MP sensor corresponding to a 4.88 μm pixel pitch. It can be seen that the 36.3 MP curve drops in value at a greater rate with respect to f-number than the 12.1 MP curve. In other words, the *advantage* of the higher pixel count is gradually lost as the f-number increases from its minimum value. At $N = 22$, the difference in MTF50 between the two curves is relatively small.

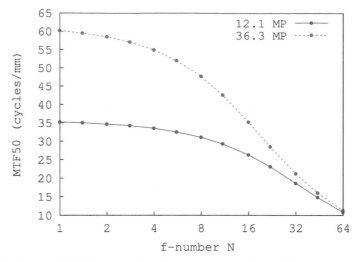

Figure 5.17. Model system MTF50 as a function of f-number for two 35 mm full-frame cameras with different pixel counts. The horizontal axis uses a base 2 logarithmic scale. Lens aberrations have not been included.

Diffraction and perceived resolution

A drop in perceived sharpness does not necessarily imply that perceived resolution will be reduced. Recall that system resolving power is defined by the spatial frequency where the system MTF drops below a small prescribed value. System resolving power will not be reduced until diffraction causes the system cut-off frequency to drop below this prescribed value. Again this will be evident when viewing the output image at 100% on a computer display, but this does not automatically imply that the effect will be noticeable at normal viewing distances and enlargements.

Since the *observer* resolving power corresponds to a spatial frequency equal to $1.22/c$ on the sensor, perceived resolution will be affected when diffraction causes the system resolving power to drop below $1.22/c$. When diffraction is the dominating factor, the system MTF is likely to be dominated by the optics MTF. Ignoring aberrations, the Rayleigh criterion for the optics cut-off frequency is given by $1/(1.22\,\lambda N)$ obtained by taking the reciprocal of equation (5.28). An upper-bound estimate for the f-number at which the system resolving power drops below $1.22/c$ can therefore be obtained by equating these values,

$$N \leqslant \frac{c}{1.22^2\lambda}. \tag{5.30}$$

Figure 5.18 shows the size of the Airy disk in relation to the CoC in this case. For a 35 mm full-frame camera, the CoC diameter $c = 0.030$ mm if the output image is enlarged to A4 size and viewed at $D_v = 250$ mm. Assuming $\lambda = 550$ nm, equation (5.30) suggests that perceived resolution will begin to drop when $N \approx 36$.

The above estimate can be tested by using the same model system MTF from the previous section. The results are shown in figure 5.19. The observer resolving power

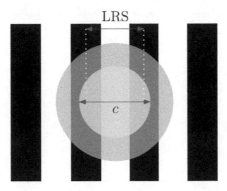

Figure 5.18. The size of the Airy disk (grey circle) in relation to the CoC (light-blue circle) when diffraction causes perceived resolution to drop, valid provided the output image is viewed under the conditions specified by the CoC. The PSF or blur distribution defined by the CoC is uniform, whereas the blur distribution defined by the Airy disk takes the form of a squared jinc function.

corresponds to a spatial frequency $1.22/c = 40\,\mathrm{lp\,mm^{-1}}$, and a prescribed system MTF value of 9% has been used to define the system resolving power. Figure 5.19(a) shows the model system MTF and its components for a 35 mm full-frame camera with 12.1 MP sensor. It is found that perceived resolution will start to reduce when $N = 30$. Figure 5.19(b) shows the results when the sensor pixel count is increased to 36.3 MP. In this case perceived resolution will start to reduce when $N = 35$. If the OLPF filter is removed, a value $N = 36$ is obtained as shown in figure 5.19(c). The difference between these values is negligible since the diffraction contribution to the system MTF dominates, in agreement with the above upper-bound estimate.

5.6 Signal-to-noise ratio

Signal-to-noise ratio (SNR) is a fundamental measure of IQ. An understanding of the techniques that exist for maximising SNR in various photographic situations will help to fully utilise the IQ potential of a camera. Reference [29] provides a detailed study of this topic.

In terms of input-referred units (electron count), SNR is a function of electron count n_e and the corresponding total signal noise $n_{e,\mathrm{noise}}$. SNR per photosite can be expressed as a ratio, or alternatively can be measured in stops or decibels,

$$\mathrm{SNR(ratio)} = \frac{n_e}{n_{e,\mathrm{noise}}} : 1 \tag{5.31a}$$

$$\mathrm{SNR(stops)} = \log_2\left(\frac{n_e}{n_{e,\mathrm{noise}}}\right) \tag{5.31b}$$

$$\mathrm{SNR(dB)} = 20\log_{10}\left(\frac{n_e}{n_{e,\mathrm{noise}}}\right). \tag{5.31c}$$

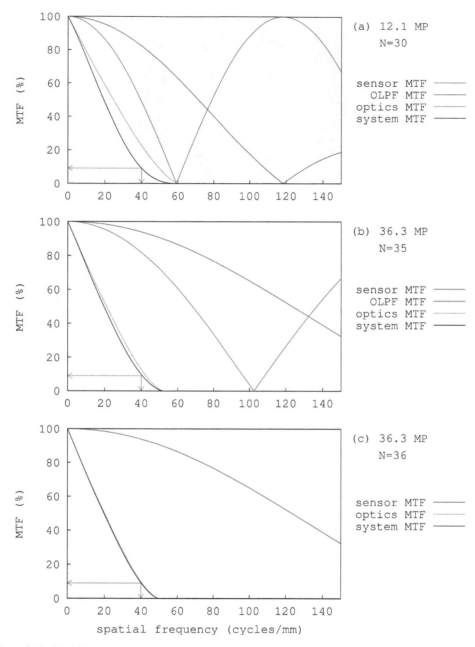

Figure 5.19. Model system MTF for FF cameras with differing pixel counts. The grey arrows show that the system MTF has dropped to 9% at 40 lp mm^{-1} for the indicated f-number N.

Sometimes only the *peak* SNR value is given. In terms of output-referred units (DN or ADU), SNR per photosite can be expressed as

$$
\begin{aligned}
\text{SNR(ratio)} &= \frac{n_{\text{DN}}}{n_{\text{DN,noise}}} : 1 \\
\text{SNR(stops)} &= \log_2\left(\frac{n_{\text{DN}}}{n_{\text{DN,noise}}}\right) \\
\text{SNR(dB)} &= 20\log_{10}\left(\frac{n_{\text{DN}}}{n_{\text{DN,noise}}}\right)
\end{aligned}
\tag{5.32}
$$

In practice, SNR can be calculated in terms of output-referred units using the raw data and the methods for measuring noise described in chapter 3. According to equation (3.53a) of chapter 3, the conversion factor or gain g can be used to convert between output-referred and input-referred units,

$$
n_{\text{DN},i} = \text{INT}\left[\frac{n_{e,i}}{g}\right].
$$

Here i is the mosaic label, and g is defined by equation (3.53b),

$$
g = \frac{U}{G_{\text{ISO}}}.
$$

The unity gain U is the ISO gain where each electron corresponds to one DN. Since g depends upon the ISO gain G_{ISO}, the relationship between input and output-referred units is dependent on the associated ISO setting S. Noise contributions such as read noise which were not part of the original detected charge can also be expressed in terms of input-referred units.

5.6.1 SNR and ISO setting

SNR varies as a function of signal and ISO setting. Recall from chapter 3 that the base ISO setting corresponds to the gain setting which uses the least analog amplification to saturate the raw output, either through FWC being utilised or ADC saturation. The base ISO setting S can be associated with an ISO gain $G_{\text{ISO}} = 1$. The value of S is determined through the SOS or REI methods which are based upon the JPEG output from the camera.

Along with noise levels due to circuitry, SNR is influenced largely by the QE and the FWC per unit photosite area. Ideally, QE should be increased as high as possible. This increases SNR at a given exposure level H because a higher photo-electron count will be generated, which in turn generates a higher signal. Equivalently, the same SNR can be achieved at a higher ISO setting for the same H. For two cameras that are identical apart from QE, the camera with the lower QE requires a greater H to achieve the same peak SNR. It should be noted that a higher QE *raises* the base ISO.

For sensors which use the same technology and have the same QE, a larger photosite area will yield a higher FWC. However, the base ISO will remain the same because the flux collection area will be correspondingly larger, as shown in figure 2.10 of chapter 2. On the other hand, sensor technology advances can raise FWC *per unit area* and therefore allow more charge to be stored per unit photosite area. This brings the following benefits:

- A higher peak SNR can be achieved because the maximum achievable signal will be higher.
- DR will be improved for a given noise floor.
- If desired, the extra DR can be traded for shadow improvement at ISO settings below the ISO-less value. This topic will be discussed later in this section.

It should be noted that a higher FWC per unit area *lowers* the base ISO.

The base ISO setting is a characteristic of a camera and is not a performance metric. A better QE and higher FWC per unit area are both favourable, however a better QE raises the base ISO whereas a higher FWC per unit area lowers the base ISO. In older cameras, a very low base ISO is characteristic of poor QE. In newer cameras which have good QE, a very low base ISO is characteristic of a very high FWC per unit area. This increases the maximum achievable signal because a higher H can be tolerated before saturation. This extra photographic capability can be utilised by taking advantage of the longer exposure times available, for example through the use of a tripod in landscape photography.

The performance metric of significance is the SNR as a function of signal at a given ISO setting. In order to present a simplified measure of SNR that relates to ISO setting, DxO® Labs [21] use a 'low-light ISO' score to rate cameras. This is defined as the highest ISO setting at which a minimum SNR is achieved while preserving a specified DR and colour depth.

JPEG comparisons

Japanese camera manufacturers are now required to use either standard output sensitivity (SOS) or recommended exposure index (REI) to specify exposure index (ISO setting) as stipulated in the CIPA DC-004 standard [30]. The aim of the ISO speed metric from ISO 12232 used previously was to ensure a minimum IQ level in the output JPEG image. In contrast, the aim of SOS is to ensure that the output JPEG image has a *standard brightness* when used with conventional metering based on average photometry. Camera manufacturers are free to the use the sensor response curve in any desired fashion provided the output JPEG image turns out to have the standard brightness [31]. In particular, the measured SOS value will take into account tone-curve processing along with the analog gain setting.

Photographers who primarily rely on JPEG output and wish to compare SNR performance between different camera models can examine data provided by camera reviewers [32]. The SNR data is usually presented pictorially so that noise can be visually inspected as a function of ISO setting for a scene metered using average photometry. This is the most appropriate way to compare the JPEG output from different camera models obtained according to the quoted ISO settings. The quality of the in-camera image-processing engine is fully taken into account, and the appearance of the noise can be judged in terms of its aesthetic appearance. For example, some camera models produce JPEG images with noise that appears more unpleasant at a given SNR compared to other models. Furthermore, there are IQ trade-offs involved when designing an in-camera image-processing engine. For example, there is a trade-off between SNR at a mid-tone DOL and highlight headroom. Camera manufacturers will choose to optimise these trade-offs differently, and so information about other aspects of the JPEG output provided by camera reviewers such as shadow and highlight DR should be taken into consideration when comparing SNR performance.

When comparing cameras with different sensor formats, the equivalence ratio should be taken into account if the aim is to compare equivalent output as defined in section 5.2. In particular, noise comparisons should be made at equivalent focal lengths, f-numbers and ISO settings. For example, ISO 800 on APS-C should be compared with ISO 1600 on 35 mm full frame. Ideally, the camera reviewer would then go on to show the additional capability that the larger format offers when the smaller format is unable to offer equivalent output.

Raw comparisons

SNR can be maximised as part of a photographic exposure strategy by using the ETTR technique in conjunction with raw output. The ETTR technique will be discussed in the final section of this chapter. The basic idea is to ensure that the raw histogram is placed as far right as possible without clipping the highlights when metering the scene.

Figure 5.20 shows SNR in terms of *output-referred* units for the Olympus® E-M1, plotted as a function of raw level (digital number or DN) at a range of ISO settings.

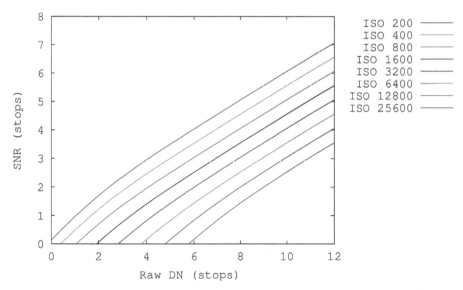

Figure 5.20. SNR plotted as a function of raw level at a variety of ISO settings for the Olympus® E-M1. Here SNR is lowered at a given raw level when the ISO setting is raised because less photometric exposure has been used to obtain the same raw data.

These curves were obtained using the experimental methods described in section 3.8 of chapter 3. Both SNR and raw level have been expressed in stops by taking the base 2 logarithm. Only read noise and photon shot noise have been included as noise sources when determining the SNR.

The first observation to make is that the peak SNR is obtained at the highest raw value for a given ISO setting. This is the premise behind the ETTR technique. Each curve rises linearly at low exposure with slope approximately equal to unity. The slope drops to one half at higher exposure levels when the square root relationship between signal and photon shot noise dominates. The main reason for the increase in SNR with H is that photon shot noise is proportional to $\sqrt{H}$ and so signal-to-*photon*-noise ratio is also proportional to $\sqrt{H}$,

$$\mathrm{SNR_{ph}} = \frac{n_e}{n_{\mathrm{ph}}} \propto \frac{H}{\sqrt{H}} \propto \sqrt{H}. \tag{5.33}$$

The second observation to make is that SNR appears to be lowered when the ISO setting is raised. Although it is commonly assumed that higher ISO settings are inherently noisier, this is not the case, as discussed previously in section 3.8 of chapter 3. In fact, the curves in figure 5.20 indicate lower SNR as the ISO setting is raised because *less photometric exposure H* has been used to obtain the same raw level at the higher ISO setting. For example, the ISO 200 curve has been obtained using one stop higher H than the ISO 400 curve. The base ISO setting offers the highest peak SNR because a higher H can be tolerated before raw saturation. In order to see that higher ISO settings can in fact offer improved SNR, it is necessary to compared curves obtained at the same exposure level rather than the same raw level. This will be shown below in the section on *shadow improvement*.

Figure 5.20 has labelled the gain settings according to the standard ISO settings which will be either SOS or REI. Camera manufacturers all correctly adhere to the CIPA and ISO standards, however SOS and REI are based on the JPEG output which may include digital gain applied to the raw data. Moreover, the quoted values are standard values obtained from rounding the measured values. When SNR as a function of raw level is compared for different camera models, some sources of camera data may instead use 'raw ISO' values, an example being DxO® Labs [21]. The aim is to place raw comparisons on an equal footing by defining ISO settings based on the raw data rather than the JPEG output.

The only available exposure index which can in principle be used with raw output is ISO speed. Although no longer used by camera manufacturers, ISO speed remains part of the ISO 12232 standard [33]. DxO® Labs use *raw ISO speed* determined via the saturation-based method described in chapter 2. Applied to the raw data, this measure ensures that half a stop of raw highlight headroom is retained when using standard metering based on average photometry and an average scene luminance that is 18% of the maximum. Importantly, *no correspondence should be expected between raw ISO values determined in this way and the ISO settings labelled on the camera*. Nevertheless, photographers who wish to use the ETTR technique in conjunction with raw output could in principle replace the labelled camera ISO settings with the raw ISO speed values. According to the analysis given in chapter 2, an average scene luminance that is 12.8% of the maximum would saturate the raw output if the scene is metered using average photometry in conjunction with the raw ISO speed.

5.6.2 Shadow improvement

Recall that the programmable gain amplifier (PGA) applies a variable analog ISO gain to the voltage signal before quantisation by the ADC. In contrast, *digital* amplification applies gain to the post-quantised signal through simple multiplication of the raw levels. It is clear that multiplication of existing raw levels simply adjusts the brightness of the image and cannot bring about any SNR advantage. However, further analysis is required to demonstrate that analog amplification can provide a SNR advantage.

Figure 5.21 shows the same data as figure 5.20 but plotted instead as a function of photometric exposure H expressed in stops. This graph has been obtained by first converting from output-referred units (DN) to input-referred units (electron count) using the appropriate conversion factor g at each ISO setting. Subsequently, the base 2 logarithm of the photoelectron count n_e has been taken. The maximum resulting value has then been normalised to 12 since this corresponds to the signal obtained from 12 stops of photometric exposure H. An equivalent method for obtaining this graph from figure 5.20 is simply to replace raw levels in stops on the horizontal axis by exposure in stops, and then to shift each curve to the left according to the difference in the maximum number of stops of exposure used compared to the base ISO setting.

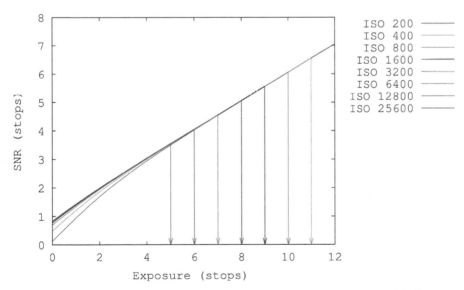

Figure 5.21. SNR plotted as a function of exposure at a variety of ISO settings for the Olympus® E-M1. For a given level of photometric exposure, higher ISO settings provide a SNR advantage in the low-exposure regions of the image. However, raw highlight headroom is lost.

When plotted in the above manner, it can be seen that higher ISO gains actually yield a *higher* SNR in the low exposure regions of an image. This advantage arises from better signal-to-*read*-noise ratio as ISO gain goes up. The ISO gain amplifies *all* of the voltage signal but only *part* of the read noise, specifically the contribution arising from readout circuitry upstream from the PGA [29, 34]. The penalty for using a higher analog gain is that the ADC will saturate before FWC can be utilised. Consequently, peak SNR and available DR will both be lowered. For the same reasons, a camera manufacturer can improve SNR at low exposures by using a higher conversion factor g. However, the ADC may saturate before FWC is utilised because of the fixed voltage of the ADC power supply. The camera manufacturer must balance these trade-offs when choosing optimal values [34].

The above analysis reveals that if photometric exposure level H is unrestricted by photographic conditions, it makes sense to use a low ISO setting. This will enable a higher H to be utilised which in turn will improve SNR. Higher H can be utilised through ETTR as described in the final section of this chapter. On the other hand, if photographic conditions restrict the photometric exposure level H to a fixed value, then SNR may be improved in the low-exposure regions of the image by using a *higher* ISO setting [29]. It will be shown later that the latter strategy can also be considered a form of ETTR known as *shadow improvement*.

5.6.3 ISO invariance

Although figure 5.21 shows that higher ISO gains yield a higher SNR in the low exposure regions of the image, the advantage gradually lessens each time the ISO gain is raised. Eventually a value is reached where the upstream read noise dominates and a higher ISO gain would bring no further advantage. For the Olympus® E-M1 used to produce figure 5.21, all curves above ISO 800 lie almost on top of each other. The precise ISO setting S above which the corresponding ISO gain would bring no SNR advantage compared with applying digital gain in post-processing is referred to as the *ISO-less* setting.

When using the ETTR technique with raw output, it is not advisable to raise the ISO setting above the ISO-less value. This follows because a drawback of using higher ISO gains is that one stop of raw highlight exposure headroom is lost each time the ISO setting is raised by one stop from its base value. This was mentioned in section 3.7.2 of chapter 3 and is explicit in figure 5.21. The Olympus® E-M1 used to produce figure 5.21 has a 12-bit ADC and a base ISO setting of 200. This means that 12 stops of exposure can be tolerated before saturation occurs at base ISO, assuming that the sensor response and ADC are both perfectly linear and that FWC corresponds to ADC saturation. At higher ISO settings, a higher signal voltage is quantised for the same exposure level. If the ISO-less setting is ISO 800, then ten stops of exposure can be tolerated before saturation at ISO 800, but only nine stops can be tolerated at ISO 1600. In other words, ISO settings above the ISO-less value bring no further SNR advantage and yet lead to further loss of exposure headroom and raw DR.

If the photographic conditions lead to underexposure at the ISO-less setting when shooting raw rather than JPEG, it makes more sense to leave the raw output underexposed and then raise the image brightness digitally when processing the raw file using the raw converter. The image produced in this way will have the same SNR as the image that would have been obtained at the higher ISO setting, but the raw converter will allow a tone curve to be applied which can utilise the greater DR available that the ISO-less setting offers [29]. Some recent cameras have such low levels of downstream read noise that the ISO-less setting is very low and the camera can be described as being *ISO invariant* [35].

5.6.4 SNR and pixel count

The discussion so far has centred on SNR per photosite (or sensor pixel). However, this metric is only comparable between cameras that have the same photosite area and sensor format. This is because SNR depends on the spatial scale at which it is measured [29, 36].

For example, consider a single photosite at the sensor plane with signal n_1 and associated temporal noise σ_1. For simplicity, assume that fixed-pattern noise (FPN) has been eliminated. The SNR for this photosite is

$$SNR_1 = \frac{n_1}{\sigma_1}.$$

If the irradiance at the sensor plane is uniform, the total signal n and total temporal noise σ for a 2×2 block of photosites will be

$$n = n_1 + n_2 + n_3 + n_4 = 4n_1$$
$$\sigma = \sqrt{\sigma_1^2 + \sigma_2^2 + \sigma_3^2 + \sigma_4^2} = \sqrt{4\sigma_1^2} = 2\sigma_1.$$

The total SNR will be

$$SNR = \frac{n}{\sigma} = 2\,SNR_1.$$

Therefore increasing the charge detection area by a factor of 4 through *pixel binning* has increased the SNR by a factor of 2. For a uniform exposure at the sensor plane, *SNR is seen to increase as the square root of the charge detection area*. For a non-uniform exposure, the increase in SNR will fall short of this value [29].

The explanation for the above lies in the fact that pixel binning is proportional to averaging over photosites. Since temporal noise is uncorrelated and is measured by the standard deviation σ from the mean value of its statistical distribution, averaging reduces temporal noise. On the other hand, the charge signal at a photosite is completely correlated with its neighbours when the irradiance at the sensor plane is uniform, and so the signal is unchanged by averaging. In areas of the photographic scene which contain details and gradients, the exposure at the corresponding areas of the sensor plane will not be uniform. In this case, averaging will smooth the signal and the reduction in temporal noise will not be as large.

SNR for cameras which have the same sensor format but different photosite areas (sensor pixel counts) should be compared at a fixed spatial scale [29]. For example, an appropriate metric is *SNR per unit area* of the sensor,

$$\text{SNR per unit area} = \frac{\text{SNR per photosite}}{A}. \tag{5.34}$$

Here A is the photosite area in microns squared. SNR per unit area depends upon factors such as:

- QE per unit area.
- FWC per unit area.
- Noise floor.

In practice, it is found that camera manufacturers are generally able to achieve the same QE per unit area over a wide range of photosite areas (sensor pixel sizes) *when using the same sensor technology*. In CCD sensors, this naturally follows from the fact that the photosensitive area at a given photosite decreases in proportion with the photosite area itself. However, in CMOS sensors the area occupied by the transistor cannot be proportionally reduced and so the QE per unit area becomes a function of photosite area. Nevertheless, the QE of small CMOS photosites can be increased through backside illumination (BSI) [19].

On the other hand, the noise floor does depend upon photosite area. In order that SNR per unit area be independent of photosite area, read noise must scale in proportion with the photosite *spacing* (square root of the photosite area) in analogy with the ideal pixel-binning example above. The deviation from this square root relationship arises in practice because read noise for a larger photosite is generally less than the read noise for the corresponding aggregate of smaller photosites. Since the read noise introduced downstream from the ISO gain amplifier is independent of photosite area, the read noise advantage of the larger photosites only becomes apparent at higher ISO settings where the read noise contribution upstream from the ISO gain amplifier dominates [29].

The latest trends in SNR performance in relation to sensor pixel count can be found by examining camera sensor performance data available online [21, 37]. However, care should be taken when comparing cameras with different sensor sizes. This is discussed in section 5.6.5 below.

SNR and downsampling
Digital images appear to be less noisy after having been downsampled. This is particularly noticeable when downsampling and subsequently downscaling an image to a small size for displaying online.

The noise reduction achieved when downsampling can be explained by the pixel binning example given above. If the downsampling algorithm is implemented correctly as described in section 5.5.2, the interpolation filter will construct the output by acting as an anti-aliasing filter rather than a reconstruction filter and will bandlimit the image spectrum to the Nyquist frequency of the new sampling grid.

The filtering operation has a similar effect to averaging, and so the signal will be smoothed when details and gradients are present in the scene. However, the temporal noise will be *reduced* by the anti-aliasing filter because temporal noise is uncorrelated. The greatest reduction in noise will occur in uniform areas of the scene.

In conclusion, downsampling yields larger pixels, and each of the new larger pixels will have a greater *SNR per pixel*. Therefore the downsampled image will have less noise at the pixel level. The noise reduction has been achieved by discarding resolution [29].

5.6.5 SNR and sensor format

Care should be taken when comparing SNR values between cameras with different sensor formats.

Consider two cameras with different sensor formats subject to the *same uniform level of exposure H*. Assume that the sensors have the same QE and read noise per unit sensor area. Since SNR is seen to increase as the square root of the charge detection area, *the larger sensor format will have a higher total SNR when measured over the entire frame*.

This SNR relationship with sensor size is commonly observed in camera reviews, for example when image noise is compared at the same ISO setting. However, it is important to remember that the cameras will not necessarily be used in the same way in practice. In particular, a *different level of exposure H* is required at the sensor plane when *equivalent* photos are taken.

As described in section 5.2, equivalent photos are defined as having the same perspective, framing, DoF, brightness, and must be taken at the same shutter speed and viewed at the same display dimensions [6]. Equivalent rather than identical settings are required on different formats in order to produce equivalent photos.

A fully comparable metric for performing cross-format SNR comparisons in this case is *SNR per percentage frame height compared at equivalent camera settings*. For example, an image taken at $f = 100$ mm, $N = 2.8$, and ISO 800 on APS-C would need to be compared with an equivalent image taken at $f = 150$ mm, $N = 4$, and ISO 1600 on 35 mm full frame. In this case, the level of exposure at the APS-C sensor plane will be double that of the 35 mm full-frame sensor plane, and so the advantage of the larger full-frame charge detection area will be neutralised. However, the larger format offers additional photographic capability and potentially higher SNR when the smaller format cannot produce equivalent output.

5.7 Dynamic range

The definition of dynamic range (DR) used in engineering was introduced briefly in chapter 2 and is expanded upon below. This section also discusses photographic DR (PDR) which is designed to provide a measure of DR that can be observed in practice.

5.7.1 Engineering dynamic range

Engineering DR can be expressed using either input-referred units (electrons) or output-referred units (DN or ADU). In general, the value will differ depending on whether it refers to *raw DR*, which is the maximum DR that can be represented in the raw data, or *sensor DR*, which is the DR that the sensor is actually capable of delivering.

Input-referred units

Raw DR describes the maximum DR that can be represented in the raw data as a function of ISO setting. Using input-referred units by expressing the signal and noise in terms of electrons, raw DR per photosite is defined as

$$
\boxed{
\begin{aligned}
\text{raw DR (ratio)} &= \frac{n_{e,\max}}{\sigma_{e,\text{read}}} : 1 \\[2mm]
\text{raw DR (stops)} &= \log_2\!\left(\frac{n_{e,\max}}{\sigma_{e,\text{read}}}\right) \\[2mm]
\text{raw DR (decibels)} &= 20 \log_{10}\!\left(\frac{n_{e,\max}}{\sigma_{e,\text{read}}}\right)
\end{aligned}
}
\tag{5.35}
$$

Here $n_{e,\max}$ is the maximum number of electrons that can be collected before the ADC saturates. This defines the *raw DR upper limit*. By using the read noise $\sigma_{e,\text{read}}$ as the noise floor, the *raw DR lower limit* is defined by the signal per photosite where the SNR is unity, SNR = 1. This is also known as *noise equivalent exposure*. When expressed in decibels, the convention adopted here is such that $1\text{stop} \equiv 20\log_{10} 2 \approx 6.02$ decibels (dB).

At base ISO, the raw DR upper limit is defined by full-well capacity (FWC), assuming that the photoelectron well completely fills before the ADC saturates. It was shown in section 3.8 of chapter 3 and in section 5.6.2 above that read noise expressed in electrons *decreases* as the ISO gain is raised from its base value, and so the raw DR lower limit is similarly lowered or improved. However, the raw DR upper limit is lowered from FWC by one stop each time the corresponding ISO setting is doubled from its base value. The overall result is that *raw DR goes down with increasing ISO gain.*

Although raw DR describes the actual DR available in the raw file as a function of ISO setting, this metric does not describe the DR which the sensor is actually capable of delivering. *Sensor DR* per photosite [29] can be defined as

$$
\boxed{
\begin{aligned}
\text{sensor DR (ratio)} &= \frac{n_{e,\text{FWC}}}{\sigma_{e,\text{read,sensor}}} : 1 \\[2mm]
\text{sensor DR (stops)} &= \log_2\!\left(\frac{n_{e,\text{FWC}}}{\sigma_{e,\text{read,sensor}}}\right) \\[2mm]
\text{sensor DR (decibels)} &= 20 \log_{10}\!\left(\frac{n_{e,\text{FWC}}}{\sigma_{e,\text{read,sensor}}}\right)
\end{aligned}
}
\tag{5.36}
$$

The *sensor DR upper limit* is defined by the signal at full-well capacity (FWC), $n_{e,\text{FWC}}$. The *sensor DR lower limit* is defined by the contribution to the total read noise arising from the sensor, $\sigma_{e,\text{read,sensor}}$. This is the contribution from components *upstream* from the PGA. In terms of photoelectrons, the read noise contribution arising from electronics downstream from the PGA is essentially zero at the ISO gain corresponding to the ISO-less setting. Therefore $\sigma_{e,\text{read,sensor}}$ can be defined as the read noise at the ISO-less setting.

Raw DR is less than sensor DR only because the standard strategy for quantising the voltage signal does not overcome the limitations imposed by the downstream electronics [29]. Camera manufacturers have recently begun to address this issue by developing more sophisticated methods for quantising the signal.

Output-referred units
Using output-referred units for the signal and noise in terms of raw levels (DN or ADU), raw DR per photosite is defined as

$$
\begin{aligned}
\text{raw DR (ratio)} &= \frac{n_{\text{DN,clip}}}{\sigma_{\text{DN,read}}} : 1 \\[2ex]
\text{raw DR (stops)} &= \log_2\!\left(\frac{n_{\text{DN,clip}}}{\sigma_{\text{DN,read}}}\right) \\[2ex]
\text{raw DR (decibels)} &= 20\,\log_{10}\!\left(\frac{n_{\text{DN,clip}}}{\sigma_{\text{DN,read}}}\right)
\end{aligned}
\tag{5.37}
$$

Here $n_{\text{DN,clip}}$ is the raw clipping point in DN, and $\sigma_{\text{DN,read}}$ is the read noise in DN.

The ISO gain compensates for reduced photometric exposure and electron count by maintaining the raw level in output-referred units at the expense of SNR. In other words, the read noise in DN goes up with increasing ISO gain while the raw clipping point remains constant. Therefore DR goes down with increasing ISO gain. This is consistent with the definition given using input-referred units.

5.7.2 Photographic dynamic range

The engineering definition of raw DR has several drawbacks in relation to photography, for example:

(i) Engineering raw DR is defined per photosite. This measure is not comparable between cameras with different sized photosites or different sensor formats.

(ii) The engineering raw DR lower limit is defined as the signal where the SNR is unity. Many observers of the output image would consider this signal to be of insufficient quality to be useful in practice.

Photographic dynamic range (PDR) is a metric which aims to provide a measure of raw DR which could be perceived in practice by an observer of the output image under specified viewing conditions. The definition introduced by reference [38] will be described in this section.

In order to address issue (i) above and account for different sized photosites along with different sensor formats, an appropriately normalised measure of SNR needs to be introduced for defining PDR. One option is to use SNR per fixed percentage of the frame height as described in section 5.6.5 earlier. An alternative option introduced by reference [38] which is particularly useful in the current context is SNR *per CoC*.

It has already been shown in section 5.6.4 that signal, noise, and therefore SNR are dependent on the spatial scale at which they are measured. Recall from section 5.1 that detail on a smaller spatial scale than the CoC cannot be resolved by an observer of the output image under the specified viewing conditions which define the CoC diameter. This suggests that the CoC is a suitable minimum spatial scale at which to measure SNR as perceived by an observer of the output image. The CoC defined by the camera or lens manufacturer assumes that the output image will be enlarged to A4 size and viewed at the least distance of distinct vision, $D_v = 250$ mm. The photographer is of course free to use a different CoC diameter based upon the intended viewing conditions. Given the SNR per photosite, SNR per CoC can be calculated in the following way:

$$\text{SNR per CoC} = \text{SNR per photosite} \times \sqrt{\frac{\pi(c/2)^2}{A}}. \tag{5.38}$$

Here A is the photosite area and c is the CoC diameter. As a metric, SNR per CoC has two important properties:

- Photosite area and therefore sensor pixel count are accounted for because the photosites are binned together up to the CoC area.
- Sensor format is accounted for because the CoC for a given format takes into account the enlargement factor from the dimensions of the optical image formed at the sensor plane to the dimensions of the viewed output image.

In order to address issue (ii) above, PDR needs to use a more appropriate DR lower limit than the signal where SNR = 1. Progress has already been made by introducing SNR per CoC since this takes into account the intended viewing conditions under which the output image will be viewed. Nevertheless, an appropriate lower limit is highly subjective because different observers will have different expectations in terms of IQ. Reference [38] defines the PDR *lower limit* by the raw level (DN) where the SNR per CoC is equal to 20. Using equation (5.38), this can be written

$$\text{PDR lower limit (DN)} \equiv \text{Raw level (DN) where}$$

$$\text{SNR per photosite} = \frac{20}{\sqrt{\frac{\pi(c/2)^2}{A}}}.$$

If raw level and SNR are both expressed in stops by taking the base 2 logarithm, the definition becomes

$$\text{PDR lower limit (stops)} \equiv \text{Raw level (stops) where}$$
$$\text{SNR per photosite} = \log_2 \frac{20}{\sqrt{\dfrac{\pi(c/2)^2}{A}}}. \qquad (5.39)$$

Again working with output-referred units, the PDR *upper limit* is defined by the raw clipping point in DN, denoted by RCP. This may be below the maximum DN corresponding to the bit-depth of the ADC. The PDR upper limit may similarly be expressed in stops,

$$\text{PDR upper limit (stops)} = \log_2 \text{RCP}.$$

Now PDR in stops can be defined as

$$\text{PDR (stops)} = \text{PDR upper limit (stops)} \\ - \text{PDR lower limit (stops)}. \qquad (5.40)$$

The PDR lower limit in output-referred units will go up as the ISO gain increases, and so PDR will go down when the ISO setting is raised from its base value. Reference [37] provides PDR values for a wide range of cameras. Some examples are shown in figure 5.22. It should be noted that the ISO values in the plot are the ISO settings on the camera and these are defined according to the camera JPEG output file rather than the raw data. Performance comparison between cameras could be improved by plotting PDR according to the *raw ISO speed* described in section 5.6.1 earlier.

Not all of the raw DR will be transferred to the output image in general. Indeed, the image DR is dependent on the output tone curve used when processing the raw file, and the image DR may subsequently be compressed or tonemapped into the DR of the display medium, as described in chapter 2. Nevertheless, the above definition of PDR describes an upper bound on the image DR which could be observed in practice under the specified viewing conditions.

5.8 Practical strategies

Acquiring a camera and lens with the highest technical IQ scores does not automatically guarantee higher IQ in practice. For a given choice of camera and lens, various photographic techniques can be employed in order to utilise the full IQ potential from the camera system.

Two fundamental aspects of IQ which can be optimised through photographic practice are resolution and noise. This section briefly describes strategies for maximising the detail captured of an object positioned in the scene, non-destructive noise-reduction techniques that can increase SNR, and the ETTR technique for maximising SNR.

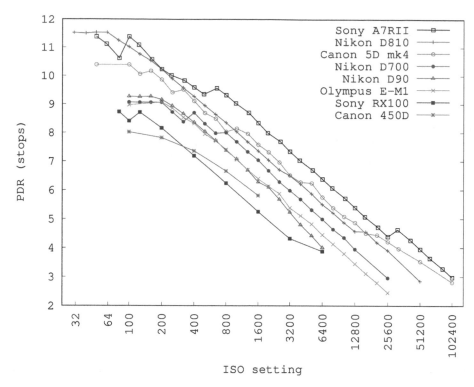

Figure 5.22. PDR as a function of ISO setting for a selection of cameras. (Data courtesy of W J Claff, http://www.photonstophotos.net.)

5.8.1 Object resolution

In order to maximise the detail captured of an object positioned at the object plane, the system resolving power should be increased as high as possible by choosing a camera with a high sensor pixel count and lens with a high resolving power.

It is also advisable to use a tripod to eliminate image blur caused by camera shake. Camera shake can be described by a jitter MTF which has a cut-off frequency [13]. Camera system resolving power will be reduced if this cut-off frequency drops below that of the combined camera and lens system.

For a given camera system, the following techniques can be used to take advantage of the available system resolving power:

For fixed magnification:

- Use light with smaller wavelengths.
- Lower the f-number.

If the magnification is allowed to vary, then additionally:

- Move closer to the object plane.
- Increase the focal length.
- Increase the refractive index of object space relative to image space.

These methods are discussed in more detail below.

1. **Use light with smaller wavelengths**

   Equation (5.27) reveals that μ_c is inversely related to λ,

   $$\mu_c = \left(\frac{n}{n'}\right)\frac{1}{\lambda N_w}.$$

   The maximum achievable resolution can therefore be increased by using light with smaller wavelengths. For this reason, near ultraviolet light is often used in microscopy.

2. **Lower the f-number**

   For fixed magnification, the bellows factor b remains fixed,

   $$b = 1 + \frac{|m|}{m_p}.$$

   Equation (5.27) can be written in the form

   $$\mu_c = \left(\frac{n}{n'}\right)\frac{1}{\lambda Nb}. \tag{5.41}$$

   Therefore μ_c can be raised by lowering the f-number N. This is equivalent to *increasing the lens entrance pupil diameter*.

   In practice, lens aberrations are more severe at the lowest f-numbers due to the increasing angular extent of the cones of light entering and exiting the lens. Although this does not change μ_c in principle, the MTF can be lowered dramatically in the region close to μ_c, as discussed in section 5.3.4. This reduces the 'effective' value of μ_c [10]. An optimum f-number or 'sweet spot' exists for a given lens. This is typically higher than the lowest f-number available.

3. **Move closer to the object plane**

   If the magnification is allowed to vary, the magnification and bellows factor b both *increase* when the object plane is brought closer to the lens, and so μ_c *decreases* according to equation (5.41). However, μ_c is the *image-space* cut-off frequency measured at the sensor plane. When the magnification changes, the scene content similarly changes and the spatial frequencies no longer correspond to those at the previous magnification.

   To see the effect on object resolution, the quantity of interest is the *object-space* cut-off frequency $\mu_c(OP)$ measured at the object plane. This is directly related to μ_c via the magnification,

   $$\mu_c(OP) = |m|\mu_c.$$

   Substituting into equation (5.41) and utilising equation (1.24) of chapter 1 yields

   $$\boxed{\mu_c(OP) = \left(\frac{n}{n'}\right)\frac{D}{\lambda(s - s_{ep})}.} \tag{5.42}$$

Here D is the diameter of the *entrance* pupil, $D = f_F/N$. The object distance s is measured from the first principal plane, and s_{ep} is the distance from the first principal plane to the entrance pupil. It can be seen that $\mu_c(OP)$ *increases* when s is reduced.

4. **Increase the focal length (for fixed object distance and f-number)**

   For a given object distance s and f-number N, increasing the focal length *increases* the cut-off frequency at the object plane, $\mu_c(OP)$. This follows from equation (5.42), and is another means of *increasing the lens entrance pupil diameter*.

5. **Increase the ratio $n : n'$**

   Object resolution can be improved by increasing the refractive index of object space relative to image space. Although not practical in everyday photography, this principle is used in microscopy through the use of object-space immersion oil with a high refractive index, typically of order $n \approx 1.5$. In this case, equation (5.42) is usually expressed in the more general form

$$\mu_c(OP) = \left(\frac{n}{n'}\right)\frac{2\sin U}{\lambda} = \frac{2NA}{n'\lambda}.$$

Here $NA = n \sin U$ is the object-space numerical aperture defined by the real marginal ray angle U, and typically $n' = 1$ (air). From equation (1.65) of chapter 1, the increase in the maximum achievable object-space resolution occurs at the expense of the image-space numerical aperture and image-plane irradiance.

5.8.2 Non-destructive noise reduction

Several non-destructive procedures can be performed on the raw data to improve SNR. Unlike noise reduction techniques used in image processing, the procedures detailed below do not filter the data and so do not reduce resolution.

Frame averaging

Temporal noise can be reduced to very low levels by frame averaging. To use this technique, the photographer must record a number of *frames* by photographing the scene a number of times in quick succession using the same framing and camera settings. The scene luminance distribution must remain constant when recording the frames and so the technique cannot be used with moving subjects.

Each of the M frames will be identical apart from the statistical variation in temporal noise. Averaging M frames leaves the original signal n_{DN} expressed in DN unchanged for a given pixel,

$$\frac{1}{M}\sum_M n_{DN} = \frac{M n_{DN}}{M} = n_{DN}.$$

On the other hand, temporal noise σ_{DN} adds in quadrature and so averaging M frames decreases the temporal noise by a factor $\sqrt{M}$,

$$\frac{1}{M} \sum_M \sigma_{DN} = \frac{1}{M} \sqrt{M \sigma_{DN}^2} = \frac{\sigma_{DN}}{\sqrt{M}}.$$

Equivalently, averaging M frames increases SNR by a factor of $\sqrt{M}$ [39]. For example, averaging 16 frames will increase SNR by a factor of 4. Some cameras do not leave a bias offset in the raw data. In this case the negative-valued noise fluctuations will be clipped to zero which complicates the procedure [29].

Dark-frame subtraction (DSNU compensation)

Dark signal non-unifomity (DSNU) refers to FPN present in the absence of illumination. Since the sensor-plane photometric exposure distribution is zero, the FPN image is known as a *dark frame*. In the absence of illumination, the exposure duration or shutter speed is referred to as the *integration time*. The major contribution to DSNU for a long integration time is dark-current non-uniformity (DCNU) which arises from variations in photosite response over the sensor plane to thermally induced dark current. Another contribution for long integration times is *amplifier glow*. Since DSNU is still present when the sensor is under illumination, scientific CCD sensors used in astrophotography are often cooled in order to reduce these contributions.

For short integration times of less than about a second, the contribution from dark current is relatively minor. However, DSNU may arise from the readout circuitry. Although read noise should in principle be purely temporal and form a Gaussian distribution about the expected signal, the read noise in some cameras is not purely Gaussian in nature but has some pattern component [29]. Although the pattern component may not be fixed from frame to frame, any overall FPN can be detected by averaging over many bias frames, a *bias frame* being a dark frame taken with zero integration time. If present, this contribution to DSNU will vary with the ISO setting.

One way to reduce DSNU is to use in-camera long-exposure noise reduction (LENR). If the photographer is using a long exposure duration, typically to photograph a night scene with the camera on a tripod, LENR functions by taking a dark frame of equal duration immediately after the normal frame. This dark frame is then subtracted from the normal frame. Because DSNU is still present when the sensor is under illumination, this procedure can help remove DSNU from the raw data. One drawback of this approach arises from the fact that the normal frame and dark frame both contain temporal noise [29]. Because temporal noise adds in quadrature, subtracting the dark frame increases temporal noise in the raw data by a factor $\sqrt{2}$,

$$\sqrt{\sigma_{DN}^2 + (-\sigma)_{DN}^2} = \sqrt{2}\ \sigma_{DN}.$$

Furthermore, it is inconvenient for the photographer to wait while the dark frame is being taken after every normal frame. For photographers who specialise in long-exposure photography, an alternative strategy is to make a set of dark-frame templates. Each template can be made by averaging together many dark frames in order to isolate DSNU. Subtracting the template from the normal frame will increase read noise by a factor $\sqrt{1 + (1/\sqrt{M})}$, where M is the number of dark frames used to make the template. This increase becomes negligible if M is large. In principle, a template should be made for each exposure duration and ISO setting, and this should be carried out periodically since sensor properties change over time. Software such as the freeware astrophotography program *iris* can be used to construct the templates[1]. Attempting to perform the dark frame subtraction after the colour demosaic will yield less than optimum results.

Flat-field correction (PRNU compensation)

Pixel response non-uniformity (PRNU) refers to FPN in the presence of illumination. It arises from slight differences in photosite response over the sensor plane. PRNU increases in proportion with photometric exposure and hence the number of photoelectrons generated,

$$n_{e,\mathrm{PRNU}} = kn_e.$$

Here k is a proportionality constant. Since the total noise will be larger than the PRNU, it follows that

$$\mathrm{SNR} \leqslant \frac{n_e}{n_{e,\mathrm{PRNU}}} = \frac{1}{k}.$$

Therefore PRNU limits the maximum achievable SNR to the value $1/k$ [29, 34].

Unlike DSNU compensation, PRNU compensation is rarely carried out in normal photographic situations. However, PRNU is often compensated for in astrophotography through the use of a *flat-field* template. This is constructed by averaging over a set of M flat-field frames, where each flat-field frame is an image of a uniform surface under uniform illumination. The averaging reduces the temporal noise. The flat-field template needs to be divided from the normal frame, and then the normal frame multiplied by the average raw value of the flat-field template. Again software such as *iris* can carry out these procedures.

5.8.3 Exposing to the right

ETTR is a very important technique which can be used by a photographer to improve SNR. The technique takes advantage of the analysis given in section 5.6, and the general concept involves ensuring that the image histogram is always pushed to the right as far as possible without clipping the highlights.

The ETTR concept takes a different form depending upon the type of photographic situation encountered. These photographic situations can be broadly classified into two types according to any restrictions on the level of photometric exposure H required at the sensor plane:

- The photographer is free to vary H.
- The photographic conditions dictate that H must be kept fixed.

---

[1] The freeware astrophotography software *iris* by C Buil is available at http://www.astrosurf.com/buil/us/iris/iris.htm.

Ideally, the ETTR technique should be used with raw output. This will enable the maximum SNR to be achieved by making full use of the sensor response curve. If necessary, any desired tone curve can subsequently be applied using the raw processing software in order to bring the image brightness down to a suitable level, but with the added benefit of the higher SNR. It is also possible to use the ETTR technique with JPEG output, however the JPEG clipping point may be positioned below the raw clipping point on the sensor response curve, and so SNR may not be maximised. The JPEG output may need to be edited in order to reduce the image brightness back down to an appropriate level.

Unfortunately for photographers who wish to base exposure decisions on raw output rather than JPEG output, digital camera LCD displays and electronic viewfinders show the histogram corresponding to the JPEG output even when shooting raw, and so it can be hard to judge how much extra ETTR can be utilised beyond the JPEG clipping point without carrying out various tests. The option for displaying a raw histogram is not currently available, however an open-source firmware solution is currently freely available for Canon® cameras [40].

The theory behind the ETTR technique will be described below for both of the above scenarios by assuming the camera is in manual mode. ETTR is achieved when the histogram is shifted as far right as possible without highlight clipping. On traditional DSLRs, the histogram can be checked after the photo has been taken. DSLRs with live view or cameras with an electronic viewfinder offer a live histogram. In manual mode, the live histogram may appear fixed according to the target exposure, and the shift indicated by the exposure compensation (EC) level.

After discussing the ETTR theory, practical ETTR strategies for manual, aperture priority and shutter priority modes will be described.

ETTR: variable H

The highest possible SNR can be obtained if the photographer is free to increase the exposure at the sensor plane, H. This follows because photon shot noise is proportional to $\sqrt{H}$, and so signal-to-*photon*-noise ratio is also proportional to $\sqrt{H}$ according to equation (5.33),

$$\text{SNR}_{\text{ph}} = \frac{n_e}{n_{\text{ph}}} \propto \frac{H}{\sqrt{H}} \propto \sqrt{H}.$$

Exposure H can typically be increased when photographing static subjects in good lighting conditions, or in low-light conditions where a tripod can be used to remove restrictions imposed by camera shake.

Assume that the camera is in manual mode and a moderate ISO setting has been selected along with a combination of N and t which avoids highlight clipping. Increasing the exposure duration t or opening up the aperture by lowering N will both increase H and shift the histogram to the right.

If the photographic conditions allow a lower N or longer t to be selected even after ETTR has been achieved at the selected ISO setting, a potentially higher SNR can be achieved by lowering the ISO setting. If the ISO setting is lowered by one stop by halving its numerical value, the right edge of the histogram will shift to the left of the ETTR limit by one stop. The SNR will typically decrease slightly, however lowering the ISO setting *increases the exposure headroom available for ETTR*. In the present example, the extra stop available at the highlight end of the histogram could be utilised by lowering N or lengthening t to increase H, leading to further improvement in SNR beyond that achievable at the higher ISO setting.

If the photographic conditions continue to allow a lower N or longer t, it logically follows that the highest possible SNR and therefore the highest possible IQ will eventually be achieved by lowering the ISO to the base value and then applying the ETTR technique. The ETTR technique at base ISO therefore ensures that that the maximum possible amount of light is captured from the scene.

If H is restricted by the photographic conditions so that ETTR cannot be achieved at the selected ISO setting, then the strategy for fixed H described below should be followed.

ETTR: fixed H

In many photographic scenarios, the photometric exposure level H must be kept fixed. Typical situations include hand-held photography in low light and action photography.

For example, consider an action photographer using the camera in manual mode. Assume that the lowest available f-number N has been selected in order to open up the aperture and achieve the shallowest possible DoF, and a fixed exposure duration t has been selected which is short enough to freeze the appearance of the moving action. If the scene lighting conditions remain fixed, the level of photometric exposure H cannot be increased any further because doing so would require the exposure duration to be lengthened, which in turn could cause subject motion blur. In other words, it is not possible to add more light to the image to increase SNR.

Nevertheless, IQ can be optimised by minimising the effect of internal noise sources such as read noise. In the present context, the ISO setting can be changed without affecting N or t because the camera is in manual mode. In fact, read noise can be reduced by *increasing* the ISO gain to push the histogram as far right as possible without clipping, provided headroom is available. The reason for this somewhat counter-intuitive behaviour was given in section 5.6.2. The ISO gain amplifies *all* of the voltage signal but only *part* of the read noise, specifically the contribution arising from readout circuitry *upstream* from the ISO gain amplifier [29]. When referred back into photoelectrons, read noise is seen to decrease with increasing ISO gain, or equivalently signal-to-*read*-noise ratio goes up. In turn, total SNR increases because *all* photon shot-noise was present at the time the photo-electrons were detected, and so photon shot-noise expressed in photoelectrons is independent of ISO gain.

The benefit from any SNR increase when using the above technique is mainly seen in the *low-exposure* regions of the image where read noise is the dominant source of noise, and leads to *shadow improvement*. The shadow improvement technique can be considered a form of ETTR because it uses the ISO setting to push the histogram to the right, and the ISO setting along with the f-number and exposure duration (or shutter speed) define the *camera exposure* variables.

Although the shadow improvement technique improves IQ, it does not increase photometric exposure H. Rather, it maximises IQ given the constraints on H. Raising H can always provide a higher achievable SNR, and so the shadow improvement technique should only be employed once the photographic conditions do not allow H to be increased any further. For the reasons described in section 5.6.3, shadow improvement should only be implemented up to the *ISO-less setting* if shooting raw.

ETTR implementation

- *Manual mode.* In order to maximise H, begin by lowering N and increasing t as much as the photographic constraints allow. Then raise the ISO setting from the base value as much as possible without causing highlight clipping. However, the ISO setting should not be raised above the ISO-less value even if the metering indicates underexposure. Subsequently, the image brightness can be adjusted digitally when processing the raw file using the raw converter.

- *Aperture priority mode.* In aperture priority mode, the photographer controls the f-number N. The camera meter recommends an exposure duration t which aims to produce a JPEG output image with standard brightness at the selected ISO setting. However, the provided t value can be shortened by applying negative EC, or lengthened by applying positive EC.

  In order to apply the ETTR technique, the desired N first needs to be selected. Starting at base ISO, apply positive EC in order to achieve ETTR if headroom is available. If the provided exposure duration t is too long to prevent camera shake or prevent subject motion blur after achieving ETTR, the ISO setting can be raised until the metered t is sufficiently short. However, it is not advisable to raise the ISO setting above the ISO-less value if shooting raw.

  It is not necessary to perform any further EC adjustments because the camera metering system is designed to maintain the position of the JPEG histogram relative to the highlight clipping point at all ISO settings above and including base ISO. Finally, the image brightness can be adjusted digitally when processing the raw file.

- *Shutter priority mode.* In shutter or time priority mode, the photographer controls the shutter speed or exposure duration t and the camera meter provides the f-number N. Positive EC lowers N, and negative EC increases N.

  In order to apply the ETTR technique in shutter priority mode, the desired t value first needs to be selected. Starting at base ISO, positive EC can be applied to achieve ETTR if headroom is available. If the recommended N value is too low to provide sufficient DoF after ETTR has been achieved, the ISO setting can be raised until N is sufficiently high. However, it is not advisable to raise the ISO setting above the ISO-less value if shooting raw.

  Again it is not necessary to perform any further EC adjustments because the camera metering system is designed to maintain the position of the JPEG histogram relative to the highlight clipping point at all ISO settings above and including base ISO. Finally, the image brightness can be adjusted digitally when processing the raw file.

Bibliography

[1] Williams J B 1990 *Image Clarity: High-Resolution Photography* (London: Focal)

[2] Nasse H H 2008 *How to Read MTF Curves* Carl Zeiss Camera Lens Division http://lenspire.zeiss.com/en/overview-technical-articles

[3] Ray S F 2002 *Applied Photographic Optics: Lenses and Optical Systems for Photography, Film, Video, Electronic and Digital Imaging* 3rd edn (London: Focal)

[4] Nasse H H 2009 *How to Read MTF Curves Part II* Carl Zeiss Camera Lens Division http://lenspire.zeiss.com/en/overview-technical-articles

[5] Smith W J 2007 *Modern Optical Engineering* 4th edn (New York: McGraw-Hill)

[6] James J *Essay on equivalence* http://www.josephjamesphotography.com/equivalence/ (Retrieved 31/01/2017)

[7] Kingslake R 1992 *Optics in Photography (SPIE Press Monograph* vol PM06*)* (Bellingham, WA: SPIE)

[8] Kingslake R and Johnson R B 2010 *Lens Design Fundamentals* 2nd edn (New York: Academic)

[9] Sasian J 2012 *Introduction to Aberrations in Optical Imaging Systems* (Cambridge: Cambridge University Press)

[10] Goodman J 2004 *Introduction to Fourier Optics* 3rd edn (Englewood CO: Roberts)

[11] Shannon R R 1997 *The Art and Science of Optical Design* (Cambridge: Cambridge University Press)

[12] Shannon R R 1994 *Optical specifications Handbook of Optics* (New York: McGraw-Hill) chapter 35

[13] Fiete R D 2010 Modeling the imaging chain of digital cameras *SPIE Tutorial Texts in Optical Engineering* vol TT92 (Bellingham, WA: SPIE)

[14] Koyama T 2006 *Image Sensors and Signal Processing for Digital Still Cameras* ed J Nakamura (Boca Raton, FL/London: CRC Press/Taylor and Francis)

[15] ISO 2000 Photography—Electronic still-picture cameras—Resolution measurements, ISO 12233:2000

[16] Burns P D 2000 Slanted-edge MTF for digital camera and scanner analysis *Proc. IS & T PICS Conf.* pp 135–8

[17] Burns P D and Williams D 2002 Refined slanted-edge measurement practical camera and scanner testing *Proc. IS & T PICS Conf.* pp 191–5

[18] Palum R 2009 *Single-Sensor Imaging: Methods and Applications for Digital Cameras* ed R Lukac (Boca Raton, FL: CRC Press)

[19] Holst G C and Lomheim T S 2011 *CMOS/CCD Sensors and Camera Systems* 2nd edn (Oviedo, FL/Bellingham, WA: JCD/SPIE)

[20] Baxter D, Cao F, Eliasson H and Phillips J 2012 Development of the I3A CPIQ spatial metrics *Proc. SPIE* **8293** 829302

[21] DxO Mark by DxO Labs http://www.dxomark.com

[22] Koren N 2009 Imatest software documentation http://www.imatest.com

[23] Granger E M and Cupery K N 1973 An optical merit function (SQF), which correlates with subjective image judgments *Photogr. Sci. Eng.* **16** 221–30

[24] Mannos J and Sakrison D 1974 The effects of a visual fidelity criterion of the encoding of images *IEEE Trans. Inform. Theory* **20** 525

[25] Wolberg G 1990 *Digital Image Warping* 1st edn (New York: IEEE Computer Society Press)

[26] Keys R G 1981 Cubic convolution interpolation for digital image processing *IEEE Trans. Acoust., Speech, Signal Process.* **29** 1153

[27] Mitchell D P and Netravali A N 1988 Reconstruction filters in computer graphics *SIGGRAPH Comput. Graph.* **22** 221

[28] Wolberg G 2004 *Computer Science Handbook* 2nd edn ed A B Tucker (London/Boca Raton, FL: Chapman and Hall/CRC Press)

[29] Martinec E 2008 Noise, dynamic range and bit depth in digital SLRs http://theory.uchicago.edu/~ejm/pix/20d/tests/noise/ and http://www.photonstophotos.net/Emil%20Martinec/noise.html

[30] CIPA DC-004 2004 Sensitivity of digital cameras (Tokyo: Camera & Imaging Products Association)

[31] Butler R 2011 Behind the scenes: extended highlights! http://www.dpreview.com/articles/2845734946

[32] Digital Photography Review http://www.dpreview.com

[33] ISO 2006 Photography—Digital still cameras— Determination of exposure index, ISO speed ratings, standard output sensitivity, and recommended exposure index, ISO 12232:2006

[34] Nakamura J 2006 *Image Sensors and Signal Processing for Digital Still Cameras* ed J Nakamura (Boca Raton, FL/London: CRC Press/Taylor and Francis)

[35] Sanyal R 2015 Sony Alpha 7R II: real-world ISO invariance study http://www.dpreview.com/articles/7450523388

[36] Chen T, Catrysse P B, Gamal A E and Wandell B A 2000 How small should pixel size be? *Proc. SPIE* **3965** 451

[37] Claff W J http://www.photonstophotos.net/

[38] Claff W J 2009 Sensor analysis primer–Engineering and photographic dynamic range http://www.photonstophotos.net/

[39] Mizoguchi T 2006 *Image Sensors and Signal Processing for Digital Still Cameras* ed J Nakamura (Boca Raton, FL/London: CRC Press/Taylor and Francis)

[40] Magic Lantern http://www.magiclantern.fm